The Fortune of the Rougons
Zola, Emile
(Translator: Ernest Alfred Vizetelly)

Published: 1871
Categorie(s): Fiction, Literary

About Zola:

Émile Zola (2 April 1840 – 29 September 1902) was an influential French novelist, the most important example of the literary school of naturalism, and a major figure in the political liberalization of France. Source: Wikipedia

Also available for Zola:
- *Nana* (1880)
- *Thérèse Raquin* (1867)
- *L'Assommoir* (1877)
- *The Fat and the Thin* (1873)
- *The Death of Olivier Becaille* (1880)
- *The Miller's Daughter* (1880)
- *Captain Burle* (1880)

Introduction

"The Fortune of the Rougons" is the initial volume of the Rougon-Macquart series. Though it was by no means M. Zola's first essay in fiction, it was undoubtedly his first great bid for genuine literary fame, and the foundation of what must necessarily be regarded as his life-work. The idea of writing the "natural and social history of a family under the Second Empire," extending to a score of volumes, was doubtless suggested to M. Zola by Balzac's immortal "Comedie Humaine." He was twenty-eight years of age when this idea first occurred to him; he was fifty-three when he at last sent the manuscript of his concluding volume, "Dr. Pascal," to the press. He had spent five-and-twenty years in working out his scheme, persevering with it doggedly and stubbornly, whatever rebuffs he might encounter, whatever jeers and whatever insults might be directed against him by the ignorant, the prejudiced, and the hypocritical. Truth was on the march and nothing could stay it; even as, at the present hour, its march, if slow, none the less continues athwart another and a different crisis of the illustrious novelist's career.

It was in the early summer of 1869 that M. Zola first began the actual writing of "The Fortune of the Rougons." It was only in the following year, however, that the serial publication of the work commenced in the columns of "Le Siecle," the Republican journal of most influence in Paris in those days of the Second Empire. The Franco-German war interrupted this issue of the story, and publication in book form did not take place until the latter half of 1871, a time when both the war and the Commune had left Paris exhausted, supine, with little or no interest in anything. No more unfavourable moment for the issue of an ambitious work of fiction could have been found. Some two or three years went by, as I well remember, before anything like a revival of literature and of public interest in literature took place. Thus, M. Zola launched his gigantic scheme under auspices which would have made many another man recoil. "The Fortune of the Rougons," and two or three subsequent volumes of his series, attracted but a moderate degree of attention, and it was only on the morrow of the publication of "L'Assommoir" that he awoke, like Byron, to find himself famous.

As previously mentioned, the Rougon-Macquart series forms twenty volumes. The last of these, "Dr. Pascal," appeared in 1893. Since then M. Zola has written "Lourdes," "Rome," and "Paris." Critics have repeated *ad nauseam* that these last works constitute a new departure on M. Zola's part, and, so far as they formed a new series, this is true. But the suggestion that he has in any way repented of the Rougon-Macquart novels is ridiculous. As he has often told me of recent years, it is, as far as possible, his plan to subordinate his style and methods to his subject. To have written a book like "Rome," so largely devoted to the ambitions of the Papal See, in the same way as he had written books dealing with the drunkenness or other vices of Paris, would have been the climax of absurdity.

Yet the publication of "Rome," was the signal for a general outcry on the part of English and American reviewers that Zolaism, as typified by the Rougon-Macquart series, was altogether a thing of the past. To my thinking this is a profound error. M. Zola has always remained faithful to himself. The only difference that I perceive between his latest work, "Paris," and certain Rougon-Macquart volumes, is that with time, experience and assiduity, his genius has expanded and ripened, and that the hesitation, the groping for truth, so to say, which may be found in some of his earlier writings, has disappeared.

At the time when "The Fortune of the Rougons" was first published, none but the author himself can have imagined that the foundation-stone of one of the great literary monuments of the century had just been laid. From the "story" point of view the book is one of M. Zola's very best, although its construction—particularly as regards the long interlude of the idyll of Miette and Silvere—is far from being perfect. Such a work when first issued might well bring its author a measure of popularity, but it could hardly confer fame. Nowadays, however, looking backward, and bearing in mind that one here has the genius of M. Zola's lifework, "The Fortune of the Rougons" becomes a book of exceptional interest and importance. This has been so well understood by French readers that during the last six or seven years the annual sales of the work have increased threefold. Where, over a course of twenty years, 1,000 copies were sold, 2,500 and 3,000 are sold to-day. How many living

English novelists can say the same of their early essays in fiction, issued more than a quarter of a century ago?

I may here mention that at the last date to which I have authentic figures, that is, Midsummer 1897 (prior, of course, to what is called "L'Affaire Dreyfus"), there had been sold of the entire Rougon-Macquart series (which had begun in 1871) 1,421,000 copies. These were of the ordinary Charpentier editions of the French originals. By adding thereto several *editions de luxe* and the widely-circulated popular illustrated editions of certain volumes, the total amounts roundly to 2,100,000. "Rome," "Lourdes," "Paris," and all M. Zola's other works, apart from the "Rougon-Macquart" series, together with the translations into a dozen different languages—English, German, Italian, Spanish, Dutch, Danish, Portuguese, Bohemian, Hungarian, and others—are not included in the above figures. Otherwise the latter might well be doubled. Nor is account taken of the many serial issues which have brought M. Zola's views to the knowledge of the masses of all Europe.

It is, of course, the celebrity attaching to certain of M. Zola's literary efforts that has stimulated the demand for his other writings. Among those which are well worthy of being read for their own sakes, I would assign a prominent place to the present volume. Much of the story element in it is admirable, and, further, it shows M. Zola as a genuine satirist and humorist. The Rougons' yellow drawing-room and its habitues, and many of the scenes between Pierre Rougon and his wife Felicite, are worthy of the pen of Douglas Jerrold. The whole account, indeed, of the town of Plassans, its customs and its notabilities, is satire of the most effective kind, because it is satire true to life, and never degenerates into mere caricature.

It is a rather curious coincidence that, at the time when M. Zola was thus portraying the life of Provence, his great contemporary, bosom friend, and rival for literary fame, the late Alphonse Daudet, should have been producing, under the title of "The Provencal Don Quixote," that unrivalled presentment of the foibles of the French Southerner, with everyone nowadays knows as "Tartarin of Tarascon." It is possible that M. Zola, while writing his book, may have read the instalments of "Le Don Quichotte Provencal" published in the Paris "Figaro," and it may be that this perusal imparted that fillip to his pen to which we owe the many amusing particulars that he gives us of the town of Plassans. Plassans, I may mention, is really the Provencal Aix, which M. Zola's father provided with water by means of a canal still bearing his name. M. Zola himself, though born in Paris, spent the greater part of his childhood there. Tarascon, as is well known, never forgave Alphonse Daudet for his "Tartarin"; and in a like way M. Zola, who doubtless counts more enemies than any other literary man of the period, has none bitterer than the worthy citizens of Aix. They cannot forget or forgive the rascally Rougon-Macquarts.

The name Rougon-Macquart has to me always suggested that splendid and amusing type of the cynical rogue, Robert Macaire. But, of course, both Rougon and Macquart are genuine French names and not inventions. Indeed, several years ago I came by chance upon them both, in an old French deed which I was examining at the Bibliotheque Nationale in Paris. I there found mention of a Rougon family and a Macquart family dwelling virtually side by side in the same village. This, however, was in Champagne, not in Provence. Both families farmed vineyards for a once famous abbey in the vicinity of Epernay, early in the seventeenth century. To me, personally, this trivial discovery meant a great deal. It somehow aroused my interest in M. Zola and his works. Of the latter I had then only glanced through two or three volumes. With M. Zola himself I was absolutely unacquainted. However, I took the liberty to inform him of my little discovery; and afterwards I read all the books that he had published. Now, as it is fairly well known, I have given the greater part of my time, for several years past, to the task of familiarising English readers with his writings. An old deed, a chance glance, followed by the great friendship of my life and years of patient labour. If I mention this matter, it is solely with the object of endorsing the truth of the saying that the most insignificant incidents frequently influence and even shape our careers.

But I must come back to "The Fortune of the Rougons." It has, as I have said, its satirical and humorous side; but it also contains a strong element of pathos. The idyll of Miette and Silvere is a very touching one, and quite in accord with the conditions of life prevailing in Provence at the period M. Zola selects for his narrative. Miette is a frank child of nature;

Silvere, her lover, in certain respects foreshadows, a quarter of a century in advance, the Abbe Pierre Fromont of "Lourdes," "Rome," and "Paris." The environment differs, of course, but germs of the same nature may readily be detected in both characters. As for the other personages of M. Zola's book—on the one hand, Aunt Dide, Pierre Rougon, his wife, Felicite, and their sons Eugene, Aristide and Pascal, and, on the other, Macquart, his daughter Gervaise of "L'Assommoir," and his son Jean of "La Terre" and "La Debacle," together with the members of the Mouret branch of the ravenous, neurotic, duplex family—these are analysed or sketched in a way which renders their subsequent careers, as related in other volumes of the series, thoroughly consistent with their origin and their upbringing. I venture to asset that, although it is possible to read individual volumes of the Rougon-Macquart series while neglecting others, nobody can really understand any one of these books unless he makes himself acquainted with the alpha and the omega of the edifice, that is, "The Fortune of the Rougons" and "Dr. Pascal."

With regard to the present English translation, it is based on one made for my father several years ago. But to convey M. Zola's meaning more accurately I have found it necessary to alter, on an average, at least one sentence out of every three. Thus, though I only claim to edit the volume, it is, to all intents and purposes, quite a new English version of M. Zola's work.

E. A. V. MERTON, SURREY: August, 1898.

Author's Preface

I wish to explain how a family, a small group of human beings, conducts itself in a given social system after blossoming forth and giving birth to ten or twenty members, who, though they may appear, at the first glance, profoundly dissimilar one from the other, are, as analysis demonstrates, most closely linked together from the point of view of affinity. Heredity, like gravity, has its laws.

By resolving the duplex question of temperament and environment, I shall endeavour to discover and follow the thread of connection which leads mathematically from one man to another. And when I have possession of every thread, and hold a complete social group in my hands, I shall show this group at work, participating in an historical period; I shall depict it in action, with all its varied energies, and I shall analyse both the will power of each member, and the general tendency of the whole.

The great characteristic of the Rougon-Macquarts, the group or family which I propose to study, is their ravenous appetite, the great outburst of our age which rushes upon enjoyment. Physiologically the Rougon-Macquarts represent the slow succession of accidents pertaining to the nerves or the blood, which befall a race after the first organic lesion, and, according to environment, determine in each individual member of the race those feelings, desires and passions—briefly, all the natural and instinctive manifestations peculiar to human- ity—whose outcome assumes the conventional name of virtue or vice. Historically the Rougon-Macquarts proceed from the masses, radiate throughout the whole of contemporary society, and ascend to all sorts of positions by the force of that impulsion of essentially modern origin, which sets the lower classes marching through the social system. And thus the dramas of their individual lives recount the story of the Second Empire, from the ambuscade of the Coup d'Etat to the treachery of Sedan.

For three years I had been collecting the necessary documents for this long work, and the present volume was even written, when the fall of the Bonapartes, which I needed artistically, and with, as if by fate, I ever found at the end of the drama, without daring to hope that it would prove so near at hand, suddenly occurred and furnished me with the terrible but necessary denouement for my work. My scheme is, at this date, completed; the circle in which my characters will revolve is perfected; and my work becomes a picture of a departed reign, of a strange period of human madness and shame.

This work, which will comprise several episodes, is therefore, in my mind, the natural and social history of a family under the Second Empire. And the first episode, here called "The Fortune of the Rougons," should scientifically be entitled "The Origin."

EMILE ZOLA PARIS, July 1, 1871.

Chapter 1

On quitting Plassans by the Rome Gate, on the southern side of the town, you will find, on the right side of the road to Nice, and a little way past the first suburban houses, a plot of land locally known as the Aire Saint-Mittre.

This Aire Saint-Mittre is of oblong shape and on a level with the footpath of the adjacent road, from which it is separated by a strip of trodden grass. A narrow blind alley fringed with a row of hovels borders it on the right; while on the left, and at the further end, it is closed in by bits of wall overgrown with moss, above which can be seen the top branches of the mulberry-trees of the Jas-Meiffren—an extensive property with an entrance lower down the road. Enclosed upon three sides, the Aire Saint-Mittre leads nowhere, and is only crossed by people out for a stroll.

In former times it was a cemetery under the patronage of Saint-Mittre, a greatly honoured Provencal saint; and in 1851 the old people of Plassans could still remember having seen the wall of the cemetery standing, although the place itself had been closed for years. The soil had been so glutted with corpses that it had been found necessary to open a new burial-ground at the other end of town. Then the old abandoned cemetery had been gradually purified by the dark thick-set vegetation which had sprouted over it every spring. The rich soil, in which the gravediggers could no longer delve without turning up some human remains, was possessed of wondrous fertility. The tall weeds overtopped the walls after the May rains and the June sunshine so as to be visible from the high road; while inside, the place presented the appearance of a deep, dark green sea studded with large blossoms of singular brilliancy. Beneath one's feet amidst the close-set stalks one could feel that the damp soil reeked and bubbled with sap.

Among the curiosities of the place at that time were some large pear-trees, with twisted and knotty boughs; but none of the housewives of Plassans cared to pluck the large fruit which grew upon them. Indeed, the townspeople spoke of this fruit with grimaces of disgust. No such delicacy, however, restrained the suburban urchins, who assembled in bands at twilight and climbed the walls to steal the pears, even before they were ripe.

The trees and the weeds with their vigorous growth had rapidly assimilated all the decomposing matter in the old cemetery of Saint-Mittre; the malaria rising from the human remains interred there had been greedily absorbed by the flowers and the fruit; so that eventually the only odour one could detect in passing by was the strong perfume of wild gillyflowers. This had merely been a question of a few summers.

At last the townspeople determined to utilise this common property, which had long served no purpose. The walls bordering the roadway and the blind alley were pulled down; the weeds and the pear-trees uprooted; the sepulchral remains were removed; the ground was dug deep, and such bones as the earth was willing to surrender were heaped up in a corner. For nearly a month the youngsters, who lamented the loss of the pear-trees, played at bowls with the skulls; and one night some practical jokers even suspended femurs and tibias to all the bell-handles of the town. This scandal, which is still remembered at Plassans, did not cease until the authorities decided to have the bones shot into a hole which had been dug for the purpose in the new cemetery. All work, however, is usually carried out with discreet dilatoriness in country towns, and so during an entire week the inhabitants saw a solitary cart removing these human remains as if they had been mere rubbish. The vehicle had to cross Plassans from end to end, and owing to the bad condition of the roads fragments of bones and handfuls of rich mould were scattered at every jolt. There was not the briefest religious ceremony, nothing but slow and brutish cartage. Never before had a town felt so disgusted.

For several years the old cemetery remained an object of terror. Although it adjoined the main thoroughfare and was open to all comers, it was left quite deserted, a prey to fresh vegetable growth. The local authorities, who had doubtless counted on selling it and seeing houses built upon it, were evidently unable to find a purchaser. The recollection of the heaps of bones and the cart persistently jolting through the streets may have made people recoil from the spot; or perhaps the indifference that was shown was due to the indolence, the repugnance to pulling down and setting up again, which is characteristic of country people. At all events the authorities still retained possession of the ground, and at last forgot their desire to dispose of it. They did not even erect a fence round it, but left it open to all comers. Then, as time rolled on, people gradually grew accustomed to this barren spot; they would sit on the grass at the edges, walk about, or gather in groups. When the grass had been worn away and the trodden soil had become grey and hard, the old cemetery resembled a badly-levelled public square. As if the more effectually to efface the memory of all objectionable associations, the inhabitants slowly changed the very appellation of the place, retaining but the name of the saint, which was likewise applied to the blind alley dipping down at one corner of the field. Thus there was the Aire Saint-Mittre and the Impasse Saint-Mittre.

All this dates, however, from some considerable time back. For more than thirty years now the Aire Saint-Mittre has presented a different appearance. One day the townspeople, far too inert and indifferent to derive any advantage from it, let it, for a trifling consideration, to some suburban wheelwrights, who turned it into a wood-yard. At the present day it is still littered with huge pieces of timber thirty or forty feet long, lying here and there in piles, and looking like lofty overturned columns. These piles of timber, disposed at intervals from one end of the yard to the other, are a continual source of delight to the local urchins. In some places the ground is covered with fallen wood, forming a kind of uneven flooring over which it is impossible to walk, unless one balance one's self with marvellous dexterity. Troops of children amuse themselves with this exercise all day long. You will see them jumping over the big beams, walking in Indian file along the narrow ends, or else crawling astride them; various games which generally terminate in blows and bellowings. Sometimes, too, a dozen of them will sit, closely packed one against the other, on the thin end of a pole raised a few feet from the ground, and will see-saw there for hours together. The Aire Saint-Mittre thus serves as a recreation ground, where for more than a quarter of a century all the little suburban ragamuffins have been in the habit of wearing out the seats of their breeches.

The strangeness of the place is increased by the circumstance that wandering gipsies, by a sort of traditional custom always select the vacant portions of it for their encampments. Whenever any caravan arrives at Plassans it takes up its quarters on the Aire Saint-Mittre. The place is consequently never empty. There is always some strange band there, some troop of wild men and withered women, among whom groups of healthy-looking children roll about on the grass. These people live in the open air, regardless of everybody, setting their pots boiling, eating nameless things, freely displaying their tattered garments, and sleeping, fighting, kissing, and reeking with mingled filth and misery.

The field, formerly so still and deserted, save for the buzzing of hornets around the rich blossoms in the heavy sunshine, has thus become a very rowdy spot, resounding with the noisy quarrels of the gipsies and the shrill cries of the urchins of the suburb. In one corner there is a primitive saw-mill for cutting the timber, the noise from which serves as a dull, continuous bass accompaniment to the sharp voices. The wood is placed on two high tressels, and a couple of sawyers, one of whom stands aloft on the timber itself, while the other underneath is half blinded by the falling sawdust, work a large saw to and fro for hours together, with rigid machine-like regularity, as if they were wire-pulled puppets. The wood they saw is stacked, plank by plank, along the wall at the end, in carefully arranged piles six or eight feet high, which often remain there several seasons, and constitute one of the charms of the Aire Saint-Mittre. Between these stacks are mysterious, retired little alleys leading to a broader path between the timber and the wall, a deserted strip of verdure whence only small patches of sky can be seen. The vigorous vegetation and the quivering, deathlike stillness of the old cemetery still reign in this path. In all the country round Plassans there is no spot more instinct with languor, solitude, and love. It is a most delightful place for love-making. When the cemetery was being cleared the bones must have been heaped up in this corner; for even to-day it

frequently happens that one's foot comes across some fragment of a skull lying concealed in the damp turf.

Nobody, however, now thinks of the bodies that once slept
under that turf. In the daytime only the children go behind the
piles of wood when playing at hide and seek. The green path
remains virginal, unknown to others who see nought but the
wood-yard crowded with timber and grey with dust. In the
morning and afternoon, when the sun is warm, the whole place
swarms with life. Above all the turmoil, above the ragamuffins
playing among the timber, and the gipsies kindling fires under
their cauldrons, the sharp silhouette of the sawyer mounted on
his beam stands out against the sky, moving to and fro with the
precision of clockwork, as if to regulate the busy activity that
has sprung up in this spot once set apart for eternal slumber.
Only the old people who sit on the planks, basking in the setting sun, speak occasionally among themselves of the bones
which they once saw carted through the streets of Plassans by
the legendary tumbrel.

When night falls the Aire Saint-Mittre loses its animation,
and looks like some great black hole. At the far end one may
just espy the dying embers of the gipsies' fires, and at times
shadows slink noiselessly into the dense darkness. The place
becomes quite sinister, particularly in winter time.

One Sunday evening, at about seven o'clock, a young man
stepped lightly from the Impasse Saint-Mittre, and, closely
skirting the walls, took his way among the timber in the wood-
yard. It was in the early part of December, 1851. The weather
was dry and cold. The full moon shone with that sharp brilliancy peculiar to winter moons. The wood-yard did not have
the forbidding appearance which it wears on rainy nights; illumined by stretches of white light, and wrapped in deep and
chilly silence, it spread around with a soft, melancholy aspect.

For a few seconds the young man paused on the edge of the
yard and gazed mistrustfully in front of him. He carried a long
gun, the butt-end of which was hidden under his jacket, while
the barrel, pointed towards the ground, glittered in the moonlight. Pressing the weapon to his side, he attentively examined
the square shadows cast by the piles of timber. The ground
looked like a chess-board, with black and white squares clearly
defined by alternate patches of light and shade. The sawyers'

tressels in the centre of the plot threw long, narrow fantastic shadows, suggesting some huge geometrical figure, upon a strip of bare grey ground. The rest of the yard, the flooring of beams, formed a great couch on which the light reposed, streaked here and there with the slender black shadows which edged the different pieces of timber. In the frigid silence under the wintry moon, the motionless, recumbent poles, stiffened, as it were, with sleep and cold, recalled the corpses of the old cemetery. The young man cast but a rapid glance round the empty space; there was not a creature, not a sound, no danger of being seen or heard. The black patches at the further end caused him more anxiety, but after a brief examination he plucked up courage and hurriedly crossed the wood-yard.

As soon as he felt himself under cover he slackened his pace. He was now in the green pathway skirting the wall behind the piles of planks. Here his very footsteps became inaudible; the frozen grass scarcely crackled under his tread. He must have loved the spot, have feared no danger, sought nothing but what was pleasant there. He no longer concealed his gun. The path stretched away like a dark trench, except that the moonrays, gliding ever and anon between the piles of timber, then streaked the grass with patches of light. All slept, both darkness and light, with the same deep, soft, sad slumber. No words can describe the calm peacefulness of the place. The young man went right down the path, and stopped at the end where the walls of the Jas-Meiffren form an angle. Here he listened as if to ascertain whether any sound might be coming from the adjoining estate. At last, hearing nothing, he stooped down, thrust a plank aside, and hid his gun in a timber-stack.

An old tombstone, which had been overlooked in the clearing of the burial-ground, lay in the corner, resting on its side and forming a high and slightly sloping seat. The rain had worn its edges, and moss was slowly eating into it. Nevertheless, the following fragment of an inscription, cut on the side which was sinking into the ground, might still have been distinguished in the moonlight: "*Here lieth ... Marie ... died ...* " The finger of time had effaced the rest.

When the young man had concealed his gun he again listened attentively, and still hearing nothing, resolved to climb upon the stone. The wall being low, he was able to rest his elbows on the coping. He could, however, perceive nothing except a flood of light beyond the row of mulberry-trees skirting the wall. The flat ground of the Jas-Meiffren spread out under the moon like an immense sheet of unbleached linen; a hundred yards away the farmhouse and its outbuildings formed a still whiter patch. The young man was still gazing anxiously in that direction when, suddenly, one of the town clocks slowly and solemnly struck seven. He counted the strokes, and then jumped down, apparently surprised and relieved.

He seated himself on the tombstone, like one who is prepared to wait some considerable time. And for about half an hour he remained motionless and deep in thought, apparently quite unconscious of the cold, while his eyes gazed fixedly at a mass of shadow. He had placed himself in a dark corner, but the beams of the rising moon had gradually reached him, and at last his head was in the full light.

He was a strong, sturdy-looking lad, with a fine mouth, and soft delicate skin that bespoke youthfulness. He looked about seventeen years of age, and was handsome in a characteristic way.

His thin, long face looked like the work of some master sculptor; his high forehead, overhanging brows, aquiline nose, broad flat chin, and protruding cheek bones, gave singularly bold relief to his countenance. Such a face would, with advancing age, become too bony, as fleshless as that of a knight errant. But at this stage of youth, with chin and cheek lightly covered with soft down, its latent harshness was attenuated by the charming softness of certain contours which had remained vague and childlike. His soft black eyes, still full of youth, also lent delicacy to his otherwise vigorous countenance. The young fellow would probably not have fascinated all women, as he was not what one calls a handsome man; but his features, as a whole, expressed such ardent and sympathetic life, such enthusiasm and energy, that they doubtless engaged the thoughts of the girls of his own part—those sunburnt girls of the South—as he passed their doors on sultry July evenings.

He remained seated upon the tombstone, wrapped in thought, and apparently quite unconscious of the moonlight which now fell upon his chest and legs. He was of middle stature, rather thick-set, with over-developed arms and a labourer's hands, already hardened by toil; his feet, shod with heavy laced boots, looked large and square-toed. His general appearance, more particularly the heaviness of his limbs, bespoke lowly origin. There was, however, something in him, in the upright bearing of his neck and the thoughtful gleams of his eyes, which seemed to indicate an inner revolt against the brutifying manual labour which was beginning to bend him to the ground. He was, no doubt, an intelligent nature buried beneath the oppressive burden of race and class; one of those delicate refined minds embedded in a rough envelope, from which they in vain struggle to free themselves. Thus, in spite of his vigour, he seemed timid and restless, feeling a kind of unconscious shame at his imperfection. An honest lad he doubtless was, whose very ignorance had generated enthusiasm, whose manly heart was impelled by childish intellect, and who could show alike the submissiveness of a woman and the courage of a hero. On the evening in question he was dressed in a coat and trousers of greenish corduroy. A soft felt hat, placed lightly on the back of his head, cast a streak of shadow over his brow.

As the neighbouring clock struck the half hour, he suddenly started from his reverie. Perceiving that the white moonlight was shining full upon him, he gazed anxiously ahead. Then he abruptly dived back into the shade, but was unable to recover the thread of his thoughts. He now realised that his hands and feet were becoming very cold, and impatience seized hold of him. So he jumped upon the stone again, and once more glanced over the Jas-Meiffren, which was still empty and silent. Finally, at a loss how to employ his time, he jumped down, fetched his gun from the pile of planks where he had concealed it, and amused himself by working the trigger. The weapon was a long, heavy carbine, which had doubtless belonged to some smuggler. The thickness of the butt and the breech of the barrel showed it to be an old flintlock which had been altered into a percussion gun by some local gunsmith. Such firearms are to be found in farmhouses, hanging against the wall over the chimney-piece. The young man caressed his weapon with affection; twenty times or more he pulled the trigger, thrust his little finger into the barrel, and examined the butt attentively. By degrees he grew full of youth enthusiasm, combined with childish frolicsomeness, and ended by levelling his weapon and aiming at space, like a recruit going through his drill.

It was now very nearly eight o'clock, and he had been holding his gun levelled for over a minute, when all at once a low, panting call, light as a breath, came from the direction of the Jas-Meiffren.

"Are you there, Silvere?" the voice asked.

Silvere dropped his gun and bounded on to the tombstone.

"Yes, yes," he replied, also in a hushed voice. "Wait, I'll help you."

Before he could stretch out his arms, however, a girl's head appeared above the wall. With singular agility the damsel had availed herself of the trunk of a mulberry-tree, and climbed aloft like a kitten. The ease and certainty with which she moved showed that she was familiar with this strange spot. In another moment she was seated on the coping of the wall. Then Silvere, taking her in his arms, carried her, though not without a struggle, to the seat.

"Let go," she laughingly cried; "let go, I can get down alone very well." And when she was seated on the stone slab she added:

"Have you been waiting for me long? I've been running, and am quite out of breath."

Silvere made no reply. He seemed in no laughing humour, but gazed sorrowfully into the girl's face. "I wanted to see you, Miette," he said, as he seated himself beside her. "I should have waited all night for you. I am going away at daybreak to-morrow morning."

Miette had just caught sight of the gun lying on the grass, and with a thoughtful air, she murmured: "Ah! so it's decided then? There's your gun!"

"Yes," replied Silvere, after a brief pause, his voice still faltering, "it's my gun. I thought it best to remove it from the house to-night; to-morrow morning aunt Dide might have seen me take it, and have felt uneasy about it. I am going to hide it, and shall fetch it just before starting."

Then, as Miette could not remove her eyes from the weapon which he had so foolishly left on the grass, he jumped up and again hid it among the woodstacks.

"We learnt this morning," he said, as he resumed his seat, "that the insurgents of La Palud and Saint Martin-de-Vaulx were on the march, and spent last night at Alboise. We have decided to join them. Some of the workmen of Plassans have already left the town this afternoon; those who still remain will join their brothers to-morrow."

He spoke the word brothers with youthful emphasis.

"A contest is becoming inevitable," he added; "but, at any rate, we have right on our side, and we shall triumph."

Miette listened to Silvere, her eyes meantime gazing in front of her, without observing anything.

"'Tis well," she said, when he had finished speaking. And after a fresh pause she continued: "You warned me, yet I still hoped... . However, it is decided."

Neither of them knew what else to say. The green path in the deserted corner of the wood-yard relapsed into melancholy stillness; only the moon chased the shadows of the piles of timber over the grass. The two young people on the tombstone remained silent and motionless in the pale light. Silvere had passed his arm round Miette's waist, and she was leaning against his shoulder. They exchanged no kisses, naught but an embrace in which love showed the innocent tenderness of fraternal affection.

Miette was enveloped in a long brown hooded cloak reaching to her feet, and leaving only her head and hands visible. The women of the lower classes in Provence—the peasantry and workpeople—still wear these ample cloaks, which are called pelisses; it is a fashion which must have lasted for ages. Miette had thrown back her hood on arriving. Living in the open air and born of a hotblooded race, she never wore a cap. Her bare head showed in bold relief against the wall, which the moonlight whitened. She was still a child, no doubt, but a child ripening into womanhood. She had reached that adorable, uncertain hour when the frolicsome girl changes to a young woman. At that stage of life a bud-like delicacy, a hesitancy of contour that is exquisitely charming, distinguishes young girls. The outlines of womanhood appear amidst girlhood's innocent slimness, and woman shoots forth at first all embarrassment, still retaining much of the child, and ever and unconsciously betraying her sex. This period is very unpropitious for some girls, who suddenly shoot up, become ugly, sallow and frail, like plants before their due season. For those, however, who, like Miette, are healthy and live in the open air, it is a time of delightful gracefulness which once passed can never be recalled.

Miette was thirteen years of age, and although strong and sturdy did not look any older, so bright and childish was the smile which lit up her countenance. However, she was nearly as tall as Silvere, plump and full of life. Like her lover, she had no common beauty. She would not have been considered ugly, but she might have appeared peculiar to many young exquisites. Her rich black hair rose roughly erect above her forehead, streamed back like a rushing wave, and flowed over her head and neck like an inky sea, tossing and bubbling capriciously. It was very thick and inconvenient to arrange. However, she twisted it as tightly as possible into coils as thick as a child's fist, which she wound together at the back of her head. She had little time to devote to her toilette, but this huge chignon, hastily contrived without the aid of any mirror, was often instinct with vigorous grace. On seeing her thus naturally helmeted with a mass of frizzy hair which hung about her neck and temples like a mane, one could readily understand why she always went bareheaded, heedless alike of rain and frost.

Under her dark locks appeared her low forehead, curved and golden like a crescent moon. Her large prominent eyes, her short tip-tilted nose with dilated nostrils, and her thick ruddy lips, when regarded apart from one another, would have looked ugly; viewed, however, all together, amidst the delightful roundness and vivacious mobility of her countenance, they formed an ensemble of strange, surprising beauty. When Miette laughed, throwing back her head and gently resting it on her right shoulder, she resembled an old-time Bacchante, her throat distending with sonorous gaiety, her cheeks round like those of a child, her teeth large and white, her twists of woolly hair tossed by every outburst of merriment, and waving like a crown of vine leaves. To realise that she was only a child of thirteen, one had to notice the innocence underlying her full womanly laughter, and especially the child-like delicacy of her chin and soft transparency of her temples. In certain lights Miette's sun-tanned face showed yellow like amber. A little soft black down already shaded her upper lip. Toil too was beginning to disfigure her small hands, which, if left idle, would have become charmingly plump and delicate.

Miette and Silvere long remained silent. They were reading their own anxious thoughts, and, as they pondered upon the unknown terrors of the morrow, they tightened their mutual embrace. Their hearts communed with each other, they understood how useless and cruel would be any verbal plaint. The girl, however, could at last no longer contain herself, and, choking with emotion, she gave expression, in one phrase, to their mutual misgivings.

"You will come back again, won't you?" she whispered, as she hung on Silvere's neck.

Silvere made no reply, but, half-stifling, and fearing lest he should give way to tears like herself, he kissed her in brotherly fashion on the cheek, at a loss for any other consolation. Then disengaging themselves they again lapsed into silence.

After a moment Miette shuddered. Now that she no longer leant against Silvere's shoulder she was becoming icy cold. Yet she would not have shuddered thus had she been in this deserted path the previous evening, seated on this tombstone, where for several seasons they had tasted so much happiness.

"I'm very cold," she said, as she pulled her hood over her head.

"Shall we walk about a little?" the young man asked her. "It's not yet nine o'clock; we can take a stroll along the road."

Miette reflected that for a long time she would probably not have the pleasure of another meeting—another of those evening chats, the joy of which served to sustain her all day long.

"Yes, let us walk a little," she eagerly replied. "Let us go as far as the mill. I could pass the whole night like this if you wanted to."

They rose from the tombstone, and were soon hidden in the shadow of a pile of planks. Here Miette opened her cloak, which had a quilted lining of red twill, and threw half of it over Silvere's shoulders, thus enveloping him as he stood there close beside her. The same garment cloaked them both, and they passed their arms round each other's waist, and became as it were but one being. When they were thus shrouded in the pelisse they walked slowly towards the high road, fearlessly crossing the vacant parts of the wood-yard, which looked white in the moonlight. Miette had thrown the cloak over Silvere, and he had submitted to it quite naturally, as though indeed the garment rendered them a similar service every evening.

The road to Nice, on either side of which the suburban houses are built, was, in the year 1851, lined with ancient elm-trees, grand and gigantic ruins, still full of vigour, which the fastidious town council has replaced, some years since, by some little plane-trees. When Silvere and Miette found themselves under the elms, the huge boughs of which cast shadows on the moonlit footpath, they met now and again black forms which silently skirted the house fronts. These, too, were amorous couples, closely wrapped in one and the same cloak, and strolling in the darkness.

This style of promenading has been instituted by the young lovers of Southern towns. Those boys and girls among the people who mean to marry sooner or later, but who do not dislike a kiss or two in advance, know no spot where they can kiss at their ease without exposing themselves to recognition and gossip. Accordingly, while strolling about the suburbs, the plots of waste land, the footpaths of the high road—in fact, all these places where there are few passers-by and numerous shady nooks—they conceal their identity by wrapping themselves in these long cloaks, which are capacious enough to cover a whole family. The parents tolerate these proceedings; however stiff may be provincial propriety, no apprehensions, seemingly, are entertained. And, on the other hand, nothing could be more charming than these lovers' rambles, which appeal so keenly to the Southerner's fanciful imagination. There is a veritable masquerade, fertile in innocent enjoyments, within the reach of the most humble. The girl clasps her sweetheart to her bosom, enveloping him in her own warm cloak; and no doubt it is delightful to be able to kiss one's sweetheart within those shrouding folds without danger of being recognised. One couple is exactly like another. And to the belated pedestrian, who sees the vague groups gliding hither and thither, 'tis merely love passing, love guessed and scarce espied. The lovers know they are safely concealed within their cloaks, they converse in undertones and make themselves quite at home; most frequently they do not converse at all, but walk along at random and in silence, content in their embrace. The climate alone is to blame for having in the first instance prompted these young lovers to retire to secluded spots in the suburbs. On fine summer nights one cannot walk round Plassans without coming across a hooded couple in every patch of shadow falling from the house walls. Certain places, the Aire Saint-Mittre, for instance, are full of these dark "dominoes" brushing past one another, gliding softly in the warm nocturnal air. One might imagine they were guests invited to some mysterious ball given by the stars to lowly lovers. When the weather is very warm and the girls do not wear cloaks, they simply turn up their over-skirts. And in the winter the more passionate lovers make light of the frosts. Thus, Miette and Silvere, as they descended the Nice road, thought little of the chill December night.

They passed through the slumbering suburb without exchanging a word, but enjoying the mute delight of their warm embrace. Their hearts were heavy; the joy which they felt in being side by side was tinged with the painful emotion which comes from the thought of approaching severance, and it seemed to them that they could never exhaust the mingled sweetness and bitterness of the silence which slowly lulled their steps. But the houses soon grew fewer, and they reached the end of the Faubourg. There stands the entrance to the Jas-Meiffren, an iron gate fixed to two strong pillars; a low row of mulberry-trees being visible through the bars. Silvere and Miette instinctively cast a glance inside as they passed on.

Beyond the Jas-Meiffren the road descends with a gentle slope to a valley, which serves as the bed of a little rivulet, the Viorne, a brook in summer but a torrent in winter. The rows of elms still extended the whole way at that time, making the high road a magnificent avenue, which cast a broad band of gigantic trees across the hill, which was planted with corn and stunted vines. On that December night, under the clear cold moonlight, the newly-ploughed fields stretching away on either hand resembled vast beds of greyish wadding which deadened every sound in the atmosphere. The dull murmur of the Viorne in the distance alone sent a quivering thrill through the profound silence of the country-side.

When the young people had begun to descend the avenue, Miette's thoughts reverted to the Jas-Meiffren which they had just left behind them.

"I had great difficulty in getting away this evening," she said. "My uncle wouldn't let me go. He had shut himself up in a cellar, where he was hiding his money, I think, for he seemed greatly frightened this morning at the events that are taking place."

Silvere clasped her yet more lovingly. "Be brave!" said he. "The time will come when we shall be able to see each other freely the whole day long. You must not fret."

"Oh," replied the girl, shaking her head, "you are very hopeful. For my part I sometimes feel very sad. It isn't the hard work which grieves me; on the contrary, I am often very glad of my uncle's severity, and the tasks he sets me. He was quite right to make me a peasant girl; I should perhaps have turned out badly, for, do you know, Silvere, there are moments when I fancy myself under a curse... . I feel, then, that I should like to be dead... . I think of you know whom."

As she spoke these last words, her voice broke into a sob. Silvere interrupted her somewhat harshly. "Be quiet," he said. "You promised not to think about it. It's no crime of yours... . We love each other very much, don't we?" he added in a gentler tone. "When we're married you'll have no more unpleasant hours."

"I know," murmured Miette. "You are so kind, you sustain me. But what am I to do? I sometimes have fears and feelings of revolt. I think at times that I have been wronged, and then I should like to do something wicked. You see I pour forth my heart to you. Whenever my father's name is thrown in my face, I feel my whole body burning. When the urchins cry at me as I pass, 'Eh, La Chantegreil,' I lose all control of myself, and feel that I should like to lay hold of them and whip them."

After a savage pause she resumed: "As for you, you're a man; you're going to fight; you're very lucky."

Silvere had let her speak on. After a few steps he observed sorrowfully: "You are wrong, Miette; yours is bad anger. You shouldn't rebel against justice. As for me, I'm going to fight in defence of our common rights, not to gratify any personal animosity."

"All the same," the young girl continued, "I should like to be a man and handle a gun. I feel that it would do me good."

Then, as Silvere remained silent, she perceived that she had displeased him. Her feverishness subsided, and she whispered in a supplicating tone: "You are not angry with me, are you? It's your departure which grieves me and awakens such ideas. I know very well you are right—that I ought to be humble."

Then she began to cry, and Silvere, moved by her tears, grasped her hands and kissed them.

"See, now, how you pass from anger to tears, like a child," he said lovingly. "You must be reasonable. I'm not scolding you. I only want to see you happier, and that depends largely upon yourself."

The remembrance of the drama which Miette had so sadly evoked cast a temporary gloom over the lovers. They continued their walk with bowed heads and troubled thoughts.

"Do you think I'm much happier than you?" Silvere at last inquired, resuming the conversation in spite of himself. "If my grandmother had not taken care of me and educated me, what would have become of me? With the exception of my Uncle Antoine, who is an artisan like myself, and who taught me to love the Republic, all my other relations seem to fear that I might besmirch them by coming near them."

He was now speaking with animation, and suddenly stopped, detaining Miette in the middle of the road.

"God is my witness," he continued, "that I do not envy or hate anybody. But if we triumph, I shall have to tell the truth to those fine gentlemen. Uncle Antoine knows all about this matter. You'll see when we return. We shall all live free and happy."

Then Miette gently led him on, and they resumed their walk.

"You dearly love your Republic?" the girl asked, essaying a joke. "Do you love me as much?"

Her smile was not altogether free from a tinge of bitterness. She was thinking, perhaps, how easily Silvere abandoned her to go and scour the country-side. But the lad gravely replied: "You are my wife, to whom I have given my whole heart. I love the Republic because I love you. When we are married we shall want plenty of happiness, and it is to procure a share of that happiness that I'm going way to-morrow morning. You surely don't want to persuade me to remain at home?"

"Oh, no!" cried the girl eagerly. "A man should be brave! Courage is beautiful! You must forgive my jealousy. I should like to be as strong-minded as you are. You would love me all the more, wouldn't you?"

After a moment's silence she added, with charming vivacity and ingenuousness: "Ah, how willingly I shall kiss you when you come back!"

This outburst of a loving and courageous heart deeply affected Silvere. He clasped Miette in his arms and printed several kisses on her cheek. As she laughingly struggled to escape him, her eyes filled with tears of emotion.

All around the lovers the country still slumbered amid the deep stillness of the cold. They were now half-way down the hill. On the top of a rather lofty hillock to the left stood the ruins of a windmill, blanched by the moon; the tower, which had fallen in on one side, alone remained. This was the limit which the young people had assigned to their walk. They had come straight from the Faubourg without casting a single glance at the fields between which they passed. When Silvere had kissed Miette's cheek, he raised his head and observed the mill.

"What a long walk we've had!" he exclaimed. "See—here is the mill. It must be nearly half-past nine. We must go home."

But Miette pouted. "Let us walk a little further," she implored; "only a few steps, just as far as the little cross-road, no farther, really."

Silvere smiled as he again took her round the waist. Then they continued to descend the hill, no longer fearing inquisitive glances, for they had not met a living soul since passing the last houses. They nevertheless remained enveloped in the long pelisse, which seemed, as it were, a natural nest for their love. It had shrouded them on so many happy evenings! Had they simply walked side by side, they would have felt small and isolated in that vast stretch of country, whereas, blended together as they were, they became bolder and seemed less puny. Between the folds of the pelisse they gazed upon the fields stretching on both sides of the road, without experiencing that crushing feeling with which far-stretching callous vistas oppress the human affections. It seemed to them as though they had brought their house with them; they felt a pleasure in viewing the country-side as from a window, delighting in the calm solitude, the sheets of slumbering light, the glimpses of nature vaguely distinguishable beneath the shroud of night and winter, the whole of that valley indeed, which while charming them could not thrust itself between their close-pressed hearts.

All continuity of conversation had ceased; they spoke no more of others, nor even of themselves. They were absorbed by the present, pressing each other's hands, uttering exclamations at the sight of some particular spot, exchanging words at rare intervals, and then understanding each other but little, for drowsiness came from the warmth of their embrace. Silvere forgot his Republican enthusiasm; Miette no longer reflected that her lover would be leaving her in an hour, for a long time, perhaps for ever. The transports of their affection lulled them into a feeling of security, as on other days, when no prospect of parting had marred the tranquility of their meetings.

They still walked on, and soon reached the little crossroad mentioned by Miette—a bit of a lane which led through the fields to a village on the banks of the Viorne. But they passed on, pretending not to notice this path, where they had agreed to stop. And it was only some minutes afterwards that Silvere whispered, "It must be very late; you will get tired."

"No; I assure you I'm not at all tired," the girl replied. "I could walk several leagues like this easily." Then, in a coaxing tone, she added: "Let us go down as far as the meadows of Sainte-Claire. There we will really stop and turn back."

Silvere, whom the girl's rhythmic gait lulled to semi-somnolence, made no objection, and their rapture began afresh. They now went on more slowly, fearing the moment when they would have to retrace their steps. So long as they walked onward, they felt as though they were advancing to the eternity of their mutual embrace; the return would mean separation and bitter leave-taking.

The declivity of the road was gradually becoming more gentle. In the valley below there are meadows extending as far as the Viorne, which runs at the other end, beneath a range of low hills. These meadows, separated from the high-road by thickset hedges, are the meadows of Sainte-Claire.

"Bah!" exclaimed Silvere this time, as he caught sight of the first patches of grass: "we may as well go as far as the bridge."

At this Miette burst out laughing, clasped the young man round the neck, and kissed him noisily.

At the spot where the hedges begin, there were in those days two elms forming the end of the long avenue, two colossal trees larger than any of the others. The treeless fields stretch out from the high road, like a broad band of green wool, as far as the willows and birches by the river. The distance from the last elms to the bridge is scarcely three hundred yards. The lovers took a good quarter of an hour to cover that space. At last, however slow their gait, they reached the bridge, and there they stopped.

The road to Nice ran up in front of them, along the opposite slope of the valley. But they could only see a small portion of it, as it takes a sudden turn about half a mile from the bridge, and is lost to view among the wooded hills. On looking round they caught sight of the other end of the road, that which they had just traversed, and which leads in a direct line from Plassans to the Viorne. In the beautiful winter moonlight it looked like a long silver ribbon, with dark edgings traced by the rows of elms. On the right and left the ploughed hill-land showed like vast, grey, vague seas intersected by this ribbon, this roadway white with frost, and brilliant as with metallic lustre. Up above, on a level with the horizon, lights shone from a few windows in the Faubourg, resembling glowing sparks. By degrees Miette and Silvere had walked fully a league. They gazed at the inter-vening road, full of silent admiration for the vast amphitheatre which rose to the verge of the heavens, and over which flowed bluish streams of light, as over the superposed rocks of a gi-gantic waterfall. The strange and colossal picture spread out amid deathlike stillness and silence. Nothing could have been of more sovereign grandeur.

Then the young people, having leant against the parapet of the bridge, gazed beneath them. The Viorne, swollen by the rains, flowed on with a dull, continuous sound. Up and down stream, despite the darkness which filled the hollows, they per-ceived the black lines of the trees growing on the banks; here and there glided the moonbeams, casting a trail of molten met-al, as it were, over the water, which glittered and danced like

rays of light on the scales of some live animal. The gleams darted with a mysterious charm along the gray torrent, betwixt
the vague phantom-like foliage. You might have thought this an
enchanted valley, some wondrous retreat where a community
of shadows and gleams lived a fantastic life.

This part of the river was familiar to the lovers; they had often come here in search of coolness on warm July nights; they
had spent hours hidden among the clusters of willows on the
right bank, at the spot where the meadows of Sainte-Claire
spread their verdant carpet to the waterside. They remembered every bend of the bank, the stones on which they
had stepped in order to cross the Viorne, at that season as narrow as a brooklet, and certain little grassy hollows where they
had indulged in their dreams of love. Miette, therefore, now
gazed from the bridge at the right bank of the torrent with
longing eyes.

"If it were warmer," she sighed, "we might go down and rest
awhile before going back up the hill." Then, after a pause, during which she kept her eyes fixed on the banks, she resumed:
"Look down there, Silvere, at that black mass yonder in front of
the lock. Do you remember? That's the brushwood where we
sat last Corpus Christi Day."

"Yes, so it is," replied Silvere, softly.

This was the spot where they had first ventured to kiss each
other on the cheek. The remembrance just roused by the girl's
words brought both of them a delightful feeling, an emotion in
which the joys of the past mingled with the hopes of the morrow. Before their eyes, with the rapidity of lightening, there
passed all the delightful evenings they had spent together, especially that evening of Corpus Christi Day, with the warm sky,
the cool willows of the Viorne, and their own loving talk. And at
the same time, whilst the past came back to their hearts full of
a delightful savour, they fancied they could plunge into the unknown future, see their dreams realised, and march through
life arm in arm—even as they had just been doing on the highway—warmly wrapped in the same cloak. Then rapture came
to them again, and they smiled in each other's eyes, alone
amidst all the silent radiance.

Suddenly, however, Silvere raised his head and, throwing off
the cloak, listened attentively. Miette, in her surprise, imitated

him, at a loss to understand why he had started so abruptly from her side.

Confused sounds had for a moment been coming from behind the hills in the midst of which the Nice road wends its way. They suggested the distant jolting of a procession of carts; but not distinctly, so loud was the roaring of the Viorne. Gradually, however, they became more pronounced, and rose at last like the tramping of an army on the march. Then amidst the continuous growing rumble one detected the shouts of a crowd, strange rhythmical blasts as of a hurricane. One could even have fancied they were the thunderclaps of a rapidly approaching storm which was already disturbing the slumbering atmosphere. Silvere listened attentively, unable to tell, however, what were those tempest-like shouts, for the hills prevented them from reaching him distinctly. Suddenly a dark mass appeared at the turn of the road, and then the "Marseillaise" burst forth, formidable, sung as with avenging fury.

"Ah, here they are!" cried Silvere, with a burst of joyous enthusiasm.

Forthwith he began to run up the hill, dragging Miette with him. On the left of the road was an embankment planted with evergreen oaks, up which he clambered with the young girl, to avoid being carried away by the surging, howling multitude.

When he had reached the top of the bank and the shadow of the brushwood, Miette, rather pale, gazed sorrowfully at those men whose distant song had sufficed to draw Silvere from her embrace. It seemed as if the whole band had thrust itself between them. They had been so happy a few minutes before, locked in each other's arms, alone and lost amidst the overwhelming silence and discreet glimmer of the moon! And now Silvere, whose head was turned away from her, who no longer seemed even conscious of her presence, had eyes only for those strangers whom he called his brothers.

The band descended the slope with a superb, irresistible stride. There could have been nothing grander than the irruption of those few thousand men into that cold, still, deathly scene. The highway became a torrent, rolling with living waves which seemed inexhaustible. At the bend in the road fresh masses ever appeared, whose songs ever helped to swell the roar of this human tempest. When the last battalions came in

sight the uproar was deafening. The "Marseillaise" filled the atmosphere as if blown through enormous trumpets by giant
mouths, which cast it, vibrating with a brazen clang, into every
corner of the valley. The slumbering country-side awoke with a
start—quivering like a beaten drum resonant to its very en-
trails, and repeating with each and every echo the passionate
notes of the national song. And then the singing was no longer
confined to the men. From the very horizon, from the distant
rocks, the ploughed land, the meadows, the copses, the smallest bits of brushwood, human voices seemed to come. The
great amphitheatre, extending from the river to Plassans, the
gigantic cascade over which the bluish moonlight flowed, was
as if filled with innumerable invisible people cheering the insurgents; and in the depths of the Viorne, along the waters
streaked with mysterious metallic reflections, there was not a
dark nook but seemed to conceal human beings, who took up
each refrain with yet greater passion. With air and earth alike
quivering, the whole country-side cried for vengeance and
liberty. So long as the little army was descending the slope, the
roar of the populace thus rolled on in sonorous waves broken
by abrupt outbursts which shook the very stones in the
roadway.

Silvere, pale with emotion, still listened and looked on. The
insurgents who led the van of that swarming, roaring stream,
so vague and monstrous in the darkness, were rapidly approaching the bridge.

"I thought," murmured Miette, "that you would not pass
through Plassans?"

"They must have altered the plan of operations," Silvere
replied; "we were, in fact, to have marched to the chief town by
the Toulon road, passing to the left of Plassans and Orcheres.
They must have left Alboise this afternoon and passed Les Tulettes this evening."

The head of the column had already arrived in front of the
young people. The little army was more orderly than one would
have expected from a band of undisciplined men. The contingents from the various towns and villages formed separate battalions, each separated by a distance of a few paces. These battalions were apparently under the orders of certain chiefs. For
the nonce the pace at which they were descending the hillside

made them a compact mass of invincible strength. There were probably about three thousand men, all united and carried away by the same storm of indignation. The strange details of the scene were not discernible amidst the shadows cast over the highway by the lofty slopes. At five or six feet from the brushwood, however, where Miette and Silvere were sheltered, the left-hand embankment gave place to a little pathway which ran alongside the Viorne; and the moonlight, flowing through this gap, cast a broad band of radiance across the road. When the first insurgents reached this patch of light they were suddenly illumined by a sharp white glow which revealed, with singular distinctness, every outline of visage or costume. And as the various contingents swept on, the young people thus saw them emerge, fiercely and without cessation, from the surrounding darkness.

As the first men passed through the light Miette instinctively clung to Silvere, although she knew she was safe, even from observation. She passed her arm round the young fellow's neck, resting her head against his shoulder. And with the hood of her pelisse encircling her pale face she gazed fixedly at that square patch of light as it was rapidly traversed by those strange faces, transfigured by enthusiasm, with dark open mouths full of the furious cry of the "Marseillaise." Silvere, whom she felt quivering at her side, then bent towards her and named the various contingents as they passed.

The column marched along eight abreast. In the van were a number of big, square-headed fellows, who seemed to possess the herculean strength and naïve confidence of giants. They would doubtless prove blind, intrepid defenders of the Republic. On their shoulders they carried large axes, whose edges, freshly sharpened, glittered in the moonlight.

"Those are the woodcutters of the forests of the Seille," said Silvere. "They have been formed into a corps of sappers. At a signal from their leaders they would march as far as Paris, battering down the gates of the towns with their axes, just as they cut down the old cork-trees on the mountain."

The young man spoke with pride of the heavy fists of his brethren. And on seeing a band of labourers and rough-bearded men, tanned by the sun, coming along behind the woodcutters, he continued: "That is the contingent from La

Palud. That was the first place to rise. The men in blouses are labourers who cut up the cork-trees; the others in velveteen jackets must be sportsmen, poachers, and charcoal-burners living in the passes of the Seille. The poachers knew your father, Miette. They have good firearms, which they handle skilfully. Ah! if all were armed in the same manner! We are short of muskets. See, the labourers have only got cudgels!"

Miette, still speechless, looked on and listened. As Silvere spoke to her of her father, the blood surged to her cheeks. Her face burnt as she scrutinised the sportsmen with a strange air of mingled indignation and sympathy. From this moment she grew animated, yielding to the feverish quiver which the insurgents' songs awakened.

The column, which had just begun the "Marseillaise" afresh, was still marching down as though lashed on by the sharp blasts of the "Mistral." The men of La Palud were followed by another troop of workmen, among whom a goodly number of middle class folks in great-coats were to be seen.

"Those are the men of Saint-Martin-de-Vaulx," Silvere resumed. "That *bourg* rose almost at the same time as La Palud. The masters joined the workmen. There are some rich men there, Miette; men whose wealth would enable them to live peacefully at home, but who prefer to risk their lives in defence of liberty. One can but admire them. Weapons are very scarce, however; they've scarcely got a few fowling-pieces. But do you see those men yonder, Miette, with red bands round their left elbows? They are the leaders."

The contingents descended the hill more rapidly than Silvere could speak. While he was naming the men from Saint-Martin-de-Vaulx, two battalions had already crossed the ray of light which blanched the roadway.

"Did you see the insurgents from Alboise and Les Tulettes pass by just now?" he asked. "I recognised Burgat the blacksmith. They must have joined the band to-day. How they do run!"

Miette was now leaning forward, in order to see more of the little bands described to her by the young man. The quiver she felt rose from her bosom to her throat. Then a battalion larger and better disciplined than the others appeared. The insurgents composing it were nearly all dressed in blue blouses, with red sashes round their waists. One would have thought they were arrayed in uniform. A man on horseback, with a sabre at his side, was in the midst of them. And most of these improvised soldiers carried guns, probably carbines and old muskets of the National Guard.

"I don't know those," said Silvere. "The man on horseback must be the chief I've heard spoken of. He brought with him the contingents from Faverolles and the neighbouring villages. The whole column ought to be equipped in the same manner."

He had no time to take breath. "Ah! see, here are the country people!" he suddenly cried.

Small groups of ten or twenty men at the most were now advancing behind the men of Faverolles. They all wore the short jacket of the Southern peasantry, and as they sang they brandished pitchforks and scythes. Some of them even only carried large navvies' shovels. Every hamlet, however, had sent its able-bodied men.

Silvere, who recognised the parties by their leaders, enumerated them in feverish tones. "The contingent from Chavanoz!" said he. "There are only eight men, but they are strong; Uncle Antoine knows them. Here's Nazeres! Here's Poujols! They're all here; not one has failed to answer the summons. Valqueyras! Hold, there's the parson amongst them; I've heard about him, he's a staunch Republican."

He was becoming intoxicated with the spectacle. Now that each battalion consisted of only a few insurgents he had to name them yet more hastily, and his precipitancy gave him the appearance of one in a frenzy.

"Ah! Miette," he continued, "what a fine march past! Rozan! Vernoux! Corbiere! And there are more still, you'll see. These have only got scythes, but they'll mow down the troops as close as the grass in their meadows—Saint-Eutrope! Mazet! Les Gardes, Marsanne! The whole north side of the Seille! Ah, we shall be victorious! The whole country is with us. Look at those men's arms, they are hard and black as iron. There's no end to them. There's Pruinas! Roches Noires! Those last are smugglers: they are carrying carbines. Still more scythes and pitchforks, the contingents of country folk are still passing. Castel-le-Vieux! Sainte-Anne! Graille! Estourmel! Murdaran!"

His voice was husky with emotion as he finished naming these men, who seemed to be borne away by a whirlwind as fast as he enumerated them. Erect, with glowing countenance, he pointed out the several contingents with a nervous gesture. Miette followed his movements. The road below attracted her like the depths of a precipice. To avoid slipping down the incline she clung to the young man's neck. A strange intoxication emanated from those men, who themselves were inebriated with clamour, courage, and confidence. Those beings, seen athwart a moonbeam, those youths and those men in their prime, those old people brandishing strange weapons and dressed in the most diverse costumes, from working smock to middle class overcoat, those endless rows of heads, which the hour and the circumstances endowed with an expression of fanatical energy and enthusiasm, gradually appeared to the girl like a whirling, impetuous torrent. At certain moments she fancied they were not of themselves moving, that they were really being carried away by the force of the "Marseillaise," by that hoarse, sonorous chant. She could not distinguish any conversation, she heard but a continuous volume of sound, alternating from bass to shrill notes, as piercing as nails driven into one's flesh. This roar of revolt, this call to combat, to death, with its outbursts of indignation, its burning thirst for liberty, its remarkable blending of bloodthirsty and sublime impulses, unceasingly smote her heart, penetrating more deeply at each fierce outburst, and filling her with the voluptuous pangs of a virgin martyr who stands erect and smiles under the lash. And the crowd flowed on ever amidst the same sonorous wave of sound. The march past, which did not really last more than a few minutes, seemed to the young people to be interminable.

Truly, Miette was but a child. She had turned pale at the approach of the band, she had wept for the loss of love, but she was a brave child, whose ardent nature was easily fired by enthusiasm. Thus ardent emotions had gradually got possession of her, and she became as courageous as a youth. She would willingly have seized a weapon and followed the insurgents. As the muskets and scythes filed past, her white teeth glistened longer and sharper between her red lips, like the fangs of a young wolf eager to bite and tear. And as she listened to Silvere enumerating the contingents from the country-side with ever-increasing haste, the pace of the column seemed to her to accelerate still more. She soon fancied it all a cloud of human dust swept along by a tempest. Everything began to whirl before her. Then she closed her eyes; big hot tears were rolling down her cheeks.

Silvere's eyelashes were also moist. "I don't see the men who left Plassans this afternoon," he murmured.

He tried to distinguish the end of the column, which was still hidden by the darkness. Suddenly he cried with joyous exultation: "Ah, here they are! They've got the banner—the banner has been entrusted to them!"

Then he wanted to leap from the slope in order to join his companions. At this moment, however, the insurgents halted. Words of command ran along the column, the "Marseillaise" died out in a final rumble, and one could only hear the confused murmuring of the still surging crowd. Silvere, as he listened, caught the orders which were passed on from one contingent to another; they called the men of Plassans to the van. Then, as each battalion ranged itself alongside the road to make way for the banner, the young man reascended the embankment, dragging Miette with him.

"Come," he said; "we can get across the river before they do."

When they were on the top, among the ploughed land, they ran along to a mill whose lock bars the river. Then they crossed the Viorne on a plank placed there by the millers, and cut across the meadows of Sainte-Claire, running hand-in-hand, without exchanging a word. The column threw a dark line over the highway, which they followed alongside the hedges. There were some gaps in the hawthorns, and at last Silvere and Miette sprang on to the road through one of them.

In spite of the circuitous way they had come, they arrived at the same time as the men of Plassans. Silvere shook hands with some of them. They must have thought he had heard of the new route they had chosen, and had come to meet them. Miette, whose face was half-concealed by her hood, was scrutinised rather inquisitively.

"Why, it's Chantegreil," at last said one of the men from the Faubourg of Plassans, "the niece of Rebufat, the *meger*[1] of the Jas-Meiffren."

"Where have you sprung from, gadabout?" cried another voice.

Silvere, intoxicated with enthusiasm, had not thought of the distress which his sweetheart would feel at the jeers of the workmen. Miette, all confusion, looked at him as if to implore his aid. But before he could even open his lips another voice rose from the crowd, brutally exclaiming:

"Her father's at the galleys; we don't want the daughter of a thief and murderer amongst us."

At this Miette turned dreadfully pale.

"You lie!" she muttered. "If my father did kill anybody, he never thieved!"

And as Silvere, pale and trembling more than she, began to clench his fists: "Stop!" she continued; "this is my affair."

Then, turning to the men, she repeated with a shout: "You lie! You lie! He never stole a copper from anybody. You know it well enough. Why do you insult him when he can't be here?"

She drew herself up, superb with indignation. With her ardent, half-wild nature she seemed to accept the charge of murder composedly enough, but that of theft exasperated her. They knew it, and that was why folks, from stupid malice, often cast the accusation in her face.

The man who had just called her father a thief was merely repeating what he had heard said for many years. The girl's defiant attitude only incited the workmen to jeer the more. Silvere still had his fists clenched, and matters might have become serious if a poacher from the Seille, who had been sitting on a heap of stones at the roadside awaiting the order to march, had not come to the girl's assistance.

"The little one's right," he said. "Chantegreil was one of us. I knew him. Nobody knows the real facts of his little matter. I always believed in the truth of his deposition before the judge. The gendarme whom he brought down with a bullet, while he was out shooting, was no doubt taking aim at him at the time. A man must defend himself! At all events Chantegreil was a decent fellow; he committed no robbery."

1.A meger is a farmer in Provence who shares the expenses and profits of his farm with the owner of the land.

As often happens in such cases, the testimony of this poacher sufficed to bring other defenders to Miette's aid. Several workmen also professed to have known Chantegreil.

"Yes, yes, it's true!" they all said. "He wasn't a thief. There are some scoundrels at Plassans who ought to be sent to prison in his place. Chantegreil was our brother. Come, now, be calm, little one."

Miette had never before heard anyone speak well of her father. He was generally referred to as a beggar, a villain, and now she found good fellows who had forgiving words for him, and declared him to be an honest man. She burst into tears, again full of the emotion awakened in her by the "Marseillaise;" and she bethought herself how she might thank these men for their kindness to her in misfortune. For a moment she conceived the idea of shaking them all by the hand like a man. But her heart suggested something better. By her side stood the insurgent who carried the banner. She touched the staff, and, to express her gratitude, said in an entreating tone, "Give it to me; I will carry it."

The simple-minded workmen understood the ingenuous sublimity of this form of gratitude.

"Yes," they all cried, "Chantegreil shall carry the banner."

However, a woodcutter remarked that she would soon get tired, and would not be able to go far.

"Oh! I'm quite strong," she retorted proudly, tucking up her sleeves and showing a pair of arms as big as those of a grown woman. Then as they handed her the flag she resumed, "Wait just a moment."

Forthwith she pulled off her cloak, and put it on again after turning the red lining outside. In the clear moonlight she appeared to be arrayed in a purple mantle reaching to her feet. The hood resting on the edge of her chignon formed a kind of Phrygian cap. She took the flag, pressed the staff to her bosom, and held herself upright amid the folds of that blood-coloured banner which waved behind her. Enthusiastic child that she was, her countenance, with its curly hair, large eyes moist with tears, and lips parted in a smile, seemed to rise with energetic pride as she turned it towards the sky. At that moment she was the virgin Liberty.

The insurgents burst into applause. The vivid imagination of those Southerners was fired with enthusiasm at the sudden apparition of this girl so nervously clasping their banner to her bosom. Shouts rose from the nearest group:

"Bravo, Chantegreil! Chantegreil for ever! She shall remain with us; she'll bring us luck!"

They would have cheered her for a long time yet had not the order to resume the march arrived. Whilst the column moved on, Miette pressed Silvere's hand and whispered in his ear: "You hear! I shall remain with you. Are you glad?"

Silvere, without replying, returned the pressure. He consented. In fact, he was deeply affected, unable to resist the enthusiasm which fired his companions. Miette seemed to him so lovely, so grand, so saintly! During the whole climb up the hill he still saw her before him, radiant, amidst a purple glory. She was now blended with his other adored mistress—the Republic. He would have liked to be in action already, with his gun on his shoulder. But the insurgents moved slowly. They had orders to make as little noise as possible. Thus the column advanced between the rows of elms like some gigantic serpent whose every ring had a strange quivering. The frosty December night had again sunk into silence, and the Viorne alone seemed to roar more loudly.

On reaching the first houses of the Faubourg, Silvere ran on in front to fetch his gun from the Aire Saint-Mittre, which he found slumbering in the moonlight. When he again joined the insurgents they had reached the Porte de Rome. Miette bent towards him, and with her childish smile observed: "I feel as if I were at the procession on Corpus Christi Day carrying the banner of the Virgin."

Chapter 2

Plassans is a sub-prefecture with about ten thousand inhabitants. Built on a plateau overlooking the Viorne, and resting on the north side against the Garrigues hills, one of the last spurs of the Alps, the town is situated, as it were, in the depths of a cul-de-sac. In 1851 it communicated with the adjoining country by two roads only, the Nice road, which runs down to the east, and the Lyons road, which rises to the west, the one continuing the other on almost parallel lines. Since that time a railway has been built which passes to the south of the town, below the hill which descends steeply from the old ramparts to the river. At the present day, on coming out of the station on the right bank of the little torrent, one can see, by raising one's head, the first houses of Plassans, with their gardens disposed in terrace fashion. It is, however, only after an uphill walk lasting a full quarter of an hour that one reaches these houses.

About twenty years ago, owing, no doubt, to deficient means of communication, there was no town that had more completely retained the pious and aristocratic character of the old Provencal cities. Plassans then had, and has even now, a whole district of large mansions built in the reigns of Louis XIV. and Louis XV., a dozen churches, Jesuit and Capuchin houses, and a considerable number of convents. Class distinctions were long perpetuated by the town's division into various districts. There were three of them, each forming, as it were, a separate and complete locality, with its own churches, promenades, customs, and landscapes.

The district of the nobility, called Saint-Marc, after the name of one of its parish churches, is a sort of miniature Versailles, with straight streets overgrown with grass, and large square houses which conceal extensive gardens. It extends to the south along the edge of the plateau. Some of the mansions built on the declivity itself have a double row of terraces whence one can see the whole valley of the Viorne, a most charming vista much vaunted in that part of the country. Then on the north-west, the old quarter, formed of the original town, rears its narrow, tortuous lanes bordered with tottering hovels. The Town-Hall, the Civil Court, the Market, and the Gendarmerie barracks are situated here. This, the most populous part of the Plassans, is inhabited by working-men and shop-keepers, all the wretched, toiling, common folk. The new town forms a sort of parallelogram to the north-east; the well-to-do, those who have slowly amassed a fortune, and those engaged in the liberal professions, here occupy houses set out in straight lines and coloured a light yellow. This district, which is embellished by the Sub-Prefecture, an ugly plaster building decorated with rose-mouldings, numbered scarcely five or six streets in 1851; it is of quite recent formation, and it is only since the construction of the railway that it has been growing in extent.

One circumstance which even at the present time tends to divide Plassans into three distinct independent parts is that the limits of the districts are clearly defined by the principal thoroughfares. The Cours Sauvaire and the Rue de Rome, which is, as it were, a narrow extension of the former, run from west to east, from the Grand'-Porte to the Porte de Rome, thus cutting the town into two portions, and dividing the quarter of the nobility from the others. The latter are themselves parted by the Rue de la Banne. This street, the finest in the locality, starts from the extremity of the Cours Sauvaire, and ascends northwards, leaving the black masses of the old quarter on its left, and the light-yellow houses of the new town on its right. It is here, about half-way along the street, that stands the Sub-Prefecture, in the rear of a small square planted with sickly trees; the people of Plassans are very proud of this edifice.

As if to keep more isolated and shut up within itself, the town is belted with old ramparts, which only serve to increase its gloom and render it more confined. These ridiculous fortifications, preyed upon by ivy and crowned with wild gillyflowers, are about as high and as thick as the walls of a convent, and could be demolished by gunshot. They have several openings, the principal of which, the Porte de Rome and the Grand'-Porte, afford access to the Nice road and the Lyons road, at the other end of town. Until 1853 these openings were furnished with huge wooden two-leaved gates, arched at the top, and strengthened with bars of iron. These gates were double-locked at eleven o'clock in summer, and ten o'clock in winter. The town having thus shot its bolts like a timid girl, went quietly to sleep. A keeper, who lived in a little cell in one of the inner corners of each gateway, was authorised to admit belated persons. But it was necessary to stand parleying a long time. The keeper would not let people in until, by the light of his lantern, he had carefully scrutinised their faces through a peep-hole. If their looks displeased him they had to sleep outside. This custom of locking the gates every evening was highly characteristic of the spirit of the town, which was a commingling of cowardice, egotism, routine, exclusiveness, and devout longing for a cloistered life. Plassans, when it had shut itself up, would say to itself, "I am at home," with the satisfaction of some pious bourgeois, who, assured of the safety of his cash-box, and certain that no noise will disturb him, duly says his prayers and retires gladly to bed. No other town, I believe, has so long persisted in thus incarcerating itself like a nun.

The population of Plassans is divided into three groups, corresponding with the same number of districts. Putting aside the functionaries—the sub-prefect, the receiver of taxes, the mortgage commissioner, and the postmaster, who are all strangers to the locality, where they are objects of envy rather than of esteem, and who live after their own fashion—the real inhabitants, those who were born there and have every intention of ending their days there, feel too much respect for traditional usages and established boundaries not to pen themselves of their own accord in one or other of the town's social divisions.

The nobility virtually cloister themselves. Since the fall of Charles X. they scarcely ever go out, and when they do they are eager to return to their large dismal mansions, and walk along furtively as though they were in a hostile country. They do not visit anyone, nor do they even receive each other. Their drawing-rooms are frequented by a few priests only. They spend the summer in the chateaux which they possess in the environs; in the winter, they sit round their firesides. They are, as it were, dead people weary of life. And thus the gloomy silence of a cemetery hangs over their quarter of the town. The doors and windows are carefully barricaded; one would think their mansions were so many convents shut off from all the tumult of the world. At rare intervals an abbe, whose measured tread adds to the gloomy silence of these sealed houses, passes by and glides like a shadow through some half-opened doorway.

The well-to-do people, the retired tradesmen, the lawyers and notaries, all those of the little easy-going, ambitious world that inhabits the new town, endeavour to infuse some liveliness into Plassans. They go to the parties given by the sub-prefect, and dream of giving similar entertainments. They eagerly seek popularity, call a workman "my good fellow," chat with the peasants about the harvest, read the papers, and walk out with their wives on Sundays. Theirs are the enlightened minds of the district, they are the only persons who venture to speak disparagingly of the ramparts; in fact, they have several times demanded of the authorities the demolition of those old walls, relics of a former age. At the same time, the most sceptical among them experience a shock of delight whenever a marquis or a count deigns to honour them with a stiff salutation. Indeed, the dream of every citizen of the new town is to be admitted to a drawing-room of the Saint-Marc quarter. They know very well that their ambition is not attainable, and it is this which makes them proclaim all the louder that they are freethinkers. But they are freethinkers in words only; firm friends of the authorities, they are ready to rush into the arms of the first deliverer at the slightest indication of popular discontent.

The group which toils and vegetates in the old quarter is not so clearly defined as the others. The labouring classes are here in a majority; but retail dealers and even a few wholesale traders are to be found among them. As a matter of fact, Plassans is far from being a commercial centre; there is only just sufficient trade to dispose of the products of the country—oil, wine, and almonds. As for industrial labour, it is represented almost entirely by three or four evil-smelling tanyards, a felt hat manufactory, and some soap-boiling works, which last are relegated to a corner of the Faubourg. This little commercial and industrial world, though it may on high days and holidays visit the people of the new district, generally takes up its quarters among the operatives of the old town. Merchants, retail traders, and artisans have common interests which unite them together. On Sundays only, the masters make themselves spruce and foregather apart. On the other hand, the labouring classes, which constitute scarcely a fifth of the population, mingle with the idlers of the district.

It is only once a week, and during the fine weather, that the three districts of Plassans come together face to face. The whole town repairs to the Cours Sauvaire on Sunday after vespers; even the nobility venture thither. Three distinct currents flow along this sort of boulevard planted with rows of plane-trees. The well-to-do citizens of the new quarter merely pass along before quitting the town by the Grand'-Porte and taking the Avenue du Mail on the right, where they walk up and down till nightfall. Meantime, the nobility and the lower classes share the Cours Sauvaire between them. For more than a century past the nobility have selected the walk on the south side, which is bordered with large mansions, and is the first to escape the heat of the sun; the lower classes have to rest content with the walk on the north, where the cafes, inns, and tobacconists' shops are located. The people and the nobility promenade the whole afternoon, walking up and down the Cours without anyone of either party thinking of changing sides. They are only separated by a distance of some seven or eight yards, yet it is as if they were a thousand leagues away from each other, for they scrupulously follow those two parallel lines, as though they must not come in contact here below. Even during the revolutionary periods each party kept to its own side. This regulation walk on Sunday and the locking of the town gates in the evening are analogous instances which suffice to indicate the character of the ten thousand people inhabiting the town.

Here, amidst these surroundings, until the year 1848, there vegetated an obscure family that enjoyed little esteem, but whose head, Pierre Rougon, subsequently played an important part in life owing to certain circumstances.

Pierre Rougon was the son of a peasant. His mother's family, the Fouques, owned, towards the end of the last century, a large plot of ground in the Faubourg, behind the old cemetery of Saint-Mittre; this ground was subsequently joined to the Jas-Meiffren. The Fouques were the richest market-gardeners in that part of the country; they supplied an entire district of Plassans with vegetables. However, their name died out a few years before the Revolution. Only one girl, Adelaide, remained; born in 1768, she had become an orphan at the age of eighteen. This girl, whose father had died insane, was a long, lank, pale creature, with a scared look and strange ways which one might have taken for shyness so long as she was a little girl. As she grew up, however, she became still stranger; she did certain things which were inexplicable even to the cleverest folk of the Faubourg, and from that time it was rumoured that she was cracked like her father.

She had scarcely been an orphan six months, in possession of a fortune which rendered her an eagerly sought heiress, when it transpired that she had married a young gardener named Rougon, a rough-hewn peasant from the Basses-Alpes. This Rougon, after the death of the last of the male Fouques, who had engaged him for a term, had remained in the service of the deceased's daughter. From the situation of salaried servant he ascended rapidly to the enviable position of husband. This marriage was a first shock to public opinion. No one could comprehend why Adelaide preferred this poor fellow, coarse, heavy, vulgar, scarce able to speak French, to those other young men, sons of well-to-do farmers, who had been seen hovering round her for some time. And, as provincial people do not allow anything to remain unexplained, they made sure there was some mystery at the bottom of this affair, alleging even that the marriage of the two young people had become an absolute necessity. But events proved the falsity of the accusation. More than a year went by before Adelaide had a son. The Faubourg was annoyed; it could not admit that it was wrong, and determined to penetrate the supposed mystery; accordingly all the gossips kept a watch upon the Rougons. They soon found ample matter for tittle-tattle. Rougon died almost suddenly, fifteen months after his marriage, from a sunstroke received one afternoon while he was weeding a bed of carrots.

Scarcely a year then elapsed before the young widow caused unheard-of scandal. It became known, as an indisputable fact, that she had a lover. She did not appear to make any secret of it; several persons asserted that they had heard her use endearing terms in public to poor Rougon's successor. Scarcely a year of widowhood and a lover already! Such a disregard of propriety seemed monstrous out of all reason. And the scandal was heightened by Adelaide's strange choice. At that time there dwelt at the end of the Impasse Saint-Mittre, in a hovel the back of which abutted on the Fouques' land, a man of bad repute, who was generally referred to as "that scoundrel Macquart." This man would vanish for weeks and then turn up some fine evening, sauntering about with his hands in his pockets and whistling as though he had just come from a short walk. And the women sitting at their doorsteps as he passed: "There's that scoundrel Macquart! He has hidden his bales and his gun in some hollow of the Viorne." The truth was, Macquart had no means, and yet ate and drank like a happy drone during his short sojourns in the town. He drank copiously and with fierce obstinacy. Seating himself alone at a table in some tavern, he would linger there evening after evening, with his eyes stupidly fixed on his glass, neither seeing nor hearing anything around him. When the landlord closed his establishment, he would retire with a firm step, with his head raised, as if he were kept yet more erect by inebriation. "Macquart walks so straight, he's surely dead drunk," people used to say, as they saw him going home. Usually, when he had had no drink, he walked with a slight stoop and shunned the gaze of curious people with a kind of savage shyness.

Since the death of his father, a journeyman tanner who had left him as sole heritage the hovel in the Impasse Saint-Mittre, he had never been known to have either relatives or friends. The proximity of the frontiers and the neighbouring forests of the Seille had turned this singular, lazy fellow into a combination of smuggler and poacher, one of those suspicious-looking characters of whom passers-by observe: "I shouldn't care to meet that man at midnight in a dark wood." Tall, with a formidable beard and lean face, Macquart was the terror of the good women of the Faubourg of Plassans; they actually accused him of devouring little children raw. Though he was hardly thirty years old, he looked fifty. Amidst his bushy beard and the locks of hair which hung over his face in poodle fashion, one could only distinguish the gleam of his brown eyes, the furtive sorrowful glance of a man of vagrant instincts, rendered vicious by wine and a pariah life. Although no crimes had actually been brought home to him, no theft or murder was ever perpetrated in the district without suspicion at once falling upon him.

And it was this ogre, this brigand, this scoundrel Macquart, whom Adelaide had chosen! In twenty months she had two children by him, first a boy and then a girl. There was no question of marriage between them. Never had the Faubourg beheld such audacious impropriety. The stupefaction was so great, the idea of Macquart having found a young and wealthy mistress so completely upset the gossips, that they even spoke gently of Adelaide. "Poor thing! She's gone quite mad," they would say. "If she had any relatives she would have been placed in confinement long ago." And as they never knew anything of the history of those strange amours, they accused that rogue Macquart of having taken advantage of Adelaide's weak mind to rob her of her money.

The legitimate son, little Pierre Rougon, grew up with his mother's other offspring. The latter, Antoine and Ursule, the young wolves as they were called in the district, were kept at home by Adelaide, who treated them as affectionately as her first child. She did not appear to entertain a very clear idea of the position in life reserved for these two poor creatures. To her they were the same in every respect as her first-born. She would sometimes go out holding Pierre with one hand and Antoine with the other, never noticing how differently the two little fellows were already regarded.

It was a strange home. For nearly twenty years everyone lived there after his or her fancy, the children like the mother. Everything went on free from control. In growing to womanhood, Adelaide had retained the strangeness which had been taken for shyness when she was fifteen. It was not that she was insane, as the people of the Faubourg asserted, but there was a lack of equilibrium between her nerves and her blood, a disorder of the brain and heart which made her lead a life out of the ordinary, different from that of the rest of the world. She was certainly very natural, very consistent with herself; but in the eyes of the neighbours her consistency became pure insanity. She seemed desirous of making herself conspicuous, it was thought she was wickedly determined to turn things at home from bad to worse, whereas with great naivete she simply acted according to the impulses of her nature.

Ever since giving birth to her first child she had been subject to nervous fits which brought on terrible convulsions. These fits recurred periodically, every two or three months. The doctors whom she consulted declared they could do nothing for her, that age would weaken the severity of the attacks. They simply prescribed a dietary regimen of underdone meat and quinine wine. However, these repeated shocks led to cerebral disorder. She lived on from day to day like a child, like a fawning animal yielding to its instincts. When Macquart was on his rounds, she passed her time in lazy, pensive idleness. All she did for her children was to kiss and play with them. Then as soon as her lover returned she would disappear.

Behind Macquart's hovel there was a little yard, separated from the Fouques' property by a wall. One morning the neighbours were much astonished to find in this wall a door which had not been there the previous evening. Before an hour had elapsed, the entire Faubourg had flocked to the neighbouring windows. The lovers must have worked the whole night to pierce the opening and place the door there. They could now go freely from one house to the other. The scandal was revived, everyone felt less pity for Adelaide, who was certainly the disgrace of the suburb; she was reproached more wrathfully for that door, that tacit, brutal admission of her union, than even for her two illegitimate children. "People should at least study appearances," the most tolerant women would say. But Adelaide did not understand what was meant by studying appearances. She was very happy, very proud of her door; she had assisted Macquart to knock the stones from the wall and had even mixed the mortar so that the work might proceed the quicker; and she came with childish delight to inspect the work by daylight on the morrow—an act which was deemed a climax of shamelessness by three gossips who observed her contemplating the masonry. From that date, whenever Macquart reappeared, it was thought, as no one then ever saw the young woman, that she was living with him in the hovel of the Impasse Saint-Mittre.

The smuggler would come very irregularly, almost always unexpectedly, to Plassans. Nobody ever knew what life the lovers led during the two or three days he spent there at distant intervals. They used to shut themselves up; the little dwelling seemed uninhabited. Then, as the gossips had declared that Macquart had simply seduced Adelaide in order to spend her money, they were astonished, after a time, to see him still lead his wonted life, ever up hill and down dale and as badly equipped as previously. Perhaps the young woman loved him all the more for seeing him at rare intervals, perhaps he had disregarded her entreaties, feeling an irresistible desire for a life of adventure. The gossips invented a thousand fables, without succeeding in giving any reasonable explanation of a connection which had originated and continued in so strange a manner. The hovel in the Impasse Saint-Mittre remained closed and preserved its secrets. It was merely guessed that Macquart had probably acquired the habit of beating Adelaide, although the sound of a quarrel never issued from the house. However, on several occasions she was seen with her face black and blue, and her hair torn away. At the same time, she did not display the least dejection or grief, nor did she seek in any way to hide her bruises. She smiled, and seemed happy. No doubt she allowed herself to be beaten without breathing a word. This existence lasted for more than fifteen years.

At times when Adelaide returned home she would find her house upside down, but would not take the least notice of it. She was utterly ignorant of the practical meaning of life, of the proper value of things and the necessity for order. She let her children grow up like those plum-trees which sprout along the highways at the pleasure of the rain and sun. They bore their natural fruits like wild stock which has never known grafting or pruning. Never was nature allowed such complete sway, never did such mischievous creatures grow up more freely under the sole influence of instinct. They rolled among the vegetables, passed their days in the open air playing and fighting like good-for-nothing urchins. They stole provisions from the house and pillaged the few fruit-trees in the enclosure; they were the plundering, squalling, familiar demons of this strange abode of lucid insanity. When their mother was absent for days together, they would make such an uproar, and hit upon such diabolical devices for annoying people, that the neighbours had to threaten them with a whipping. Moreover, Adelaide did not inspire them with much fear; if they were less obnoxious to other people when she was at home, it was because they made her their victim, shirking school five or six times a week and doing everything they could to receive some punishment which would allow them to squall to their hearts' content. But she never beat them, nor even lost her temper; she lived on very well, placidly, indolently, in a state of mental abstraction amidst all the uproar. At last, indeed, this uproar became indispensable to her, to fill the void in her brain. She smiled complacently when she heard anyone say, "Her children will beat her some day, and it will serve her right." To all remarks, her utter indifference seemed to reply, "What does it matter?" She troubled even less about her property than about her children. The Fouques' enclosure, during the many years that this singular existence lasted would have become a piece of waste ground if the young woman had not luckily entrusted the cultivation of her vegetables to a clever market-gardener. This man, who was to share the profits with her, robbed her impudently, though she never noticed it. This circumstance had its advantages, however; for, in order to steal the more, the gardener drew as much as possible from the land, which in the result almost doubled in value.

Pierre, the legitimate son, either from secret instinct or from his knowledge of the different manner in which he and the others were regarded by the neighbours, domineered over his brother and sister from an early age. In their quarrels, although he was much weaker than Antoine, he always got the better of the contest, beating the other with all the authority of a master. With regard to Ursule, a poor, puny, wan little creature, she was handled with equal roughness by both the boys. Indeed, until they were fifteen or sixteen, the three children fraternally beat each other without understanding their vague, mutual hatred, without realising how foreign they were to one another. It was only in youth that they found themselves face to face with definite, self-conscious personalities.

At sixteen, Antoine was a tall fellow, a blend of Macquart's and Adelaide's failings. Macquart, however, predominated in him, with his love of vagrancy, his tendency to drunkenness, and his brutish savagery. At the same time, under the influence of Adelaide's nervous nature, the vices which in the father assumed a kind of sanguinary frankness were in the son tinged with an artfulness full of hypocrisy and cowardice. Antoine resembled his mother by his total want of dignified will, by his effeminate voluptuous egotism, which disposed him to accept any bed of infamy provided he could lounge upon it at his ease and sleep warmly in it. People said of him: "Ah! the brigand! He hasn't even the courage of his villainy like Macquart; if ever he commits a murder, it will be with pin pricks." Physically, Antoine inherited Adelaide's thick lips only; his other features resembled those of the smuggler, but they were softer and more prone to change of expression.

In Ursule, on the other hand, physical and moral resemblance to the mother predominated. There was a mixture of certain characteristics in her also; but born the last, at a time when Adelaide's love was warmer than Macquart's, the poor little thing seemed to have received with her sex a deeper impress of her mother's temperament. Moreover, hers was not a fusion of the two natures, but rather a juxtaposition, a remarkably close soldering. Ursule was whimsical, and displayed at times the shyness, the melancholy, and the transports of a pariah; then she would often break out into nervous fits of laughter, and muse lazily, like a woman unsound both in head and heart. Her eyes, which at times had a scared expression like those of Adelaide, were as limpid as crystal, similar to those of kittens doomed to die of consumption.

In presence of those two illegitimate children Pierre seemed a stranger; to one who had not penetrated to the roots of his being he would have appeared profoundly dissimilar. Never did child's nature show a more equal balance of the characteristics of its parents. He was the exact mean between the peasant Rougon and the nervous Adelaide. Paternal grossness was attenuated by the maternal influence. One found in him the first phase of that evolution of temperaments which ultimately brings about the amelioration or deterioration of a race. Although he was still a peasant, his skin was less coarse, his face less heavy, his intellect more capacious and more supple. In him the defects of his father and his mother had advantageously reacted upon each other. If Adelaide's nature, rendered exquisitely sensitive by her rebellious nerves, had combated and lessened Rougon's full-bodied ponderosity, the latter had successfully prevented the young woman's tendency to cerebral disorder from being implanted in the child. Pierre knew neither the passions nor the sickly ravings of Macquart's young whelps. Very badly brought up, unruly and noisy, like all children who are not restrained during their infancy, he nevertheless possessed at bottom such sense and intelligence as would always preserve him from perpetrating any unproductive folly. His vices, his laziness, his appetite for indulgence, lacked the instinctiveness which characterised Antoine's; he meant to cultivate and gratify them honourably and openly. In his plump person of medium height, in his long pale face, in which the features derived from his father had acquired some of the maternal refinement, one could already detect signs of sly and crafty ambition and insatiable desire, with the hardness of heart and envious hatred of a peasant's son whom his mother's means and nervous temperament had turned into a member of the middle classes.

When, at the age of seventeen, Pierre observed and was able to understand Adelaide's disorders and the singular position of Antoine and Ursule, he seemed neither sorry nor indignant, but simply worried as to the course which would best serve his own interests. He was the only one of the three children who had pursued his studies with any industry. When a peasant begins to feel the need of instruction he most frequently becomes a fierce calculator. At school Pierre's playmates roused his first suspicions by the manner in which they treated and hooted his brother. Later on he came to understand the significance of many looks and words. And at last he clearly saw that the house was being pillaged. From that time forward he regarded Antoine and Ursule as shameless parasites, mouths that were devouring his own substance. Like the people of the Faubourg, he thought that his mother was a fit subject for a lunatic asylum, and feared she would end by squandering all her money, if he did not take steps to prevent it. What gave him the finishing stroke was the dishonesty of the gardener who cultivated the land. At this, in one day, the unruly child was transformed into a thrifty, selfish lad, hurriedly matured, as regards his instincts, by the strange improvident life which he could no longer bear to see around him without a feeling of anguish. Those vegetables, from the sale of which the market-gardener derived the largest profits, really belonged to him; the wine which his mother's offspring drank, the bread they ate, also belonged to him. The whole house, the entire fortune, was his by right; according to his boorish logic, he alone, the legitimate son, was the heir. And as his riches were in danger, as everybody was greedily gnawing at his future fortune, he sought a means of turning them all out—mother, brother, sister, servants—and of succeeding immediately to his inheritance.

The conflict was a cruel one; the lad knew that he must first strike his mother. Step by step, with patient tenacity, he executed a plan whose every detail he had long previously thought out. His tactics were to appear before Adelaide like a living reproach—not that he flew into a passion, or upbraided her for her misconduct; but he had acquired a certain manner of looking at her, without saying a word, which terrified her. Whenever she returned from a short sojourn in Macquart's hovel she could not turn her eyes on her son without a shudder. She felt his cold glances, as sharp as steel blades pierce her deeply and pitilessly. The severe, taciturn demeanour of the child of the man whom she had so soon forgotten strangely troubled her poor disordered brain. She would fancy at times that Rougon had risen from the dead to punish her for her dissoluteness. Every week she fell into one of those nervous fits which were shattering her constitution. She was left to struggle until she recovered consciousness, after which she would creep about more feebly than ever. She would also often sob the whole night long, holding her head in her hands, and accepting the wounds that Pierre dealt her with resignation, as if they had been the strokes of an avenging deity. At other times she repudiated him; she would not acknowledge her own flesh and blood in that heavy-faced lad, whose calmness chilled her own feverishness so painfully. She would a thousand times rather have been beaten than glared at like that. Those implacable looks, which followed her everywhere, threw her at last into such unbearable torments that on several occasions she determined to see her lover no more. As soon, however, as Macquart returned she forgot her vows and hastened to him. The conflict with her son began afresh, silent and terrible, when she came back home. At the end of a few months she fell completely under his sway. She stood before him like a child doubtful of her behaviour and fearing that she deserves a whipping. Pierre had skilfully bound her hand and foot, and made a very submissive servant of her, without opening his lips, without once entering into difficult and compromising explanations.

When the young man felt that his mother was in his power, that he could treat her like a slave, he began, in his own interest, to turn her cerebral weakness and the foolish terror with which his glances inspired her to his own advantage. His first care, as soon as he was master at home, was to dismiss the market-gardener and replace him by one of his own creatures. Then he took upon himself the supreme direction of the household, selling, buying, and holding the cash-box. On the other hand, he made no attempt to regulate Adelaide's actions, or to correct Antoine and Ursule for their laziness. That mattered little to him, for he counted upon getting rid of these people as soon as an opportunity presented itself. He contented himself with portioning out their bread and water. Then, having already got all the property in his own hands, he awaited an event which would permit him to dispose of it as he pleased.

Circumstances proved singularly favourable. He escaped the conscription on the ground of being a widow's eldest son. But two years later Antoine was called out. His bad luck did not affect him much; he counted on his mother purchasing a substitute for him. Adelaide, in fact, wished to save him from serving; Pierre, however, who held the money, turned a deaf ear to her. His brother's compulsory departure would be a lucky event for him, and greatly assist the accomplishment of his plans. When his mother mentioned the matter to him, he gave her such a look that she did not venture to pursue it. His glance plainly signified, "Do you wish, then, to ruin me for the sake of your illegitimate offspring?" Forthwith she selfishly abandoned Antoine, for before everything else she sought her own peace and quietness. Pierre, who did not like violent measures, and who rejoiced at being able to eject his brother without a disturbance, then played the part of a man in despair: the year had been a bad one, money was scarce, and to raise any he would be compelled to sell a portion of the land, which would be the beginning of their ruin. Then he pledged his word of honour to Antoine that he would buy him out the following year, though he meant to do nothing of the kind. Antoine then went off, duped, and half satisfied.

Pierre got rid of Ursule in a still more unexpected manner. A journeyman hatter of the Faubourg, named Mouret, conceived a real affection for the girl, whom he thought as white and delicate as any young lady from the Saint-Marc quarter. He married her. On his part it was a love match, free from all sordid motives. As for Ursule, she accepted the marriage in order to escape a home where her eldest brother rendered life intolerable. Her mother, absorbed in her own courses, and using her remaining energy to defend her own particular interests, regarded the matter with absolute indifference. She was even glad of Ursule's departure from the house, hoping that Pierre, now that he had no further cause for dissatisfaction, would let her live in peace after her own fashion. No sooner had the young people been married than Mouret perceived that he would have to quit Plassans, if he did not wish to hear endless disparaging remarks about his wife and his mother-in-law. Taking Ursule with him, he accordingly repaired to Marseilles, where he worked at his trade. It should be mentioned that he had not asked for one sou of dowry. When Pierre, somewhat surprised by this disinterestedness, commenced to stammer out some explanations, Mouret closed his mouth by saying that he preferred to earn his wife's bread. Nevertheless the worthy son of the peasant remained uneasy; Mouret's indifference seemed to him to conceal some trap.

Adelaide now remained to be disposed of. Nothing in the world would have induced Pierre to live with her any longer. She was compromising him; it was with her that he would have liked to make a start. But he found himself between two very embarrassing alternatives: to keep her, and thus, in a measure, share her disgrace, and bind a fetter to his feet which would arrest him in his ambitious flight; or to turn her out, with the certainty of being pointed at as a bad son, which would have robbed him of the reputation for good nature which he desired. Knowing that he would be in want of everybody, he desired to secure an untarnished name throughout Plassans. There was but one method to adopt, namely, to induce Adelaide to leave of her own accord. Pierre neglected nothing to accomplish this end. He considered his mother's misconduct a sufficient excuse for his own hard-heartedness. He punished her as one would chastise a child. The tables were turned. The poor woman cowered under the stick which, figuratively, was constantly held over her. She was scarcely forty-two years old, and already had the stammerings of terror, and vague, pitiful looks of an old woman in her dotage. Her son continued to stab her with his piercing glances, hoping that she would run away when her courage was exhausted. The unfortunate woman suffered terribly from shame, restrained desire and enforced cowardice, receiving the blows dealt her with passive resignation, and nevertheless returning to Macquart with the determination to die on the spot rather than submit. There were nights when she would have got out of bed, and thrown herself into the Viorne, if with her weak, nervous, nature she had not felt the greatest fear of death. On several occasions she thought of running away and joining her lover on the frontier. It was only because she did not know whither to go that she remained in the house, submitting to her son's contemptuous silence and secret brutality. Pierre divined that she would have left long ago if she had only had a refuge. He was waiting an opportunity to take a little apartment for her somewhere, when a fortuitous occurrence, which he had not ventured to anticipate, abruptly brought about the realisation of his desires. Information reached the Faubourg that Macquart had just been killed on the frontier by a shot from a custom-house officer, at the moment when he was endeavouring to smuggle a load of Geneva watches into France. The story was true. The smuggler's body was not even brought home, but was interred in the cemetery of a little mountain village. Adelaide's grief plunged her into stupor. Her son, who watched her curiously, did not see her shed a tear. Macquart had made her sole legatee. She inherited his hovel in the Impasse Saint-Mittre, and his carbine, which a fellow-smuggler, braving the balls of the custom-house officers, loyally brought back to her. On the following day she retired to the little house, hung the carbine above the mantelpiece, and lived there estranged from all the world, solitary and silent.

Pierre was at last sole master of the house. The Fouques' land belonged to him in fact, if not in law. He never thought of establishing himself on it. It was too narrow a field for his ambition. To till the ground and cultivate vegetables seemed to him boorish, unworthy of his faculties. He was in a hurry to divest himself of everything recalling the peasant. With his nature refined by his mother's nervous temperament, he felt an irresistible longing for the enjoyments of the middle classes. In all his calculations, therefore, he had regarded the sale of the Fouques' property as the final consummation. This sale, by placing a round sum of money in his hands, would enable him to marry the daughter of some merchant who would take him into partnership. At this period the wars of the First Empire were greatly thinning the ranks of eligible young men. Parents were not so fastidious as previously in the choice of a son-in-law. Pierre persuaded himself that money would smooth all difficulties, and that the gossip of the Faubourg would be overlooked; he intended to pose as a victim, as an honest man suffering from a family disgrace, which he deplored, without being soiled by it or excusing it.

For several months already he had cast his eyes on a certain Felicite Puech, the daughter of an oil-dealer. The firm of Puech & Lacamp, whose warehouses were in one of the darkest lanes of the old quarter, was far from prosperous. It enjoyed but doubtful credit in the market, and people talked vaguely of bankruptcy. It was precisely in consequence of these evil reports that Pierre turned his batteries in this direction. No well-to-do trader would have given him his daughter. He meant to appear on the scene at the very moment when old Puech should no longer know which way to turn; he would then purchase Felicite of him, and re-establish the credit of the house by his own energy and intelligence. It was a clever expedient for ascending the first rung of the social ladder, for raising himself above his station. Above all things, he wished to escape from that frightful Faubourg where everybody reviled his family, and to obliterate all these foul legends, by effacing even the very name of the Fouques' enclosure. For that reason the filthy streets of the old quarter seemed to him perfect paradise. There, only, he would be able to change his skin.

The moment which he had been awaiting soon arrived. The firm of Puech and Lacamp seemed to be at the last gasp. The young man then negotiated the match with prudent skill. He was received, if not as a deliverer, at least as a necessary and acceptable expedient. The marriage agreed upon, he turned his attention to the sale of the ground. The owner of the Jas-Meiffren, desiring to enlarge his estate, had made him repeated offers. A low, thin, party-wall alone separated the two estates. Pierre speculated on the eagerness of his wealthy neighbour, who, to gratify his caprice, offered as much as fifty thousand francs for the land. It was double its value. Pierre, whoever, with the craftiness of a peasant, pulled a long face, and said that he did not care to sell; that his mother would never consent to get rid of the property where the Fouques had lived from father to son for nearly two centuries. But all the time that he was seemingly holding back he was really making preparations for the sale. Certain doubts had arisen in his mind. According to his own brutal logic, the property belonged to him; he had the right to dispose of it as he chose. Beneath this assurance, however, he had vague presentiments of legal complications. So he indirectly consulted a lawyer of the Faubourg.

He learnt some fine things from him. According to the lawyer, his hands were completely tied. His mother alone could alienate the property, and he doubted whether she would. But what he did not know, what came as a heavy blow to him, was that Ursule and Antoine, those young wolves, had claims on the estate. What! they would despoil him, rob him, the legitimate child! The lawyer's explanations were clear and precise, however; Adelaide, it is true, had married Rougon under the common property system; but as the whole fortune consisted of land, the young woman, according to law, again came into possession of everything at her husband's death. Moreover, Macquart and Adelaide had duly acknowledged their children when declaring their birth for registration, and thus these children were entitled to inherit from their mother. For sole consolation, Pierre learnt that the law reduced the share of illegitimate children in favour of the others. This, however, did not console him at all. He wanted to have everything. He would not have shared ten sous with Ursule and Antoine.

This vista of the intricacies of the Code opened up a new horizon, which he scanned with a singularly thoughtful air. He soon recognised that a shrewd man must always keep the law on his side. And this is what he devised without consulting anyone, even the lawyer, whose suspicions he was afraid of arousing. He knew how to turn his mother round his finger. One fine morning he took her to a notary and made her sign a deed of sale. Provided she were left the hovel in the Impasse Saint-Mittre, Adelaide would have sold all Plassans. Besides, Pierre assured her an annual income of six hundred francs, and made the most solemn promises to watch over his brother and sister. This oath satisfied the good woman. She recited, before the notary, the lesson which it had pleased her son to teach her. On the following day the young man made her place her name at the foot of a document in which she acknowledged having received fifty thousand francs as the price of the property. This was his stroke of genius, the act of a rogue. He contented himself with telling his mother, who was a little surprised at signing such a receipt when she had not seen a centime of the fifty thousand francs, that it was a pure formality of no consequence whatever. As he slipped the paper into his pocket, he thought to himself, "Now, let the young wolves ask me to render an account. I will tell them the old woman has squandered everything. They will never dare to go to law with me about it." A week afterwards, the party-wall no longer existed: a plough had turned up the vegetable beds; the Fouques' enclosure, in accordance with young Rougon's wish, was about to become a thing of the past. A few months later, the owner of the Jas-Meiffren even had the old market-gardener's house, which was falling to pieces, pulled down.

When Pierre had secured the fifty thousand francs he married Felicite Puech with as little delay as possible. Felicite was a short, dark woman, such as one often meets in Provence. She looked like one of those brown, lean, noisy grasshoppers, which in their sudden leaps often strike their heads against the almond-trees. Thin, flat-breasted, with pointed shoulders and a face like that of a pole-cat, her features singularly sunken and attenuated, it was not easy to tell her age; she looked as near fifteen as thirty, although she was in reality only nineteen, four years younger than her husband. There was much feline slyness in the depths of her little black eyes, which suggested gimlet holes. Her low, bumpy forehead, her slightly depressed nose with delicate quivering nostrils, her thin red lips and prominent chin, parted from her cheeks by strange hollows, all suggested the countenance of an artful dwarf, a living mask of intrigue, an active, envious ambition. With all her ugliness, however, Felicite possessed a sort of gracefulness which rendered her seductive. People said of her that she could be pretty or ugly as she pleased. It would depend on the fashion in which she tied her magnificent hair; but it depended still more on the triumphant smile which illumined her golden complexion when she thought she had got the better of somebody. Born under an evil star, and believing herself ill-used by fortune, she was generally content to appear an ugly creature. She did not, however, intend to abandon the struggle, for she had vowed that she would some day make the whole town burst with envy, by an insolent display of happiness and luxury. Had she been able to act her part on a more spacious stage, where full play would have been allowed her ready wit, she would have quickly brought her dream to pass. Her intelligence was far superior to that of the girls of her own station and education. Evil tongues asserted that her mother, who had died a few years after she was born, had, during the early period of her married life, been familiar with the Marquis de Carnavant, a young nobleman of the Saint-Marc quarter. In fact, Felicite had the hands and feet of a marchioness, and, in this respect, did not appear to belong to that class of workers from which she was descended.

Her marriage with Pierre Rougon, that semi-peasant, that man of the Faubourg, whose family was in such bad odour, kept the old quarter in a state of astonishment for more than a month. She let people gossip, however, receiving the stiff congratulations of her friends with strange smiles. Her calculations had been made; she had chosen Rougon for a husband as one would choose an accomplice. Her father, in accepting the young man, had merely had eyes for the fifty thousand francs which were to save him from bankruptcy. Felicite, however, was more keen-sighted. She looked into the future, and felt that she would be in want of a robust man, even if he were somewhat rustic, behind whom she might conceal herself, and whose limbs she would move at will. She entertained a deliberate hatred for the insignificant little exquisites of provincial towns, the lean herd of notaries' clerks and prospective barristers, who stand shivering with cold while waiting for clients. Having no dowry, and despairing of ever marrying a rich merchant's son, she by far preferred a peasant whom she could use as a passive tool, to some lank graduate who would overwhelm her with his academical superiority, and drag her about all her life in search of hollow vanities. She was of opinion that the woman ought to make the man. She believed herself capable of carving a minister out of a cow-herd. That which had attracted her in Rougon was his broad chest, his heavy frame, which was not altogether wanting in elegance. A man thus built would bear with ease and sprightliness the mass of intrigues which she dreamt of placing on his shoulders. However, while she appreciated her husband's strength and vigour, she also perceived that he was far from being a fool; under his coarse flesh she had divined the cunning suppleness of his mind. Still she was a long way from really knowing her Rougon; she thought him far stupider than he was. A few days after her marriage, as she was by chance fumbling in the drawer of a secretaire, she came across the receipt for fifty thousand francs which Adelaide had signed. At sight of it she understood things, and felt rather frightened; her own natural average honesty rendered her hostile to such expedients. Her terror, however, was not unmixed with admiration; Rougon became in her eyes a very smart fellow.

The young couple bravely sought to conquer fortune. The firm of Puech & Lacamp was not, after all, so embarrassed as Pierre had thought. Its liabilities were small, it was merely in want of ready-money. In the provinces, traders adopt prudent courses to save them from serious disasters. Puech & Lacamp were prudent to an excessive degree; they never risked a thousand crowns without the greatest fear, and thus their house, a veritable hole, was an unimportant one. The fifty thousand francs that Pierre brought into it sufficed to pay the debts and extend the business. The beginnings were good. During three successive years the olive harvest was an abundant one. Felicite, by a bold stroke which absolutely frightened both Pierre and old Puech, made them purchase a considerable quantity of oil, which they stored in their warehouse. During the following years, as the young woman had foreseen, the crops failed, and a considerable rise in prices having set in, they realised large profits by selling out their stock.

A short time after this haul, Puech & Lacamp retired from the firm, content with the few sous they had just secured, and ambitious of living on their incomes.

The young couple now had sole control of the business, and thought that they had at last laid the foundation of their fortune. "You have vanquished my ill-luck," Felicite would sometimes say to her husband.

One of the rare weaknesses of her energetic nature was to believe herself stricken by misfortune. Hitherto, so she asserted, nothing had been successful with either herself or her father, in spite of all their efforts. Goaded by her southern superstition, she prepared to struggle with fate as one struggles with somebody who is endeavouring to strangle one. Circumstances soon justified her apprehensions in a singular manner. Ill-luck returned inexorably. Every year some fresh disaster shook Rougon's business. A bankruptcy resulted in the loss of a few thousand francs; his estimates of crops proved incorrect, through the most incredible circumstances; the safest speculations collapsed miserably. It was a truceless, merciless combat.

"You see I was born under an unlucky star!" Felicite would bitterly exclaim.

And yet she still struggled furiously, not understanding how it was that she, who had shown such keen scent in a first speculation, could now only give her husband the most deplorable advice.

Pierre, dejected and less tenacious than herself, would have gone into liquidation a score of times had it not been for his wife's firm obstinacy. She longed to be rich. She perceived that her ambition could only be attained by fortune. As soon as they possessed a few hundred thousand francs they would be masters of the town. She would get her husband appointed to an important post, and she would govern. It was not the attainment of honours which troubled her; she felt herself marvellously well armed for such a combat. But she could do nothing to get together the first few bags of money which were needed. Though the ruling of men caused her no apprehensions, she felt a sort of impotent rage at the thought of those inert, white, cold, five-franc pieces over which her intriguing spirit had no power, and which obstinately resisted her.

The battle lasted for more than thirty years. The death of Puech proved another heavy blow. Felicite, who had counted upon an inheritance of about forty thousand francs, found that the selfish old man, in order to indulge himself in his old age, had sunk all his money in a life annuity. The discovery made her quite ill. She was gradually becoming soured, she was growing more lean and harsh. To see her, from morning till night, whirling round the jars of oil, one would have thought she believed that she could stimulate the sales by continually flitting about like a restless fly. Her husband, on the contrary, became heavier; misfortune fattened him, making him duller and more indolent. These thirty years of combat did not, however, bring him to ruin. At each annual stock-taking they managed to make both ends meet fairly well; if they suffered any loss during one season, they recouped themselves the next. However, it was precisely this living from hand to mouth which exasperated Felicite. She would, by far, have preferred a big failure. They would then, perhaps, have been able to commence life over again, instead of obstinately persisting in their petty business, working themselves to death to gain the bare necessaries of life. During one third of a century they did not save fifty thousand francs.

It should be mentioned that, from the very first years of their married life, they had a numerous family, which in the long run became a heavy burden to them. In the course of five years, from 1811 to 1815, Felicite gave birth to three boys. Then during the four ensuing years she presented her husband with two girls. These had but an indifferent welcome; daughters are a terrible embarrassment when one has no dowry to give them.

However, the young woman did not regard this troop of children as the cause of their ruin. On the contrary, she based on her sons' heads the building of the fortune which was crumbling in her own hands. They were hardly ten years old before she discounted their future careers in her dreams. Doubting whether she would ever succeed herself, she centred in them all her hopes of overcoming the animosity of fate. They would provide satisfaction for her disappointed vanity, they would give her that wealthy, honourable position which she had hitherto sought in vain. From that time forward, without abandoning the business struggle, she conceived a second plan for obtaining the gratification of her domineering instincts. It seemed to her impossible that, amongst her three sons, there should not be a man of superior intellect, who would enrich them all. She felt it, she said. Accordingly, she nursed the children with a fervour in which maternal severity was blended with an usurer's solicitude. She amused herself by fattening them as though they constituted a capital which, later on, would return a large interest.

"Enough!" Pierre would sometimes exclaim, "all children are ungrateful. You are spoiling them, you are ruining us."

When Felicite spoke of sending them to college, he got angry. Latin was a useless luxury, it would be quite sufficient if they went through the classes of a little neighbouring school The young woman, however, persisted in her design. She possessed certain elevated instincts which made her take a great pride in surrounding herself with accomplished children; moreover, she felt that her sons must never remain as illiterate as her husband, if she wished to see them become prominent men. She fancied them all three in Paris in high positions, which she did not clearly define. When Rougon consented, and the three youngsters had entered the eighth class, Felicite felt the most lively satisfaction she had ever experienced. She listened with delight as they talked of their professors and their studies. When she heard her eldest son make one of his brothers decline *Rosa, a rose*, it sounded like delicious music to her. It is only fair to add that her delight was not tarnished by any sordid calculations. Even Rougon felt the satisfaction which an illiterate man experiences on perceiving his sons grow more learned than himself. Then the fellowship which grew up between their sons and those of the local big-wigs completed the parents' gratification. The youngsters were soon on familiar terms with the sons of the Mayor and the Sub-Prefect, and even with two or three young noblemen whom the Saint-Marc quarter had deigned to send to the Plassans College. Felicite was at a loss how to repay such an honour. The education of the three lads weighed seriously on the budget of the Rougon household.

Until the boys had taken their degrees, their parents, who kept them at college at enormous sacrifices, lived in hopes of their success. When they had obtained their diplomas Felicite wished to continue her work, and even persuaded her husband to send the three to Paris. Two of them devoted themselves to the study of law, and the third passed through the School of Medicine. Then, when they were men, and had exhausted the resources of the Rougon family and were obliged to return and establish themselves in the provinces, their parents' disenchantment began. They idled about and grew fat. And Felicite again felt all the bitterness of her ill-luck. Her sons were failing her. They had ruined her, and did not return any interest on the capital which they represented. This last blow of fate was the heaviest, as it fell on her ambition and her maternal vanity alike. Rougon repeated to her from morning till night, "I told you so!" which only exasperated her the more.

One day, as she was bitterly reproaching her eldest son with the large amount of money expended on his education, he said to her with equal bitterness, "I will repay you later on if I can. But as you had no means, you should have brought us up to a trade. We are out of our element, we are suffering more than you."

Felicite understood the wisdom of these words. From that time she ceased to accuse her children, and turned her anger against fate, which never wearied of striking her. She started her old complaints afresh, and bemoaned more and more the want of means which made her strand, as it were, in port. Whenever Rougon said to her, "Your sons are lazy fellows, they will eat up all we have," she sourly replied, "Would to God I had more money to give them; if they do vegetate, poor fellows, it's because they haven't got a sou to bless themselves with."

At the beginning of the year 1848, on the eve of the Revolution of February, the three young Rougons held very precarious positions at Plassans. They presented most curious and profoundly dissimilar characteristics, though they came of the same stock. They were in reality superior to their parents. The race of the Rougons was destined to become refined through its female side. Adelaide had made Pierre a man of moderate enterprise, disposed to low ambitions; Felicite had inspired her sons with a higher intelligence, with a capacity for greater vices and greater virtues.

At the period now referred to the eldest, Eugene, was nearly forty years old. He was a man of middle height, slightly bald, and already disposed to obesity. He had his father's face, a long face with broad features; beneath his skin one could divine the fat to which were due the flabby roundness of his features, and his yellowish, waxy complexion. Though his massive square head still recalled the peasant, his physiognomy was transfigured, lit up from within as it were, when his drooping eyelids were raised and his eyes awoke to life. In the son's case, the father's ponderousness had turned to gravity. This big fellow, Eugene, usually preserved a heavy somnolent demeanour. At the same time, certain of his heavy, languid movements suggested those of a giant stretching his limbs pending the time for action. By one of those alleged freaks of nature, of which, however, science is now commencing to discover the laws, if physical resemblance to Pierre was perfect in Eugene, Felicite on her side seemed to have furnished him with his brains. He offered an instance of certain moral and intellectual qualities of maternal origin being embedded in the coarse flesh he had derived from his father. He cherished lofty ambitions, possessed domineering instincts, and showed singular contempt for trifling expedients and petty fortunes.

He was a proof that Plassans was perhaps not mistaken in suspecting that Felicite had some blue blood in her veins. The passion for indulgence, which became formidably developed in the Rougons, and was, in fact, the family characteristic, attained in his case its highest pitch; he longed for self-gratification, but in the form of mental enjoyment such as would gratify his burning desire for domination. A man such as this was never intended to succeed in a provincial town. He vegetated there for fifteen years, his eyes turned towards Paris, watching his opportunities. On his return home he had entered his name on the rolls, in order to be independent of his parents. After that he pleaded from time to time, earning a bare livelihood, without appearing to rise above average mediocrity. At Plassans his voice was considered thick, his movements heavy. He generally wandered from the question at issue, rambled, as the wiseacres expressed it. On one occasion particularly, when he was pleading in a case for damages, he so forgot himself as to stray into a political disquisition, to such a point that the presiding judge interfered, whereupon he immediately sat down with a strange smile. His client was condemned to pay a considerable sum of money, a circumstance which did not, however, seem to cause Eugene the least regret for his irrelevant digression. He appeared to regard his speeches as mere exercises which would be of use to him later on. It was this that puzzled and disheartened Felicite. She would have liked to see her son dictating the law to the Civil Court of Plassans. At last she came to entertain a very unfavourable opinion of her first-born. To her mind this lazy fellow would never be the one to shed any lustre on the family. Pierre, on the contrary, felt absolute confidence in him, not that he had more intuition than his wife, but because external appearances sufficed him, and he flattered himself by believing in the genius of a son who was his living image. A month prior to the Revolution of February, 1848, Eugene became restless; some special inspiration made him anticipate the crisis. From that time forward he seemed to feel out of his element at Plassans. He would wander about the streets like a distressed soul. At last he formed a sudden resolution, and left for Paris, with scarcely five hundred francs in his pocket.

Aristide, the youngest son, was, so to speak, diametrically opposed to Eugene. He had his mother's face, and a covetousness and slyness of character prone to trivial intrigues, in which his father's instincts predominated. Nature has need of symmetry. Short, with a pitiful countenance suggesting the knob of a stick carved into a Punch's head, Aristide ferretted and fumbled everywhere, without any scruples, eager only to gratify himself. He loved money as his eldest brother loved power. While Eugene dreamed of bending a people to his will, and intoxicated himself with visions of future omnipotence, the other fancied himself ten times a millionaire, installed in a princely mansion, eating and drinking to his heart's content, and enjoying life to the fullest possible extent. Above all things, he longed to make a rapid fortune. When he was building his castles in the air, they would rise in his mind as if by magic; he would become possessed of tons of gold in one night. These visions agreed with his indolence, as he never troubled himself about the means, considering those the best which were the most expeditious. In his case the race of the Rougons, of those coarse, greedy peasants with brutish appetites, had matured too rapidly; every desire for material indulgence was found in him, augmented threefold by hasty education, and rendered the more insatiable and dangerous by the deliberate way in which the young man had come to regard their realisation as his set purpose. In spite of her keen feminine intuition, Felicite preferred this son; she did not perceive the greater affinity between herself and Eugene; she excused the follies and indolence of her youngest son under the pretext that he would some day be the superior genius of the family, and that such a man was entitled to live a disorderly life until his intellectual strength should be revealed.

Aristide subjected her indulgence to a rude test. In Paris he led a low, idle life; he was one of those students who enter their names at the taverns of the Quartier Latin. He did not remain there, however, more than two years; his father, growing apprehensive, and seeing that he had not yet passed a single examination, kept him at Plassans and spoke of finding a wife for him, hoping that domestic responsibility would make him more steady. Aristide let himself be married. He had no very clear idea of his own ambitions at this time; provincial life did not displease him; he was battening in his little town—eating, sleeping, and sauntering about. Felicite pleaded his cause so earnestly that Pierre consented to board and lodge the newly-married couple, on condition that the young man should turn his attention to the business. From that time, however, Aristide led a life of ease and idleness. He spent his days and the best part of his nights at the club, again and again slipping out of his father's office like a schoolboy to go and gamble away the few louis that his mother gave him clandestinely.

It is necessary to have lived in the depths of the French provinces to form an idea of the four brutifying years which the young fellow spent in this fashion. In every little town there is a group of individuals who thus live on their parents, pretending at times to work, but in reality cultivating idleness with a sort of religious zeal. Aristide was typical of these incorrigible drones. For four years he did little but play ecarte. While he passed his time at the club, his wife, a fair-complexioned nerveless woman, helped to ruin the Rougon business by her inordinate passion for showy gowns and her formidable appetite, a rather remarkable peculiarity in so frail a creature. Angele, however, adored sky-blue ribbons and roast beef. She was the daughter of a retired captain who was called Commander Sicardot, a good-hearted old gentleman, who had given her a dowry of ten thousand francs—all his savings. Pierre, in selecting Angele for his son had considered that he had made an unexpected bargain, so lightly did he esteem Aristide. However, that dowry of ten thousand francs, which determined his choice, ultimately became a millstone round his neck. His son, who was already a cunning rogue, deposited the ten thousand francs with his father, with whom he entered into partnership, declining, with the most sincere professions of devotion, to keep a single copper.

"We have no need of anything," he said; "you will keep my wife and myself, and we will reckon up later on."

Pierre was short of money at the time, and accepted, not, however, without some uneasiness at Aristide's disinterestedness. The latter calculated that it would be years before his father would have ten thousand francs in ready money to repay him, so that he and his wife would live at the paternal expense so long as the partnership could not be dissolved. It was an admirable investment for his few bank-notes. When the oil-dealer understood what a foolish bargain he had made he was not in a position to rid himself of Aristide; Angele's dowry was involved in speculations which were turning out unfavourably. He was exasperated, stung to the heart, at having to provide for his daughter-in-law's voracious appetite and keep his son in idleness. Had he been able to buy them out of the business he would twenty times have shut his doors on those bloodsuckers, as he emphatically expressed it. Felicite secretly defended them; the young man, who had divined her dreams of ambition, would every evening describe to her the elaborate plans by which he would shortly make a fortune. By a rare chance she had remained on excellent terms with her daughter-in-law. It must be confessed that Angele had no will of her own—she could be moved and disposed of like a piece of furniture.

Meantime Pierre became enraged whenever his wife spoke to him of the success their youngest son would ultimately achieve; he declared that he would really bring them to ruin. During the four years that the young couple lived with him he stormed in this manner, wasting his impotent rage in quarrels, without in the least disturbing the equanimity of Aristide and Angele. They were located there, and there they intended to remain like blocks of wood. At last Pierre met with a stroke of luck which enabled him to return the ten thousand francs to his son. When, however, he wanted to reckon up accounts with him, Aristide interposed so much chicanery that he had to let the couple go without deducting a copper for their board and lodging. They installed themselves but a short distance off, in a part of the old quarter called the Place Saint-Louis. The ten thousand francs were soon consumed. They had everything to get for their new home. Moreover Aristide made no change in his mode of living as long as any money was left in the house. When he had reached the last hundred-franc note he felt rather nervous. He was seen prowling about the town in a suspicious manner. He no longer took his customary cup of coffee at the club; he watched feverishly whilst play was going on, without touching a card. Poverty made him more spiteful than he would otherwise have been. He bore the blow for a long time, obstinately refusing to do anything in the way of work.

In 1840 he had a son, little Maxime, whom his grandmother Felicite fortunately sent to college, paying his fees clandestinely. That made one mouth less at home; but poor Angele was dying of hunger, and her husband was at last compelled to seek a situation. He secured one at the Sub-Prefecture. He remained there nearly ten years, and only attained a salary of eighteen hundred francs per annum. From that time forward it was with ever increasing malevolence and rancour that he hungered for the enjoyments of which he was deprived. His lowly position exasperated him; the paltry hundred and fifty francs which he received every month seemed to him an irony of fate. Never did man burn with such desire for self-gratification. Felicite, to whom he imparted his sufferings, was by no means grieved to see him so eager. She thought his misery would stimulate his energies. At last, crouching in ambush as it were, with his ears wide open, he began to look about him like a thief seeking his opportunity. At the beginning of 1848, when his brother left for Paris, he had a momentary idea of following him. But Eugene was a bachelor; and he, Aristide, could not take his wife so far without money. So he waited, scenting a catastrophe, and ready to fall on the first prey that might come within his reach.

The other son, Pascal, born between Eugene and Aristide, did not appear to belong to the family. He was one of those frequent cases which give the lie to the laws of heredity. During the evolution of a race nature often produces some one being whose every element she derives from her own creative powers. Nothing in the moral or physical constitution of Pascal recalled the Rougons. Tall, with a grave and gentle face, he had an uprightness of mind, a love of study, a retiring modesty which contrasted strangely with the feverish ambitions and unscrupulous intrigues of his relatives. After acquitting himself admirably of his medical studies in Paris, he had retired, by preference, to Plassans, notwithstanding the offers he received from his professors. He loved a quiet provincial life; he maintained that for a studious man such a life was preferable to the excitement of Paris. Even at Plassans he did not exert himself to extend his practice. Very steady, and despising fortune, he contented himself with the few patients sent him by chance. All his pleasures were centred in a bright little house in the new town, where he shut himself up, lovingly devoting his whole time to the study of natural history. He was particularly fond of physiology. It was known in the town that he frequently purchased dead bodies from the hospital grave-digger, a circumstance which rendered him an object of horror to delicate ladies and certain timid gentlemen. Fortunately, they did not actually look upon him as a sorcerer; but his practice diminished, and he was regarded as an eccentric character, to whom people of good society ought not to entrust even a finger-tip, for fear of being compromised. The mayor's wife was one day heard to say: "I would sooner die than be attended by that gentleman. He smells of death."

From that time, Pascal was condemned. He seemed to rejoice at the mute terror which he inspired. The fewer patients he had, the more time he could devote to his favourite sciences. As his fees were very moderate, the poorer people remained faithful to him; he earned just enough to live, and lived contentedly, a thousand leagues away from the rest of the country, absorbed in the pure delight of his researches and discoveries. From time to time he sent a memoir to the Academie des Sciences at Paris. Plassans did not know that this eccentric character, this gentleman who smelt of death was well-known and highly-esteemed in the world of science. When people saw him starting on Sundays for an excursion among the Garrigues hills, with a botanist's bag hung round his neck and a geologist's hammer in his hand, they would shrug their shoulders and institute a comparison between him and some other doctor of the town who was noted for his smart cravat, his affability to the ladies, and the delicious odour of violets which his garments always diffused. Pascal's parents did not understand him any better than other people. When Felicite saw him adopting such a strange, unpretentious mode of life she was stupefied, and reproached him for disappointing her hopes. She, who tolerated Aristide's idleness because she thought it would prove fertile, could not view without regret the slow progress of Pascal, his partiality for obscurity and contempt for riches, his determined resolve to lead a life of retirement. He was certainly not the child who would ever gratify her vanities.

"But where do you spring from?" she would sometimes say to him. "You are not one of us. Look at your brothers, how they keep their eyes open, striving to profit by the education we have given them, whilst you waste your time on follies and trifles. You make a very poor return to us, who have ruined ourselves for your education. No, you are certainly not one of us."

Pascal, who preferred to laugh whenever he was called upon to feel annoyed, replied cheerfully, but not without a sting of irony: "Oh, you need not be frightened, I shall never drive you to the verge of bankruptcy; when any of you are ill, I will attend you for nothing."

Moreover, though he never displayed any repugnance to his relatives, he very rarely saw them, following in this wise his natural instincts. Before Aristide obtained a situation at the Sub-Prefecture, Pascal had frequently come to his assistance. For his part he had remained a bachelor. He had not the least suspicion of the grave events that were preparing. For two or three years he had been studying the great problem of heredity, comparing the human and animal races together, and becoming absorbed in the strange results which he obtained. Certain observations which he had made with respect to himself and his relatives had been, so to say, the starting-point of his studies. The common people, with their natural intuition, so well understood that he was quite different from the other Rougons, that they invariably called him Monsieur Pascal, without ever adding his family name.

Three years prior to the Revolution of 1848 Pierre and Felicite retired from business. Old age was coming on apace; they were both past fifty and were weary enough of the struggle. In face of their ill fortune, they were afraid of being ultimately ruined if they obstinately persisted in the fight. Their sons, by disappointing their expectations, had dealt them the final blow. Now that they despaired of ever being enriched by them, they were anxious to make some little provision for old age. They retired with forty thousand francs at the utmost. This sum provided an annual income of two thousand francs, just sufficient to live in a small way in the provinces. Fortunately, they were by themselves, having succeeded in marrying their daughters Marthe and Sidonie, the former of whom resided at Marseilles and the latter in Paris.

After they had settled their affairs they would much have liked to take up their abode in the new town, the quarter of the retired traders, but they dared not do so. Their income was too small; they were afraid that they would cut but a poor figure there. So, as a sort of compromise, they took apartments in the Rue de la Banne, the street which separates the old quarter from the new one. As their abode was one of the row of houses bordering the old quarter, they still lived among the common people; nevertheless, they could see the town of the richer classes from their windows, so that they were just on the threshold of the promised land.

Their apartments, situated on the second floor, consisted of three large rooms—dining-room, drawing-room, and bedroom. The first floor was occupied by the owner of the house, a stick and umbrella manufacturer, who had a shop on the ground floor. The house, which was narrow and by no means deep, had only two storeys. Felicite moved into it with a bitter pang. In the provinces, to live in another person's house is an avowal of poverty. Every family of position at Plassans has a house of its own, landed property being very cheap there. Pierre kept the purse-strings well tied; he would not hear of any embellishments. The old furniture, faded, worn, damaged though it was, had to suffice, without even being repaired. Felicite, however, who keenly felt the necessity for this parsimony, exerted herself to give fresh polish to all the wreckage; she herself knocked nails into some of the furniture which was more dilapidated than the rest, and darned the frayed velvet of the armchairs.

The dining-room, which, like the kitchen, was at the back of the house, was nearly bare; a table and a dozen chairs were lost in the gloom of this large apartment, whose window faced the grey wall of a neighbouring building. As no strangers ever went into the bedroom, Felicite had stowed all her useless furniture there; thus, besides a bedstead, wardrobe, secretaire, and wash-stand, it contained two cradles, one perched atop of the other, a sideboard whose doors were missing, and an empty bookcase, venerable ruins which the old woman could not make up her mind to part with. All her cares, however, were bestowed upon the drawing-room, and she almost succeeded in making it comfortable and decent. The furniture was covered with yellowish velvet with satin flowers; in the middle stood a round table with a marble top, while a couple of pier tables, surmounted by mirrors, leant against the walls at either end of the room. There was even a carpet, which just covered the middle of the floor, and a chandelier in a white muslin cover which the flies had spotted with black specks. On the walls hung six lithographs representing the great battles of Napoleon I. Moreover, the furniture dated from the first years of the Empire. The only embellishment that Felicite could obtain was to have the walls hung with orange-hued paper covered with large flowers. Thus the drawing room had a strange yellow glow, which filled it with an artificial dazzling light. The furniture, the paper, and the window curtains were yellow; the carpet and even the marble table-tops showed touches of yellow. However, when the curtains were drawn the colours harmonised fairly well and the drawing-room looked almost decent.

But Felicite had dreamed of quite a different kind of luxury. She regarded with mute despair this ill-concealed misery. She usually occupied the drawing-room, the best apartment in the house, and the sweetest and bitterest of her pastimes was to sit at one of the windows which overlooked the Rue de la Banne and gave her a side view of the square in front of the Sub-Prefecture. That was the paradise of her dreams. That little, neat, tidy square, with its bright houses, seemed to her a Garden of Eden. She would have given ten years of her life to possess one of those habitations. The house at the left-hand corner, in which the receiver of taxes resided, particularly tempted her. She contemplated it with eager longing. Sometimes, when the windows of this abode were open, she could catch a glimpse of rich furniture and tasteful elegance which made her burn with envy.

At this period the Rougons passed through a curious crisis of vanity and unsatiated appetite. The few proper feelings which they had once entertained had become embittered. They posed as victims of evil fortune, not with resignation, however, for they seemed still more keenly determined that they would not die before they had satisfied their ambitions. In reality, they did not abandon any of their hopes, notwithstanding their advanced age. Felicite professed to feel a presentiment that she would die rich. However, each day of poverty weighed them down the more. When they recapitulated their vain attempts—when they recalled their thirty years' struggle, and the defection of their children—when they saw their airy castles end in this yellow drawing-room, whose shabbiness they could only conceal by drawing the curtains, they were overcome with bitter rage. Then, as a consolation, they would think of plans for making a colossal fortune, seeking all sorts of devices. Felicite would fancy herself the winner of the grand prize of a hundred thousand francs in some lottery, while Pierre pictured himself carrying out some wonderful speculation. They lived with one sole thought—that of making a fortune immediately, in a few hours—of becoming rich and enjoying themselves, if only for a year. Their whole beings tended to this, stubbornly, without a pause. And they still cherished some faint hopes with regard to their sons, with that peculiar egotism of parents who cannot bear to think that they have sent their children to college without deriving some personal advantage from it.

Felicite did not appear to have aged; she was still the same dark little woman, ever on the move, buzzing about like a grasshopper. Any person walking behind her on the pavement would have thought her a girl of fifteen, from the lightness of her step and the angularity of her shoulders and waist. Even her face had scarcely undergone any change; it was simply rather more sunken, rather more suggestive of the snout of a pole-cat.

As for Pierre Rougon, he had grown corpulent, and had become a highly respectable looking citizen, who only lacked a decent income to make him a very dignified individual. His pale, flabby face, his heaviness, his languid manner, seemed redolent of wealth. He had one day heard a peasant who did not know him say: "Ah! he's some rich fellow, that fat old gentleman there. He's no cause to worry about his dinner!" This was a remark which stung him to the heart, for he considered it cruel mockery to be only a poor devil while possessing the bulk and contented gravity of a millionaire. When he shaved on Sundays in front of a small five-sou looking-glass hanging from the fastening of a window, he would often think that in a dress coat and white tie he would cut a far better figure at the Sub-Prefect's than such or such a functionary of Plassans. This peasant's son, who had grown sallow from business worries, and corpulent from a sedentary life, whose hateful passions were hidden beneath naturally placid features, really had that air of solemn imbecility which gives a man a position in an official salon. People imagined that his wife held a rod over him, but they were mistaken. He was as self-willed as a brute. Any determined expression of extraneous will would drive him into a violent rage. Felicite was far too supple to thwart him openly; with her light fluttering nature she did not attack obstacles in front. When she wished to obtain something from her husband, or drive him the way she thought best, she would buzz round him in her grasshopper fashion, stinging him on all sides, and returning to the charge a hundred times until he yielded almost unconsciously. He felt, moreover, that she was shrewder than he, and tolerated her advice fairly patiently. Felicite, more useful than the coach fly, would sometimes do all the work while she was thus buzzing round Pierre's ears. Strange to say, the husband and wife never accused each other of their ill-success. The only bone of contention between them was the education lavished on their children.

The Revolution of 1848 found all the Rougons on the lookout, exasperated by their bad luck, and disposed to lay violent hands on fortune if ever they should meet her in a byway. They were a family of bandits lying in wait, ready to rifle and plunder. Eugene kept an eye on Paris; Aristide dreamed of strangling Plassans; the mother and father, perhaps the most eager of the lot, intended to work on their own account, and reap some additional advantage from their sons' doings. Pascal alone, that discreet wooer of science, led the happy, indifferent life of a lover in his bright little house in the new town.

Chapter 3

In that closed, sequestered town of Plassans, where class dis-
tinction was so clearly marked in 1848, the commotion caused
by political events was very slight. Even at the present day the
popular voice sounds very faintly there; the middle classes
bring their prudence to bear in the matter, the nobility their
mute despair, and the clergy their shrewd cunning. Kings may
usurp thrones, or republics may be established, without
scarcely any stir in the town. Plassans sleeps while Paris fights.
But though on the surface the town may appear calm and indifferent, in the depths hidden work goes on which it is curious to
study. If shots are rare in the streets, intrigues consume the
drawing-rooms of both the new town and the Saint-Marc
quarter. Until the year 1830 the masses were reckoned of no
account. Even at the present time they are similarly ignored.
Everything is settled between the clergy, the nobility, and the
bourgeoisie. The priests, who are very numerous, give the cue
to the local politics; they lay subterranean mines, as it were,
and deal blows in the dark, following a prudent tactical system,
which hardly allows of a step in advance or retreat even in the
course of ten years. The secret intrigues of men who desire
above all things to avoid noise requires special shrewdness, a
special aptitude for dealing with small matters, and a patient
endurance such as one only finds in persons callous to all passions. It is thus that provincial dilatoriness, which is so freely
ridiculed in Paris, is full of treachery, secret stabs, hidden vic-
tories and defeats. These worthy men, particularly when their
interests are at stake, kill at home with a snap of the fingers,
as we, the Parisians, kill with cannon in the public
thoroughfares.

The political history of Plassans, like that of all little towns in
Provence, is singularly characteristic. Until 1830, the inhabitants remained observant Catholics and fervent royalists; even

the lower classes only swore by God and their legitimate sovereigns. Then there came a sudden change; faith departed, the working and middle classes deserted the cause of legitimacy, and gradually espoused the great democratic movement of our time. When the Revolution of 1848 broke out, the nobility and the clergy were left alone to labour for the triumph of Henri V. For a long time they had regarded the accession of the Orleanists as a ridiculous experiment, which sooner or later would bring back the Bourbons; although their hopes were singularly shaken, they nevertheless continued the struggle, scandalised by the defection of their former allies, whom they strove to win back to their cause. The Saint-Marc quarter, assisted by all the parish priests, set to work. Among the middle classes, and especially among the people, the enthusiasm was very great on the morrow of the events of February; these apprentice republicans were in haste to display their revolutionary fervour. As regards the gentry of the new town, however, the conflagration, bright though it was, lasted no longer than a fire of straw. The small houseowners and retired tradespeople who had had their good days, or had made snug little fortunes under the monarchy, were soon seized with panic; the Republic, with its constant shocks and convulsions, made them tremble for their money and their life of selfishness.

Consequently, when the Clerical reaction of 1849 declared itself, nearly all the middle classes passed over to the Conservative party. They were received with open arms. The new town had never before had such close relations with the Saint-Marc quarter: some of the nobility even went so far as to shake hands with lawyers and retired oil-dealers. This unexpected familiarity kindled the enthusiasm of the new quarter, which henceforward waged bitter warfare against the republican government. To bring about such a coalition, the clergy had to display marvellous skill and endurance. The nobility of Plassans for the most part lay prostrate, as if half dead. They retained their faith, but lethargy had fallen on them, and they preferred to remain inactive, allowing the heavens to work their will. They would gladly have contented themselves with silent protest, feeling, perhaps, a vague presentiment that their divinities were dead, and that there was nothing left for them to do but rejoin them. Even at this period of confusion, when the catastrophe of 1848 was calculated to give them a momentary hope of the return of the Bourbons, they showed themselves spiritless and indifferent, speaking of rushing into the melee, yet never quitting their hearths without a pang of regret.

The clergy battled indefatigably against this feeling of impotence and resignation. They infused a kind of passion into their work: a priest, when he despairs, struggles all the more fiercely. The fundamental policy of the Church is to march straight forward; even though she may have to postpone the accomplishment of her projects for several centuries, she never wastes a single hour, but is always pushing forward with increasing energy. So it was the clergy who led the reaction of Plassans; the nobility only lent them their name, nothing more. The priests hid themselves behind the nobles, restrained them, directed them, and even succeeded in endowing them with a semblance of life. When they had induced them to overcome their repugnance so far as to make common cause with the middle classes, they believed themselves certain of victory. The ground was marvellously well prepared. This ancient royalist town, with its population of peaceful householders and timorous tradespeople, was destined to range itself, sooner or later, on the side of law and order. The clergy, by their tactics, hastened the conversion. After gaining the landlords of the new town to their side, they even succeeded in convincing the little retail-dealers of the old quarter. From that time the reactionary movement obtained complete possession of the town. All opinions were represented in this reaction; such a mixture of embittered Liberals, Legitimists, Orleanists, Bonapartists, and Clericals had never before been seen. It mattered little, however, at that time. The sole object was to kill the Republic; and the Republic was at the point of death. Only a fraction of the people—a thousand workmen at most, out of the ten thousand souls in the town—still saluted the tree of liberty planted in the middle of the square in front of the Sub-Prefecture.

The shrewdest politicians of Plassans, those who led the reactionary movement, did not scent the approach of the Empire until very much later. Prince Louis Napoleon's popularity seemed to them a mere passing fancy of the multitude. His person inspired them with but little admiration. They reckoned him a nonentity, a dreamer, incapable of laying his hands on

France, and especially of maintaining his authority. To them he was only a tool whom they would make use of, who would clear the way for them, and whom they would turn out as soon as the hour arrived for the rightful Pretender to show himself.[2] However, months went by, and they became uneasy. It was only then that they vaguely perceived they were being duped: they had no time, however, to take any steps; the Coup d'Etat burst over their heads, and they were compelled to applaud. That great abomination, the Republic, had been assassinated; that, at least, was some sort of triumph. So the clergy and the nobility accepted accomplished facts with resignation; postponing, until later, the realisation of their hopes, and making amends for their miscalculations by uniting with the Bonapartists for the purpose of crushing the last Republicans.

It was these events that laid the foundation of the Rougons' fortune. After being mixed up with the various phases of the crisis, they rose to eminence on the ruins of liberty. These bandits had been lying in wait to rob the Republic; as soon as it had been strangled, they helped to plunder it.

After the events of February 1848, Felicite, who had the keenest scent of all the members of the family, perceived that they were at last on the right track. So she began to flutter round her husband, goading him on to bestir himself. The first rumours of the Revolution that had overturned King Louis Philippe had terrified Pierre. When his wife, however, made him understand that they had little to lose and much to gain from a convulsion, he soon came round to her way of thinking.

"I don't know what you can do," Felicite repeatedly said, "but it seems to me that there's plenty to be done. Did not Monsieur de Carnavant say to us one day that he would be rich if ever Henri V. should return, and that this sovereign would magnificently recompense those who had worked for his restoration? Perhaps our fortune lies in that direction. We may yet be lucky."

The Marquis de Carnavant, the nobleman who, according to the scandalous talk of the town, had been on very familiar terms with Felicite's mother, used occasionally to visit the Rougons. Evil tongues asserted that Madame Rougon resembled him. He was a little, lean, active man, seventy-five

---

2. The Count de Chambord, "Henri V."

years old at that time, and Felicite certainly appeared to be taking his features and manner as she grew older. It was said that the wreck of his fortune, which had already been greatly diminished by his father at the time of the Emigration, had been squandered on women. Indeed, he cheerfully acknowledged his poverty. Brought up by one of his relatives, the Count de Valqueyras, he lived the life of a parasite, eating at the count's table and occupying a small apartment just under his roof.

"Little one," he would often say to Felicite, as he patted her on the cheek, "if ever Henri V. gives me a fortune, I will make you my heiress!"

He still called Felicite "little one," even when she was fifty years old. It was of these friendly pats, of these repeated promises of an inheritance, that Madame Rougon was thinking when she endeavoured to drive her husband into politics. Monsieur de Carnavant had often bitterly lamented his inability to render her any assistance. No doubt he would treat her like a father if ever he should acquire some influence. Pierre, to whom his wife half explained the situation in veiled terms, declared his readiness to move in any direction indicated.

The marquis's peculiar position qualified him to act as an energetic agent of the reactionary movement at Plassans from the first days of the Republic. This bustling little man, who had everything to gain from the return of his legitimate sovereigns, worked assiduously for their cause. While the wealthy nobility of the Saint-Marc quarter were slumbering in mute despair, fearing, perhaps that they might compromise themselves and again be condemned to exile, he multiplied himself, as it were, spread the propaganda and rallied faithful ones together. He was a weapon whose hilt was held by an invisible hand. From that time forward he paid daily visits to the Rougons. He required a centre of operations. His relative, Monsieur de Valqueyras, had forbidden him to bring any of his associates into his house, so he had chosen Felicite's yellow drawing-room. Moreover, he very soon found Pierre a valuable assistant. He could not go himself and preach the cause of Legitimacy to the petty traders and workmen of the old quarter; they would have hooted him. Pierre, on the other hand, who had lived among these people, spoke their language and knew their wants, was able to catechise them in a friendly way. He thus became an indispensable man. In less than a fortnight the Rougons were more determined royalists than the king himself. The marquis, perceiving Pierre's zeal, shrewdly sheltered himself behind him. What was the use of making himself conspicuous, when a man with such broad shoulders was willing to bear on them the burden of all the follies of a party? He allowed Pierre to reign, puff himself out with importance and speak with authority, content to restrain or urge him on, according to the necessities of the cause. Thus, the old oil-dealer soon became a personage of mark. In the evening, when they were alone, Felicite used to say to him: "Go on, don't be frightened. We're on the right track. If this continues we shall be rich; we shall have a drawing-room like the tax-receiver's, and be able to entertain people."

A little party of Conservatives had already been formed at the Rougons' house, and meetings were held every evening in the yellow drawing-room to declaim against the Republic.

Among those who came were three or four retired merchants who trembled for their money, and clamoured with all their might for a wise and strong government. An old almond-dealer, a member of the Municipal Council, Monsieur Isidore Granoux, was the head of this group. His hare-lipped mouth was cloven a little way from the nose; his round eyes, his air of mingled satisfaction and astonishment, made him resemble a fat goose whose digestion is attended by wholesome terror of the cook. He spoke little, having no command of words; and he only pricked up his ears when anyone accused the Republicans of wishing to pillage the houses of the rich; whereupon he would colour up to such a degree as to make one fear an approaching apoplectic fit, and mutter low imprecations, in which the words "idlers," "scoundrels," "thieves," and "assassins" frequently recurred.

All those who frequented the yellow drawing-room were not, however, as heavy as this fat goose. A rich landowner, Monsieur Roudier, with a plump, insinuating face, used to discourse there for hours altogether, with all the passion of an Orleanist whose calculations had been upset by the fall of Louis Philippe. He had formerly been a hosier at Paris, and a purveyor to the Court, but had now retired to Plassans. He had made his son a magistrate, relying on the Orleanist party to promote him to the highest dignities. The revolution having ruined all his hopes, he had rushed wildly into the reaction. His fortune, his former commercial relations with the Tuileries, which he transformed into friendly intercourse, that prestige which is enjoyed by every man in the provinces who has made his money in Paris and deigns to come and spend it in a far away department, gave him great influence in the district; some persons listened to him as though he were an oracle.

However, the strongest intellect of the yellow drawing-room was certainly Commander Sicardot, Aristide's father-in-law. Of Herculean frame, with a brick-red face, scarred and planted with tufts of grey hair, he was one of the most glorious old dolts of the Grande Armee. During the February Revolution he had been exasperated with the street warfare and never wearied of referring to it, proclaiming with indignation that this kind of fighting was shameful: whereupon he recalled with pride the grand reign of Napoleon.

Another person seen at the Rougons' house was an individual with clammy hands and equivocal look, one Monsieur Vuillet, a bookseller, who supplied all the devout ladies of the town with holy images and rosaries. Vuillet dealt in both classical and religious works; he was a strict Catholic, a circumstance which insured him the custom of the numerous convents and parish churches. Further, by a stroke of genius he had added to his business the publication of a little bi-weekly journal, the "Gazette de Plassans," which was devoted exclusively to the interests of the clergy. This paper involved an annual loss of a thousand francs, but it made him the champion of the Church, and enabled him to dispose of his sacred unsaleable stock. Though he was virtually illiterate and could not even spell correctly, he himself wrote the articles of the "Gazette" with a humility and rancour that compensated for his lack of talent. The marquis, in entering on the campaign, had perceived immediately the advantage that might be derived from the co-operation of this insipid sacristan with the coarse, mercenary pen. After the February Revolution the articles in the "Gazette" contained fewer mistakes; the marquis revised them.

One can now imagine what a singular spectacle the Rougons' yellow drawing-room presented every evening. All opinions met there to bark at the Republic. Their hatred of that institution made them agree together. The marquis, who never missed a meeting, appeased by his presence the little squabbles which occasionally arose between the commander and the other adherents. These plebeians were inwardly flattered by the handshakes which he distributed on his arrival and departure. Roudier, however, like a free-thinker of the Rue Saint-Honore, asserted that the marquis had not a copper to bless himself with, and was disposed to make light of him. M. de Carnavant on his side preserved the amiable smile of a nobleman lowering himself to the level of these middle class people, without making any of those contemptuous grimaces which any other resident of the Saint-Marc quarter would have thought fit under such circumstances. The parasite life he had led had rendered him supple. He was the life and soul of the group, commanding in the name of unknown personages whom he never revealed. "They want this, they don't want that," he would say. The concealed divinities who thus watched over the destinies of Plassans from behind some cloud, without appearing to interfere directly in public matters, must have been certain priests, the great political agents of the country. When the marquis pronounced that mysterious word "they," which inspired the assembly with such marvellous respect, Vuillet confessed, with a gesture of pious devotion, that he knew them very well.

The happiest person in all this was Felicite. At last she had people coming to her drawing-room. It was true she felt a little ashamed of her old yellow velvet furniture. She consoled herself, however, thinking of the rich things she would purchase when the good cause should have triumphed. The Rougons had, in the end, regarded their royalism as very serious. Felicite went as far as to say, when Roudier was not present, that if they had not made a fortune in the oil business the fault lay in the monarchy of July. This was her mode of giving a political tinge to their poverty. She had a friendly word for everybody, even for Granoux, inventing each evening some new polite method of waking him up when it was time for departure.

The drawing-room, that little band of Conservatives belonging to all parties, and daily increasing in numbers, soon wielded powerful influence. Owing to the diversified characters of its members, and especially to the secret impulse which each one received from the clergy, it became the centre of the reactionary movement and spread its influence throughout Plassans. The policy of the marquis, who sank his own personality, transformed Rougon into the leader of the party. The meetings were held at his house, and this circumstance sufficed in the eyes of most people to make him the head of the group, and draw public attention to him. The whole work was attributed to him; he was believed to be the chief artisan of the movement which was gradually bringing over to the Conservative party those who had lately been enthusiastic Republicans. There are some situations which benefit only persons of bad repute. These lay the foundations of their fortune where men of better position and more influence would never dare to risk theirs. Roudier, Granoux, and the others, all men of means and respectability, certainly seemed a thousand times preferable to Pierre as the acting leaders of the Conservative party. But none of them would have consented to turn his drawing-room into a political centre. Their convictions did not go so far as to induce them to compromise themselves openly; in fact, they were only so many provincial babblers, who liked to inveigh against the Republic at a neighbour's house as long as the neighbour was willing to bear the responsibility of their chatter. The game was too risky. There was no one among the middle classes of Plassans who cared to play it except the Rougons, whose ungratified longings urged them on to extreme measures.

In the month of April, 1849, Eugene suddenly left Paris, and came to stay with his father for a fortnight. Nobody ever knew the purpose of this journey. It is probable that Eugene wanted to sound his native town, to ascertain whether he might successfully stand as a candidate for the legislature which was about to replace the Constituent Assembly. He was too shrewd to risk a failure. No doubt public opinion appeared to him little in his favour, for he abstained from any attempt. It was not known at Plassans what had become of him in Paris, what he was doing there. On his return to his native place, folks found him less heavy and somnolent than formerly. They surrounded him and endeavoured to make him speak out concerning the political situation. But he feigned ignorance and compelled them to talk. A little perspicacity would have detected that beneath his apparent unconcern there was great anxiety with regard to the political opinions of the town. However, he seemed to be sounding the ground more on behalf of a party than on his own account.

Although he had renounced all hope for himself, he remained at Plassans until the end of the month, assiduously attending the meetings in the yellow drawing-room. As soon as the bell rang, announcing the first visitor, he would take up his position in one of the window recesses as far as possible from the lamp. And he remained there the whole evening, resting his chin on the palm of his right hand, and listening religiously. The greatest absurdities did not disturb his equanimity. He nodded approval even to the wild grunts of Granoux. When anyone asked him his own opinion, he politely repeated that of the majority. Nothing seemed to tire his patience, neither the hollow dreams of the marquis, who spoke of the Bourbons as if 1815 were a recent date, nor the effusions of citizen Roudier, who grew quite pathetic when he recounted how many pairs of socks he had supplied to the citizen king, Louis Philippe. On the contrary, he seemed quite at his ease in this Tower of Babel. Sometimes, when these grotesque personages were storming against the Republic, his eyes would smile, while his lips retained their expression of gravity. His meditative manner of listening, and his invariable complacency, had earned him the sympathy of everyone. He was considered a nonentity, but a very decent fellow. Whenever an old oil or almond dealer failed to get a hearing, amidst the clamour, for some plan by which he could save France if he were only a master, he took himself off to Eugene and shouted his marvellous suggestions in his ear. And Eugene gently nodded his head, as though delighted with the grand projects he was listening to. Vuillet, alone, regarded him with a suspicious eye. This bookseller, half-sacristan and half-journalist, spoke less than the others, but was more observant. He had noticed that Eugene occasionally conversed at times in a corner with Commander Sicardot. So he determined to watch them, but never succeeded in overhearing a word. Eugene silenced the commander by a wink whenever Vuillet approached them. From that time, Sicardot never spoke of the Napoleons without a mysterious smile.

Two days before his return to Paris, Eugene met his brother Aristide, on the Cours Sauvaire, and the latter accompanied him for a short distance with the importunity of a man in search of advice. As a matter of fact, Aristide was in great perplexity. Ever since the proclamation of the Republic, he had manifested the most lively enthusiasm for the new government. His intelligence, sharpened by two years' stay at Paris, enabled him to see farther than the thick heads of Plassans. He divined the powerlessness of the Legitimists and Orleanists, without clearly distinguishing, however, what third thief would come and juggle the Republic away. At all hazard he had ranged himself on the side of the victors, and he had severed his connection with his father, whom he publicly denounced as an old fool, an old dolt whom the nobility had bamboozled.

"Yet my mother is an intelligent woman," he would add. "I should never have thought her capable of inducing her husband to join a party whose hopes are simply chimerical. They are taking the right course to end their lives in poverty. But then women know nothing about politics."

For his part he wanted to sell himself as dearly as possible. His great anxiety as to the direction in which the wind was blowing, so that he might invariably range himself on the side of that party, which, in the hour of triumph, would be able to reward him munificently. Unfortunately, he was groping in the dark. Shut up in his far away province, without a guide, without any precise information, he felt quite lost. While waiting for events to trace out a sure and certain path, he preserved the enthusiastic republican attitude which he had assumed from the very first day. Thanks to this demeanour, he remained at the Sub-Prefecture; and his salary was even raised. Burning, however, with the desire to play a prominent part, he persuaded a bookseller, one of Vuillet's rivals, to establish a democratic journal, to which he became one of the most energetic contributors. Under his impulse the "Independant" waged merciless warfare against the reactionaries. But the current gradually carried him further than he wished to go; he ended by writing inflammatory articles, which made him shudder when he re-perused them. It was remarked at Plassans that he directed a series of attacks against all whom his father was in the habit of receiving of an evening in his famous yellow drawing-room. The fact is that the wealth of Roudier and Granoux exasperated Aristide to such a degree as to make him forget all prudence. Urged on by his jealous, insatiate bitterness, he had already made the middle classes his irreconcilable enemy, when Eugene's arrival and demeanour at Plassans caused him great consternation. He confessed to himself that his brother was a skilful man. According to him, that big, drowsy fellow always slept with one eye open, like a cat lying in wait before a mouse-hole. And now here was Eugene spending entire evenings in the yellow drawing-room, and devoting himself to those same grotesque personages whom he, Aristide, had so mercilessly ridiculed. When he discovered from the gossip of the town that his brother shook hands with Granoux and the marquis, he asked himself, with considerable anxiety, what was the meaning of it? Could he himself have been deceived? Had the Legitimists or the Orleanists really any chance of success? The thought terrified him. He lost his equilibrium, and, as frequently happens, he fell upon the Conservatives with increased rancour, as if to avenge his own blindness.

On the evening prior to the day when he stopped Eugene on the Cours Sauvaire, he had published, in the "Independant," a terrible article on the intrigues of the clergy, in response to a short paragraph from Vuillet, who had accused the Republicans of desiring to demolish the churches. Vuillet was Aristide's bugbear. Never a week passed but these two journalists exchanged the greatest insults. In the provinces, where a periphrastic style is still cultivated, polemics are clothed in high-sounding phrases. Aristide called his adversary "brother Judas," or "slave of Saint-Anthony." Vuillet gallantly retorted by terming the Republican "a monster glutted with blood whose ignoble purveyor was the guillotine."

In order to sound his brother, Aristide, who did not dare to appear openly uneasy, contented himself with asking: "Did you read my article yesterday? What do you think of it?"

Eugene lightly shrugged his shoulders. "You're a simpleton, brother," was his sole reply.

"Then you think Vuillet right?" cried the journalist, turning pale; "you believe in Vuillet's triumph?"

"I!—Vuillet——"

He was certainly about to add, "Vuillet is as big a fool as you are." But, observing his brother's distorted face anxiously extended towards him, he experienced sudden mistrust. "Vuillet has his good points," he calmly replied.

On parting from his brother, Aristide felt more perplexed than before. Eugene must certainly have been making game of him, for Vuillet was really the most abominable person imaginable. However, he determined to be prudent and not tie himself down any more; for he wished to have his hands free should he ever be called upon to help any party in strangling the Republic.

Eugene, on the morning of his departure, an hour before getting into the diligence, took his father into the bedroom and had a long conversation with him. Felicite, who remained in the drawing-room, vainly tried to catch what they were saying. They spoke in whispers, as if they feared lest a single word should be heard outside. When at last they quitted the bedroom they seemed in high spirits. After kissing his father and mother, Eugene, who usually spoke in a drawling tone, exclaimed with vivacity: "You have understood me, father? There lies our fortune. We must work with all our energy in that direction. Trust in me."

"I'll follow your instructions faithfully," Rougon replied. "Only don't forget what I asked you as the price of my cooperation."

"If we succeed your demands shall be satisfied, I give you my word. Moreover, I will write to you and guide you according to the direction which events may take. Mind, no panic or excitement. You must obey me implicitly."

"What have you been plotting there?" Felicite asked inquisitively.

"My dear mother," Eugene replied with a smile, "you have had too little faith in me thitherto to induce me to confide in you my hopes, particularly as at present they are only based on probabilities. To be able to understand me you would require faith. However, father will inform you when the right time comes."

Then, as Felicite assumed the demeanour of a woman who feels somewhat piqued, he added in her ear, as he kissed her once more: "I take after you, although you disowned me. Too much intelligence would be dangerous at the present moment.

When the crisis comes, it is you who will have to manage the business."

He then quitted the room, but, suddenly re-opening the door, exclaimed in an imperious tone: "Above all things, do not trust Aristide; he is a mar-all, who would spoil everything. I have studied him sufficiently to feel certain that he will always fall on his feet. Don't have any pity; if we make a fortune, he'll know well enough how to rob us of his share."

When Eugene had gone, Felicite endeavoured to ferret out the secret that was being hidden from her. She knew her husband too well to interrogate him openly. He would have angrily replied that it was no business of hers. In spite, however, of the clever tactics she pursued, she learnt absolutely nothing. Eugene had chosen a good confidant for those troubled times, when the greatest discretion was necessary. Pierre, flattered by his son's confidence, exaggerated that passive ponderosity which made him so impenetrable. When Felicite saw she would not learn anything from him, she ceased to flutter round him. On one point only did she remain inquisitive, but in this respect her curiosity was intense. The two men had mentioned a price stipulated by Pierre himself. What could that price be? This after all was the sole point of interest for Felicite, who did not care a rap for political matters. She knew that her husband must have sold himself dearly, but she was burning to know the nature of the bargain. One evening, when they had gone to bed, finding Pierre in a good humour, she brought the conversation round to the discomforts of their poverty.

"It's quite time to put an end to this," she said. "We have been ruining ourselves in oil and fuel since those gentlemen have been coming here. And who will pay the reckoning? Nobody perhaps."

Her husband fell into the trap, and smiled with complacent superiority. "Patience," said he. And with an air of shrewdness he looked into his wife's eyes and added: "Would you be glad to be the wife of a receiver of taxes?"

Felicite's face flushed with a joyous glow. She sat up in bed and clapped her old withered little hands like a child.

"Really?" she stammered. "At Plassans?"

Pierre, without replying, gave a long affirmative nod. He enjoyed his consort's astonishment and emotion.

"But," she at last resumed, half sitting, "you would have to deposit an enormous sum as security. I have heard that our neighbour, Monsieur Peirotte, had to deposit eighty thousand francs with the Treasury."

"Eh!" said the retired oil-dealer, "that's nothing to do with me; Eugene will see to that. He will get the money advanced by a banker in Paris. You see, I selected an appointment bringing in a good income. Eugene at first made a wry face, saying one must be rich to occupy such posts, to which influential men were usually nominated. I persisted, however, and he yielded. To be a receiver of taxes one need not know either Greek or Latin. I shall have a representative, like Monsieur Peirotte, and he will do all the work."

Felicite listened to him with rapture.

"I guessed, however," he continued, "what it was that worried our dear son. We're not much liked here. People know that we have no means, and will make themselves obnoxious. But all sorts of things occur in a time of crisis. Eugene wished to get me an appointment in another town. However, I objected; I want to remain at Plassans."

"Yes, yes, we must remain here," the old woman quickly replied. "We have suffered here, and here we must triumph. Ah! I'll crush them all, those fine ladies on the Mail, who scornfully eye my woollen dresses! I didn't think of the appointment of receiver of taxes at all; I thought you wanted to become mayor."

"Mayor! Nonsense. That appointment is honorary. Eugene also mentioned the mayoralty to me. I replied: 'I'll accept, if you give me an income of fifteen thousand francs.'"

This conversation, in which high figures flew about like rockets, quite excited Felicite. She felt delightfully buoyant. But at last she put on a devout air, and gravely said: "Come, let us reckon it out. How much will you earn?"

"Well," said Pierre, "the fixed salary, I believe, is three thousand francs."

"Three thousand," Felicite counted.

"Then there is so much per cent on the receipts, which at Plassans, may produce the sum of twelve thousand francs."

"That makes fifteen thousand."

"Yes, about fifteen thousand francs. That's what Peirotte earns. That's not all. Peirotte does a little banking business on his own account. It's allowed. Perhaps I shall be disposed to make a venture when I feel luck on my side."

"Well, let us say twenty thousand. Twenty thousand francs a year!" repeated Felicite, overwhelmed by the amount.

"We shall have to repay the advances," Pierre observed.

"That doesn't matter," Felicite replied, "we shall be richer than many of those gentlemen. Are the marquis and the others going to share the cake with you?"

"No, no; it will be all for us," he replied.

Then, as she continued to importune him with her questions, Pierre frowned, thinking that she wanted to wrest his secret from him. "We've talked enough," he said, abruptly. "It's late, let us go to sleep. It will bring us bad luck to count our chickens beforehand. I haven't got the place yet. Above all things, be prudent."

When the lamp was extinguished, Felicite could not sleep. With her eyes closed she built the most marvellous castles in the air. Those twenty thousand francs a year danced a diabolical dance before her in the darkness. She occupied splendid apartments in the new town, enjoyed the same luxuries as Monsieur Peirotte, gave parties, and bespattered the whole place with her wealth. That, however, which tickled her vanity most was the high position that her husband would then occupy. He would pay their state dividends to Granoux, Roudier, and all those people who now came to her house as they might come to a cafe, to swagger and learn the latest news. She had noticed the free-and-easy manner in which these people entered her drawing-room, and it had made her take a dislike to them. Even the marquis, with his ironical politeness, was beginning to displease her. To triumph alone, therefore, to keep the cake for themselves, as she expressed it, was a revenge which she fondly cherished. Later on, when all those ill-bred persons presented themselves, hats off, before Monsieur Rougon the receiver of taxes, she would crush them in her turn. She was busy with these thoughts all night; and on the morrow, as she opened the shutters, she instinctively cast her first glance across the street towards Monsieur Peirotte's house, and smiled as she contemplated the broad damask curtains hanging in the windows.

Felicite's hopes, in becoming modified, had grown yet more intense. Like all women, she did not object to a tinge of mystery. The secret object that her husband was pursuing excited her far more than the Legitimist intrigues of Monsieur de Carnavant had ever done. She abandoned, without much regret, the calculations she had based on the marquis's success now that her husband declared he would be able to make large profits by other means. She displayed, moreover, remarkable prudence and discretion.

In reality, she was still tortured by anxious curiosity; she studied Pierre's slightest actions, endeavouring to discover their meaning. What if by chance he were following the wrong track? What if Eugene were dragging them in his train into some break-neck pit, whence they would emerge yet more hungry and impoverished? However, faith was dawning on her. Eugene had commanded with such an air of authority that she ultimately came to believe in him. In this case again some unknown power was at work. Pierre would speak mysteriously of the high personages whom their eldest son visited in Paris. For her part she did not know what he could have to do with them, but on the other hand she was unable to close her eyes to Aristide's ill-advised acts at Plassans. The visitors to her drawing-room did not scruple to denounce the democratic journalist with extreme severity. Granoux muttered that he was a brigand, and Roudier would three or four times a week repeat to Felicite: "Your son is writing some fine articles. Only yesterday he attacked our friend Vuillet with revolting scurrility."

The whole room joined in the chorus, and Commander Sicardot spoke of boxing his son-in-law's ears, while Pierre flatly disowned him. The poor mother hung her head, restraining her tears. For an instant she felt an inclination to burst forth, to tell Roudier that her dear child, in spite of his faults, was worth more than he and all the others put together. But she was tied down, and did not wish to compromise the position they had so laboriously attained. Seeing the whole town so bitter against Aristide, she despaired of his future, thinking he was hopelessly ruining himself. On two occasions she spoke to him in secret, imploring him to return to them, and not to irritate the yellow drawing-room any further. Aristide replied that she did not understand such matters; that she was the one who had committed a great blunder in placing her husband at the service of the marquis. So she had to abandon her son to his own courses, resolving, however that if Eugene succeeded she would compel him to share the spoils with the poor fellow who was her favourite child.

After the departure of his eldest son, Pierre Rougon pursued his reactionary intrigues. Nothing seemed to have changed in the opinions of the famous yellow drawing-room. Every evening the same men came to join in the same propaganda in favour of the establishment of a monarchy, while the master of the house approved and aided them with as much zeal as in the past. Eugene had left Plassans on May 1. A few days later, the yellow drawing-room was in raptures. The gossips were discussing the letter of the President of the Republic to General Oudinot, in which the siege of Rome had been decided upon. This letter was regarded as a brilliant victory, due to the firm demeanour of the reactionary party. Since 1848 the Chambers had been discussing the Roman question; but it had been reserved for a Bonaparte to stifle a rising Republic by an act of intervention which France, if free, would never have countenanced. The marquis declared, however, that one could not better promote the cause of legitimacy, and Vuillet wrote a superb article on the matter. The enthusiasm became unbounded when, a month later, Commander Sicardot entered the Rougons' house one evening and announced to the company that the French army was fighting under the walls of Rome. Then, while everybody was raising exclamations at this news, he went up to Pierre, and shook hands with him in a significant manner. And when he had taken a seat, he began to sound the praises of the President of the Republic, who, said he, was the only person able to save France from anarchy.

"Let him save it, then, as quickly as possible," interrupted the marquis, "and let him then understand his duty by restoring it to its legitimate masters."

Pierre seemed to approve this fine retort, and having thus given proof of his ardent royalism, he ventured to remark that Prince Louis Bonaparte had his entire sympathy in the matter.

He thereupon exchanged a few short sentences with the commander, commending the excellent intentions of the President, which sentences one might have thought prepared and learnt beforehand. Bonapartism now, for the first time, made its entry into the yellow drawing-room. It is true that since the election of December 10 the Prince had been treated there with a certain amount of consideration. He was preferred a thousand times to Cavaignac, and the whole reactionary party had voted for him. But they regarded him rather as an accomplice than a friend; and, as such, they distrusted him, and even began to accuse him of a desire to keep for himself the chestnuts which he had pulled out of the fire. On that particular evening, however, owing to the fighting at Rome, they listened with favour to the praises of Pierre and the commander.

The group led by Granoux and Roudier already demanded that the President should order all republican rascals to be shot; while the marquis, leaning against the mantelpiece, gazed meditatively at a faded rose on the carpet. When he at last lifted his head, Pierre, who had furtively watched his countenance as if to see the effect of his words, suddenly ceased speaking. However, Monsieur de Carnavant merely smiled and glanced at Felicite with a knowing look. This rapid by-play was not observed by the other people. Vuillet alone remarked in a sharp tone:

"I would rather see your Bonaparte at London than at Paris. Our affairs would get along better then."

At this the old oil-dealer turned slightly pale, fearing that he had gone too far. "I'm not anxious to retain 'my' Bonaparte," he said, with some firmness; "you know where I would send him to if I were the master. I simply assert that the expedition to Rome was a good stroke."

Felicite had followed this scene with inquisitive astonishment. However, she did not speak of it to her husband, which proved that she adopted it as the basis of secret study. The marquis's smile, the significance of which escaped her, set her thinking.

From that day forward, Rougon, at distant intervals, whenever the occasion offered, slipped in a good word for the President of the Republic. On such evenings, Commander Sicardot acted the part of a willing accomplice. At the same time,

Clerical opinions still reigned supreme in the yellow drawing-room. It was more particularly in the following year that this group of reactionaries gained decisive influence in the town, thanks to the retrograde movement which was going on at Paris. All those anti-Liberal laws which the country called "the Roman expedition at home" definitively secured the triumph of the Rougon faction. The last enthusiastic bourgeois saw the Republic tottering, and hastened to rally round the Conservatives. Thus the Rougons' hour had arrived; the new town almost gave them an ovation on the day when the tree of Liberty, planted on the square before the Sub-Prefecture, was sawed down. This tree, a young poplar brought from the banks of the Viorne, had gradually withered, much to the despair of the republican working-men, who would come every Sunday to observe the progress of the decay without being able to comprehend the cause of it. A hatter's apprentice at last asserted that he had seen a woman leave Rougon's house and pour a pail of poisoned water at the foot of the tree. It thenceforward became a matter of history that Felicite herself got up every night to sprinkle the poplar with vitriol. When the tree was dead the Municipal Council declared that the dignity of the Republic required its removal. For this, as they feared the displeasure of the working classes, they selected an advanced hour of the night. However, the conservative householders of the new town got wind of the little ceremony, and all came down to the square before the Sub-Prefecture in order to see how the tree of Liberty would fall. The frequenters of the yellow drawing-room stationed themselves at the windows there. When the poplar cracked and fell with a thud in the darkness, as tragically rigid as some mortally stricken hero, Felicite felt bound to wave a white handkerchief. This induced the crowd to applaud, and many responded to the salute by waving their handkerchiefs likewise. A group of people even came under the window shouting: "We'll bury it, we'll bury it."

They meant the Republic, no doubt. Such was Felicite's emotion, that she almost had a nervous attack. It was a fine evening for the yellow drawing-room.

However, the marquis still looked at Felicite with the same mysterious smile. This little old man was far too shrewd to be ignorant of whither France was tending. He was among the first to scent the coming of the Empire. When the Legislative Assembly, later on, exhausted its energies in useless squabbling, when the Orleanists and the Legitimists tacitly accepted the idea of the Coup d'Etat, he said to himself that the game was definitely lost. In fact, he was the only one who saw things clearly. Vuillet certainly felt that the cause of Henry V., which his paper defended, was becoming detestable; but it mattered little to him; he was content to be the obedient creature of the clergy; his entire policy was framed so as to enable him to dispose of as many rosaries and sacred images as possible. As for Roudier and Granoux, they lived in a state of blind scare; it was not certain whether they really had any opinions; all that they desired was to eat and sleep in peace; their political aspirations went no further. The marquis, though he had bidden farewell to his hopes, continued to come to the Rougons' as regularly as ever. He enjoyed himself there. The clash of rival ambitions among the middle classes, and the display of their follies, had become an extremely amusing spectacle to him. He shuddered at the thought of again shutting himself in the little room which he owed to the beneficence of the Count de Valqueyras. With a kind of malicious delight, he kept to himself the conviction that the Bourbons' hour had not yet arrived. He feigned blindness, working as hitherto for the triumph of Legitimacy, and still remaining at the orders of the clergy and nobility, though from the very first day he had penetrated Pierre's new course of action, and believed that Felicite was his accomplice.

One evening, being the first to arrive, he found the old lady alone in the drawing-room. "Well! little one," he asked, with his smiling familiarity, "are your affairs going on all right? Why the deuce do you make such mysteries with me?"

"I'm not hiding anything from you," Felicite replied, somewhat perplexed.

"Come, do you think you can deceive an old fox like me, eh? My dear child, treat me as a friend. I'm quite ready to help you secretly. Come now, be frank!"

A bright idea struck Felicite. She had nothing to tell; but perhaps she might find out something if she kept quiet.

"Why do you smile?" Monsieur de Carnavant resumed. "That's the beginning of a confession, you know. I suspected that you must be behind your husband. Pierre is too stupid to invent the pretty treason you are hatching. I sincerely hope the Bonapartists will give you what I should have asked for you from the Bourbons."

This single sentence confirmed the suspicions which the old woman had entertained for some time past.

"Prince Louis has every chance, hasn't he?" she eagerly inquired.

"Will you betray me if I tell you that I believe so?" the marquis laughingly replied. "I've donned my mourning over it, little one. I'm simply a poor old man, worn out and only fit to be laid on the shelf. It was for you, however, that I was working. Since you have been able to find the right track without me, I shall feel some consolation in seeing you triumph amidst my own defeat. Above all things, don't make any more mysteries. Come to me if you are ever in trouble."

And he added, with the sceptical smile of a nobleman who has lost caste: "Pshaw! I also can go in for a little treachery!"

At this moment the clan of retired oil and almond dealers arrived.

"Ah! the dear reactionaries!" Monsieur de Carnavant continued in an undertone. "You see, little one, the great art of politics consists in having a pair of good eyes when other people are blind. You hold all the best cards in the pack."

On the following day, Felicite, incited by this conversation, desired to make sure on the matter. They were then in the first days of the year 1851. For more than eighteen months, Rougon had been in the habit of receiving a letter from his son Eugene regularly every fortnight. He would shut himself in the bedroom to read these letters, which he then hid at the bottom of an old secretaire, the key of which he carefully kept in his waistcoat pocket. Whenever his wife questioned him about their son he would simply answer: "Eugene writes that he is going on all right." Felicite had long since thought of laying hands on her son's letters. So early on the morning after her chat with the marquis, while Pierre was still asleep, she got up on tiptoes, took the key of the secretaire from her husband's waistcoat and substituted in its place that of the chest of drawers, which was of the same size. Then, as soon as her husband had gone out, she shut herself in the room in her turn, emptied the drawer, and read all the letters with feverish curiosity.

Monsieur de Carnavant had not been mistaken, and her own suspicions were confirmed. There were about forty letters, which enabled her to follow the course of that great Bonapartist movement which was to terminate in the second Empire. The letters constituted a sort of concise journal, narrating events as they occurred, and drawing hopes and suggestions from each of them. Eugene was full of faith. He described Prince Louis Bonaparte to his father as the predestined necessary man who alone could unravel the situation. He had believed in him prior even to his return to France, at a time when Bonapartism was treated as a ridiculous chimera. Felicite understood that her son had been a very active secret agent since 1848. Although he did not clearly explain his position in Paris, it was evident that he was working for the Empire, under the orders of personages whose names he mentioned with a sort of familiarity. Each of his letters gave information as to the progress of the cause, to which an early denouement was foreshadowed; and usually concluded by pointing out the line of action that Pierre should pursue at Plassans. Felicite could now comprehend certain words and acts of her husband, whose significance had previously escaped her; Pierre was obeying his son, and blindly following his recommendations.

When the old woman had finished reading, she was convinced. Eugene's entire thoughts were clearly revealed to her. He reckoned upon making his political fortune in the squabble, and repaying his parents the debt he owed them for his education, by throwing them a scrap of the prey as soon as the quarry was secured. However small the assistance his father might render to him and to the cause, it would not be difficult to get him appointed receiver of taxes. Nothing would be refused to one who like Eugene had steeped his hands in the most secret machinations. His letters were simply a kind attention on his part, a device to prevent the Rougons from committing any act of imprudence, for which Felicite felt deeply grateful. She read certain passages of the letters twice over, notably those in which Eugene spoke, in vague terms, of "a final catastrophe." This catastrophe, the nature or bearings of which she could not well conceive became a sort of end of the world for her. God would range the chosen ones on His right hand and the damned on His left, and she placed herself among the former.

When she succeeded in replacing the key in her husband's waistcoat pocket on the following night, she made up her mind to employ the same expedient for reading every fresh letter that arrived. She resolved, likewise, to profess complete ignorance. This plan was an excellent one. Henceforward, she gave her husband the more assistance as she appeared to render it unconsciously. When Pierre thought he was working alone it was she who brought the conversation round to the desired topic, recruiting partisans for the decisive moment. She felt hurt at Eugene's distrust of her. She wanted to be able to say to him, after the triumph: "I knew all, and so far from spoiling anything, I have secured the victory." Never did an accomplice make less noise or work harder. The marquis, whom she had taken into her confidence, was astounded at it.

The fate of her dear Aristide, however, continued to make her uneasy. Now that she shared the faith of her eldest son, the rabid articles of the "Independant" alarmed her all the more. She longed to convert the unfortunate republican to Napoleonist ideas; but she did not know how to accomplish this in a discreet manner. She recalled the emphasis with which Eugene had told them to be on their guard against Aristide. At last she submitted the matter to Monsieur de Carnavant, who was entirely of the same opinion.

"Little one," he said to her, "in politics one must know how to look after one's self. If you were to convert your son, and the 'Independant' were to start writing in defence of Bonapartism, it would deal the party a rude blow. The 'Independant' has already been condemned, its title alone suffices to enrage the middle classes of Plassans. Let dear Aristide flounder about; this only moulds young people. He does not appear to me to be cut out for carrying on the role of a martyr for any length of time."

However, in her eagerness to point out the right way to her family, now that she believed herself in possession of the truth, Felicite even sought to convert her son Pascal. The doctor, with the egotism of a scientist immersed in his researches, gave little heed to politics. Empires might fall while he was making an experiment, yet he would not have deigned to turn his head. He at last yielded, however, to certain importunities of his mother, who accused him more than ever of living like an unsociable churl.

"If you were to go into society," she said to him, "you would get some well-to-do patients. Come, at least, and spend some evenings in our drawing-room. You will make the acquaintance of Messieurs Roudier, Granoux, and Sicardot, all gentlemen in good circumstances, who will pay you four or five francs a visit. The poor people will never enrich you."

The idea of succeeding in life, of seeing all her family attain to fortune, had become a form of monomania with Felicite. Pascal, in order to be agreeable to her, came and spent a few evenings in the yellow drawing-room. He was much less bored there than he had apprehended. At first he was rather stupefied at the degree of imbecility to which sane men can sink. The old oil and almond dealers, the marquis and the commander even, appeared to him so many curious animals, which he had not hitherto had an opportunity of studying. He looked with a naturalist's interest at their grimacing faces, in which he discerned traces of their occupations and appetites; he listened also to their inane chatter, just as he might have tried to catch the meaning of a cat's mew or a dog's bark. At this period he was occupied with comparative natural history, applying to the human race the observations which he had made upon animals with regard to the working of heredity. While he was in the yellow drawing-room, therefore, he amused himself with the belief that he had fallen in with a menagerie. He established comparisons between the grotesque creatures he found there and certain animals of his acquaintance. The marquis, with his leanness and small crafty-looking head, reminded him exactly of a long green grasshopper. Vuillet impressed him as a pale, slimy toad. He was more considerate for Roudier, a fat sheep, and for the commander, an old toothless mastiff. But the prodigious Granoux was a perpetual cause of astonishment to him. He spent a whole evening measuring this imbecile's facial angle. When he heard him mutter indistinct imprecations against those blood-suckers the Republicans, he always expected to hear him moan like a calf; and he could never see him rise from his chair without imagining that he was about to leave the room on all fours.

"Talk to them," his mother used to say in an undertone; "try and make a practice out of these gentlemen."

"I am not a veterinary surgeon," he at last replied, exasperated.

One evening Felicite took him into a corner and tired to catechise him. She was glad to see him come to her house rather assiduously. She thought him reconciled to Society, not suspecting for a moment the singular amusement that he derived from ridiculing these rich people. She cherished the secret project of making him the fashionable doctor of Plassans. It would be sufficient if men like Granoux and Roudier consented to give him a start. She wished, above all, to impart to him the political views of the family, considering that a doctor had everything to gain by constituting himself a warm partisan of the regime which was to succeed the Republic.

"My dear boy," she said to him, "as you have now become reasonable, you must give some thought to the future. You are accused of being a Republican, because you are foolish enough to attend all the beggars of the town without making any charge. Be frank, what are your real opinions?"

Pascal looked at his mother with naïve astonishment, then with a smile replied: "My real opinions? I don't quite know—I am accused of being a Republican, did you say? Very well! I don't feel at all offended. I am undoubtedly a Republican, if you understand by that word a man who wishes the welfare of everybody."

"But you will never attain to any position," Felicite quickly interrupted. "You will be crushed. Look at your brothers, they are trying to make their way."

Pascal then comprehended that he was not called upon to defend his philosophic egotism. His mother simply accused him of not speculating on the political situation. He began to laugh somewhat sadly, and then turned the conversation into another channel. Felicite could never induce him to consider the chances of the various parties, nor to enlist in that one of them which seemed likely to carry the day. However, he still occasionally came to spend an evening in the yellow drawing-room. Granoux interested him like an antediluvian animal.

In the meantime, events were moving. The year 1851 was a year of anxiety and apprehension for the politicians of Plassans, and the cause which the Rougons served derived advantage from this circumstance. The most contradictory news arrived from Paris; sometimes the Republicans were in the ascendant, sometimes the Conservative party was crushing the Republic. The echoes of the squabbles which were rending the Legislative Assembly reached the depths of the provinces, now in an exaggerated, now in an attenuated form, varying so greatly as to obscure the vision of the most clear-sighted. The only general feeling was that a denouement was approaching. The prevailing ignorance as to the nature of this denouement kept timid middle class people in a terrible state of anxiety. Everybody wished to see the end. They were sick of uncertainty, and would have flung themselves into the arms of the Grand Turk, if he would have deigned to save France from anarchy.

The marquis's smile became more acute. Of an evening, in the yellow drawing-room, when Granoux's growl was rendered indistinct by fright, he would draw near to Felicite and whisper in her ear: "Come, little one, the fruit is ripe—but you must make yourself useful."

Felicite, who continued to read Eugene's letters, and knew that a decisive crisis might any day occur, had already often felt the necessity of making herself useful, and reflected as to the manner in which the Rougons should employ themselves. At last she consulted the marquis.

"It all depends upon circumstances," the little old man replied. "If the department remains quiet, if no insurrection occurs to terrify Plassans, it will be difficult for you to make yourselves conspicuous and render any services to the new government. I advise you, in that case, to remain at home, and peacefully await the bounties of your son Eugene. But if the people rise, and our brave bourgeois think themselves in danger, there will be a fine part to play. Your husband is somewhat heavy—"

"Oh!" said Felicite, "I'll undertake to make him supple. Do you think the department will revolt?"

"To my mind it's a certainty. Plassans, perhaps, will not make a stir; the reaction has secured too firm a hold here for that.

But the neighbouring towns, especially the small ones and the villages, have long been worked by certain secret societies, and belong to the advanced Republican party. If a Coup d'Etat should burst forth, the tocsin will be heard throughout the entire country, from the forests of the Seille to the plateau of Sainte-Roure."

Felicite reflected. "You think, then," she resumed, "that an insurrection is necessary to ensure our fortune!"

"That's my opinion," replied Monsieur de Carnavant. And he added, with a slightly ironical smile: "A new dynasty is never founded excepting upon an affray. Blood is good manure. It will be a fine thing for the Rougons to date from a massacre, like certain illustrious families."

These words, accompanied by a sneer, sent a cold chill through Felicite's bones. But she was a strong-minded woman, and the sight of Monsieur Peirotte's beautiful curtains, which she religiously viewed every morning, sustained her courage. Whenever she felt herself giving way, she planted herself at the window and contemplated the tax-receiver's house. For her it was the Tuileries. She had determined upon the most extreme measures in order to secure an entree into the new town, that promised land, on the threshold of which she had stood with burning longing for so many years.

The conversation which she had held with the marquis had at last clearly revealed the situation to her. A few days afterwards, she succeeded in reading one of Eugene's letters, in which he, who was working for the Coup d'Etat, seemed also to rely upon an insurrection as the means of endowing his father with some importance. Eugene knew his department well. All his suggestions had been framed with the object of placing as much influence as possible in the hands of the yellow drawing-room reactionaries, so that the Rougons might be able to hold the town at the critical moment. In accordance with his desires, the yellow drawing-room was master of Plassans in November, 1851. Roudier represented the rich citizens there, and his attitude would certainly decide that of the entire new town. Granoux was still more valuable; he had the Municipal Council behind him: he was its most powerful member, a fact which will give some idea of its other members. Finally, through Commander Sicardot, whom the marquis had succeeded in getting appointed as chief of the National Guard, the yellow drawing-room had the armed forces at their disposal.

The Rougons, those poor disreputable devils, had thus succeeded in rallying round themselves the instruments of their own fortune. Everyone, from cowardice or stupidity, would have to obey them and work in the dark for their aggrandisement. They simply had to fear those other influences which might be working with the same object as themselves, and might partially rob them of the merit of victory. That was their great fear, for they wanted to reserve to themselves the role of deliverers. They knew beforehand that they would be aided rather than hindered by the clergy and the nobility. But if the sub-prefect, the mayor, and the other functionaries were to take a step in advance and at once stifle the insurrection they would find themselves thrown into the shade, and even arrested in their exploits; they would have neither time nor means to make themselves useful. What they longed for was complete abstention, general panic among the functionaries. If only all regular administration should disappear, and they could dispose of the destinies of Plassans for a single day, their fortune would be firmly established.

Happily for them, there was not a man in the government service whose convictions were so firm or whose circumstances were so needy as to make him disposed to risk the game. The sub-prefect was a man of liberal spirit whom the executive had forgetfully left at Plassans, owing, no doubt, to the good repute of the town. Of timid character and incapable of exceeding his authority, he would no doubt be greatly embarrassed in the presence of an insurrection. The Rougons, who knew that he was in favour of the democratic cause, and who consequently never dreaded his zeal, were simply curious to know what attitude he would assume. As for the municipality, this did not cause them much apprehension. The mayor, Monsieur Garconnet, was a Legitimist whose nomination had been procured by the influence of the Saint-Marc quarter in 1849. He detested the Republicans and treated them with undisguised disdain; but he was too closely united by bonds of friendship with certain members of the church to lend any active hand in a Bonapartist Coup d'Etat. The other functionaries were in exactly the same position. The justices of the peace, the post-master, the tax-collector, as well as Monsieur Peirotte, the chief receiver of taxes, were all indebted for their posts to the Clerical reaction, and could not accept the Empire with any great enthusiasm. The Rougons, though they did not quite see how they might get rid of these people and clear the way for themselves, nevertheless indulged in sanguine hopes on finding there was little likelihood of anybody disputing their role as deliverers.

The denouement was drawing near. In the last few days of November, as the rumour of a Coup d'Etat was circulating, the prince-president was accused of seeking the position of emperor.

"Eh! we'll call him whatever he likes," Granoux exclaimed, "provided he has those Republican rascals shot!"

This exclamation from Granoux, who was believed to be asleep, caused great commotion. The marquis pretended not to have heard it; but all the bourgeois nodded approval. Roudier, who, being rich, did not fear to applaud the sentiment aloud, went so far as to declare, while glancing askance at Monsieur de Carnavant, that the position was no longer tenable, and that France must be chastised as soon as possible, never mind by what hand.

The marquis still maintained a silence which was interpreted as acquiescence. And thereupon the Conservative clan, abandoning the cause of Legitimacy, ventured to offer up prayers in favour of the Empire.

"My friends," said Commander Sicardot, rising from his seat, "only a Napoleon can now protect threatened life and property. Have no fear, I've taken the necessary precautions to preserve order at Plassans."

As a matter of fact the commander, in concert with Rougon, had concealed, in a kind of cart-house near the ramparts, both a supply of cartridges and a considerable number of muskets; he had also taken steps to secure the co-operation of the National Guard, on which he believed he could rely. His words produced a very favourable impression. On separating for the evening, the peaceful citizens of the yellow drawing-room spoke of massacring the "Reds" if they should dare to stir.

On December 1, Pierre Rougon received a letter from Eugene which he went to read in his bedroom, in accordance with his prudent habit. Felicite observed, however, that he was very agitated when he came out again. She fluttered round the secretaire all day. When night came, she could restrain her impatience no longer. Her husband had scarcely fallen asleep, when she quietly got up, took the key of the secretaire from the waistcoat pocket, and gained possession of the letter with as little noise as possible. Eugene, in ten lines, warned his father that the crisis was at hand, and advised him to acquaint his mother with the situation of affairs. The hour for informing her had arrived; he might stand in need of her advice.

Felicite awaited, on the morrow, a disclosure which did not come. She did not dare to confess her curiosity; but continued to feign ignorance, though enraged at the foolish distrust of her husband, who, doubtless, considered her a gossip, and weak like other women. Pierre, with that marital pride which inspires a man with the belief in his own superiority at home, had ended by attributing all their past ill-luck to his wife. From the time that he fancied he had been conducting matters alone everything seemed to him to have gone as he desired. He had decided, therefore, to dispense altogether with his consort's counsels, and to confide nothing to her, in spite of his son's recommendations.

Felicite was piqued to such a degree that she would have upset the whole affair had she not desired the triumph as ardently as Pierre. So she continued to work energetically for victory, while endeavouring to take her revenge.

"Ah! if he could only have some great fright," thought she; "if he would only commit some act of imprudence! Then I should see him come to me and humbly ask for advice; it would be my turn to lay down the law."

She felt somewhat uneasy at the imperious attitude Pierre would certainly assume if he were to triumph without her aid. On marrying this peasant's son, in preference to some notary's clerk, she had intended to make use of him as a strongly made puppet, whose strings she would pull in her own way; and now, at the decisive moment, the puppet, in his blind stupidity, wanted to work alone! All the cunning, all the feverish activity within the old woman protested against this. She knew Pierre was quite capable of some brutal resolve such as that which he had taken when he compelled his mother to sign the receipt for fifty thousand francs; the tool was indeed a useful and unscrupulous one; but she felt the necessity for guiding it, especially under present circumstances, when considerable suppleness was requisite.

The official news of the Coup d'Etat did not reach Plassans until the afternoon of December 3—a Thursday. Already, at seven o'clock in the evening, there was a full meeting in the yellow drawing-room. Although the crisis had been eagerly desired, vague uneasiness appeared on the faces of the majority. They discussed events amid endless chatter. Pierre, who like the others was slightly pale, thought it right, as an extreme measure of prudence, to excuse Prince Louis's decisive act to the Legitimists and Orleanists who were present.

"There is talk of an appeal to the people," he said; "the nation will then be free to choose whatever government it likes. The president is a man to retire before our legitimate masters."

The marquis, who had retained his aristocratic coolness, was the only one who greeted these words with a smile. The others, in the enthusiasm of the moment, concerned themselves very little about what might follow. All their opinions foundered. Roudier, forgetting the esteem which as a former shopkeeper he had entertained for the Orleanists, stopped Pierre rather abruptly. And everybody exclaimed: "Don't argue the matter. Let us think of preserving order."

These good people were terribly afraid of the Republicans. There had, however been very little commotion in the town on the announcement of the events in Paris. People had collected in front of the notices posted on the door of the Sub-Prefecture; it was also rumoured that a few hundred workmen had left their work and were endeavouring to organise resistance. That was all. No serious disturbance seemed likely to occur. The course which the neighbouring towns and rural districts might take seemed more likely to occasion anxiety; however, it was not yet known how they had received the news of the Coup d'Etat.

Granoux arrived at about nine o'clock, quite out of breath. He had just left a sitting of the Municipal Council which had been hastily summoned together. Choking with emotion, he announced that the mayor, Monsieur Garconnet, had declared, while making due reserves, that he was determined to preserve order by the most stringent measures. However, the intelligence which caused the noisiest chattering in the yellow drawing-room was that of the resignation of the sub-prefect. This functionary had absolutely refused to communicate the despatches of the Minister of the Interior to the inhabitants of Plassans; he had just left the town, so Granoux asserted, and it was thanks to the mayor that the messages had been posted. This was perhaps the only sub-prefect in France who ever had the courage of his democratic opinions.

Although Monsieur Garconnet's firm demeanour caused the Rougons some secret anxiety, they rubbed their hands at the flight of the sub-prefect, which left the post vacant for them. It was decided on this memorable evening that the yellow drawing-room party should accept the Coup d'Etat and openly declare that it was in favour of accomplished facts. Vuillet was commissioned to write an article to that effect, and publish it on the morrow in the "Gazette." Neither he nor the marquis raised any objection. They had, no doubt, received instructions from the mysterious individuals to whom they sometimes made pious allusions. The clergy and the nobility were already resigned to the course of lending a strong hand to the victors, in order to crush their common enemy, the Republic.

While the yellow drawing-room was deliberating on the evening in question, Aristide was perspiring with anxiety. Never had gambler, staking his last louis on a card, felt such anguish. During the day the resignation of his chief, the sub-prefect, had given him much matter for reflection. He had heard him repeat several times that the Coup d'Etat must prove a failure. This functionary, endowed with a limited amount of honesty, believed in the final triumph of the democracy, though he had not the courage to work for that triumph by offering resistance. Aristide was in the habit of listening at the doors of the Sub-Prefecture, in order to get precise information, for he felt that he was groping in the dark, and clung to the intelligence which he gleaned from the officials. The sub-prefect's opinion struck him forcibly; but he remained perplexed. He thought to himself: "Why does the fellow go away if he is so certain that the prince-president will meet with a check?" However, as he was compelled to espouse one side or the other, he resolved to continue his opposition. He wrote a very hostile article on the Coup d'Etat, and took it to the "Independant" the same evening for the following morning's issue. He had corrected the proofs of this article, and was returning home somewhat calmed, when, as he passed along the Rue de la Banne, he instinctively raised his head and glanced at the Rougons' windows. Their windows were brightly lighted up.

"What can they be plotting up there?" the journalist asked himself, with anxious curiosity.

A fierce desire to know the opinion of the yellow drawing-room with regard to recent events then assailed him. He credited this group of reactionaries with little intelligence; but his doubts recurred, he was in that frame of mind when one might seek advice from a child. He could not think of entering his father's home at that moment, after the campaign he had waged against Granoux and the others. Nevertheless, he went upstairs, reflecting what a singular figure he would cut if he were surprised on the way by anyone. On reaching the Rougons' door, he could only catch a confused echo of voices.

"What a child I am," said he, "fear makes me stupid." And he was going to descend again, when he heard the approach of his mother, who was about to show somebody out. He had barely time to hide in a dark corner formed by a little staircase leading to the garrets of the house. The Rougons' door opened, and the marquis appeared, followed by Felicite. Monsieur de Carnavant usually left before the gentlemen of the new town did, in order no doubt to avoid having to shake hands with them in the street.

"Eh! little one," he said on the landing, in a low voice, "these men are greater cowards than I should have thought. With such men France will always be at the mercy of whoever dares to lay his hands upon her!" And he added, with some bitterness, as though speaking to himself: "The monarchy is decidedly becoming too honest for modern times. Its day is over."

"Eugene announced the crisis to his father," replied Felicite. "Prince Louis's triumph seems to him certain."

"Oh, you can proceed without fear," the marquis replied, as he descended the first steps. "In two or three days the country will be well bound and gagged. Good-bye till to-morrow, little one."

Felicite closed the door again. Aristide had received quite a shock in his dark corner. However, without waiting for the marquis to reach the street, he bounded down the staircase, four steps at a time, rushed outside like a madman, and turned his steps towards the printing-office of the "Independant." A flood of thoughts surged through his mind. He was enraged, and accused his family of having duped him. What! Eugene kept his parents informed of the situation, and yet his mother had never given him any of his eldest brother's letters to read, in order that he might follow the advice given therein! And it was only now he learnt by chance that his eldest brother regarded the success of the Coup d'Etat as certain! This circumstance, moreover, confirmed certain presentiments which that idiot of a sub-prefect had prevented him from obeying. He was especially exasperated against his father, whom he had thought stupid enough to be a Legitimist, but who revealed himself as a Bonapartist at the right moment.

"What a lot of folly they have allowed me to perpetrate," he muttered as he ran along. "I'm a fine fellow now. Ah! what a lesson! Granoux is more capable than I."

He entered the office of the "Independant" like a hurricane, and asked for his article in a choking voice. The article had already been imposed. He had the forme unlocked and would not rest until he had himself destroyed the setting, mixing the type in a furious manner, like a set of dominoes. The bookseller who managed the paper looked at him in amazement. He was, in reality, rather glad of the incident, as the article had seemed to him somewhat dangerous. But he was absolutely obliged to have some copy, if the "Independant" was to appear.

"Are you going to give me something else?" he asked.

"Certainly," replied Aristide.

He sat down at the table and began a warm panegyric on the Coup d'Etat. At the very first line, he swore that Prince Louis had just saved the Republic; but he had hardly written a page before he stopped and seemed at a loss how to continue. A troubled look came over his pole-cat face.

"I must go home," he said at last. "I will send you this immediately. Your paper can appear a little later, if necessary."

He walked slowly on his way home, lost in meditation. He was again giving way to indecision. Why should he veer round so quickly? Eugene was an intelligent fellow, but his mother had perhaps exaggerated the significance of some sentence in his letter. In any case, it would be better to wait and hold his tongue.

An hour later Angele called at the bookseller's, feigning deep emotion.

"My husband has just severely injured himself," she said. "He jammed his four fingers in a door as he was coming in. In spite of his sufferings, he has dictated this little note, which he begs you to publish to-morrow."

On the following day the "Independant," made up almost entirely of miscellaneous items of news, appeared with these few lines at the head of the first column:

"A deplorable accident which has occurred to our eminent contributor Monsieur Aristide Rougon will deprive us of his articles for some time. He will suffer at having to remain silent in the present grave circumstances. None of our readers will doubt, however, the good wishes which he offers up with patriotic feelings for the welfare of France."

This burlesque note had been maturely studied. The last sentence might be interpreted in favour of all parties. By this expedient, Aristide devised a glorious return for himself on the morrow of battle, in the shape of a laudatory article on the victors. On the following day he showed himself to the whole town, with his arm in a sling. His mother, frightened by the notice in the paper, hastily called upon him, but he refused to show her his hand, and spoke with a bitterness which enlightened the old woman.

"It won't be anything," she said in a reassuring and somewhat sarcastic tone, as she was leaving. "You only want a little rest."

It was no doubt owing to this pretended accident, and the sub-prefect's departure, that the "Independant" was not interfered with, like most of the democratic papers of the departments.

The 4th day of the month proved comparatively quiet at Plassans. In the evening there was a public demonstration which the mere appearance of the gendarmes sufficed to disperse. A band of working-men came to request Monsieur Garconnet to communicate the despatches he had received from Paris, which the latter haughtily refused to do; as it retired the band shouted: "Long live the Republic! Long live the Constitution!" After this, order was restored. The yellow drawing-room, after commenting at some length on this innocent parade, concluded that affairs were going on excellently.

The 5th and 6th were, however, more disquieting. Intelligence was received of successive risings in small neighbouring towns; the whole southern part of the department had taken up arms; La Palud and Saint-Martin-de-Vaulx had been the first to rise, drawing after them the villages of Chavanos, Nazeres, Poujols, Valqueyras and Vernoux. The yellow drawing-room party was now becoming seriously alarmed. It felt particularly uneasy at seeing Plassans isolated in the very midst of the revolt. Bands of insurgents would certainly scour the country and cut off all communications. Granoux announced, with a terrified look, that the mayor was without any news. Some people even asserted that blood had been shed at Marseilles, and that a formidable revolution had broken out in Paris. Commander Sicardot, enraged at the cowardice of the bourgeois, vowed he would die at the head of his men.

On Sunday the 7th the terror reached a climax. Already at six o'clock the yellow drawing-room, where a sort of reactionary committee sat *en permanence*, was crowded with pale, trembling men, who conversed in undertones, as though they were in a chamber of death. It had been ascertained during the day that a column of insurgents, about three thousand strong, had assembled at Alboise, a big village not more than three leagues away. It was true that this column had been ordered to make for the chief town of the department, leaving Plassans on its left; but the plan of campaign might at any time be altered; moreover, it sufficed for these cowardly cits to know that there were insurgents a few miles off, to make them feel the horny hands of the toilers already tightened round their throats. They had had a foretaste of the revolt in the morning; the few Republicans at Plassans, seeing that they would be unable to make any determined move in the town, had resolved to join their brethren of La Palud and Saint-Martin-de-Vaulx; the first group had left at about eleven o'clock, by the Porte de Rome, shouting the "Marseillaise" and smashing a few windows. Granoux had had one broken. He mentioned the circumstance with stammerings of terror.

Meantime, the most acute anxiety agitated the yellow drawing-room. The commander had sent his servant to obtain some information as to the exact movements of the insurgents, and the others awaited this man's return, making the most astonishing surmises. They had a full meeting. Roudier and Granoux, sinking back in their arm-chairs, exchanged the most pitiable glances, whilst behind them moaned a terror-stricken group of retired tradesmen. Vuillet, without appearing over scared, reflected upon what precautions he should take to protect his shop and person; he was in doubt whether he should hide himself in his garret or cellar, and inclined towards the latter. For their part Pierre and the commander walked up and down, exchanging a word ever and anon. The old oil-dealer clung to this friend Sicardot as if to borrow a little courage from him. He, who had been awaiting the crisis for such a long time, now endeavoured to keep his countenance, in spite of the emotion which was stifling him. As for the marquis, more spruce and smiling than usual, he conversed in a corner with Felicite, who seemed very gay.

At last a ring came. The gentlemen started as if they had heard a gun-shot. Dead silence reigned in the drawing-room when Felicite went to open the door, towards which their pale, anxious faces were turned. Then the commander's servant appeared on the threshold, quite out of breath, and said abruptly to his master: "Sir, the insurgents will be here in an hour."

This was a thunderbolt. They all started up, vociferating, and raising their arms towards the ceiling. For several minutes it was impossible to hear one's self speak. The company surrounded the messenger, overwhelming him with questions.

"Damnation!" the commander at length shouted, "don't make such a row. Be calm, or I won't answer for anything."

Everyone sank back in his chair again, heaving long-drawn sighs. They then obtained a few particulars. The messenger had met the column at Les Tulettes, and had hastened to return.

"There are at least three thousand of them," said he. "They are marching in battalions, like soldiers. I thought I caught sight of some prisoners in their midst."

"Prisoners!" cried the terrified bourgeois.

"No doubt," the marquis interrupted in his shrill voice. "I've heard that the insurgents arrest all persons who are known to have conservative leanings."

This information gave a finishing touch to the consternation of the yellow drawing-room. A few bourgeois got up and stealthily made for the door, reflecting that they had not too much time before them to gain a place of safety.

The announcement of the arrests made by the Republicans appeared to strike Felicite. She took the marquis aside and asked him: "What do these men do with the people they arrest?"

"Why, they carry them off in their train," Monsieur de Carnavant replied. "They no doubt consider them excellent hostages."

"Ah!" the old woman rejoined, in a strange tone.

Then she again thoughtfully watched the curious scene of panic around her. The bourgeois gradually disappeared; soon there only remained Vuillet and Roudier, whom the approaching danger inspired with some courage. As for Granoux, he likewise remained in his corner, his legs refusing to perform their office.

"Well, I like this better," Sicardot remarked, as he observed the flight of the other adherents. "Those cowards were exasperating me at last. For more than two years they've been speaking of shooting all the Republicans in the province, and to-day they wouldn't even fire a halfpenny cracker under their noses."

Then he took up his hat and turned towards the door. "Let's see," he continued, "time presses. Come, Rougon." Felicite, it seemed, had been waiting for this moment. She placed herself between the door and her husband, who, for that matter, was not particularly eager to follow the formidable Sicardot.

"I won't have you go out," she cried, feigning sudden despair. "I won't let you leave my side. Those scoundrels will kill you."

The commander stopped in amazement.

"Hang it all!" he growled, "if the women are going to whine now—Come along, Rougon!'

"No, no," continued the old woman, affecting increase of terror, "he sha'n't follow you. I will hang on to his clothes and prevent him."

The marquis, very much surprised at the scene, looked inquiringly at Felicite. Was this really the woman who had just now been conversing so merrily? What comedy was she playing? Pierre, meantime, seeing that his wife wanted to detain him, deigned a determination to force his way out.

"I tell you you shall not go," the old woman reiterated, as she clung to one of his arms. And turning towards the commander, she said to him: "How can you think of offering any resistance? They are three thousand strong, and you won't be able to collect a hundred men of any spirit. You are rushing into the cannon's mouth to no purpose."

"Eh! that is our duty," said Sicardot, impatiently.

Felicite burst into sobs.

"If they don't kill him, they'll make him a prisoner," she continued, looked fixedly at her husband. "Good heavens! What will become of me, left alone in an abandoned town?"

"But," exclaimed the commander, "we shall be arrested just the same if we allow the insurgents to enter the town unmolested. I believe that before an hour has elapsed the mayor and all the functionaries will be prisoners, to say nothing of your husband and the frequenters of this drawing-room."

The marquis thought he saw a vague smile play about Felicite's lips as she answered, with a look of dismay: "Do you really think so?"

"Of course!" replied Sicardot; "the Republicans are not so stupid as to leave enemies behind them. To-morrow Plassans will be emptied of its functionaries and good citizens."

At these words, which she had so cleverly provoked, Felicite released her husband's arms. Pierre no longer looked as if he wanted to go out. Thanks to his wife, whose skilful tactics escaped him, however, and whose secret complicity he never for a moment suspected, he had just lighted on a whole plan of campaign.

"We must deliberate before taking any decision," he said to the commander. "My wife is perhaps not wrong in accusing us of forgetting the true interests of our families."

"No, indeed, madame is not wrong," cried Granoux, who had been listening to Felicite's terrified cries with the rapture of a coward.

Thereupon the commander energetically clapped his hat on his head, and said in a clear voice: "Right or wrong, it matters little to me. I am commander of the National Guard. I ought to have been at the mayor's before now. Confess that you are afraid, that you leaven me to act alone... . Well, good-night."

He was just turning the handle of the door, when Rougon forcibly detained him.

"Listen, Sicardot," he said.

He drew him into a corner, on seeing Vuillet prick up his big ears. And there he explained to him, in an undertone, that it would be a good plan to leave a few energetic men behind the insurgents, so as to restore order in the town. And as the fierce commander obstinately refused to desert his post, Pierre offered to place himself at the head of such a reserve corps.

"Give me the key of the cart-shed in which the arms and ammunition are kept," he said to him, "and order some fifty of our men not to stir until I call for them."

Sicardot ended by consenting to these prudent measures. He entrusted Pierre with the key of the cart-shed, convinced as he was of the inexpediency of present resistance, but still desirous of sacrificing himself.

During this conversation, the marquis had whispered a few words in Felicite's ear with a knowing look. He complimented her, no doubt, on her theatrical display. The old woman could not repress a faint smile. But, as Sicardot shook hands with Rougon and prepared to go, she again asked him with an air of fright: "Are you really determined to leave us?"

"It is not for one of Napoleon's old soldiers to let himself be intimidated by the mob," he replied.

He was already on the landing, when Granoux hurried after him, crying: "If you go to the mayor's tell him what's going on. I'll just run home to my wife to reassure her."

Then Felicite bent towards the marquis's ear, and whispered with discreet gaiety: "Upon my word, it is best that devil of a commander should go and get himself arrested. He's far too zealous."

However, Rougon brought Granoux back to the drawing-room. Roudier, who had quietly followed the scene from his corner, making signs in support of the proposed measures of prudence, got up and joined them. When the marquis and Vuillet had likewise risen, Pierre began:

"Now that we are alone, among peaceable men, I propose that we should conceal ourselves so as to avoid certain arrest, and be at liberty as soon as ours again becomes the stronger party."

Granoux was ready to embrace him. Roudier and Vuillet breathed more easily.

"I shall want you shortly, gentlemen," the oil-dealer continued, with an important air. "It is to us that the honour of restoring order in Plassans is reserved."

"You may rely upon us!" cried Vuillet, with an enthusiasm which disturbed Felicite.

Time was pressing. These singular defenders of Plassans, who hid themselves the better to protect the town, hastened away, to bury themselves in some hole or other. Pierre, on being left alone with his wife, advised her not to make the mistake of barricading herself indoors, but to reply, if anybody came to question her, that he, Pierre, had simply gone on a short journey. And as she acted the simpleton, feigning terror and asking what all this was coming to, he replied abruptly: "It's nothing to do with you. Let me manage our affairs alone. They'll get on all the better."

A few minutes later he was rapidly threading his way along the Rue de la Banne. On reaching the Cours Sauvaire, he saw a band of armed workmen coming out of the old quarter and singing the "Marseillaise."

"The devil!" he thought. "It was quite time, indeed; here's the town itself in revolt now!"

He quickened his steps in the direction of the Porte de Rome. Cold perspiration came over him while he waited there for the dilatory keeper to open the gate. Almost as soon as he set foot on the high road, he perceived in the moonlight at the other end of the Faubourg the column of insurgents, whose gun barrels gleamed like white flames. So it was at a run that he dived into the Impasse Saint-Mittre, and reached his mother's house, which he had not visited for many a long year.

Chapter 4

Antoine Macquart had returned to Plassans after the fall of the first Napoleon. He had had the incredible good fortune to escape all the final murderous campaigns of the Empire. He had moved from barracks to barracks, dragging on his brutifying military life. This mode of existence brought his natural vices to full development. His idleness became deliberate; his intemperance, which brought him countless punishments, became, to his mind, a veritable religious duty. But that which above all made him the worst of scapegraces was the supercilious disdain which he entertained for the poor devils who had to earn their bread.

"I've got money waiting for me at home," he often said to his comrades; "when I've served my time, I shall be able to live like a gentleman."

This belief, together with his stupid ignorance, prevented him from rising even to the grade of corporal.

Since his departure he had never spent a day's furlough at Plassans, his brother having invented a thousand pretexts to keep him at a distance. He was therefore completely ignorant of the adroit manner in which Pierre had got possession of their mother's fortune. Adelaide, with her profound indifference, did not even write to him three times to tell him how she was going on. The silence which generally greeted his numerous requests for money did not awaken the least suspicion in him; Pierre's stinginess sufficed to explain the difficulty he experienced in securing from time to time a paltry twenty-franc piece. This, however, only increased his animosity towards his brother, who left him to languish in military service in spite of his formal promise to purchase his discharge. He vowed to himself that on his return home he would no longer submit like a child, but would flatly demand his share of the fortune to enable him to live as he pleased. In the diligence which conveyed him home he dreamed of a delightful life of idleness. The shattering of his castles in the air was terrible. When he reached the Faubourg, and could no longer even recognise the Fouques' plot of ground, he was stupefied. He was compelled to ask for his mother's new address. There a terrible scene occurred. Adelaide calmly informed him of the sale of the property. He flew into a rage, and even raised his hand against her.

The poor woman kept repeating: "Your brother has taken everything; it is understood that he will take care of you."

At last he left her and ran off to see Pierre, whom he had previously informed of his return, and who was prepared to receive him in such a way as to put an end to the matter at the first word of abuse.

"Listen," the oil-dealer said to him, affecting distant coldness; "don't rouse my anger, or I'll turn you out. As a matter of fact, I don't know you. We don't bear the same name. It's quite misfortune enough for me that my mother misconducted herself, without having her offspring coming here and insulting me. I was well disposed towards you, but since you are insolent I shall do nothing for you, absolutely nothing."

Antoine was almost choking with rage.

"And what about my money," he cried; "will you give it up, you thief, or shall I have to drag you before the judges?"

Pierre shrugged his shoulders.

"I've got no money of yours," he replied, more calmly than ever. "My mother disposed of her fortune as she thought proper. I am certainly not going to poke my nose into her business. I willingly renounced all hope of inheritance. I am quite safe from your foul accusations."

And as his brother, exasperated by this composure, and not knowing what to think, muttered something, Pierre thrust Adelaide's receipt under his nose. The reading of this scrap of paper completed Antoine's dismay.

"Very well," he said, in a calmer voice, "I know now what I have to do."

The truth was, however, he did not know what to do. His inability to hit upon any immediate expedient for obtaining his share of the money and satisfying his desire of revenge increased his fury. He went back to his mother and subjected her to a disgraceful cross-examination. The wretched woman could do nothing but again refer him to Pierre.

"Do you think you are going to make me run to and fro like a shuttle?" he cried, insolently. "I'll soon find out which of you two has the hoard. You've already squandered it, perhaps?"

And making an allusion to her former misconduct he asked her if there were still not some low fellow to whom she gave her last sous? He did not even spare his father, that drunkard Macquart, as he called him, who must have lived on her till the day of his death, and who left his children in poverty. The poor woman listened with a stupefied air; big tears rolled down her cheeks. She defended herself with the terror of a child, replying to her son's questions as though he were a judge; she swore that she was living respectably, and reiterated with emphasis that she had never had a sou of the money, that Pierre had taken everything. Antoine almost came to believe it at last.

"Ah! the scoundrel!" he muttered; "that's why he wouldn't purchase my discharge."

He had to sleep at his mother's house, on a straw mattress flung in a corner. He had returned with his pockets perfectly empty, and was exasperated at finding himself destitute of resources, abandoned like a dog in the streets, without hearth or home, while his brother, as he thought, was in a good way of business, and living on the fat of the land. As he had no money to buy clothes with, he went out on the following day in his regimental cap and trousers. He had the good fortune to find, at the bottom of a cupboard, an old yellowish velveteen jacket, threadbare and patched, which had belonged to Macquart. In this strange attire he walked about the town, relating his story to everyone, and demanding justice.

The people whom he went to consult received him with a contempt which made him shed tears of rage. Provincial folks are inexorable towards fallen families. In the general opinion it was only natural that the Rougon-Macquarts should seek to devour each other; the spectators, instead of separating them, were more inclined to urge them on. Pierre, however, was at that time already beginning to purify himself of his early stains. People laughed at his roguery; some even went so far as to say that he had done quite right, if he really had taken possession of the money, and that it would be a good lesson to the dissolute folks of the town.

Antoine returned home discouraged. A lawyer had advised him, in a scornful manner, to wash his dirty linen at home, though not until he had skilfully ascertained whether Antoine possessed the requisite means to carry on a lawsuit. According to this man, the case was very involved, the pleadings would be very lengthy, and success was doubtful. Moreover, it would require money, and plenty of it.

Antoine treated his mother yet more harshly that evening. Not knowing on whom else to wreak his vengeance, he repeated his accusation of the previous day; he kept the wretched woman up till midnight, trembling with shame and fright. Adelaide having informed him that Pierre made her an allowance, he now felt certain that his brother had pocketed the fifty thousand francs. But, in his irritation, he still affected to doubt it, and did not cease to question the poor woman, again and again reproaching her with misconduct.

Antoine soon found out that, alone and without resources, he could not successfully carry on a contest with his brother. He then endeavoured to gain Adelaide to his cause; an accusation lodged by her might have serious consequences. But, at Antoine's first suggestion of it, the poor, lazy, lethargic creature firmly refused to bring trouble on her eldest son.

"I am an unhappy woman," she stammered; "it is quite right of you to get angry. But I should feel too much remorse if I caused one of my sons to be sent to prison. No; I'd rather let you beat me."

He saw that he would get nothing but tears out of her, and contented himself with saying that she was justly punished, and that he had no pity for her. In the evening, upset by the continual quarrels which her son had sought with her, Adelaide had one of those nervous attacks which kept her as rigid as if she had been dead. The young man threw her on her bed, and then began to rummage the house to see if the wretched woman had any savings hidden away. He found about forty francs. He took possession of them, and, while his mother still lay there, rigid and scarce able to breathe, he quietly took the diligence to Marseilles.

He had just bethought himself that Mouret, the journeyman hatter who had married his sister Ursule, must be indignant at Pierre's roguery, and would no doubt be willing to defend his wife's interests. But he did not find in him the man he expected. Mouret plainly told him that he had become accustomed to look upon Ursule as an orphan, and would have no contentions with her family at any price. Their affairs were prospering. Antoine was received so coldly that he hastened to take the diligence home again. But, before leaving, he was anxious to revenge himself for the secret contempt which he read in the workman's eyes; and, observing that his sister appeared rather pale and dejected, he said to her husband, in a slyly cruel way, as he took his departure: "Have a care, my sister was always sickly, and I find her much changed for the worse; you may lose her altogether."

The tears which rushed to Mouret's eyes convinced him that he had touched a sore wound. But then those work-people made too great a display of their happiness.

When he was back again in Plassans, Antoine became the more menacing from the conviction that his hands were tied. During a whole month he was seen all over the place. He paraded the streets, recounting his story to all who would listen to him. Whenever he succeeded in extorting a franc from his mother, he would drink it away at some tavern, where he would revile his brother, declaring that the rascal should shortly hear from him. In places like these, the good-natured fraternity which reigns among drunkards procured him a sympathetic audience; all the scum of the town espoused his cause, and poured forth bitter imprecations against that rascal Rougon, who left a brave soldier to starve; the discussion generally terminating with an indiscriminate condemnation of the rich. Antoine, the better to revenge himself, continued to march about in his regimental cap and trousers and his old yellow velvet jacket, although his mother had offered to purchase some more becoming clothes for him. But no; he preferred to make a display of his rags, and paraded them on Sundays in the most frequented parts of the Cours Sauvaire.

One of his most exquisite pleasures was to pass Pierre's shop ten times a day. He would enlarge the holes in his jacket with his fingers, slacken his step, and sometimes stand talking in front of the door, so as to remain longer in the street. On these occasions, too, he would bring one of his drunken friends and gossip to him; telling him about the theft of the fifty thousand francs, accompanying his narrative with loud insults and menaces, which could be heard by everyone in the street, and taking particular care that his abuse should reach the furthest end of the shop.

"He'll finish by coming to beg in front of our house," Felicite used to say in despair.

The vain little woman suffered terribly from this scandal. She even at this time felt some regret at ever having married Rougon; his family connections were so objectionable. She would have given all she had in the world to prevent Antoine from parading his rags. But Pierre, who was maddened by his brother's conduct, would not allow his name to be mentioned. When his wife tried to convince him that it would perhaps be better to free himself from all annoyance by giving Antoine a little money: "No, nothing; not a sou," he cried with rage. "Let him starve!"

He confessed, however, at last that Antoine's demeanour was becoming intolerable. One day, Felicite, desiring to put an end to it, called to "that man," as she styled him with a disdainful curl on her lip. "That man" was in the act of calling her a foul name in the middle of the street, where he stood with one of his friends, even more ragged than himself. They were both drunk.

"Come, they want us in there," said Antoine to his companion in a jeering tone.

But Felicite drew back, muttering: "It's you alone we wish to speak to."

"Bah!" the young man replied, "my friend's a decent fellow. You needn't mind him hearing. He'll be my witness."

The witness sank heavily on a chair. He did not take off his hat, but began to stare around him, with the maudlin, stupid grin of drunkards and coarse people who know that they are insolent. Felicite was so ashamed that she stood in front of the shop door in order that people outside might not see what strange company she was receiving. Fortunately her husband came to the rescue. A violent quarrel ensued between him and his brother. The latter, after stammering insults, reiterated his old grievances twenty times over. At last he even began to cry, and his companion was near following his example. Pierre had defended himself in a very dignified manner.

"Look here," he said at last, "you're unfortunate, and I pity you. Although you have cruelly insulted me, I can't forget that we are children of the same mother. If I give you anything, however, you must understand I give it you out of kindness, and not from fear. Would you like a hundred francs to help you out of your difficulties?"

This abrupt offer of a hundred francs dazzled Antoine's companion. He looked at the other with an air of delight, which clearly signified: "As the gentleman offers a hundred francs, it is time to leave off abusing him." But Antoine was determined to speculate on his brother's favourable disposition. He asked him whether he took him for a fool; it was his share, ten thousand francs, that he wanted.

"You're wrong, you're wrong," stuttered his friend.

At last, as Pierre, losing all patience, was threatening to turn them both out, Antoine lowered his demands and contented himself with claiming one thousand francs. They quarrelled for another quarter of an hour over this amount. Finally, Felicite interfered. A crowd was gathering round the shop.

"Listen," she said, excitedly; "my husband will give you two hundred francs. I'll undertake to buy you a suit of clothes, and hire a room for a year for you."

Rougon got angry at this. But Antoine's comrade cried, with transports of delight: "All right, it's settled, then; my friend accepts."

Antoine did, in fact, declare, in a surly way, that he would accept. He felt he would not be able to get any more. It was arranged that the money and clothes should be sent to him on the following day, and that a few days later, as soon as Felicite should have found a room for him, he would take up his quarters there. As they were leaving, the young man's sottish companion became as respectful as he had previously been insolent. He bowed to the company more than a dozen times, in an awkward and humble manner, muttering many indistinct thanks, as if the Rougons' gifts had been intended for himself.

A week later Antoine occupied a large room in the old quarter, in which Felicite, exceeding her promises, had placed a bed, a table, and some chairs, on the young man formally undertaking not to molest them in future. Adelaide felt no regret at her son leaving her; the short stay he had made with her had condemned her to bread and water for more than three months. However, Antoine had soon eaten and drunk the two hundred francs he received from Pierre. He never for a moment thought of investing them in some little business which would have helped him to live. When he was again penniless, having no trade, and being, moreover, unwilling to work, he again sought to slip a hand into the Rougons' purse. Circumstances were not the same as before, however, and he failed to intimidate them. Pierre even took advantage of this opportunity to turn him out, and forbade him ever to set foot in his house again. It was of no avail for Antoine to repeat his former accusations. The townspeople, who were acquainted with his brother's munificence from the publicity which Felicite had given to it, declared him to be in the wrong, and called him a lazy, idle fellow. Meantime his hunger was pressing. He threatened to turn smuggler like his father, and perpetrate some crime which would dishonour his family. At this the Rougons shrugged their shoulders; they knew he was too much of a coward to risk his neck. At last, blindly enraged against his relatives in particular and society in general, Antoine made up his mind to seek some work.

In a tavern of the Faubourg he made the acquaintance of a basket-maker who worked at home. He offered to help him. In a short time he learnt to plait baskets and hampers—a coarse and poorly-paid kind of labour which finds a ready market. He was very soon able to work on his own account. This trade pleased him, as it was not over laborious. He could still indulge his idleness, and that was what he chiefly cared for. He would only take to his work when he could no longer do otherwise; then he would hurriedly plait a dozen baskets and go and sell them in the market. As long as the money lasted he lounged about, visiting all the taverns and digesting his drink in the sunshine. Then, when he had fasted a whole day, he would once more take up his osier with a low growl and revile the wealthy who lived in idleness. The trade of a basket-maker, when followed in such a manner, is a thankless one. Antoine's work would not have sufficed to pay for his drinking bouts if he had not contrived a means of procuring his osier at low cost. He never bought any at Plassans, but used to say that he went each month to purchase a stock at a neighbouring town, where he pretended it was sold cheaper. The truth, however, was that he supplied himself from the osier-grounds of the Viorne on dark nights. A rural policeman even caught him once in the very act, and Antoine underwent a few days' imprisonment in consequence. It was from that time forward that he posed in the town as a fierce Republican. He declared that he had been quietly smoking his pipe by the riverside when the rural policeman arrested him. And he added: "They would like to get me out of the way because they know what my opinions are. But I'm not afraid of them, those rich scoundrels."

At last, at the end of ten years of idleness, Antoine considered that he had been working too hard. His constant dream was to devise some expedient by which he might live at his ease without having to do anything. His idleness would never have rested content with bread and water; he was not like certain lazy persons who are willing to put up with hunger provided they can keep their hands in their pockets. He liked good feeding and nothing to do. He talked at one time of taking a situation as servant in some nobleman's house in the Saint-Marc quarter. But one of his friends, a groom, frightened him by describing the exacting ways of his masters. Finally Macquart, sick of his baskets, and seeing the time approach when he would be compelled to purchase the requisite osier, was on the point of selling himself as an army substitute and resuming his military life, which he preferred a thousand times to that of an artisan, when he made the acquaintance of a woman, an acquaintance which modified his plans.

Josephine Gavaudan, who was known throughout the town by the familiar diminutive of Fine, was a tall, strapping wench of about thirty. With a square face of masculine proportions, and a few terribly long hairs about her chin and lips, she was cited as a doughty woman, one who could make the weight of her fist felt. Her broad shoulders and huge arms consequently inspired the town urchins with marvellous respect; and they did not even dare to smile at her moustache. Notwithstanding all this, Fine had a faint voice, weak and clear like that of a child. Those who were acquainted with her asserted that she was as gentle as a lamb, in spite of her formidable appearance. As she was very hard-working, she might have put some money aside if she had not had a partiality for liqueurs. She adored aniseed, and very often had to be carried home on Sunday evenings.

On week days she would toil with the stubbornness of an animal. She had three or four different occupations; she sold fruit or boiled chestnuts in the market, according to the season; went out charring for a few well-to-do people; washed up plates and dishes at houses when parties were given, and employed her spare time in mending old chairs. She was more particularly known in the town as a chair-mender. In the South large numbers of straw-bottomed chairs are used.

Antoine Macquart formed an acquaintance with Fine at the market. When he went to sell his baskets in the winter he would stand beside the stove on which she cooled her chestnuts and warm himself. He was astonished at her courage, he who was frightened of the least work. By degrees he discerned, beneath the apparent roughness of this strapping creature, signs of timidity and kindliness. He frequently saw her give handfuls of chestnuts to the ragged urchins who stood in ecstasy round her smoking pot. At other times, when the market inspector hustled her, she very nearly began to cry, apparently forgetting all about her heavy fists. Antoine at last decided that she was exactly the woman he wanted. She would work for both and he would lay down the law at home. She would be his beast of burden, an obedient, indefatigable animal. As for her partiality for liqueurs, he regarded this as quite natural. After well weighing the advantages of such an union, he declared himself to Fine, who was delighted with his proposal. No man had ever yet ventured to propose to her. Though she was told that Antoine was the most worthless of vagabonds, she lacked the courage to refuse matrimony. The very evening of the nuptials the young man took up his abode in his wife's lodgings in the Rue Civadiere, near the market. These lodgings, consisting of three rooms, were much more comfortably furnished than his own, and he gave a sigh of satisfaction as he stretched himself out on the two excellent mattresses which covered the bedstead.

Everything went on very well for the first few days. Fine attended to her various occupations as in the past; Antoine, seized with a sort of marital self-pride which astonished even himself, plaited in one week more baskets than he had ever before done in a month. On the first Sunday, however, war broke out. The couple had a goodly sum of money in the house, and they spent it freely. During the night, when they were both drunk, they beat each other outrageously, without being able to remember on the morrow how it was that the quarrel had commenced. They had remained on most affectionate terms until about ten o'clock, when Antoine had begun to beat Fine brutally, whereupon the latter, growing exasperated and forgetting her meekness, had given him back as much as she received. She went to work again bravely on the following day, as though nothing had happened. But her husband, with sullen rancour, rose late and passed the remainder of the day smoking his pipe in the sunshine.

From that time forward the Macquarts adopted the kind of life which they were destined to lead in the future. It became, as it were, tacitly understood between them that the wife should toil and moil to keep her husband. Fine, who had an instinctive liking for work, did not object to this. She was as patient as a saint, provided she had had no drink, thought it quite natural that her husband should remain idle, and even strove to spare him the most trifling labour. Her little weakness, aniseed, did not make her vicious, but just. On the evenings when she had forgotten herself in the company of a bottle of her favourite liqueur, if Antoine tried to pick a quarrel with her, she would set upon him with might and main, reproaching him with his idleness and ingratitude. The neighbours grew accustomed to the disturbances which periodically broke out in the couple's room. The two battered each other conscientiously; the wife slapped like a mother chastising a naughty child; but the husband, treacherous and spiteful as he was, measured his blows, and, on several occasions, very nearly crippled the unfortunate woman.

"You'll be in a fine plight when you've broken one of my arms or legs," she would say to him. "Who'll keep you then, you lazy fellow?"

Excepting for these turbulent scenes, Antoine began to find his new mode of existence quite endurable. He was well clothed, and ate and drank his fill. He had laid aside the basket work altogether; sometimes, when he was feeling over-bored, he would resolve to plait a dozen baskets for the next market day; but very often he did not even finish the first one. He kept, under a couch, a bundle of osier which he did not use up in twenty years.

The Macquarts had three children, two girls and a boy. Lisa,[3] born the first, in 1827, one year after the marriage, remained but little at home. She was a fine, big, healthy, full-blooded child, greatly resembling her mother. She did not, however, inherit the latter's animal devotion and endurance. Macquart had implanted in her a most decided longing for ease and comfort. While she was a child she would consent to work for a whole day in return for a cake. When she was scarcely seven years old, the wife of the postmaster, who was a neighbour of the Macquarts, took a liking to her. She made a little maid of her. And when she lost her husband in 1839, and went to live in Paris, she took Lisa with her. The parents had almost given her their daughter.

The second girl, Gervaise,[4] born the following year, was a cripple from birth. Her right thigh was smaller than the left and showed signs of curvature, a curious hereditary result of the brutality which her mother had to endure during her fierce drunken brawls with Macquart. Gervaise remained puny, and Fine, observing her pallor and weakness, put her on a course of aniseed, under the pretext that she required something to strengthen her. But the poor child became still more emaciated. She was a tall, lank girl, whose frocks, invariably too large, hung round her as if they had nothing under them. Above a deformed and puny body she had a sweet little doll-like head, a tiny round face, pale and exquisitely delicate. Her infirmity almost became graceful. Her body swayed gently at every step with a sort of rhythmical swing.

The Macquarts' son, Jean,[5] was born three years later. He was a robust child, in no respect recalling Gervaise. Like the eldest girl, he took after his mother, without having any physical resemblance to her. He was the first to import into the

---

3. The pork-butcher's wife in Le Ventre de Paris (The Fat and the Thin).
4. Both Francois and Marthe figure largely in The Conquest of Plassans.
5. Figures prominently in La Terre (The Earth) and La Debacle (The Downfall).

Rougon-Macquart stock a fat face with regular features, which showed all the coldness of a grave yet not over-intelligent nature. This boy grew up with the determination of some day making an independent position for himself. He attended school diligently, and tortured his dull brain to force a little arithmetic and spelling into it. After that he became an apprentice, repeating much the same efforts with a perseverance that was the more meritorious as it took him a whole day to learn what others acquired in an hour.

As long as these poor little things remained a burden to the house, Antoine grumbled. They were useless mouths that lessened his own share. He vowed, like his brother, that he would have no more children, those greedy creatures who bring their parents to penury. It was something to hear him bemoan his lot when they sat five at table, and the mother gave the best morsels to Jean, Lisa, and Gervaise.

"That's right," he would growl; "stuff them, make them burst!"

Whenever Fine bought a garment or a pair of boots for them, he would sulk for days together. Ah! if he had only known, he would never had had that pack of brats, who compelled him to limit his smoking to four sous' worth of tobacco a day, and too frequently obliged him to eat stewed potatoes for dinner, a dish which he heartily detested.

Later on, however, as soon as Jean and Gervaise earned their first francs, he found some good in children after all. Lisa was no longer there. He lived upon the earnings of the two others without compunction, as he had already lived upon their mother. It was a well-planned speculation on his part. As soon as little Gervaise was eight years old, she went to a neighbouring dealer's to crack almonds; she there earned ten sous a day, which her father pocketed right royally, without even a question from Fine as to what became of the money. The young girl was next apprenticed to a laundress, and as soon as she received two francs a day for her work, the two francs strayed in a similar manner into Macquart's hands. Jean, who had learnt the trade of a carpenter, was likewise despoiled on pay-days, whenever Macquart succeeded in catching him before he had handed the money to his mother. If the money escaped Macquart, which sometimes happened, he became frightfully surly. He would glare at his wife and children for a whole week, picking a quarrel for nothing, although he was, as yet, ashamed to confess the real cause of his irritations. On the next pay-day, however, he would station himself on the watch, and as soon as he had succeeded in pilfering the youngster's earnings, he disappeared for days together.

Gervaise, beaten and brought up in the streets among all the lads of the neighbourhood, became a mother when she was fourteen years of age. The father of her child was not eighteen years old. He was a journeyman tanner named Lantier. At first Macquart was furious, but he calmed down somewhat when he learnt that Lantier's mother, a worthy woman, was willing to take charge of the child. He kept Gervaise, however; she was then already earning twenty-five sous a day, and he therefore avoided all question of marriage. Four years later she had a second child, which was likewise taken in by Lantier's mother. This time Macquart shut his eyes altogether. And when Fine timidly suggested that it was time to come to some understanding with the tanner, in order to end a state of things which made people chatter, he flatly declared that his daughter should not leave him, and that he would give her to her lover later on, "when he was worthy of her, and had enough money to furnish a home."

This was a fine time for Antoine Macquart. He dressed like a gentleman, in frock-coats and trousers of the finest cloth. Cleanly shaved, and almost fat, he was no longer the emaciated ragged vagabond who had been wont to frequent the taverns. He dropped into cafes, read the papers, and strolled on the Cours Sauvaire. He played the gentleman as long as he had any money in his pocket. At times of impecuniosity he remained at home, exasperated at being kept in his hovel and prevented from taking his customary cup of coffee. On such occasions he would reproach the whole human race with his poverty, making himself ill with rage and envy, until Fine, out of pity, would often give him the last silver coin in the house so that he might spend his evening at the cafe. This dear fellow was fiercely selfish. Gervaise, who brought home as much as sixty francs a month, wore only thin cotton frocks, while he had black satin waistcoats made for him by one of the best tailors in Plassans.

Jean, the big lad who earned three or four francs a day, was perhaps robbed even more impudently. The cafe where his father passed entire days was just opposite his master's work-shop, and while he had plane or saw in hand he could see "Monsieur" Macquart on the other side of the way, sweetening his coffee or playing piquet with some petty annuitant. It was his money that the lazy old fellow was gambling away. He, Jean, never stepped inside a cafe, he never had so much as five sous to pay for a drink. Antoine treated him like a little girl, never leaving him a centime, and always demanding an exact account of the manner in which he had employed his time. If the unfortunate lad, led away by some of his mates, wasted a day somewhere in the country, on the banks of the Viorne, or on the slopes of Garrigues, his father would storm and raise his hand, and long bear him a grudge on account of the four francs less that he received at the end of the fortnight. He thus held his son in a state of dependence, sometimes even looking upon the sweethearts whom the young carpenter courted as his own. Several of Gervaise's friends used to come to the Macquarts' house, work-girls from sixteen to eighteen years of age, bold and boisterous girls who, on certain evenings, filled the room with youth and gaiety. Poor Jean, deprived of all pleasure, ever kept at home by the lack of money, looked at these girls with longing eyes; but the childish life which he was compelled to lead had implanted invincible shyness in him; in playing with his sister's friends, he was hardly bold enough to touch them with the tips of his fingers. Macquart used to shrug his shoulders with pity.

"What a simpleton!" he would mutter, with an air of ironical superiority.

And it was he who would kiss the girls, when his wife's back was turned. He carried his attentions even further with a little laundress whom Jean pursued rather more earnestly than the others. One fine evening he stole her almost from his arms. The old rogue prided himself on his gallantry.

There are some men who live upon their mistresses. Antoine Macquart lived on his wife and children with as much shame-lessness and impudence. He did not feel the least compunction in pillaging the home and going out to enjoy himself when the house was bare. He still assumed a supercilious air, returning from the cafe only to rail against the poverty and wretchedness that awaited him at home. He found the dinner detestable, he called Gervaise a blockhead, and declared that Jean would never be a man. Immersed in his own selfish indulgence, he rubbed his hands whenever he had eaten the best piece in the dish; and then he smoked his pipe, puffing slowly, while the two poor children, overcome with fatigue, went to sleep with their heads resting on the table. Thus Macquart passed his days in lazy enjoyment. It seemed to him quite natural that he should be kept in idleness like a girl, to sprawl about on the benches of some tavern, or stroll in the cool of the day along the Cours or the Mail. At last he went so far as to relate his amorous escapades in the presence of his son, who listened with glistening eyes. The children never protested, accustomed as they were to see their mother humble herself before her husband.

Fine, that strapping woman who drubbed him soundly when they were both intoxicated, always trembled before him when she was sober, and allowed him to rule despotically at home. He robbed her in the night of the coppers which she had earned during the day at the market, but she never dared to protest, except by veiled rebukes. Sometimes, when he had squandered the week's money in advance, he accused her, poor thing, who worked herself to death, of being stupid and not knowing how to manage. Fine, as gentle as a lamb, replied, in her soft, clear voice, which contrasted so strangely with her big figure, that she was no longer twenty years old, and that money was becoming hard to earn. In order to console herself, she would buy a pint of aniseed, and drink little glassfuls of it with her daughter of an evening, after Antoine had gone back to the cafe. That was their dissipation. Jean went to bed, while the two women remained at the table, listening attentively in order to remove the bottle and glasses at the first sound.

When Macquart was late, they often became intoxicated by the many "nips" they thus thoughtlessly imbibed. Stupefied and gazing at each other with vague smiles, this mother and daughter would end by stuttering. Red patches appeared on Gervaise's cheeks; her delicate doll-like face assumed a look of maudlin beatitude. Nothing could be more heart-rending than to see this wretched, pale child, aglow with drink and wearing the idiotic smile of a confirmed sot about her moist lips. Fine, huddled up on her chair, became heavy and drowsy. They sometimes forgot to keep watch, or even lacked the strength to remove the bottle and glasses when Antoine's footsteps were heard on the stairs. On these occasions blows were freely exchanged among the Macquarts. Jean had to get up to separate his father and mother and make his sister go to bed, as otherwise she would have slept on the floor.

Every political party numbers its grotesques and its villains. Antoine Macquart, devoured by envy and hatred, and meditating revenge against society in general, welcomed the Republic as a happy era when he would be allowed to fill his pockets from his neighbour's cash-box, and even strangle the neighbour if the latter manifested any displeasure. His cafe life and all the newspaper articles he had read without understanding them had made him a terrible ranter who enunciated the strangest of political theories. It is necessary to have heard one of those malcontents who ill digest what they read, haranguing the company in some provincial taproom, in order to conceive the degree of hateful folly at which Macquart had arrived. As he talked a good deal, had seen active service, and was naturally regarded as a man of energy and spirit, he was much sought after and listened to by simpletons. Although he was not the chief of any party, he had succeeded in collecting round him a small group of working-men who took his jealous ravings for expressions of honest and conscientious indignation.

Directly after the Revolution of February '48, he persuaded himself that Plassans was his own, and, as he strolled along the streets, the jeering manner in which he regarded the little retail traders who stood terrified at their shop doors clearly signified: "Our day has come, my little lambs; we are going to lead you a fine dance!" He had grown insolent beyond belief; he acted the part of a victorious despot to such a degree that he ceased to pay for his drinks at the cafe, and the landlord, a simpleton who trembled whenever Antoine rolled his eyes, dared not present his bill. The number of cups of coffee he consumed during this period was incalculable; sometimes he invited his friends, and shouted for hours together that the people were dying of hunger, and that the rich ought to share their wealth with them. He himself would never have given a sou to a beggar.

That which chiefly converted him into a fierce Republican was the hope of at last being able to revenge himself on the Rougons, who had openly ranged themselves on the side of the reactionary party. Ah, what a triumph if he could only hold Pierre and Felicite at his mercy! Although the latter had not succeeded over well in business, they had at last become gentlefolks, while he, Macquart, had still remained a working-man. That exasperated him. Perhaps he was still more mortified because one of their sons was a barrister, another a doctor, and the third a clerk, while his son Jean merely worked at a carpenter's shop, and his daughter Gervaise at a washerwoman's. When he compared the Macquarts with the Rougons, he was still more ashamed to see his wife selling chestnuts in the market, and mending the greasy old straw-seated chairs of the neighbourhood in the evening. Pierre, after all, was but his brother, and had no more right than himself to live fatly on his income. Moreover, this brother was actually playing the gentleman with money stolen from him. Whenever Macquart touched upon this subject, he became fiercely enraged; he clamoured for hours together, incessantly repeating his old accusations, and never wearying of exclaiming: "If my brother was where he ought to be, I should be the moneyed man at the present time!"

And when anyone asked him where his brother ought to be, he would reply, "At the galleys!" in a formidable voice.

His hatred further increased when the Rougons had gathered the Conservatives round them, and thus acquired a certain influence in Plassans. The famous yellow drawing-room became, in his hare-brained chatter at the cafe, a cave of bandits, an assembly of villains who every evening swore on their daggers that they would murder the people. In order to incite the starvelings against Pierre, Macquart went so far as to circulate a report that the retired oil-dealer was not so poor as he pretended, but that he concealed his treasures through avarice and fear of robbery. His tactics thus tended to rouse the poor people by a repetition of absurdly ridiculous tales, which he often came to believe in himself. His personal animosity and his desire for revenge were ill concealed beneath his professions of patriotism; but he was heard so frequently, and he had such a loud voice, that no one would have dared to doubt the genuineness of his convictions.

At bottom, all the members of this family had the same brutish passions. Felicite, who clearly understood that Macquart's wild theories were simply the fruit of restrained rage and embittered envy, would much have liked to purchase his silence. Unfortunately, she was short of money, and did not dare to interest him in the dangerous game which her husband was playing. Antoine now injured them very much among the well-to-do people of the new town. It sufficed that he was a relation of theirs. Granoux and Roudier often scornfully reproached them for having such a man in their family. Felicite consequently asked herself with anguish how they could manage to cleanse themselves of such a stain.

It seemed to her monstrous and indecent that Monsieur Rougon should have a brother whose wife sold chestnuts, and who himself lived in crapulous idleness. She at last even trembled for the success of their secret intrigues, so long as Antoine seemingly took pleasure in compromising them. When the diatribes which he levelled at the yellow drawing-room were reported to her, she shuddered at the thought that he was capable of becoming desperate and ruining all their hopes by force of scandal.

Antoine knew what consternation his demeanour must cause the Rougons, and it was solely for the purpose of exhausting their patience that he from day to day affected fiercer opinions. At the cafe he frequented he used to speak of "my brother Pierre" in a voice which made everybody turn round; and if he happened to meet some reactionary from the yellow drawing-room in the street, he would mutter some low abuse which the worthy citizen, amazed at such audacity, would repeat to the Rougons in the evening, as though to make them responsible for his disagreeable encounter.

One day Granoux arrived in a state of fury.

"Really," he exclaimed, when scarcely across the threshold, "it's intolerable; one can't move a step without being insulted." Then, addressing Pierre, he added: "When one has a brother like yours, sir, one should rid society of him. I was just quietly walking past the Sub-Prefecture, when that rascal passed me muttering something in which I could clearly distinguish the words 'old rogue.'"

Felicite turned pale, and felt it necessary to apologise to Granoux, but he refused to accept any excuses, and threatened to leave altogether. The marquis, however, exerted himself to arrange matters.

"It is very strange," he said, "that the wretched fellow should have called you an old rogue. Are you sure that he intended the insult for you?"

Granoux was perplexed; he admitted at last, however, that Antoine might have muttered: "So you are again going to that old rogue's?"

At this Monsieur de Carnavant stroked his chin to conceal the smile which rose to his lips in spite of himself.

Then Rougon, with superb composure, replied: "I thought as much; the 'old rogue' was no doubt intended for me. I've very glad that this misunderstanding is now cleared up. Gentlemen, pray avoid the man in question, whom I formally repudiate."

Felicite, however, did not take matters so coolly; every fresh scandal caused by Macquart made her more and more uneasy; she would sometimes pass the whole night wondering what those gentlemen must think of the matter.

A few months before the Coup d'Etat, the Rougons received an anonymous letter, three pages of foul insults, in which they were warned that if their party should ever triumph, the scandalous story of Adelaide's amours would be published in some newspaper, together with an account of the robbery perpetrated by Pierre, when he had compelled his mother, driven out of her senses by debauchery, to sign a receipt for fifty thousand francs. This letter was a heavy blow for Rougon himself. Felicite could not refrain from reproaching her husband with his disreputable family; for the husband and wife never for a moment doubted that this letter was Antoine's work.

"We shall have to get rid of the blackguard at any price," said Pierre in a gloomy tone. "He's becoming too troublesome by far."

In the meantime, Macquart, resorting to his former tactics, looked round among his own relatives for accomplices who would join him against the Rougons. He had counted upon Aristide at first, on reading his terrible articles in the

"Independant." But the young man, in spite of all his jealous rage, was not so foolish as to make common cause with such a fellow as his uncle. He never even minced matters with him, but invariably kept him at a distance, a circumstance which induced Antoine to regard him suspiciously. In the taverns, where Macquart reigned supreme, people went so far as to say the journalist was paid to provoke disturbances.

Baffled on this side, Macquart had no alternative but to sound his sister Ursule's children. Ursule had died in 1839, thus fulfilling her brother's evil prophecy. The nervous affection which she had inherited from her mother had turned into slow consumption, which gradually killed her. She left three children; a daughter, eighteen years of age, named Helene, who married a clerk, and two boys, the elder, Francois, a young man of twenty-three, and the younger, a sickly little fellow scarcely six years old, named Silvere. The death of his wife, whom he adored, proved a thunderbolt to Mouret. He dragged on his existence for another year, neglecting his business and losing all the money he had saved. Then, one morning, he was found hanging in a cupboard where Ursule's dresses were still suspended. His elder son, who had received a good commercial training, took a situation in the house of his uncle Rougon, where he replaced Aristide, who had just left.

Rougon, in spite of his profound hatred for the Macquarts, gladly welcomed this nephew, whom he knew to be industrious and sober. He was in want of a youth whom he could trust, and who would help him to retrieve his affairs. Moreover, during the time of Mouret's prosperity, he had learnt to esteem the young couple, who knew how to make money, and thus he had soon become reconciled with his sister. Perhaps he thought he was making Francois some compensation by taking him into his business; having robbed the mother, he would shield himself from remorse by giving employment to the son; even rogues make honest calculations sometimes. It was, however, a good thing for him. If the house of Rougon did not make a fortune at this time, it was certainly through no fault of that quiet, punctilious youth, Francois, who seemed born to pass his life behind a grocer's counter, between a jar of oil and a bundle of dried cod-fish. Although he physically resembled his mother, he inherited from his father a just if narrow mind, with an instinctive liking for a methodical life and the safe speculations of a small business.

Three months after his arrival, Pierre, pursuing his system of compensation, married him to his young daughter Marthe,[6] whom he did not know how to dispose of. The two young people fell in love with each other quite suddenly, in a few days. A peculiar circumstance had doubtless determined and enhanced their mutual affection. There was a remarkably close resemblance between them, suggesting that of brother and sister. Francois inherited, through Ursule, the face of his grandmother Adelaide. Marthe's case was still more curious; she was an equally exact portrait of Adelaide, although Pierre Rougon had none of his mother's features distinctly marked; the physical resemblance had, as it were, passed over Pierre, to reappear in his daughter. The similarity between husband and wife went, however, no further than their faces; if the worthy son of a steady matter-of-fact hatter was distinguishable in Francois, Marthe showed the nervousness and mental weakness of her grandmother. Perhaps it was this combination of physical resemblance and moral dissimilarity which threw the young people into each other's arms. From 1840 to 1844 they had three children. Francois remained in his uncle's employ until the latter retired. Pierre had desired to sell him the business, but the young man knew what small chance there was of making a fortune in trade at Plassans; so he declined the offer and repaired to Marseilles, where he established himself with his little savings.

Macquart soon had to abandon all hope of dragging this big industrious fellow into his campaign against the Rougons; whereupon, with all the spite of a lazybones, he regarded him as a cunning miser. He fancied, however, that he had discovered the accomplice he was seeking in Mouret's second son, a lad of fifteen years of age. Young Silvere had never even been to school at the time when Mouret was found hanging among his wife's skirts. His elder brother, not knowing what to do with him, took him also to his uncle's. The latter made a wry face on beholding the child; he had no intention of carrying his compensation so far as to feed a useless mouth. Thus Silvere, to whom Felicite also took a dislike, was growing up in tears,

---

6.Both Francois and Marthe figure largely in The Conquest of Plassans.

like an unfortunate little outcast, when his grandmother Adelaide, during one of the rare visits she paid the Rougons, took pity on him, and expressed a wish to have him with her. Pierre was delighted; he let the child go, without even suggesting an increase of the paltry allowance that he made Adelaide, and which henceforward would have to suffice for two.

Adelaide was then nearly seventy-five years of age. Grown old while leading a cloistered existence, she was no longer the lanky ardent girl who formerly ran to embrace the smuggler Macquart. She had stiffened and hardened in her hovel in the Impasse Saint-Mittre, that dismal silent hole where she lived entirely alone on potatoes and dry vegetables, and which she did not leave once in the course of a month. On seeing her pass, you might have thought her to be one of those delicately white old nuns with automatic gait, whom the cloister has kept apart from all the concerns of this world. Her pale face, always scrupulously girt with a white cap, looked like that of a dying woman; a vague, calm countenance it was, wearing an air of supreme indifference. Prolonged taciturnity had made her dumb; the darkness of her dwelling and the continual sight of the same objects had dulled her glance and given her eyes the limpidity of spring water. Absolute renunciation, slow physical and moral death, had little by little converted this crazy *amorosa* into a grave matron. When, as often happened, a blank stare came into her eyes, and she gazed before her without seeing anything, one could detect utter, internal void through those deep bright cavities.

Nothing now remained of her former voluptuous ardour but weariness of the flesh and a senile tremor of the hands. She had once loved like a she-wolf, but was now wasted, already sufficiently worn out for the grave. There had been strange workings of her nerves during her long years of chastity. A dissolute life would perhaps have wrecked her less than the slow hidden ravages of unsatisfied fever which had modified her organism.

Sometimes, even now, this moribund, pale old woman, who seemed to have no blood left in her, was seized with nervous fits like electric shocks, which galvanised her, and for an hour brought her atrocious intensity of life. She would lie on her bed rigid, with her eyes open; then hiccoughs would come upon her and she would writhe and struggle, acquiring the frightful strength of those hysterical madwomen whom one has to tie down in order to prevent them from breaking their heads against a wall. This return to former vigour, these sudden attacks, gave her a terrible shock. When she came to again, she would stagger about with such a scared, stupefied look, that the gossips of the Faubourg used to say: "She's been drinking, the crazy old thing!"

Little Silvere's childish smile was for her the last pale ray which brought some warmth to her frozen limbs. Weary of solitude, and frightened at the thought of dying alone in one of her fits, she had asked to have the child. With the little fellow running about near her, she felt secure against death. Without relinquishing her habits of taciturnity, or seeking to render her automatic movements more supple, she conceived inexpressible affection for him. Stiff and speechless, she would watch him playing for hours together, listening with delight to the intolerable noise with which he filled the old hovel. That tomb had resounded with uproar ever since Silvere had been running about it, bestriding broomsticks, knocking up against the doors, and shouting and crying. He brought Adelaide back to the world, as it were; she looked after him with the most adorable awkwardness; she who, in her youth, had neglected the duties of a mother, now felt the divine pleasures of maternity in washing his face, dressing him, and watching over his sickly life. It was a reawakening of love, a last soothing passion which heaven had granted to this woman who had been so ravaged by the want of some one to love; the touching agony of a heart that had lived amidst the most acute desires, and which was now dying full of love for a child.

She was already too far gone to pour forth the babble of good plump grandmothers; she adored the child in secret with the bashfulness of a young girl, without knowing how to fondle him. Sometimes she took him on her knees, and gazed at him for a long time with her pale eyes. When the little one, frightened by her mute white visage, began to cry, she seemed perplexed by what she had done, and quickly put him down upon the floor without even kissing him. Perhaps she recognised in him a faint resemblance to Macquart the poacher.

Silvere grew up, ever tete-a-tete with Adelaide. With childish cajolery he used to call her aunt Dide, a name which ultimately clung to the old woman; the word "aunt" employed in this way is simply a term of endearment in Provence. The child entertained singular affection, not unmixed with respectful terror, for his grandmother. During her nervous fits, when he was quite a little boy, he ran away from her, crying, terrified by her disfigured countenance; and he came back very timidly after the attack, ready to run away again, as though the old woman were disposed to beat him. Later on, however, when he was twelve years old, he would stop there bravely and watch in order that she might not hurt herself by falling off the bed. He stood for hours holding her tightly in his arms to subdue the rude shocks which distorted her. During intervals of calmness he would gaze with pity on her convulsed features and withered frame, over which her skirts lay like a shroud. These hidden dramas, which recurred every month, this old woman as rigid as a corpse, this child bent over her, silently watching for the return of consciousness, made up amidst the darkness of the hovel a strange picture of mournful horror and broken-hearted tenderness.

When aunt Dide came round, she would get up with difficulty, and set about her work in the hovel without even questioning Silvere. She remembered nothing, and the child, from a sort of instinctive prudence, avoided the least allusion to what had taken place. These recurring fits, more than anything else, strengthened Silvere's deep attachment for his grandmother. In the same manner as she adored him without any garrulous effusiveness, he felt a secret, almost bashful, affection for her. While he was really very grateful to her for having taken him in and brought him up, he could not help regarding her as an extraordinary creature, a prey to some strange malady, whom he ought to pity and respect. No doubt there was not sufficient life left in Adelaide; she was too white and too stiff for Silvere to throw himself on her neck. Thus they lived together amidst melancholy silence, in the depths of which they felt the tremor of boundless love.

The sad, solemn atmosphere, which he had breathed from childhood, gave Silvere a strong heart, in which gathered every form of enthusiasm. He early became a serious, thoughtful little man, seeking instruction with a kind of stubbornness. He only learnt a little spelling and arithmetic at the school of the Christian Brothers, which he was compelled to leave when he was but twelve years old, on account of his apprenticeship. He never acquired the first rudiments of knowledge. However, he read all the odd volumes which fell into his hands, and thus provided himself with strange equipment; he had some notions of a multitude of subjects, ill-digested notions, which he could never classify distinctly in his head. When he was quite young, he had been in the habit of playing in the workshop of a master wheelwright, a worthy man named Vian, who lived at the entrance of the blind-alley in front of the Aire Saint-Mittre where he stored his timber. Silvere used to jump up on the wheels of the tilted carts undergoing repair, and amuse himself by dragging about the heavy tools which his tiny hands could scarcely lift. One of his greatest pleasures, too, was to assist the workmen by holding some piece of wood for them, or bringing them the iron-work which they required. When he had grown older he naturally became apprenticed to Vian. The latter had taken a liking to the little fellow who was always kicking about his heels, and asked Adelaide to let him come, refusing to take anything for his board and lodging. Silvere eagerly accepted, already foreseeing the time when he would be able to make his poor aunt Dide some return for all she had spent upon him.

In a short time he became an excellent workman. He cherished, however, much higher ambitions. Having once seen, at a coachbuilder's at Plassans, a fine new carriage, shining with varnish, he vowed that he would one day build carriages himself. He remembered this carriage as a rare and unique work of art, an ideal towards which his aspirations should tend. The tilted carts at which he worked in Vian's shop, those carts which he had lovingly cherished, now seemed unworthy of his affections. He began to attend the local drawing-school, where he formed a connection with a youngster who had left college, and who lent him an old treatise on geometry. He plunged into this study without a guide, racking his brains for weeks together in order to grasp the simplest problem in the world. In this matter he gradually became one of those learned workmen who can hardly sign their name and yet talk about algebra as though it were an intimate friend.

Nothing unsettles the mind so much as this desultory kind of education, which reposes on no firm basis. Most frequently such scraps of knowledge convey an absolutely false idea of the highest truths, and render persons of limited intellect insufferably stupid. In Silvere's case, however, his scraps of stolen knowledge only augmented his liberal aspirations. He was conscious of horizons which at present remained closed to him. He formed for himself divine conceptions of things beyond his reach, and lived on, regarding in a deep, innocent, religious way the noble thoughts and grand conceptions towards which he was raising himself, but which he could not as yet comprehend. He was one of the simple-minded, one whose simplicity was divine, and who had remained on the threshold of the temple, kneeling before the tapers which from a distance he took for stars.

The hovel in the Impasse Saint-Mittre consisted, in the first place, of a large room into which the street door opened. The only pieces of furniture in this room, which had a stone floor, and served both as a kitchen and a dining-room, were some straw-seated chairs, a table on trestles, and an old coffer which Adelaide had converted into a sofa, by spreading a piece of woollen stuff over the lid. In the left hand corner of the large fireplace stood a plaster image of the Holy Virgin, surrounded by artificial flowers; she is the traditional good mother of all old Provencal women, however irreligious they may be. A passage led from the room into a yard situated at the rear of the house; in this yard there was a well. Aunt Dide's bedroom was on the left side of the passage; it was a little apartment containing an iron bedstead and one chair; Silvere slept in a still smaller room on the right hand side, just large enough for a trestle bedstead; and he had been obliged to plan a set of shelves, reaching up to the ceiling, to keep by him all those dear odd volumes which he saved his sous to purchase from a neighbouring general dealer. When he read at night-time, he would hang his lamp on a nail at the head of the bed. If his grandmother had an attack, he merely had to leap out at the first gasp to be at her side in a moment.

The young man led the life of a child. He passed his existence in this lonely spot. Like his father, he felt a dislike for taverns and Sunday strolling. His mates wounded his delicate susceptibilities by their coarse jokes. He preferred to read, to rack his rain over some simple geometrical problem. Since aunt Dide had entrusted him with the little household commissions she did not go out at all, but ceased all intercourse even with her family. The young man sometimes thought of her forlornness; he reflected that the poor old woman lived but a few steps from the children who strove to forget her, as though she were dead; and this made him love her all the more, for himself and for the others. When he at times entertained a vague idea that aunt Dide might be expiating some former transgressions, he would say to himself: "I was born to pardon her."

A nature such as Silvere's, ardent yet self-restrained, naturally cherished the most exalted republican ideas. At night, in his little hovel, Silvere would again and again read a work of Rousseau's which he had picked up at the neighbouring dealer's among a number of old locks. The reading of this book kept him awake till daylight. Amidst his dream of universal happiness so dear to the poor, the words liberty, equality, fraternity, rang in his ears like those sonorous sacred calls of the bells, at the sound of which the faithful fall upon their knees. When, therefore, he learnt that the Republic had just been proclaimed in France he fancied that the whole world would enjoy a life of celestial beatitude. His knowledge, though imperfect, made him see farther than other workmen; his aspirations did not stop at daily bread; but his extreme ingenuousness, his complete ignorance of mankind, kept him in the dreamland of theory, a Garden of Eden where universal justice reigned. His paradise was for a long time a delightful spot in which he forgot himself.

When he came to perceive that things did not go on quite satisfactorily in the best of republics he was sorely grieved, and indulged in another dream, that of compelling men to be happy even by force. Every act which seemed to him prejudicial to the interest of the people roused him to revengeful indignation. Though he was as gentle as a child, he cherished the fiercest political animosity. He would not have killed a fly, and yet he was for ever talking of a call to arms. Liberty was his passion, an unreasoning, absolute passion, to which he gave all the feverish ardour of his blood. Blinded by enthusiasm, he was both too ignorant and too learned to be tolerant, and would not allow for men's weaknesses; he required an ideal government of perfect justice and perfect liberty. It was at this period that Antoine Macquart thought of setting him against the Rougons. He fancied that this young enthusiast would work terrible havoc if he were only exasperated to the proper pitch. This calculation was not altogether devoid of shrewdness.

Such being Antoine's scheme, he tried to induce Silvere to visit him, by professing inordinate admiration for the young man's ideas. But he very nearly compromised the whole matter at the outset. He had a way of regarding the triumph of the Republic as a question of personal interest, as an era of happy idleness and endless junketing, which chilled his nephew's purely moral aspirations. However, he perceived that he was on the wrong track, and plunged into strange bathos, a string of empty but high-sounding words, which Silvere accepted as a satisfactory proof of his civism. Before long the uncle and the nephew saw each other two or three times a week. During their long discussions, in which the fate of the country was flatly settled, Antoine endeavoured to persuade the young man that the Rougons' drawing-room was the chief obstacle to the welfare of France. But he again made a false move by calling his mother "old jade" in Silvere's presence. He even repeated to him the early scandals about the poor woman. The young man blushed for shame, but listened without interruption. He had not asked his uncle for this information; he felt heartbroken by such confidences, which wounded his feeling of respectful affection for aunt Dide. From that time forward he lavished yet more attention upon his grandmother, greeting her always with pleasant smiles and looks of forgiveness. However, Macquart felt that he had acted foolishly, and strove to take advantage of Silvere's affection for Adelaide by charging the Rougons with her forlornness and poverty. According to him, he had always been the best of sons, whereas his brother had behaved disgracefully; Pierre had robbed his mother, and now, when she was penniless, he was ashamed of her. He never ceased descanting on this subject. Silvere thereupon became indignant with his uncle Pierre, much to the satisfaction of his uncle Antoine.

The scene was much the same every time the young man called. He used to come in the evening, while the Macquarts were at dinner. The father would be swallowing some potato stew with a growl, picking out the pieces of bacon, and watching the dish when it passed into the hands of Jean and Gervaise.

"You see, Silvere," he would say with a sullen rage which was ill-concealed beneath his air of cynical indifference, "more potatoes, always potatoes! We never eat anything else now. Meat is only for rich people. It's getting quite impossible to make both ends meet with children who have the devil's appetite and their own too."

Gervaise and Jean bent over their plates, no longer even daring to cut some bread. Silvere, who in his dream lived in heaven, did not grasp the situation. In a calm voice he pronounced these storm-laden words:

"But you should work, uncle."

"Ah! yes," sneered Macquart, stung to the quick. "You want me to work, eh! To let those beggars, the rich folk, continue to prey upon me. I should earn probably twenty sous a day, and ruin my constitution. It's worth while, isn't it?"

"Everyone earns what he can," the young man replied. "Twenty sous are twenty sous; and it all helps in a home. Besides, you're an old soldier, why don't you seek some employment?"

Fine would then interpose, with a thoughtlessness of which she soon repented.

"That's what I'm always telling him," said she. "The market inspector wants an assistant; I mentioned my husband to him, and he seems well disposed towards us."

But Macquart interrupted her with a fulminating glance. "Eh! hold your tongue," he growled with suppressed anger. "Women never know what they're talking about! Nobody would have me; my opinions are too well-known."

Every time he was offered employment he displayed similar irritation. He did not cease, however, to ask for situations, though he always refused such as were found for him, assigning the most extraordinary reasons. When pressed upon the point he became terrible.

If Jean were to take up a newspaper after dinner he would at once exclaim: "You'd better go to bed. You'll be getting up late to-morrow, and that'll be another day lost. To think of that young rascal coming home with eight francs short last week! However, I've requested his master not give him his money in future; I'll call for it myself."

Jean would go to bed to avoid his father's recriminations. He had but little sympathy with Silvere; politics bored him, and he thought his cousin "cracked." When only the women remained, if they unfortunately started some whispered converse after clearing the table, Macquart would cry: "Now, you idlers! Is there nothing that requires mending? we're all in rags. Look here, Gervaise, I was at your mistress's to-day, and I learnt some fine things. You're a good-for-nothing, a gad-about."

Gervaise, now a grown girl of more than twenty, coloured up at thus being scolded in the presence of Silvere, who himself felt uncomfortable. One evening, having come rather late, when his uncle was not at home, he had found the mother and daughter intoxicated before an empty bottle. From that time he could never see his cousin without recalling the disgraceful spectacle she had presented, with the maudlin grin and large red patches on her poor, pale, puny face. He was not less shocked by the nasty stories that circulated with regard to her. He sometimes looked at her stealthily, with the timid surprise of a schoolboy in the presence of a disreputable character.

When the two women had taken up their needles, and were ruining their eyesight in order to mend his old shirts, Macquart, taking the best seat, would throw himself back with an air of delicious comfort, and sip and smoke like a man who relishes his laziness. This was the time when the old rogue generally railed against the wealthy for living on the sweat of the poor man's brow. He was superbly indignant with the gentlemen of the new town, who lived so idly, and compelled the poor to keep them in luxury. The fragments of communistic notions which he culled from the newspapers in the morning became grotesque and monstrous on falling from his lips. He would talk of a time near at hand when no one would be obliged to work. He always, however, kept his fiercest animosity for the Rougons. He never could digest the potatoes he had eaten.

"I saw that vile creature Felicite buying a chicken in the market this morning," he would say. "Those robbers of inheritances must eat chicken, forsooth!"

"Aunt Dide," interposed Silvere, "says that uncle Pierre was very kind to you when you left the army. Didn't he spend a large sum of money in lodging and clothing you?"

"A large sum of money!" roared Macquart in exasperation; "your grandmother is mad. It was those thieves who spread those reports themselves, so as to close my mouth. I never had anything."

Fine again foolishly interfered, reminding him that he had received two hundred francs, besides a suit of clothes and a year's rent. Antoine thereupon shouted to her to hold her tongue, and continued, with increasing fury: "Two hundred francs! A fine thing! I want my due, ten thousand francs. Ah! yes, talk of the hole they shoved me into like a dog, and the old frock-coat which Pierre gave me because he was ashamed to wear it any longer himself, it was so dirty and ragged!"

He was not speaking the truth; but, seeing the rage that he was in, nobody ventured to protest any further. Then, turning towards Silvere: "It's very stupid of you to defend them!" he added. "They robbed your mother, who, good woman, would be alive now if she had had the means of taking care of herself."

"Oh! you're not just, uncle," the young man said; "my mother did not die for want of attention, and I'm certain my father would never have accepted a sou from his wife's family!"

"Pooh! don't talk to me! your father would have taken the money just like anybody else. We were disgracefully plundered, and it's high time we had our rights."

Then Macquart, for the hundredth time, began to recount the story of the fifty thousand francs. His nephew, who knew it by heart, and all the variations with which he embellished it, listened to him rather impatiently.

"If you were a man," Antoine would say in conclusion, "you would come some day with me, and we would kick up a nice row at the Rougons. We would not leave without having some money given us."

Silvere, however, grew serious, and frankly replied: "If those wretches robbed us, so much the worse for them. I don't want their money. You see, uncle, it's not for us to fall on our relatives. If they've done wrong, well, one of these days they'll be severely punished for it."

"Ah! what a big simpleton you are!" the uncle cried. "When we have the upper hand, you'll see whether I sha'n't settle my own little affairs myself. God cares a lot about us indeed! What a foul family ours is! Even if I were starving to death, not one of those scoundrels would throw me a dry crust."

Whenever Macquart touched upon this subject, he proved inexhaustible. He bared all his bleeding wounds of envy and covetousness. He grew mad with rage when he came to think that he was the only unlucky one in the family, and was forced to eat potatoes, while the others had meat to their heart's content. He would pass all his relations in review, even his grand-nephews, and find some grievance and reason for threatening every one of them.

"Yes, yes," he repeated bitterly, "they'd leave me to die like a dog."

Gervaise, without raising her head or ceasing to ply her needle, would sometimes say timidly: "Still, father, cousin Pascal was very kind to us, last year, when you were ill."

"He attended you without charging a sou," continued Fine, coming to her daughter's aid, "and he often slipped a five-franc piece into my hand to make you some broth."

"He! he'd have killed me if I hadn't had a strong constitution!" Macquart retorted. "Hold your tongues, you fools! You'd let yourselves be twisted about like children. They'd all like to see me dead. When I'm ill again, I beg you not to go and fetch my nephew, for I didn't feel at all comfortable in his hands. He's only a twopenny-halfpenny doctor, and hasn't got a decent patient in all his practice."

When once Macquart was fully launched, he could not stop. "It's like that little viper, Aristide," he would say, "a false brother, a traitor. Are you taken in by his articles in the 'Independant,' Silvere? You would be a fine fool if you were. They're not even written in good French; I've always maintained that this contraband Republican is in league with his worthy father to humbug us. You'll see how he'll turn his coat. And his brother, the illustrious Eugene, that big blockhead of whom the Rougons make such a fuss! Why, they've got the impudence to assert that he occupies a good position in Paris! I know something about his position; he's employed at the Rue de Jerusalem; he's a police spy."

"Who told you so? You know nothing about it," interrupted Silvere, whose upright spirit at last felt hurt by his uncle's lying accusations.

"Ah! I know nothing about it? Do you think so? I tell you he is a police spy. You'll be shorn like a lamb one of these days, with your benevolence. You're not manly enough. I don't want to say anything against your brother Francois; but, if I were in your place, I shouldn't like the scurvy manner in which he treats you. He earns a heap of money at Marseilles, and yet he never sends you a paltry twenty-franc pierce for pocket money. If ever you become poor, I shouldn't advise you to look to him for anything."

"I've no need of anybody," the young man replied in a proud and slightly injured tone of voice. "My own work suffices for aunt Dide and myself. You're cruel, uncle."

"I only say what's true, that's all. I should like to open your eyes. Our family is a disreputable lot; it's sad but true. Even that little Maxime, Aristide's son, that little nine-year-old brat, pokes his tongue out at me when me meets me. That child will some day beat his own mother, and a good job too! Say what you like, all those folks don't deserve their luck; but it's always like this in families, the good ones suffer while the bad ones make their fortunes."

All this dirty linen, which Macquart washed with such complacency before his nephew, profoundly disgusted the young man. He would have liked to soar back into his dream. As soon as he began to show unmistakable signs of impatience, Antoine would employ strong expedients to exasperate him against their relatives.

"Defend them! Defend them!" he would say, appearing to calm down. "I, for my part, have arranged to have nothing more to do with them. I only mention the matter out of pity for my poor mother, whom all that gang treat in a most revolting manner."

"They are wretches!" Silvere murmured.

"Oh! you don't know, you don't understand. These Rougons pour all sorts of insults and abuse on the good woman. Aristide has forbidden his son even to recognise her. Felicite talks of having her placed in a lunatic asylum."

The young man, as white as a sheet, abruptly interrupted his uncle: "Enough!" he cried. "I don't want to know any more about it. There will have to be an end to all this."

"I'll hold my tongue, since it annoys you," the old rascal replied, feigning a good-natured manner. "Still, there are some things that you ought not to be ignorant of, unless you want to play the part of a fool."

Macquart, while exerting himself to set Silvere against the Rougons, experienced the keenest pleasure on drawing tears of anguish from the young man's eyes. He detested him, perhaps, more than he did the others, and this because he was an excellent workman and never drank. He brought all his instincts of refined cruelty into play, in order to invent atrocious falsehoods which should sting the poor lad to the heart; then he revelled in his pallor, his trembling hands and his heart-rending looks, with the delight of some evil spirit who measures his stabs and finds that he has struck his victim in the right place. When he thought that he had wounded and exasperated Silvere sufficiently, he would at last touch upon politics.

"I've been assured," he would say, lowering his voice, "that the Rougons are preparing some treachery."

"Treachery?" Silvere asked, becoming attentive.

"Yes, one of these nights they are going to seize all the good citizens of the town and throw them into prison."

The young man was at first disposed to doubt it, but his uncle gave precise details; he spoke of lists that had been drawn up, he mentioned the persons whose names were on these lists, he indicated in what manner, at what hour, and under what circumstances the plot would be carried into effect. Silvere gradually allowed himself to be taken in by this old woman's tale, and was soon raving against the enemies of the Republic.

"It's they that we shall have to reduce to impotence if they persist in betraying the country!" he cried. "And what do they intend to do with the citizens whom they arrest?"

"What do they intend to do with them? Why, they will shoot them in the lowest dungeons of the prison, of course," replied Macquart, with a hoarse laugh. And as the young man, stupefied with horror, looked at him without knowing what to say:

"This will not be the first lot to be assassinated there," he continued. "You need only go and prowl about the Palais de Justice of an evening to hear the shots and groans."

"Oh, the wretches!" Silvere murmured.

Thereupon uncle and nephew launched out into high politics. Fine and Gervaise, on finding them hotly debating things, quietly went to bed without attracting their attention. Then the two men remained together till midnight, commenting on the news from Paris and discussing the approaching and inevitable struggle. Macquart bitterly denounced the men of his own party, Silvere dreamed his dream of ideal liberty aloud, and for himself only. Strange conversations these were, during which the uncle poured out many a little nip for himself, and from which the nephew emerged quite intoxicated with enthusiasm. Antoine, however, never succeeded in obtaining from the young Republican any perfidious suggestion or play of warfare against the Rougons. In vain he tried to goad him on; he seldom heard him suggest aught but an appeal to eternal justice, which sooner or later would punish the evil-doers.

The ingenuous youth did indeed speak warmly of taking up arms and massacring the enemies of the Republic; but, as soon as these enemies strayed out of his dream or became personified in his uncle Pierre or any other person of his acquaintance, he relied upon heaven to spare him the horror of shedding blood. It is very probable that he would have ceased visiting Macquart, whose jealous fury made him so uncomfortable, if he had not tasted the pleasure of being able to speak freely of his dear Republic there. In the end, however, his uncle exercised decisive influence over his destiny; he irritated his nerves by his everlasting diatribes, and succeeded in making him eager for an armed struggle, the conquest of universal happiness by violence.

When Silvere reached his sixteenth year, Macquart had him admitted into the secret society of the Montagnards, a powerful association whose influence extended throughout Southern France. From that moment the young Republican gazed with longing eyes at the smuggler's carbine, which Adelaide had hung over her chimney-piece. Once night, while his grandmother was asleep, he cleaned and put it in proper condition. Then he replaced it on its nail and waited, indulging in brilliant reveries, fancying gigantic epics, Homeric struggles, and knightly tournaments, whence the defenders of liberty would emerge victorious and acclaimed by the whole world.

Macquart meantime was not discouraged. He said to himself that he would be able to strangle the Rougons alone if he could ever get them into a corner. His envious rage and slothful greed were increased by certain successive accidents which compelled him to resume work. In the early part of 1850 Fine died, almost suddenly, from inflammation of the lungs, which she had caught by going one evening to wash the family linen in the Viorne, and carrying it home wet on her back. She returned soaked with water and perspiration, bowed down by her load, which was terribly heavy, and she never recovered.

Her death filled Macquart with consternation. His most reliable source of income was gone. When, a few days later, he sold the caldron in which his wife had boiled her chestnuts, and the wooden horse which she used in reseating old chairs, he foully accused the Divinity of having robbed him of that strong strapping woman of whom he had often felt ashamed, but whose real worth he now appreciated. He now also fell upon the children's earnings with greater avidity than ever. But, a month later, Gervaise, tired of his continual exactions, ran away with her two children and Lantier, whose mother was dead. The lovers took refuge in Paris. Antoine, overwhelmed, vented his rage against his daughter by expressing the hope that she might die in hospital like most of her kind. This abuse did not, however, improve the situation, which was decidedly becoming bad. Jean soon followed his sister's example. He waited for pay-day to come round, and then contrived to receive the money himself. As he was leaving he told one of his friends, who repeated it to Antoine, that he would no longer keep his lazy father, and that if the latter should take it into his head to have him brought back by the gendarmes he would touch neither saw nor plane.

On the morrow, when Antoine, having vainly sought him, found himself alone and penniless in the house where for twenty years he had been comfortably kept, he flew into the most frantic rage, kicked the furniture about, and yelled the vilest imprecations. Then he sank down exhausted, and began to drag himself about and moan like a convalescent. The fear of having to earn his bread made him positively ill. When Silvere came to see him, he complained, with tears, of his children's ingratitude. Had he not always been a good father to them? Jean and Gervaise were monsters, who had made him an evil return for all he had done for them. Now they abandoned him because he was old, and they could not get anything more out of him!

"But uncle," said Silvere, "you are not yet too old to work!"

Macquart, coughing and stooping, shook his head mournfully, as if to say that he could not bear the least fatigue for any length of time. Just as his nephew was about to withdraw, he borrowed ten francs of him. Then for a month he lived by taking his children's old clothes, one by one, to a second-hand dealer's, and in the same way, little by little, he sold all the small articles in the house. Soon nothing remained but a table, a chair, his bed, and the clothes on his back. He ended by exchanging the walnut-wood bedstead for a plain strap one. When he had exhausted all his resources, he cried with rage; and, with the fierce pallor of a man who is resigned to suicide, he went to look for the bundle of osier that he had forgotten in some corner for a quarter of a century past. As he took it up he seemed to be lifting a mountain. However, he again began to plait baskets and hampers, while denouncing the human race for their neglect.

It was particularly at this time that he talked of dividing and sharing the riches of the wealthy. He showed himself terrible. His speeches kept up a constant conflagration in the tavern, where his furious looks secured him unlimited credit. Moreover, he only worked when he had been unable to get a five-franc piece out of Silvere or a comrade. He was no longer "Monsieur" Macquart, the clean-shaven workman, who wore his Sunday clothes every day and played the gentleman; he again became the big slovenly devil who had once speculated on his rags. Felicite did not dare to go to market now that he was so often coming there to sell his baskets. He once had a violent quarrel with her there. His hatred against the Rougons grew with his wretchedness. He swore, with horrible threats, that he would wreak justice himself, since the rich were leagued together to compel him to toil.

In this state of mind, he welcomed the Coup d'Etat with the ardent, obstreperous delight of a hound scenting the quarry. As the few honest Liberals in the town had failed to arrive at an understanding amongst themselves, and therefore kept apart, he became naturally one of the most prominent agents of the insurrection. The working classes, notwithstanding the unfavourable opinion which they at last entertained of this lazy fellow, would, when the time arrived, have to accept him as a rallying flag. On the first few days, however, the town remained quiet, and Macquart thought that his plans were frustrated. It was not until the news arrived of the rising of the rural districts that he recovered hope. For his own part he would not have left Plassans for all the world; accordingly he invented some pretext for not following those workmen who, on the Sunday morning, set off to join the insurrectionary band of La Palud and Saint-Martin-de-Vaulx.

On the evening of the same day he was sitting in some disreputable tavern of the old quarter with a few friends, when a comrade came to inform him that the insurgents were only a few miles from Plassans. This news had just been brought by an express, who had succeeded in making his way into the town, and had been charged to get the gates opened for the column. There was an outburst of triumph. Macquart, especially, appeared to be delirious with enthusiasm. The unforeseen arrival of the insurgents seemed to him a delicate attention of Providence for his own particular benefit. His hands trembled at the idea that he would soon hold the Rougons by the throat.

He hastily quitted the tavern with his friends. All the Republicans who had not yet left the town were soon assembled on the Cours Sauvaire. It was this band that Rougon had perceived as he was hastening to conceal himself in his mother's house. When the band had reached the top of the Rue de la Banne, Macquart, who had stationed himself at the rear, detained four of his companions, big fellows who were not overburdened with brains and whom he swayed by his tavern bluster. He easily persuaded them that the enemies of the Republic must be arrested immediately if they wished to prevent the greatest calamities. The truth was that he feared Pierre might escape him in the midst of the confusion which the entry of the insurgents would produce. However, the four big fellows followed him with exemplary docility, and knocked violently at the door of the Rougons' abode. In this critical situation Felicite displayed admirable courage. She went down and opened the street door herself.

"We want to go upstairs into your rooms," Macquart said to her brutally.

"Very well, gentlemen, walk up," she replied with ironical politeness, pretending that she did not recognise her brother-in-law.

Once upstairs, Macquart ordered her to fetch her husband.

"My husband is not here," she said with perfect calmness; "he is travelling on business. He took the diligence for Marseilles at six o'clock this evening."

Antoine at this declaration, which Felicite uttered in a clear voice, made a gesture of rage. He rushed through the drawing-room, and then into the bedroom, turned the bed up, looked behind the curtains and under the furniture. The four big fellows assisted him. They searched the place for a quarter of an hour. Felicite meantime quietly seated herself on the drawing-room sofa, and began to fasten the strings of her petticoats, like a person who has been surprised in her sleep and has not had time to dress properly.

"It's true then, he's run away, the coward!" Macquart muttered on returning to the drawing-room.

Nevertheless, he continued to look about him with a suspicious air. He felt a presentiment that Pierre could not have given up the game at the decisive moment. At last he approached Felicite, who was yawning: "Show us the place where your husband is hidden," he said to her, "and I promise no harm shall be done to him."

"I have told you the truth," she replied impatiently. "I can't deliver my husband to you, as he's not here. You have searched everywhere, haven't you? Then leave me alone now."

Macquart, exasperated by her composure, was just going to strike her, when a rumbling noise arose from the street. It was the column of insurgents entering the Rue de la Banne.

He then had to leave the yellow drawing-room, after shaking his fist at his sister-in-law, calling her an old jade, and threatening that he would soon return. At the foot of the staircase, he took one of the men who accompanied him, a navvy named Cassoute, the most wooden-headed of the four, and ordered him to sit on the first step, and remain there.

"You must come and inform me," he said to him, "if you see the scoundrel from upstairs return."

The man sat down heavily. When Macquart reached the pavement, he raised his eyes and observed Felicite leaning out of the window of the yellow-drawing room, watching the march past of the insurgents, as if it was nothing but a regiment passing through the town to the strains of its band. This last sign of perfect composure irritated him to such a degree that he was almost tempted to go up again and throw the old woman into the street. However, he followed the column, muttering in a hoarse voice: "Yes, yes, look at us passing. We'll see whether you will station yourself at your balcony to-morrow."

It was nearly eleven o'clock at night when the insurgents entered the town by the Porte de Rome. The workmen remaining in Plassans had opened the gate for them, in spite of the wailings of the keeper, from whom they could only wrest the keys by force. This man, very jealous of his office, stood dumbfounded in the presence of the surging crowd. To think of it! he, who never allowed more than one person to pass in at a time, and then only after a prolonged examination of his face! And he murmured that he was dishonoured. The men of Plassans were still marching at the head of the column by way of guiding the others; Miette, who was in the front rank, with Silvere on her left, held up her banner more proudly than ever now that she could divine behind the closed blinds the scared looks of well-to-do bourgeois startled out of their sleep. The insurgents passed along the Rue de Rome and the Rue de la Banne slowly and warily; at every crossway, although they well knew the quiet disposition of the inhabitants, they feared they might be received with bullets. The town seemed lifeless, however; there was scarcely a stifled exclamation to be heard at the windows. Only five or six shutters opened. Some old householder then appeared in his night-shirt, candle in hand, and leant out to obtain a better view; but as soon as he distinguished the tall red girl who appeared to be drawing that crowd of black demons behind her, he hastily closed his window again, terrified by such a diabolical apparition.

The silence of the slumbering town reassured the insurgents, who ventured to make their way through the lanes of the old quarter, and thus reached the market-place and the Place de l'Hotel-de-Ville, which was connected by a short but broad street. These open spaces, planted with slender trees, were brilliantly illumined by the moon. Against the clear sky the recently restored town-hall appeared like a large patch of crude whiteness, the fine black lines of the wrought-iron arabesques of the first-floor balcony showing in bold relief. Several persons could be plainly distinguished standing on this balcony, the mayor, Commander Sicardot, three or four municipal councillors, and other functionaries. The doors below were closed. The three thousand Republicans, who covered both open spaces, halted with upraised heads, ready to force the doors with a single push.

The arrival of the insurrectionary column at such an hour took the authorities by surprise. Before repairing to the mayor's, Commander Sicardot had taken time to don his uniform. He then had to run and rouse the mayor. When the keeper of the Porte de Rome, who had been left free by the insurgents, came to announce that the villains were already in the town, the commander had so far only managed to assemble a score of the national guards. The gendarmes, though their barracks were close by, could not even be warned. It was necessary to shut the town-hall doors in all haste, in order to deliberate. Five minutes later a low continuous rumbling announced the approach of the column.

Monsieur Garconnet, out of hatred to the Republic, would have greatly liked to offer resistance. But he was of a prudent nature, and comprehended the futility of a struggle on finding only a few pale men, who were scarcely awake, around him. So the deliberations did not last long. Sicardot alone was obstinate; he wanted to fight, asserting that twenty men would suffice to bring these three thousand villains to reason. At this Monsieur Garconnet shrugged his shoulders, and declared that the only step to take was to make an honourable capitulation. As the uproar of the mob increased, he went out on the balcony, followed by all the persons present. Silence was gradually obtained. Below, among the black, quivering mass of insurgents, the guns and scythes glittered in the moonlight.

"Who are you, and what do you want?" cried the mayor in a loud voice.

Thereupon a man in a greatcoat, a landowner of La Palud, stepped forward.

"Open the doors," he said, without replying to Monsieur Garconnet's question. "Avoid a fratricidal conflict."

"I call upon you to withdraw," the mayor continued. "I protest in the name of the law."

These words provoked deafening shouts from the crowd. When the tumult had somewhat abated, vehement calls ascended to the balcony. Voices shouted: "It is in the name of the law that we have come here!"

"Your duty as a functionary is to secure respect for the fundamental law of the land, the constitution, which has just been outrageously violated."

"Long live the constitution! Long live the Republic!"

Then as Monsieur Garconnet endeavoured to make himself heard, and continued to invoke his official dignity, the landowner of La Palud, who was standing under the balcony, interrupted him with great vehemence: "You are now nothing but the functionary of a fallen functionary; we have come to dismiss you from your office."

Hitherto, Commander Sicardot had been ragefully biting his moustache, and muttering insulting words. The sight of the cudgels and scythes exasperated him; and he made desperate efforts to restrain himself from treating these twopenny-halfpenny soldiers, who had not even a gun apiece, as they deserved. But when he heard a gentleman in a mere greatcoat speak of deposing a mayor girded with his scarf, he could no longer contain himself and shouted: "You pack of rascals! If I only had four men and a corporal, I'd come down and pull your ears for you, and make you behave yourselves!"

Less than this was needed to raise a serious disturbance. A long shout rose from the mob as it made a rush for the doors. Monsieur Garconnet, in consternation, hastily quitted the balcony, entreating Sicardot to be reasonable unless he wished to have them massacred. But in two minutes the doors gave way, the people invaded the building and disarmed the national guards. The mayor and the other functionaries present were arrested. Sicardot, who declined to surrender his sword, had to be protected from the fury of some insurgents by the chief of the contingent from Les Tulettes, a man of great self-possession. When the town-hall was in the hands of the Republicans, they led their prisoners to a small cafe in the market-place, and there kept them closely watched.

The insurrectionary army would have avoided marching through Plassans if its leaders had not decided that a little food and a few hours' rest were absolutely necessary for the men. Instead of pushing forward direct to the chief town of the department, the column, owing to the inexcusable weakness and the inexperience of the improvised general who commanded it, was now diverging to the left, making a detour which was destined, ultimately, to lead it to destruction. It was bound for the heights of Sainte-Roure, still about ten leagues distant, and it was in view of this long march that it had been decided to pass through Plassans, notwithstanding the lateness of the hour. It was now half-past eleven.

When Monsieur Garconnet learnt that the band was in quest of provisions, he offered his services to procure them. This functionary formed, under very difficult circumstances, a proper estimate of the situation. Those three thousand starving men would have to be satisfied; it would never do for Plassans, on waking up, to find them still squatting on the pavements; if they withdrew before daybreak they would simply have passed through the slumbering town like an evil dream, like one of those nightmares which depart with the arrival of dawn. And so, although he remained a prisoner, Monsieur Garconnet, followed by two guards, went about knocking at the bakers' doors, and had all the provisions that he could find distributed among the insurgents.

Towards one o'clock the three thousand men began to eat, squatting on the ground, with their weapons between their legs. The market-place and the neighbourhood of the town-hall were turned into vast open-air refectories. In spite of the bitter cold, humorous sallies were exchanged among the swarming multitude, the smallest groups of which showed forth in the brilliant moonlight. The poor famished fellows eagerly devoured their portions while breathing on their fingers to warm them; and, from the depths of adjoining streets, where vague black forms sat on the white thresholds of the houses, there came sudden bursts of laughter. At the windows emboldened, inquisitive women, with silk handkerchiefs tied round their heads, watched the repast of those terrible insurgents, those blood-suckers who went in turn to the market pump to drink a little water in the hollows of their hands.

While the town-hall was being invaded, the gendarmes' barracks, situated a few steps away, in the Rue Canquoin, which leads to the market, had also fallen into the hands of the mob. The gendarmes were surprised in their beds and disarmed in a few minutes. The impetus of the crowd had carried Miette and Silvere along in this direction. The girl, who still clasped her flagstaff to her breast, was pushed against the wall of the barracks, while the young man, carried away by the human wave, penetrated into the interior, and helped his comrades to wrest from the gendarmes the carbines which they had hastily caught up. Silvere, waxing ferocious, intoxicated by the onslaught, attacked a big devil of a gendarme named Rengade, with whom for a few moments he struggled. At last, by a sudden jerk, he succeeded in wresting his carbine from him. But the barrel struck Rengade a violent blow in the face, which put his right eye out. Blood flowed, and, some of it splashing Silvere's hands, quickly brought him to his senses. He looked at his hands, dropped the carbine, and ran out, in a state of frenzy, shaking his fingers.

"You are wounded!" cried Miette.

"No, no," he replied in a stifled voice, "I've just killed a gendarme."

"Is he really dead?" asked Miette.

"I don't know," replied Silvere, "his face was all covered with blood. Come quickly."

Then he hurried the girl away. On reaching the market, he made her sit down on a stone bench, and told her to wait there for him. He was still looking at his hands, muttering something at the same time. Miette at last understood from his disquieted words that he wished to go and kiss his grandmother before leaving.

"Well, go," she said; "don't trouble yourself about me. Wash your hands."

But he went quickly away, keeping his fingers apart, without thinking of washing them at the pump which he passed. Since he had felt Rengade's warm blood on his skin, he had been possessed by one idea, that of running to Aunt Dide's and dipping his hands in the well-trough at the back of the little yard. There only, he thought, would he be able to wash off the stain of that blood. Moreover, all his calm, gentle childhood seemed to return to him; he felt an irresistible longing to take refuge in his grandmother's skirts, if only for a minute. He arrived quite out of breath. Aunt Dide had not gone to bed, a circumstance which at any other time would have greatly surprised Silvere. But on entering he did not even see his uncle Rougon, who was seated in a corner on the old chest. He did not wait for the poor old woman's questions. "Grandmother," he said quickly, "you must forgive me; I'm going to leave with the others. You see I've got blood on me. I believe I've killed a gendarme."

"You've killed a gendarme?" Aunt Dide repeated in a strange voice.

Her eyes gleamed brightly as she fixed them on the red stains. And suddenly she turned towards the chimney-piece. "You've taken the gun," she said; "where's the gun?"

Silvere, who had left the weapon with Miette, swore to her that it was quite safe. And for the very first time, Adelaide made an allusion to the smuggler Macquart in her grandson's presence.

"You'll bring the gun back? You promise me!" she said with singular energy. "It's all I have left of him. You've killed a gendarme; ah, it was the gendarmes who killed him!"

She continued gazing fixedly at Silvere with an air of cruel satisfaction, and apparently without thought of detaining him. She never asked him for any explanation, nor wept like those good grandmothers who always imagine, at sight of the least scratch, that their grandchildren are dying. All her nature was concentrated in one unique thought, to which she at last gave expression with ardent curiosity: "Did you kill the gendarme with the gun?"

Either Silvere did not quite catch what she said, or else he misunderstood her.

"Yes!" he replied. "I'm going to wash my hands."

It was only on returning from the well that he perceived his uncle. Pierre had turned pale on hearing the young man's words. Felicite was indeed right; his family took a pleasure in

compromising him. One of his nephews had now killed a gendarme! He would never get the post of receiver of taxes, if he
did not prevent this foolish madman from rejoining the insurgents. So he planted himself in front of the door, determined to
prevent Silvere from going out.

"Listen," he said to the young fellow, who was greatly surprised to find him there. "I am the head of the family, and I forbid you to leave this house. You're risking both your honour
and ours. To-morrow I will try to get you across the frontier."

But Silvere shrugged his shoulders. "Let me pass," he calmly
replied. "I'm not a police-spy; I shall not reveal your hiding-
place, never fear." And as Rougon continued to speak of the
family dignity and the authority with which his seniority invested him: "Do I belong to your family?" the young man continued. "You have always disowned me. To-day, fear has driven
you here, because you feel that the day of judgment has arrived. Come, make way! I don't hide myself; I have a duty to
perform."

Rougon did not stir. But Aunt Dide, who had listened with a
sort of delight to Silvere's vehement language, laid her
withered hand on her son's arm. "Get out of the way, Pierre,"
she said; "the lad must go."

The young man gave his uncle a slight shove, and dashed
outside. Then Rougon, having carefully shut the door again,
said to his mother in an angry, threatening tone: "If any mis-
chief happens to him it will be your fault. You're an old madwoman; you don't know what you've just done."

Adelaide, however, did not appear to hear him. She went and
threw some vine-branches on the fire, which was going out,
and murmured with a vague smile: "I'm used to it. He would
remain away for months together, and then come back to me in
much better health."

She was no doubt speaking of Macquart.

In the meantime, Silvere hastily regained the market-place.
As he approached the spot where he had left Miette, he heard
a loud uproar of voices and saw a crowd which made him
quicken his steps. A cruel scene had just occurred. Some inquisitive people were walking among the insurgents, while the
latter quietly partook of their meal. Amongst these onlookers
was Justin Rebufat, the son of the farmer of the Jas-Meiffren, a

youth of twenty years old, a sickly, squint-eyed creature, who harboured implacable hatred against his cousin Miette. At home he grudged her the bread she ate, and treated her like a beggar picked up from the gutter out of charity. It is probable that the young girl had rejected his advances. Lank and pale, with ill-proportioned limbs and face all awry, he revenged himself upon her for his own ugliness, and the contempt which the handsome, vigorous girl must have evinced for him. He ardently longed to induce his father to send her about her business; and for this reason he was always spying upon her. For some time past, he had become aware of the meetings with Silvere, and had only awaited a decisive opportunity to reveal everything to his father, Rebufat.

On the evening in question, having seen her leave home at about eight o'clock, Justin's hatred had overpowered him, and he had been unable to keep silent any longer. Rebufat, on hearing his story, fell into a terrible rage, and declared that he would kick the gadabout out of his house should she have the audacity to return. Justin then went to bed, relishing beforehand the fine scene which would take place on the morrow. Then, however, a burning desire came upon him for some immediate foretaste of his revenge. So he dressed himself again and went out. Perhaps he might meet Miette. In that case he was resolved to treat her insolently. This is how he came to witness the arrival of the insurgents, whom he followed to the town-hall with a vague presentiment that he would find the lovers there. And, indeed, he at last caught sight of his cousin on the seat where she was waiting for Silvere. Seeing her wrapped in her long pelisse, with the red flag at her side, resting against a market pillar, he began to sneer and deride her in foul language. The girl, thunderstruck at seeing him, was unable to speak. She wept beneath his abuse, and whist she was overcome by sobbing, bowing her head and hiding her face, Justin called her a convict's daughter, and shouted that old Rebufat would give her a good thrashing should she ever dare to return to Jas-Meiffren.

For a quarter of an hour he thus kept her smarting and trembling. Some people had gathered round, and grinned stupidly at the painful scene. At last a few insurgents interfered, and threatened the young man with exemplary chastisement if he did not leave Miette alone. But Justin, although he retreated, declared that he was not afraid of them. It was just at this moment that Silvere came up. Young Rebufat, on catching sight of him, made a sudden bound, as if to take flight; for he was afraid of him, knowing that he was much stronger than himself. He could not, however, resist the temptation to cast a parting insult on the girl in her lover's presence.

"Ah! I knew very well," he cried, "that the wheelwright could not be far off! You left us to run after that crack-brained fellow, eh? You wretched girl! When's the baptism to be?"

Then he retreated a few steps further on seeing Silvere clench his fists.

"And mind," he continued, with a vile sneer, "don't come to our house again. My father will kick you out if you do! Do you hear?"

But he ran away howling, with bruised visage. For Silvere had bounded upon him and dealt him a blow full in the face. The young man did not pursue him. When he returned to Miette he found her standing up, feverishly wiping her tears away with the palm of her hand. And as he gazed at her tenderly, in order to console her, she made a sudden energetic gesture. "No," she said, "I'm not going to cry any more, you'll see. I'm very glad of it. I don't feel any regret now for having left home. I am free."

She took up the flag and led Silvere back into the midst of the insurgents. It was now nearly two o'clock in the morning. The cold was becoming so intense that the Republicans had risen to their feet and were marching to and fro in order to warm themselves while they finished their bread. At last their leaders gave orders for departure. The column formed again. The prisoners were placed in the middle of it. Besides Monsieur Garconnet and Commander Sicardot, the insurgents had arrested Monsieur Peirotte, the receiver of taxes, and several other functionaries, all of whom they led away.

At this moment Aristide was observed walking about among the groups. In presence of this formidable rising, the dear fellow had thought it imprudent not to remain on friendly terms with the Republicans; but as, on the other hand, he did not desire to compromise himself too much, he had come to bid them farewell with his arm in a sling, complaining bitterly of the accursed injury which prevented him from carrying a weapon. As he walked through the crowd he came across his brother Pascal, provided with a case of surgical instruments and a little portable medicine chest. The doctor informed him, in his quiet, way, that he intended to follow the insurgents. At this Aristide inwardly pronounced him a great fool. At last he himself slunk away, fearing lest the others should entrust the care of the town to him, a post which he deemed exceptionally perilous.

The insurgents could not think of keeping Plassans in their power. The town was animated by so reactionary a spirit that it seemed impossible even to establish a democratic municipal commission there, as had already been done in other places. So they would simply have gone off without taking any further steps if Macquart, prompted and emboldened by his own private animosities, had not offered to hold Plassans in awe, on condition that they left him twenty determined men. These men were given him, and at their head he marched off triumphantly to take possession of the town-hall. Meantime the column of insurgents was wending its way along the Cours Sauvaire, and making its exit by the Grand'-Porte, leaving the streets, which it had traversed like a tempest, silent and deserted in its rear. The high road, whitened by the moonshine, stretched far into the distance. Miette had refused the support of Silvere's arm; she marched on bravely, steady and upright, holding the red flag aloft with both hands, without complaining of the cold which was turning her fingers blue.

Chapter 5

The high roads stretched far way, white with moonlight.

The insurrectionary army was continuing its heroic march through the cold, clear country. It was like a mighty wave of enthusiasm. The thrill of patriotism, which transported Miette and Silvere, big children that they were, eager for love and liberty, sped, with generous fervour, athwart the sordid intrigues of the Macquarts and the Rougons. At intervals the trumpet-voice of the people rose and drowned the prattle of the yellow drawing-room and the hateful discourses of uncle Antoine. And vulgar, ignoble farce was turned into a great historical drama.

On quitting Plassans, the insurgents had taken the road to Orcheres. They expected to reach that town at about ten o'clock in the morning. The road skirts the course of the Viorne, following at some height the windings of the hillocks, below which the torrent flows. On the left, the plain spreads out like an immense green carpet, dotted here and there with grey villages. On the right, the chain of the Garrigues rears its desolate peaks, its plateaux of stones, its huge rusty boulders that look as though they had been reddened by the sun. The high road, embanked along the riverside, passes on amidst enormous rocks, between which glimpses of the valley are caught at every step. Nothing could be wilder or more strikingly grand than this road out of the hillside. At night time, especially, it inspires one with a feeling of deep awe. The insurgents advanced under the pale light, along what seemed the chief street of some ruined town, bordered on either side with fragments of temples. The moon turned each rock into a broken column, crumbling capital, or stretch of wall pierced with mysterious arches. On high slumbered the mass of the Garrigues, suffused with a milky tinge, and resembling some immense Cyclopean city whose towers, obelisks, houses and high terraces hid one half of the heavens; and in the depths below, on the side of the plain, was a spreading ocean of diffused light, vague and limitless, over which floated masses of luminous haze. The insurrectionary force might well have thought they were following some gigantic causeway, making their rounds along some military road built on the shore of a phosphorescent sea, and circling some unknown Babel.

On the night in question, the Viorne roared hoarsely at the foot of the rocks bordering the route. Amidst the continuous rumbling of the torrent, the insurgents could distinguish the sharp, wailing notes of the tocsin. The villages scattered about the plain, on the other side of the river, were rising, sounding alarm-bells, and lighting signal fires. Till daybreak the marching column, which the persistent tolling of a mournful knell seemed to pursue in the darkness, thus beheld the insurrection spreading along the valley, like a train of powder. The fires showed in the darkness like stains of blood; echoes of distant songs were wafted to them; the whole vague distance, blurred by the whitish vapours of the moon, stirred confusedly, and suddenly broke into a spasm of anger. For leagues and leagues the scene remained the same.

These men, marching on under the blind impetus of the fever with which the events in Paris had inspired Republican hearts, became elated at seeing that long stretch of country quivering with revolt. Intoxicated with enthusiastic belief in the general insurrection of which they dreamed, they fancied that France was following them; on the other side of the Viorne, in that vast ocean of diffused light, they imagined there were endless files of men rushing like themselves to the defence of the Republic. All simplicity and delusion, as multitudes so often are, they imagined, in their uncultured minds, that victory was easy and certain. They would have seized and shot as a traitor any one who had then asserted that they were the only ones who had the courage of their duty, and that the rest of the country, overwhelmed with fright, was pusillanimously allowing itself to be garrotted.

They derived fresh courage, too, from the welcome accorded to them by the few localities that lay along their route on the slopes of the Garrigues. The inhabitants rose *en masse* immediately the little army drew near; women ran to meet them, wishing them a speedy victory, while men, half clad, seized the first weapons they could find and rushed to join their ranks. There was a fresh ovation at every village, shouts of welcome and farewell many times reiterated.

Towards daybreak the moon disappeared behind the Garrigues and the insurgents continued their rapid march amidst the dense darkness of a winter night. They were now unable to distinguish the valley or the hills; they heard only the hoarse plaints of the bells, sounding through the deep obscurity like invisible drums, hidden they knew not where, but ever goading them on with despairing calls.

Miette and Silvere went on, all eagerness like the others. Towards daybreak, the girl suffered greatly from fatigue; she could only walk with short hurried steps, and was unable to keep up with the long strides of the men who surrounded her. Nevertheless she courageously strove to suppress all complaints; it would have cost her too much to confess that she was not as strong as a boy. During the first few leagues of the march Silvere gave her his arm; then, seeing that the standard was gradually slipping from her benumbed hands, he tried to take it in order to relieve her; but she grew angry, and would only allow him to hold it with one hand while she continued to carry it on her shoulder. She thus maintained her heroic demeanour with childish stubbornness, smiling at the young man each time he gave her a glance of loving anxiety. At last, when the moon hid itself, she gave way in the sheltering darkness. Silvere felt her leaning more heavily on his arm. He now had to carry the flag, and hold her round the waist to prevent her from stumbling. Nevertheless she still made no complaint.

"Are you very tired, poor Miette?" Silvere asked her.

"Yea, a little tired," she replied in a weary tone.

"Would you like to rest a bit?"

She made no reply; but he realised that she was staggering. He thereupon handed the flag to one of the other insurgents and quitted the ranks, almost carrying the girl in his arms. She struggled a little, she felt so distressed at appearing such a child. But he calmed her, telling her that he knew of a crossroad which shortened the distance by one half. They would be able to take a good hour's rest and reach Orcheres at the same time as the others.

It was then six o'clock. There must have been a slight mist rising from the Viorne, for the darkness seemed to be growing denser. The young people groped their way along the slope of the Garrigues, till they came to a rock on which they sat down. Around them lay an abyss of darkness. They were stranded, as it were, on some reef above a dense void. And athwart that void, when the dull tramp of the little army had died away, they only heard two bells, the one clear toned and ringing doubtless at their feet, in some village across the road; and the other far-off and faint, responding, as it were, with distant sobs to the feverish plaints of the first. One might have thought that these bells were recounting to each other, through the empty waste, the sinister story of a perishing world.

Miette and Silvere, warmed by their quick march, did not at first feel the cold. They remained silent, listening in great dejection to the sounds of the tocsin, which made the darkness quiver. They could not even see one another. Miette felt frightened, and, seeking for Silvere's hand, clasped it in her own. After the feverish enthusiasm which for several hours had carried them along with the others, this sudden halt and the solitude in which they found themselves side by side left them exhausted and bewildered as though they had suddenly awakened from a strange dream. They felt as if a wave had cast them beside the highway, then ebbed back and left them stranded. Irresistible reaction plunged them into listless stupor; they forgot their enthusiasm; they thought no more of the men whom they had to rejoin; they surrendered themselves to the melancholy sweetness of finding themselves alone, hand in hand, in the midst of the wild darkness.

"You are not angry with me?" the girl at length inquired. "I could easily walk the whole night with you; but they were running too quickly, I could hardly breathe."

"Why should I be angry with you?" the young man said.

"I don't know. I was afraid you might not love me any longer. I wish I could have taken long strides like you, and have walked along without stopping. You will think I am a child."

Silvere smiled, and Miette, though the darkness prevented her from seeing him, guessed that he was doing so. Then she continued with determination: "You must not always treat me like a sister. I want to be your wife some day."

Forthwith she clasped Silvere to her bosom, and, still with her arms about him, murmured: "We shall grow so cold; come close to me that we may be warm."

Then they lapsed into silence. Until that troublous hour, they had loved one another with the affection of brother and sister. In their ignorance they still mistook their feelings for tender friendship, although beneath their guileless love their ardent blood surged more wildly day by day. Given age and experience, a violent passion of southern intensity would at last spring from this idyll. Every girl who hangs on a youth's neck is already a woman, a woman unconsciously, whom a caress may awaken to conscious womanhood. When lovers kiss on the cheeks, it is because they are searching, feeling for one another's lips. Lovers are made by a kiss. It was on that dark and cold December night, amid the bitter wailing of the tocsin, that Miette and Silvere exchanged one of those kisses that bring all the heart's blood to the lips.

They remained silent, close to one another. A gentle glow soon penetrated them, languor overcame them, and steeped them in feverish drowsiness. They were quite warm at last, and lights seemed to flit before their closed eyelids, while a buzzing mounted to their brains. This state of painful ecstasy, which lasted some minutes, seemed endless to them. Then, in a kind of dream, their lips met. The kiss they exchanged was long and greedy. It seemed to them as if they had never kissed before. Yet their embrace was fraught with suffering and they released one another. And the chilliness of the night having cooled their fever, they remained in great confusion at some distance one from the other.

Meantime the bells were keeping up their sinister converse in the dark abyss which surrounded the young people. Miette, trembling and frightened, did not dare to draw near to Silvere again. She did not even know if he were still there, for she could no longer hear him move. The stinging sweetness of their kiss still clung to their lips, to which passionate phrases surged, and they longed to kiss once more. But shame restrained them from the expression of any such desire. They felt that they would rather never taste that bliss again than speak of it aloud. If their blood had not been lashed by their rapid march, if the darkness had not offered complicity, they would, for a long time yet, have continued kissing each other on the cheeks like old playfellows. Feelings of modesty were coming to Miette. She remembered Justin's coarseness. A few hours previously she had listened, without a blush, to that fellow who called her a shameless girl. She had wept without understanding his meaning, she had wept simply because she guessed that what he spoke of must be base. Now that she was becoming a woman, she wondered in a last innocent transport whether that kiss, whose burning smart she could still feel, would not perhaps suffice to cover her with the shame to which her cousin had referred. Thereupon she was seized with remorse, and burst into sobs.

"What is the matter; why are you crying?" asked Silvere in an anxious voice.

"Oh, leave me," she faltered, "I do not know."

Then in spite of herself, as it were, she continued amidst her tears: "Ah! what an unfortunate creature I am! When I was ten years old people used to throw stones at me. To-day I am treated as the vilest of creatures. Justin did right to despise me before everybody. We have been doing wrong, Silvere."

The young man, quite dismayed, clasped her in his arms again, trying to console her. "I love you," he whispered, "I am your brother. Why say that we have been doing wrong? We kissed each other because we were cold. You know very well that we used to kiss each other every evening before separating."

"Oh! not as we did just now," she whispered. "It must be wrong, for a strange feeling came over me. The men will laugh at me now as I pass, and they will be right in doing so. I shall not be able to defend myself."

The young fellow remained silent, unable to find a word to calm the agitation of this big child, trembling at her first kiss of love. He clasped her gently, imagining that he might calm her by his embrace. She struggled, however, and continued: "If you like, we will go away; we will leave the province. I can never return to Plassans; my uncle would beat me; all the townspeople would point their fingers at me—" And then, as if seized with sudden irritation, she added: "But no! I am cursed!

I forbid you to leave aunt Dide to follow me. You must leave me on the highway."

"Miette, Miette!" Silvere implored; "don't talk like that."

"Yes. I want to please you. Be reasonable. They have turned me out like a vagabond. If I went back with you, you would always be fighting for my sake, and I don't want that."

At this the young man again pressed a kiss upon her lips, murmuring: "You shall be my wife, and nobody will then dare to hurt you."

"Oh! please, I entreat you!" she said, with a stifled cry; "don't kiss me so. You hurt me."

Then, after a short silence: "You know quite well that I cannot be your wife now. We are too young. You would have to wait for me, and meanwhile I should die of shame. You are wrong in protesting; you will be forced to leave me in some corner."

At this Silvere, his fortitude exhausted, began to cry. A man's sobs are fraught with distressing hoarseness. Miette, quite frightened as she felt the poor fellow shaking in her arms, kissed him on the face, forgetting she was burning her lips. But it was all her fault. She was a little simpleton to have let a kiss upset her so completely. She now clasped her lover to her bosom as if to beg forgiveness for having pained him. These weeping children, so anxiously clasping one another, made the dark night yet more woeful than before. In the distance, the bells continued to complain unceasingly in panting accents.

"It is better to die," repeated Silvere, amidst his sobs; "it is better to die."

"Don't cry; forgive me," stammered Miette. "I will be brave; I will do all you wish."

When the young man had dried his tears: "You are right," he said; "we cannot return to Plassans. But the time for cowardice has not yet come. If we come out of the struggle triumphant, I will go for aunt Dide, and we will take her ever so far away with us. If we are beaten——"

He stopped.

"If we are beaten?" repeated Miette, softly.

"Then be it as God wills!" continued Silvere, in a softer voice. "I most likely shall not be there. You will comfort the poor woman. That would be better."

"Ah! as you said just now," the young girl murmured, "it would be better to die."

At this longing for death they tightened their embrace. Miette relied upon dying with Silvere; he had only spoken of himself, but she felt that he would gladly take her with him into the earth. They would there be able to love each other more freely than under the sun. Aunt Dide would die likewise and join them. It was, so to say, a rapid presentiment, a desire for some strange voluptuousness, to which Heaven, by the mournful accents of the tocsin, was promising early gratification. To die! To die! The bells repeated these words with increasing passion, and the lovers yielded to the calls of the darkness; they fancied they experienced a foretaste of the last sleep, in the drowsiness into which they again sank, whilst their lips met once more.

Miette no longer turned away. It was she, now, who pressed her lips to Silvere's, who sought with mute ardour for the delight whose stinging smart she had not at first been able to endure. The thought of approaching death had excited her; she no longer felt herself blushing, but hung upon her love, while he in faltering voice repeated: "I love you! I love you!"

But at this Miette shook her head, as if to say it was not true. With her free and ardent nature she had a secret instinct of the meaning and purposes of life, and though she was right willing to die she would fain have known life first. At last, growing calmer, she gently rested her head on the young man's shoulder, without uttering a word. Silvere kissed her again. She tasted those kisses slowly, seeking their meaning, their hidden sweetness. As she felt them course through her veins, she interrogated them, asking if they were all love, all passion. But languor at last overcame her, and she fell into gentle slumber. Silvere had enveloped her in her pelisse, drawing the skirt around himself at the same time. They no longer felt cold. The young man rejoiced to find, from the regularity of her breathing, that the girl was now asleep; this repose would enable them to proceed on their way with spirit. He resolved to let her slumber for an hour. The sky was still black, and the approach of day was but faintly indicated by a whitish line in the east. Behind the lovers there must have been a pine wood whose musical awakening it was that the young man heard amidst the morning breezes. And meantime the wailing of the bells grew more sonorous in the quivering atmosphere, lulling Miette's slumber even as it had accompanied her passionate fever.

Until that troublous night, these young people had lived through one of those innocent idylls that blossom among the toiling masses, those outcasts and folks of simple mind amidst whom one may yet occasionally find amours as primitive as those of the ancient Greek romances.

Miette had been scarcely nine years old at the time when her father was sent to the galleys for shooting a gendarme. The trial of Chantegreil had remained a memorable case in the province. The poacher boldly confessed that he had killed the gendarme, but he swore that the latter had been taking aim at him. "I only anticipated him," he said, "I defended myself; it was a duel, not a murder." He never desisted from this line of argument. The presiding Judge of the Assizes could not make him understand that, although a gendarme has the right to fire upon a poacher, a poacher has no right to fire upon a gendarme. Chantegreil escaped the guillotine, owing to his obviously sincere belief in his own innocence, and his previous good character. The man wept like a child when his daughter was brought to him prior to his departure for Toulon. The little thing, who had lost her mother in her infancy, dwelt at this time with her grandfather at Chavanoz, a village in the passes of the Seille. When the poacher was no longer there, the old man and the girl lived upon alms. The inhabitants of Chavanoz, all sportsmen and poachers, came to the assistance of the poor creatures whom the convict had left behind him. After a while, however, the old man died of grief, and Miette, left alone by herself, would have had to beg on the high roads, if the neighbours had not remembered that she had an aunt at Plassans. A charitable soul was kind enough to take her to this aunt, who did not, however, receive her very kindly.

Eulalie Chantegreil, the spouse of *meger* Rebufat, was a big, dark, stubborn creature, who ruled the home. She led her husband by the noise, said the people of the Faubourg of Plassans. The truth was, Rebufat, avaricious and eager for work and gain, felt a sort of respect for this big creature, who combined uncommon vigour with strict sobriety and economy.

Thanks to her, the household thrived. The *meger* grumbled one evening when, on returning home from work, he found Miette installed there. But his wife closed his mouth by saying in her gruff voice: "Bah, the little thing's strongly built, she'll do for a servant; we'll keep her and save wages."

This calculation pleased Rebufat. He went so far as to feel the little thing's arms, and declared with satisfaction that she was sturdy for her age. Miette was then nine years old. From the very next day he made use of her. The work of the peasant-woman in the South of France is much lighter than in the North. One seldom sees them employed in digging the ground, carrying loads, or doing other kinds of men's work. They bind sheaves, gather olives and mulberry leaves; perhaps their most laborious work is that of weeding. Miette worked away willingly. Open-air life was her delight, her health. So long as her aunt lived she was always smiling. The good woman, in spite of her roughness, at last loved her as her own child; she forbade her doing the hard work which her husband sometimes tried to force upon her, saying to the latter:

"Ah! you're a clever fellow! You don't understand, you fool, that if you tire her too much to-day, she won't be able to do anything to-morrow!"

This argument was decisive. Rebufat bowed his head, and carried the load which he had desired to set on the young girl's shoulders.

The latter would have lived in perfect happiness under the secret protection of her aunt Eulalie, but for the teasing of her cousin, who was then a lad of sixteen, and employed his idle hours in hating and persecuting her. Justin's happiest moments were those when by means of some gross falsehood he succeeded in getting her scolded. Whenever he could tread on her feet, or push her roughly, pretending not to have seen her, he laughed and felt the delight of those crafty folks who rejoice at other people's misfortunes. Miette, however, would stare at him with her large black childish eyes gleaming with anger and silent scorn, which checked the cowardly youngster's sneers. In reality he was terribly afraid of his cousin.

The young girl was just attaining her eleventh year when her aunt Eulalie suddenly died. From that day everything changed in the house. Rebufat gradually come to treat her like a farm-labourer. He overwhelmed her with all sorts of rough work, and made use of her as a beast of burden. She never even complained, however, thinking that she had a debt of gratitude to repay him. In the evening, when she was worn out with fatigue, she mourned for her aunt, that terrible woman whose latent kindliness she now realised. However, it was not the hard work that distressed her, for she delighted in her strength, and took a pride in her big arms and broad shoulders. What distressed her was her uncle's distrustful surveillance, his continual reproaches, and the irritated employer-like manner he assumed towards her. She had now become a stranger in the house. Yet even a stranger would not have been so badly treated as she was. Rebufat took the most unscrupulous advantage of this poor little relative, whom he pretended to keep out of charity. She repaid his harsh hospitality ten times over with her work, and yet never a day passed but he grudged her the bread she ate. Justin especially excelled in wounding her. Since his mother had been dead, seeing her without a protector, he had brought all his evil instincts into play in trying to make the house intolerable to her. The most ingenious torture which he invented was to speak to Miette of her father. The poor girl, living away from the world, under the protection of her aunt, who had forbidden any one ever to mention the words "galleys" or "convict" before her, hardly understood their meaning. It was Justin who explained it to her by relating, in his own manner, the story of the murder of the gendarme, and Chantegreil's conviction. There was no end to the horrible particulars he supplied: the convicts had a cannonball fastened to one ankle by a chain, they worked fifteen hours a day, and all died under their punishment; their prison, too, was a frightful place, the horrors of which he described minutely. Miette listened to him, stupefied, her eyes full of tears. Sometimes she was roused to sudden violence, and Justin quickly retired before her clenched fists. However, he took a savage delight in thus instructing her as to the nature of prison life. When his father flew into a passion with the child for any little negligence, he chimed in, glad to be able to insult her without danger. And if she attempted to defend herself, he would exclaim: "Bah! bad blood always shows itself. You'll end at the galleys like your father."

At this Miette sobbed, stung to the heart, powerless and overwhelmed with shame.

She was already growing to womanhood at this period. Of precocious nature, she endured her martyrdom with extraordinary fortitude. She rarely gave way, excepting when her natural pride succumbed to her cousin's outrages. Soon even, she was able to bear, without a tear, the incessant insults of this cowardly fellow, who ever watched her while he spoke, for fear lest she should fly at his face. Then, too, she learnt to silence him by staring at him fixedly. She had several times felt inclined to run away from the Jas-Meiffren; but she did not do so, as her courage could not brook the idea of confessing that she was vanquished by the persecution she endured. She certainly earned her bread, she did not steal the Rebufats' hospitality; and this conviction satisfied her pride. So she remained there to continue the struggle, stiffening herself and living on with the one thought of resistance. Her plan was to do her work in silence, and revenge herself for all harsh treatment by mute contempt. She knew that her uncle derived too much advantage from her to listen readily to the insinuations of Justin, who longed to get her turned out of doors. And in a defiant spirit she resolved that she would not go away of her own accord.

Her continuous voluntary silence was full of strange fancies. Passing her days in the enclosure, isolated from all the world, she formed ideas for herself which would have strangely shocked the good people of the Faubourg. Her father's fate particularly occupied her thoughts. All Justin's abuse recurred to her; and she ended by accepting the charge of murder, saying to herself, however, that her father had done well to kill the gendarme who had tried to kill him. She had learnt the real story from a labourer who had worked for a time at the Jas-Meiffren. From that moment, on the few occasions when she went out, she no longer even turned if the ragamuffins of the Faubourg followed her, crying: "Hey! La Chantegreil!"

She simply hastened her steps homeward, with lips compressed, and black, fierce eyes. Then after shutting the gate, she perhaps cast one long glance at the gang of urchins. She would have become vicious, have lapsed into fierce pariah savagery, if her childishness had not sometimes gained the mastery. Her extreme youth brought her little girlish weaknesses which relieved her. She would then cry with shame for herself and her father. She would hide herself in a stable so that she might sob to her heart's content, for she knew that, if the others saw her crying, they would torment her all the more. And when she had wept sufficiently, she would bathe her eyes in the kitchen, and then again subside into uncomplaining silence. It was not interest alone, however, which prompted her to hide herself; she carried her pride in her precocious strength so far that she was unwilling to appear a child. In time she would have become very unhappy. Fortunately she was saved by discovering the latent tenderness of her loving nature.

The well in the yard of the house occupied by aunt Dide and Silvere was a party-well. The wall of the Jas-Meiffren cut it in halves. Formerly, before the Fouques' property was united to the neighbouring estate, the market-gardeners had used this well daily. Since the transfer of the Fouques' ground, however, as it was at some distance from the outhouses, the inmates of the Jas, who had large cisterns at their disposal, did not draw a pail of water from it in a month. On the other side, one could hear the grating of the pulley every morning when Silvere drew the water for aunt Dide.

One day the pulley broke. The young wheelwright made a good strong one of oak, and put it up in the evening after his day's work. To do this he had to climb upon the wall. When he had finished the job he remained resting astride the coping, and surveyed with curiosity the large expanse of the Jas-Meiffren. At last a peasant-girl, who was weeding the ground a few feet from him, attracted his attention. It was in July, and the air was broiling, although the sun had already sank to the horizon. The peasant-girl had taken off her jacket. In a white bodice, with a coloured neckerchief tied over her shoulders, and the sleeves of her chemise turned up as far as her elbows, she was squatting amid the folds of her blue cotton skirt, which was secured to a pair of braces crossed behind her back. She crawled about on her knees as she pulled up the tares and threw them into a basket. The young man could only see her bare, suntanned arms stretching out right and left to seize some overlooked weed. He followed this rapid play of her arms complacently, deriving a singular pleasure from seeing them so firm and quick. The young person had slightly raised herself on noticing that he was no longer at work, but had again lowered her head before he could distinguish her features. This shyness kept him in suspense. Like an inquisitive lad he wondered who this weeder could be, and while he lingered there, whistling and beating time with a chisel, the latter suddenly slipped out of his hand. It fell into the Jas-Meiffren, striking the curb of the well, and then bounding a few feet from the wall. Silvere looked at it, leaning forward and hesitating to get over. But the peasant-girl must have been watching the young man askance, for she jumped up without saying anything, picked up the chisel, and handed it to Silvere, who then perceived that she was a mere child. He was surprised and rather intimidated. The young girl raised herself towards him in the red glare of the sunset. The wall at this spot was low, but nevertheless too high for her to reach him. So he bent low over the coping, while she still raised herself on tiptoes. They did not speak, but looked at each other with an air of smiling confusion. The young man would indeed have liked to keep the girl in that position. She turned to him a charming head, with handsome black eyes, and red lips, which quite astonished and stirred him. He had never before seen a girl so near; he had not known that lips and eyes could be so pleasant to look at. Everything about the girl seemed to possess a strange fascination for him—her coloured neckerchief, her white bodice, her blue cotton skirt hanging from braces which stretched with the motion of her shoulders. Then his glance glided along the arm which was handing him the tool; as far as the elbow this arm was of a golden brown, as though clothed with sun-burn; but higher up, in the shadow of the tucked-up sleeve, Silvere perceived a bare, milk-white roundness. At this he felt confused; however, he leant further over, and at last managed to grasp the chisel. The little peasant-girl was becoming embarrassed. Still they remained there, smiling at each other, the child beneath with up-turned face, and the lad half reclining on the coping of the wall. They could not part from each other. So far they had not exchanged a word, and Silvere even forgot to say, "Thank you."

"What's your name?" he asked.

"Marie," replied the peasant-girl; "but everybody calls me Miette."

Again she raised herself slightly, and in a clear voice inquired in her turn: "And yours?"

"My name is Silvere," the young workman replied.

A pause ensued, during which they seemed to be listening complacently to the music of their names.

"I'm fifteen years old," resumed Silvere. "And you?"

"I!" said Miette; "oh, I shall be eleven on All Saints' Day."

The young workman made a gesture of surprise. "Ah! really!" he said, laughing, "and to think I took you for a woman! You've such big arms."

She also began to laugh, as she lowered her eyes to her arms. Then they ceased speaking. They remained for another moment gazing and smiling at each other. And finally, as Silvere seemingly had no more questions to ask her, Miette quietly withdrew and went on plucking her weeds, without raising her head. The lad for his part remained on the wall for a while. The sun was setting; a stream of oblique rays poured over the yellow soil of the Jas-Meiffren, which seemed to be all ablaze—one would have said that a fire was running along the ground—and, in the midst of the flaming expanse, Silvere saw the little stooping peasant-girl, whose bare arms had resumed their rapid motion. The blue cotton skirt was now becoming white; and rays of light streamed over the child's copper-coloured arms. At last Silvere felt somewhat ashamed of remaining there, and accordingly got off the wall.

In the evening, preoccupied with his adventure, he endeavoured to question aunt Dide. Perhaps she would know who this Miette was who had such black eyes and such red lips. But, since she had lived in the house in the alley, the old woman had never once given a look behind the wall of the little yard. It was, to her, like an impassable rampart, which shut off her past. She did not know—she did not want to know—what there might now be on the other side of that wall, in that old enclosure of the Fouques, where she had buried her love, her heart and her flesh. As soon as Silvere began to question her she looked at him with childish terror. Was he, then, going to stir up the ashes of those days now dead and gone, and make her weep like her son Antoine had done?

"I don't know," she said in a hasty voice; "I no longer go out, I never see anybody."

Silvere waited the morrow with considerable impatience. And as soon as he got to his master's workshop, he drew his fellow-workmen into conversation. He did not say anything about his interview with Miette; but spoke vaguely of a girl whom he had seen from a distance in the Jas-Meiffren.

"Oh! that's La Chantegreil!" cried one of the workmen.

There was no necessity for Silvere to question them further, for they told him the story of the poacher Chantegreil and his daughter Miette, with that unreasoning spite which is felt for social outcasts. The girl, in particular, they treated in a foul manner; and the insulting gibe of "daughter of a galley-slave" constantly rose to their lips like an incontestable reason for condemning the poor, dear innocent creature to eternal disgrace.

However, wheelwright Vian, an honest, worthy fellow, at last silenced his men.

"Hold your tongues, you foul mouths!" he said, as he let fall the shaft of a cart that he had been examining. "You ought to be ashamed of yourselves for being so hard upon the child. I've seen her, the little thing looks a very good girl. Besides, I'm told she doesn't mind work, and already does as much as any woman of thirty. There are some lazy fellows here who aren't a match for her. I hope, later on, that she'll get a good husband who'll stop this evil talk."

Silvere, who had been chilled by the workmen's gross jests and insults, felt tears rise to his eyes at the last words spoken by Vian. However, he did not open his lips. He took up his hammer, which he had laid down near him, and began with all his might to strike the nave of a wheel which he was binding with iron.

In the evening, as soon as he had returned home from the workshop, he ran to the wall and climbed upon it. He found Miette engaged upon the same labour as the day before. He called her. She came to him, with her smile of embarrassment, and the charming shyness of a child who from infancy had grown up in tears.

"You're La Chantegreil, aren't you?" he asked her, abruptly.

She recoiled, she ceased smiling, and her eyes turned sternly black, gleaming with defiance. So this lad was going to insult her, like the others! She was turning her back upon him, without giving an answer, when Silvere, perplexed by her sudden change of countenance, hastened to add: "Stay, I beg you—I don't want to pain you—I've got so many things to tell you!"

She turned round, still distrustful. Silvere, whose heart was full, and who had resolved to relieve it, remained for a moment speechless, not knowing how to continue, for he feared lest he should commit a fresh blunder. At last he put his whole heart in one phrase: "Would you like me to be your friend?" he said, in a voice full of emotion. And as Miette, in surprise, raised her eyes, which were again moist and smiling, he continued with animation: "I know that people try to vex you. It's time to put a stop to it. I will be your protector now. Shall I?"

The child beamed with delight. This proffered friendship roused her from all her evil dreams of taciturn hatred. Still she shook her head and answered: "No, I don't want you to fight on my account. You'd have too much to do. Besides which, there are persons from whom you cannot protect me."

Silvere wished to declare that he would defend her against the whole world, but she closed his mouth with a coaxing gesture, as she added: "I am satisfied to have you as a friend."

They then conversed together for a few minutes, lowering their voices as much as possible. Miette spoke to Silvere of her uncle and her cousin. For all the world she would not have liked them to catch him astride the coping of the wall. Justin would be implacable with such a weapon against her. She spoke of her misgivings with the fright of a schoolgirl on meeting a friend with whom her mother has forbidden her to associate. Silvere merely understood, however, that he would not be able to see Miette at his pleasure. This made him very sad. Still, he promised that he would not climb upon the wall any more. They were both endeavouring to find some expedient for seeing each other again, when Miette suddenly begged him to go away; she had just caught sight of Justin, who was crossing the grounds in the direction of the wall. Silvere quickly descended. When he was in the little yard again, he remained by the wall to listen, irritated by his flight. After a few minutes he ventured to climb again and cast a glance into the Jas-Meiffren, but he saw Justin speaking with Miette, and quickly withdrew his head. On the following day he could see nothing of his friend, not even in the distance; she must have finished her work in that part of the Jas. A week passed in this fashion, and the young people had no opportunity of exchanging a single word. Silvere was in despair; he thought of boldly going to the Rebufats to ask for Miette.

The party-well was a large one, but not very deep. On either side of the wall the curb formed a large semicircle. The water was only ten or twelve feet down at the utmost. This slumbering water reflected the two apertures of the well, two half-moons between which the shadow of the wall cast a black streak. On leaning over, one might have fancied in the vague light that the half-moons were two mirrors of singular clearness and brilliance. Under the morning sunshine, when the dripping of the ropes did not disturb the surface of the water, these mirrors, these reflections of the heavens, showed like white patches on the green water, and in them the leaves of the ivy which had spread along the wall over the well were repeated with marvellous exactness.

One morning, at an early hour, Silvere, as he came to draw water for aunt Dide, bent over the well mechanically, just as he was taking hold of the rope. He started, and then stood motionless, still leaning over. He had fancied that he could distinguish in the well the face of a young girl who was looking at him with a smile; however, he had shaken the rope, and the disturbed water was now but a dim mirror that no longer reflected anything clearly. Silvere, who did not venture to stir, and whose heart beat rapidly, then waited for the water to settle. As its ripples gradually widened and died away, he perceived the image reappearing. It oscillated for a long time, with a swing which lent a vague, phantom-like grace to its features, but at last it remained stationary. It was the smiling countenance of Miette, with her head and shoulders, her coloured neckerchief, her white bodice, and her blue braces. Silvere next perceived his own image in the other mirror. Then, knowing that they could see each other, they nodded their heads. For the first moment, they did not even think of speaking. At last they exchanged greetings.

"Good morning, Silvere."

"Good morning, Miette."

They were surprised by the strange sound of their voices, which became singularly soft and sweet in that damp hole. The sound seemed, indeed, to come from a distance, like the soft music of voices heard of an evening in the country. They understood that it would suffice to speak in a whisper in order to hear each other. The well echoed the faintest breath. Leaning over its brink, they conversed while gazing at one another's reflection. Miette related how sad she had been the last week. She was now working at the other end of the Jas, and could only get out early in the morning. Then she made a pout of annoyance which Silvere distinguished perfectly, and to which he replied by nodding his head with an air of vexation. They were exchanging all those gestures and facial expressions that speech entails. They cared but little for the wall which separated them now that they could see each other in those hidden depths.

"I knew," continued Miette, with a knowing look, "that you came here to draw water every morning at the same hour. I can hear the grating of the pulley from the house. So I made an excuse, I pretended that the water in this well boiled the vegetables better. I thought that I might come here every morning to draw water at the same time as you, so as to say good morning to you without anyone suspecting it."

She smiled innocently, as though well pleased with her device, and ended by saying: "But I did not imagine we should see each other in the water."

It was, in fact, this unhoped-for pleasure which so delighted them. They only spoke to see their lips move, so greatly did this new frolic amuse their childish natures. And they resolved to use all means in their power to meet here every morning. When Miette had said that she must go away, she told Silvere that he could draw his pail of water. But he did not dare to shake the rope; Miette was still leaning over—he could see her smiling face, and it was too painful to him to dispel that smile. As he slightly stirred his pail, the water murmured, and the smile faded. Then he stopped, seized with a strange fear; he fancied that he had vexed her and made her cry. But the child called to him, "Go on! go on!" with a laugh which the echo prolonged and rendered more sonorous. She herself then nosily sent down a pail. There was a perfect tempest. Everything disappeared under the black water. And Silvere made up his mind to fill two pitchers, while listening to the retreating steps of Miette on the other side of the wall.

From that day, the young people never missed their assignations. The slumbering water, the white mirrors in which they gazed at one another, imparted to their interviews a charm which long sufficed their playful, childish imaginations. They had no desire to see each other face to face: it seemed much more amusing to them to use the well as a mirror, and confide their morning greetings to its echo. They soon came to look upon the well as an old friend. They loved to bend over the motionless water that resembled molten silver. A greenish glimmer hovered below, in a mysterious half light, and seemed to change the damp hole into some hiding-place in the depths of a wood. They saw each other in a sort of greenish nest bedecked with moss, in the midst of fresh water and foliage. And all the strangeness of the deep spring, the hollow tower over which they bent, trembling with fascination, added unconfessed and delightful fear to their merry laughter. The wild idea occurred to them of going down and seating themselves on a row of large stones which formed a kind of circular bench at a few inches above the water. They would dip their feet in the latter, converse there for hours, and no one would think of coming to look for them in such a spot. But when they asked each other what there might be down there, their vague fears returned; they thought it quite sufficient to let their reflected images descend into the depths amidst those green glimmers which tinged the stones with strange moire-like reflections, and amidst those mysterious noises which rose from the dark corners. Those sounds issuing from the invisible made them particularly uneasy; they often fancied that voices were replying to their own; and then they would remain silent, detecting a thousand faint plaints which they could not understand. These came from the secret travail of the moisture, the sighs of the atmosphere, the drops that glided over the stones, and fell below with the sonorousness of sobs. They would nod affectionately to each other in order to reassure themselves. Thus the attraction which kept them leaning over the brink had a tinge

of secret terror, like all poignant charms. But the well still remained their old friend. It was such an excellent pretext for
meeting! Justin, who watched Miette's every movement, never
suspected the cause of her eagerness to go and draw some water every morning. At times, he saw her from the distance,
leaning over and loitering. "Ah! the lazy thing!" he muttered;
"how fond she is of dawdling about!" How could he suspect
that, on the other side of the wall, there was a wooer contemplating the girl's smile in the water, and saying to her: "If that
red-haired donkey Justin should illtreat you, just tell me of it,
and he shall hear from me!"

This amusement lasted for more than a month. It was July
then; the mornings were sultry; the sun shone brightly, and it
was quite a pleasure to come to that damp spot. It was delightful to feel the cold breath of the well on one's face, and make
love amidst this spring water while the skies were kindling
their fires. Miette would arrive out of breath after crossing the
stubble fields; as she ran along, her hair fell down over her
forehead and temples; and it was with flushed face and
dishevelled locks that she would lean over, shaking with
laughter, almost before she had had time to set her pitcher
down. Silvere, who was almost always the first at the well, felt,
as he suddenly saw her smiling face in the water, as keen a joy
as he would have experienced had she suddenly thrown herself
into his arms at the bend of a pathway. Around them the radiant morning hummed with mirth; a wave of warm light, sonorous with the buzzing of insects, beat against the old wall, the
posts, and the curbstone. They, however, no longer saw the
shower of morning sunshine, nor heard the thousand sounds
rising from the ground; they were in the depths of their green
hiding-place, under the earth, in that mysterious and awesome
cavity, and quivered with pleasure as they lingered there enjoying its fresh coolness and dim light.

On some mornings, Miette, who by nature could not long
maintain a contemplative attitude, began to tease; she would
shake the rope, and make drops of water fall in order to ripple
the mirrors and deface the reflections. Silvere would then entreat her to remain still; he, whose fervour was deeper than
hers, knew no keener pleasure than that of gazing at his love's
image reflected so distinctly in every feature. But she would

not listen to him; she would joke and feign a rough old bogey's voice, to which the echo imparted a raucous melodiousness.

"No, no," she would say in chiding fashion; "I don't love you to-day! I'm making faces at you; see how ugly I am."

And she laughed at seeing the fantastic forms which their spreading faces assumed as they danced upon the disturbed water.

One morning she got angry in real earnest. She did not find Silvere at the trysting-place, and waited for him for nearly a quarter of an hour, vainly making the pulley grate. She was just about to depart in a rage when he arrived. As soon as she perceived him she let a perfect tempest loose in the well, shook her pail in an irritated manner, and made the blackish water whirl and splash against the stones. In vain did Silvere try to explain that aunt Dide had detained him. To all his excuses she replied: "You've vexed me; I don't want to see you."

The poor lad, in despair, vainly questioned that sombre cavity, now so full of lamentable sounds, where, on other days, such a bright vision usually awaited him amid the silence of the stagnant water. He had to go away without seeing Miette. On the morrow, arriving before the time, he gazed sadly into the well, hearing nothing, and thinking that the obstinate girl would not come, when she, who was already on the other side slyly watching his arrival, bent over suddenly with a burst of laughter. All was at once forgotten.

In this wise the well was the scene of many a little drama and comedy. That happy cavity, with its gleaming mirrors and musical echoes, quickly ripened their love. They endowed it with such strange life, so filled it with their youthful love, that, long after they had ceased to come and lean over the brink, Silvere, as he drew water every morning, would fancy he could see Miette's smiling face in the dim light that still quivered with the joy they had set there.

That month of playful love rescued Miette from her mute despair. She felt a revival of her affections, her happy childish carelessness, which had been held in check by the hateful loneliness in which she lived. The certainty that she was loved by somebody, and that she was no longer alone in the world, enabled her to endure the persecutions of Justin and the Faubourg urchins. A song of joy, whose glad notes drowned their hootings, now sounded in her heart. She thought of her father with tender compassion, and did not now so frequently yield to dreams of bitter vengeance. Her dawning love cooled her feverish broodings like the fresh breezes of the dawn. At the same time she acquired the instinctive cunning of a young girl in love. She felt that she must maintain her usual silent and rebellious demeanour if she were to escape Justin's suspicions. But, in spite of her efforts, her eyes retained a sweet unruffled expression when the lad bullied her; she was no longer able to put on her old black look of indignant anger. One morning he heard her humming to herself at breakfast-time.

"You seem very gay, Chantegreil!" he said to her suspiciously, glancing keenly at her from his lowering eyes. "I bet you've been up to some of your tricks again!"

She shrugged her shoulders, but she trembled inwardly; and she did all she could to regain her old appearance of rebellious martyrdom. However, though Justin suspected some secret happiness, it was long before he was able to discover how his victim had escaped him.

Silvere, on his side, enjoyed profound happiness. His daily meetings with Miette made his idle hours pass pleasantly away. During his long silent companionship with aunt Dide, he recalled one by one his remembrances of the morning, revelling in their most trifling details. From that time forward, the fulness of his heart cloistered him yet more in the lonely existence which he had adopted with his grandmother. He was naturally fond of hidden spots, of solitary retirement, where he could give himself up to his thoughts. At this period already he had eagerly begun to read all the old odd volumes which he could pick up at brokers' shops in the Faubourg, and which were destined to lead him to a strange and generous social religion and morality. His reading—ill-digested and lacking all solid foundation—gave him glimpses of the world's vanities and pleasures, especially with regard to women, which would have seriously troubled his mind if his heart had not been contented. When Miette came, he received her at first as a companion, then as the joy and ambition of his life. In the evening, when he had retired to the little nook where he slept, and hung his lamp at the head of his strap-bedstead, he would find Miette on every page of the dusty old volume which he had taken at random from a shelf above his head and was reading devoutly. He never came across a young girl, a good and beautiful creature, in his reading, without immediately identifying her with his sweetheart. And he would set himself in the narrative as well. If he were reading a love story, it was he who married Miette at the end, or died with her. If, on the contrary, he were perusing some political pamphlet, some grave dissertation on social economy, works which he preferred to romances, for he had that singular partiality for difficult subjects which characterises persons of imperfect scholarship, he still found some means of associating her with the tedious themes which frequently he could not even understand. For instance, he tried to persuade himself that he was learning how to be good and kind to her when they were married. He thus associated her with all his visionary dreamings. Protected by the purity of his affection against the obscenity of certain eighteenth-century tales which fell into his hands, he found particular pleasure in shutting himself up with her in those humanitarian Utopias which some great minds of our own time, infatuated by visions of universal happiness have imagined. Miette, in his mind, became quite essential to the abolition of pauperism and the definitive triumph of the principles of the Revolution. There were nights of feverish reading, when his mind could not tear itself from his book, which he would lay down and take up at least a score of times, nights of voluptuous weariness which he enjoyed till daybreak like some secret orgie, cramped up in that tiny room, his eyes troubled by the flickering yellow light, while he yielded to the fever of insomnia and schemed out new social schemes of the most absurdly ingenuous nature, in which woman, always personified by Miette, was worshipped by the nations on their knees.

He was predisposed to Utopian ideas by certain hereditary influences; his grandmother's nervous disorders became in him so much chronic enthusiasm, striving after everything that was grandiose and impossible. His lonely childhood, his imperfect education, had developed his natural tendencies in a singular manner. However, he had not yet reached the age when the fixed idea plants itself in a man's mind. In the morning, after he had dipped his head in a bucket of water, he remembered his thoughts and visions of the night but vaguely; nothing remained of his dreams save a childlike innocence, full of trustful confidence and yearning tenderness. He felt like a child again. He ran to the well, solely desirous of meeting his sweetheart's smile, and tasting the delights of the radiant morning. And during the day, when thoughts of the future sometimes made him silent and dreamy, he would often, prompted by some sudden impulse, spring up and kiss aunt Dide on both cheeks, whereat the old woman would gaze at him anxiously, perturbed at seeing his eyes so bright, and gleaming with a joy which she thought she could divine.

At last, as time went on, Miette and Silvere began to tire of only seeing each other's reflection. The novelty of their play was gone, and now they began to dream of keener pleasures than the well could afford them. In this longing for reality which came upon them, there was the wish to see each other face to face, to run through the open fields, and return out of breath with their arms around each other's waist, clinging closely together in order that they might the better feel each other's love. One morning Silvere spoke of climbing over the wall, and walking in the Jas with Miette. But the child implored him not to perpetrate such folly, which would place her at Justin's mercy. He then promised to seek some other means.

The wall in which the well was set made a sudden bend a few paces further on, thereby forming a sort of recess, where the lovers would be free from observation, if they were to take shelter there. The question was how to reach this recess. Silvere could no longer entertain the idea of climbing over, as Miette had appeared so afraid. He secretly thought of another plan. The little door which Macquart and Adelaide had set up one night long years previously had remained forgotten in this remote corner. The owner of the Jas-Meiffren had not even thought of blocking it up. Blackened by damp and green with moss, its lock and hinges eaten away with rust, it looked like a part of the old wall. Doubtless the key was lost; the grass growing beside the lower boards, against which slight mounds had formed, amply proved that no one had passed that way for many a long year. However, it was the lost key that Silvere hoped to find. He knew with what devotion his aunt Dide allowed the relics of the past to lie rotting wherever they might be. He searched the house for a week without any result, and went stealthily night by night to see if he had at last put his hand on the right key during the daytime. In this way he tried more than thirty keys which had doubtless come from the old property of the Fouques, and which he found all over the place, against the walls, on the floors, and at the bottom of drawers. He was becoming disheartened, when all at once he found the precious key. It was simply tied by a string to the street door latch-key, which always remained in the lock. It had hung there for nearly forty years. Aunt Dide must every day have touched it with her hand, without ever making up her mind to throw it away, although it could now only carry her back sorrowfully into the past. When Silvere had convinced himself that it really opened the little door, he awaited the ensuing day, dreaming of the joyful surprise which he was preparing for Miette. He had not told her for what he had been searching.

On the morrow, as soon as he heard the girl set her pitcher down, he gently opened the door, sweeping away with a push the tall weeds which covered the threshold. Stretching out his head, he saw Miette leaning over the brink of the well, looking into the water, absorbed in expectation. Thereupon, in a couple of strides, he reached the recess formed by the wall, and thence called, "Miette! Miette!" in a soft voice, which made her tremble. She raised her head, thinking he was on the coping of the wall. But when she saw him in the Jas, at a few steps from her, she gave a faint cry of surprise, and ran up to him. They took each other's hand, and looked at one another, delighted to be so near, thinking themselves far handsomer like this, in the warm sunshine. It was the middle of August, the Feast of the Assumption. In the distance, the bells were pealing in the limpid atmosphere that so often accompanies great days of festival, an atmosphere full of bright gaiety.

"Good morning, Silvere!"

"Good morning, Miette!"

The voices in which they exchanged their morning greetings sounded strange to them. They knew only the muffled accents transmitted by the echo of the well. And now their voices seemed to them as clear as the notes of a lark. And ah! how delightful it was in that warm corner, in that holiday atmosphere! They still held each other's hands. Silvere leaning against the wall, Miette with her figure slightly thrown backwards. They were about to tell each other all the soft things which they had not dared to confide to the reverberations of the well, when Silvere, hearing a slight noise, started, and, turning pale, dropped Miette's hands. He had just seen aunt Dide standing before him erect and motionless on the threshold of the doorway.

The grandmother had come to the well by chance. And on perceiving, in the old black wall, the white gap formed by the doorway which Silvere had left wide open, she had experienced a violent shock. That open gap seemed to her like a gulf of light violently illumining her past. She once more saw herself running to the door amidst the morning brightness, and crossing the threshold full of the transports of her nervous love. And Macquart was there awaiting her. She hung upon his neck and pressed against his bosom, whilst the rising sun, following her through the doorway, which she had left open in her hurry, enveloped them with radiance. It was a sudden vision which roused her cruelly from the slumber of old age, like some supreme chastisement, and awakened a multitude of bitter memories within her. Had the well, had the entire wall, disappeared beneath the earth, she would not have been more stupefied. She had never thought that this door would open again. In her mind it had been walled up ever since the hour of Macquart's death. And amidst her amazement she felt angry, indignant with the sacrilegious hand that had penetrated this violation, and left that white open space agape like a yawning tomb. She stepped forward, yielding to a kind of fascination, and halted erect within the framework of the door.

Then she gazed out before her, with a feeling of dolorous surprise. She had certainly been told that the old enclosure of the Fouques was now joined to the Jas-Meiffren; but she would never have thought the associations of her youth could have vanished so completely. It seemed as though some tempest had carried off everything that her memory cherished. The old dwelling, the large kitchen-garden, the beds of green vegetables, all had disappeared. Not a stone, not a tree of former times remained. And instead of the scene amidst which she had grown up, and which in her mind's eye she had seen but yesterday, there lay a strip of barren soil, a broad patch of stubbles, bare like a desert. Henceforward, when, on closing her eyes, she might try to recall the objects of the past, that stubble would always appear to her like a shroud of yellowish drugget spread over the soil, in which her youth lay buried. In the presence of that unfamiliar commonplace scene her heart died, as it were, a second time. Now all was completely, finally ended. She was robbed even of her dreams of the past. Then she began to regret that she had yielded to the attraction of that white opening, of that doorway gaping upon the days which were now for ever lost.

She was about to retire and close the accursed door, without even seeking to discover who had opened it, when she suddenly perceived Miette and Silvere. And the sight of the two young lovers, who, with hanging heads, nervously awaited her glance, kept her on the threshold, quivering with yet keener pain. She now understood all. To the very end, she was destined to picture herself there, clasped in Macquart's arms in the bright sunshine. Yet a second time had the door served as an accomplice. Where love had once passed, there was it passing again. 'Twas the eternal and endless renewal, with present joys and future tears. Aunt Dide could only see the tears, and a sudden presentiment showed her the two children bleeding, with stricken hearts. Overwhelmed by the recollection of her life's sorrow, which this spot had just awakened within her, she grieved for her dear Silvere. She alone was guilty; if she had not formerly had that door made Silvere would not now be at a girl's feet in that lonely nook, intoxicating himself with a bliss which prompts and angers the jealousy of death.

After a brief pause, she went up to the young man, and, without a word, took him by the hand. She might, perhaps, have left them there, chattering under the wall, had she not felt that she herself was, to some extent, an accomplice in this fatal love. As she came back with Silvere, she turned on hearing the light footfall of Miette, who, having quickly taken up her pitcher, was hastening across the stubble. She was running wildly, glad at having escaped so easily. And aunt Dide smiled involuntarily as she watched her bound over the ground like a runaway goat.

"She is very young," she murmured, "she has plenty of time."

She meant, no doubt, that Miette had plenty of time before her to suffer and weep. Then, turning her eyes upon Silvere, who with a glance of ecstasy had followed the child as she ran off in the bright sunshine, she simply added: "Take care, my boy; this sort of thing sometimes kills one."

These were the only words she spoke with reference to the incident which had awakened all the sorrows that lay slumbering in the depths of her being. Silence had become a real religion with her. When Silvere came in, she double-locked the door, and threw the key down the well. In this wise she felt certain that the door would no longer make her an accomplice. She examined it for a moment, glad at seeing it reassume its usual gloomy, barrier-like aspect. The tomb was closed once more; the white gap was for ever boarded up with that damp-stained mossy timber over which the snails had shed silvery tears.

In the evening, aunt Dide had another of those nervous attacks which came upon her at intervals. At these times she would often talk aloud and ramble incoherently, as though she was suffering from nightmare. That evening, while Silvere held her down on her bed, he heard her stammer in a panting voice such words as "custom-house officer," "fire," and "murder." And she struggled, and begged for mercy, and dreamed aloud of vengeance. At last, as always happened when the attack was drawing to a close, she fell into a strange fright, her teeth chattering, while her limbs quivered with abject terror. Finally, after raising herself into a sitting posture, she cast a haggard look of astonishment at one and another corner of the room, and then fell back upon the pillow, heaving deep sighs. She was, doubtless, a prey to some hallucination. However, she drew Silvere to her bosom, and seemed to some degree to recognise him, though ever and anon she confused him with someone else.

"There they are!" she stammered. "Do you see? They are going to take you, they will kill you again. I don't want them to—Send them away, tell them I won't; tell them they are hurting me, staring at me like that—"

Then she turned to the wall, to avoid seeing the people of whom she was talking. And after an interval of silence, she continued: "You are near me, my child, aren't you? You must not leave me. I thought I was going to die just now. We did wrong to make an opening in the wall. I have suffered ever since. I was certain that door would bring us further misfortune—Oh! the innocent darlings, what sorrow! They will kill them as well, they will be shot down like dogs."

Then she relapsed into catalepsy; she was no longer even aware of Silvere's presence. Suddenly, however, she sat up, and gazed at the foot of her bed, with a fearful expression of terror.

"Why didn't you send them away?" she cried, hiding her white head against the young man's breast. "They are still there. The one with the gun is making signs that he is going to fire."

Shortly afterwards she fell into the heavy slumber that usually terminated these attacks. On the next day, she seemed to have forgotten everything. She never again spoke to Silvere of the morning on which she had found him with a sweetheart behind the wall.

The young people did not see each other for a couple of days. When Miette ventured to return to the well, they resolved not to recommence the pranks which had upset aunt Dide. However, the meeting which had been so strangely interrupted had filled them with a keen desire to meet again in some happy solitude. Weary of the delights afforded by the well, and unwilling to vex aunt Dide by seeing Miette again on the other side of the wall, Silvere begged the girl to meet him somewhere else. She required but little pressing; she received the proposal with the willing smile of a frolicsome lass who has no thought of evil. What made her smile was the idea of outwitting that spy of a Justin. When the lovers had come to agreement, they discussed at length the choice of a favourable spot. Silvere proposed the most impossible trysting-places. He planned regular journeys, and even suggested meeting the young girl at midnight in the barns of the Jas-Meiffren. Miette, who was much more practical, shrugged her shoulders, declaring she would try to think of some spot. On the morrow, she tarried but a minute at the well, just time enough to smile at Silvere and tell him to be at the far end of the Aire Saint-Mittre at about ten o'clock in the evening. One may be sure that the young man was punctual. All day long Miette's choice had puzzled him, and his curiosity increased when he found himself in the narrow lane formed by the piles of planks at the end of the plot of ground. "She will come this way," he said to himself, looking along the road to Nice. But he suddenly heard a loud shaking of boughs behind the wall, and saw a laughing head, with tumbled hair, appear above the coping, whilst a joyous voice called out: "It's me!"

And it was, in fact, Miette, who had climbed like an urchin up one of the mulberry-trees, which even nowadays still border the boundary of the Jas-Meiffren. In a couple of leaps she reached the tombstone, half buried in the corner at the end of the lane. Silvere watched her descend with delight and surprise, without even thinking of helping her. As soon as she had alighted, however, he took both her hands in his, and said: "How nimble you are!—you climb better than I do."

It was thus that they met for the first time in that hidden corner where they were destined to pass such happy hours. From that evening forward they saw each other there nearly every night. They now only used the well to warn each other of unforeseen obstacles to their meetings, of a change of time, and of all the trifling little news that seemed important in their eyes, and allowed of no delay. It sufficed for the one who had a communication to make to set the pulley in motion, for its creaking noise could be heard a long way off. But although, on certain days, they summoned one another two or three times in succession to speak of trifles of immense importance, it was only in the evening in that lonely little passage that they tasted real happiness. Miette was exceptionally punctual. She fortunately slept over the kitchen, in a room where the winter provisions had been kept before her arrival, and which was reached by a little private staircase. She was thus able to go out at all hours, without being seen by Rebufat or Justin. Moreover, if the latter should ever see her returning she intended to tell him some tale or other, staring at him the while with that stern look which always reduced him to silence.

Ah! how happy those warm evenings were! The lovers had now reached the first days of September, a month of bright sunshine in Provence. It was hardly possible for them to join each other before nine o'clock. Miette arrived from over the wall, in surmounting which she soon acquired such dexterity that she was almost always on the old tombstone before Silvere had time to stretch out his arms. She would laugh at her own strength and agility as, for a moment, with her hair in disorder, she remained almost breathless, tapping her skirt to make it fall. Her sweetheart laughingly called her an impudent urchin. In reality he much admired her pluck. He watched her jump over the wall with the complacency of an older brother supervising the exercises of a younger one. Indeed, there was yet much that was childlike in their growing love. On several occasions they spoke of going on some bird's-nesting expedition on the banks of the Viorne.

"You'll see how I can climb," said Miette proudly. "When I lived at Chavanoz, I used to go right up to the top of old Andre's walnut-trees. Have you ever taken a magpie's nest? It's very difficult!"

Then a discussion arose as to how one ought to climb a poplar. Miette stated her opinions, with all a boy's confidence.

However, Silvere, clasping her round the knees, had by this time lifted her to the ground, and then they would walk on, side by side, their arms encircling each other's waist. Though they were but children, fond of frolicsome play and chatter, and knew not even how to speak of love, yet they already partook of love's delight. It sufficed them to press each other's hands. Ignorant whither their feelings and their hearts were drifting, they did not seek to hide the blissful thrills which the slightest touch awoke. Smiling, often wondering at the delight they experienced, they yielded unconsciously to the sweetness of new feelings even while talking, like a couple of schoolboys, of the magpies' nests which are so difficult to reach.

And as they talked they went down the silent path, between the piles of planks and the wall of the Jas-Meiffren. They never went beyond the end of that narrow blind alley, but invariably retraced their steps. They were quite at home there. Miette, happy in the knowledge of their safe concealment, would often pause and congratulate herself on her discovery.

"Wasn't I lucky!" she would gleefully exclaim. "We might walk a long way without finding such a good hiding-place."

The thick grass muffled the noise of their footsteps. They were steeped in gloom, shut in between two black walls, and only a strip of dark sky, spangled with stars, was visible above their heads. And as they stepped along, pacing this path which resembled a dark stream flowing beneath the black star-sprent sky, they were often thrilled with undefinable emotion, and lowered their voices, although there was nobody to hear them. Surrendering themselves as it were to the silent waves of night, over which they seemed to drift, they recounted to one another, with lovers' rapture, the thousand trifles of the day.

At other times, on bright nights, when the moonlight clearly outlined the wall and the timber-stacks, Miette and Silvere would romp about with all the carelessness of children. The path stretched out, alight with white rays, and retaining no suggestion of secrecy, and the young people laughed and chased each other like boys at play, at times venturing even to climb upon the piles of timber. Silvere was occasionally obliged to frighten Miette by telling her that Justin might be watching her from over the wall. Then, quite out of breath, they would stroll side by side, and plan how they might some day go for a scamper in the Sainte-Claire meadows, to see which of the two would catch the other.

Their growing love thus accommodated itself to dark and clear nights. Their hearts were ever on the alert, and a little shade sufficed to sweeten the pleasure of their embrace, and soften their laughter. This dearly-loved retreat—so gay in the moonshine, so strangely thrilling in the gloom—seemed an inexhaustible source of both gaiety and silent emotion. They would remain there until midnight, while the town dropped off to sleep and the lights in the windows of the Faubourg went out one by one.

They were never disturbed in their solitude. At that late hour children were no longer playing at hide-and-seek behind the piles of planks. Occasionally, when the young couple heard sounds in the distance—the singing of some workmen as they passed along the road, or conversation coming from the neighbouring sidewalks—they would cast stealthy glances over the Aire Saint-Mittre. The timber-yard stretched out, empty of all, save here and there some falling shadows. On warm evenings they sometimes caught glimpses of loving couples there, and of old men sitting on the big beams by the roadside. When the evenings grew colder, all that they ever saw on the melancholy, deserted spot was some gipsy fire, before which, perhaps, a few black shadows passed to and fro. Through the still night air words and sundry faint sounds were wafted to them, the "good-night" of a townsman shutting his door, the closing of a window-shutter, the deep striking of a clock, all the parting sounds of a provincial town retiring to rest. And when Plassans was slumbering, they might still hear the quarrelling of the gipsies and the crackling of their fires, amidst which suddenly rose the guttural voices of girls singing in a strange tongue, full of rugged accents.

But the lovers did not concern themselves much with what went on in the Aire Saint-Mittre; they hastened back into their own little privacy, and again walked along their favourite retired path. Little did they care for others, or for the town itself! The few planks which separated them from the wicked world seemed to them, after a while, an insurmountable rampart. They were so secluded, so free in this nook, situated though it was in the very midst of the Faubourg, at only fifty paces from the Rome Gate, that they sometimes fancied themselves far away in some hollow of the Viorne, with the open country around them. Of all the sounds which reached them, only one made them feel uneasy, that of the clocks striking slowly in the darkness. At times, when the hour sounded, they pretended not to hear, at other moments they stopped short as if to protest. However, they could not go on for ever taking just another ten minutes, and so the time came when they were at last obliged to say good-night. Then Miette reluctantly climbed upon the wall again. But all was not ended yet, they would linger over their leave-taking for a good quarter of an hour. When the girl had climbed upon the wall, she remained there with her elbows on the coping, and her feet supported by the branches of the mulberry-tree, which served her as a ladder. Silvere, perched on the tombstone, was able to take her hands again, and renew their whispered conversation. They repeated "till to-morrow!" a dozen times, and still and ever found something more to say. At last Silvere began to scold.

"Come, you must get down, it is past midnight."

But Miette, with a girl's waywardness, wished him to descend first; she wanted to see him go away. And as he persisted in remaining, she ended by saying abruptly, by way of punishment, perhaps: "Look! I am going to jump down."

Then she sprang from the mulberry-tree, to the great consternation of Silvere. He heard the dull thud of her fall, and the burst of laughter with which she ran off, without choosing to reply to his last adieu. For some minutes he would remain watching her vague figure as it disappeared in the darkness, then, slowly descending, he regained the Impasse Saint-Mittre.

During two years they came to the path every day. At the time of their first meetings they enjoyed some beautiful warm nights. They might almost have fancied themselves in the month of May, the month of seething sap, when a pleasant odour of earth and fresh leaves pervades the warm air. This *renouveau*, this second spring, was like a gift from heaven which allowed them to run freely about the path and tighten their bonds of affection.

At last came rain, and snow, and frost. But the disagreeableness of winter did not keep them away. Miette put on her long brown pelisse, and they both made light of the bad weather. When the nights were dry and clear, and puffs of wind raised the hoar frost beneath their footsteps and fell on their faces like taps from a switch, they refrained from sitting down. They walked quickly to and fro, wrapped in the pelisse, their cheeks blue with cold, and their eyes watering; and they laughed heartily, quite quivering with mirth, at the rapidity of their march through the freezing atmosphere. One snowy evening they amused themselves with making an enormous snowball, which they rolled into a corner. It remained there fully a month, which caused them fresh astonishment each time they met in the path. Nor did the rain frighten them. They came to see each other through the heaviest downpours, though they got wet to the skin in doing so. Silvere would hasten to the spot, saying to himself that Miette would never be mad enough to come; and when Miette arrived, he could not find it in his heart to scold her. In reality he had been expecting her. At last he sought some shelter against the inclement weather, knowing quite well that they would certainly come out, however much they might promise one another not to do so when it rained. To find a shelter he only had to disturb one of the timber-stacks; pulling out several pieces of wood and arranging them so that they would move easily, in such wise that he could displace and replace them at pleasure.

From that time forward the lovers possessed a sort of low and narrow sentry-box, a square hole, which was only big enough to hold them closely squeezed together on a beam which they had left at the bottom of the little cell. Whenever it rained, the first to arrive would take shelter here; and on finding themselves together again they would listen with delight to the rain beating on the piles of planks. Before and around them, through the inky blackness of the night, came a rush of water which they could not see, but which resounded continuously like the roar of a mob. They were nevertheless quite alone, as though they had been at the end of the world or beneath the sea. They never felt so happy, so isolated, as when they found themselves in that timber-stack, in the midst of some such deluge which threatened to carry them away at every moment. Their bent knees almost reached the opening, and though they thrust themselves back as far as possible, the spray of the rain bathed their cheeks and hands. The big drops, falling from the planks, splashed at regular intervals at their feet. The brown pelisse kept them warm, and the nook was so small that Miette was compelled to sit almost on Silvere's knees. And they would chatter and then lapse into silence, overcome with languor, lulled by the warmth of their embrace and the monotonous beating of the shower. For hours and hours they remained there, with that same enjoyment of the rain which prompts little children to stroll along solemnly in stormy weather with open umbrellas in their hands. After a while they came to prefer the rainy evenings, though their parting became more painful on those occasions. Miette was obliged to climb the wall in the driving rain, and cross the puddles of the Jas-Meiffren in perfect darkness. As soon as she had left his arms, she was lost to Silvere amidst the gloom and the noise of the falling water. In vain he listened, he was deafened, blinded. However, the anxiety caused by this brusque separation proved an additional charm, and, until the morrow, each would be uneasy lest anything should have befallen the other in such weather, when one would not even have turned a dog out of doors. Perchance one of them had slipped, or lost the way; such were the mutual fears which possessed them, and rendered their next interview yet more loving.

At last the fine days returned, April brought mild nights, and the grass in the green alley sprouted up wildly. Amidst the stream of life flowing from heaven and rising from the earth, amidst all the intoxication of the budding spring-time, the lovers sometimes regretted their winter solitude, the rainy evenings and the freezing nights, during which they had been so isolated so far from all human sounds. At present the days did not draw to a close soon enough, and they grew impatient with the lagging twilights. When the night had fallen sufficiently for Miette to climb upon the wall without danger of being seen, and they could at last glide along their dear path, they no longer found there the solitude congenial to their shy, childish love. People began to flock to the Aire Saint-Mittre, the urchins of the Faubourg remained there, romping about the beams, and shouting, till eleven o'clock at night. It even happened occasionally that one of them would go and hide behind the piles of timber, and assail Miette and Silvere with boyish jeers. The fear of being surprised amidst that general awakening of life as the season gradually grew warmer, tinged their meetings with anxiety.

Then, too, they began to stifle in the narrow lane. Never had it throbbed with so ardent a quiver; never had that soil, in which the last bones left of the former cemetery lay mouldering, sent forth such oppressive and disturbing odours. They were still too young to relish the voluptuous charm of that secluded nook which the springtide filled with fever. The grass grew to their knees, they moved to and fro with difficulty, and certain plants, when they crushed their young shoots, sent forth a pungent odour which made them dizzy. Then, seized with strange drowsiness and staggering with giddiness, their feet as though entangled in the grass, they would lean against the wall, with half-closed eyes, unable to move a step. All the soft languor from the skies seemed to penetrate them.

With the petulance of beginners, impatient and irritated at this sudden faintness, they began to think their retreat too confined, and decided to ramble through the open fields. Every evening came fresh frolics. Miette arrived with her pelisse; they wrapped themselves in it, and then, gliding past the walls, reached the high-road and the open country, the broad fields where the wind rolled with full strength, like the waves at high tide. And here they no longer felt stifled; they recovered all their youthfulness, free from the giddy intoxication born of the tall rank weeds of the Aire Saint-Mittre.

During two summers they rambled through the district. Every rock ledge, every bed of turf soon knew them; there was not a cluster of trees, a hedge, or a bush, which did not become their friend. They realized their dreams: they chased each other wildly over the meadows of Sainte-Claire, and Miette ran so well that Silvere had to put his best foot forward to catch her. Sometimes, too, they went in search of magpies' nests. Headstrong Miette, wishing to show how she had climbed trees at Chavanoz, would tie up her skirts with a piece of string, and ascend the highest poplars; while Silvere stood trembling beneath, with his arms outstretched to catch her should she slip. These frolics so turned them from thoughts of love that one evening they almost fought like a couple of lads coming out of school. But there were nooks in the country side which were not healthful for them. So long as they rambled on they were continually shouting with laughter, pushing and teasing one another. They covered miles and miles of ground; sometimes they went as far as the chain of the Garrigues, following the narrowest paths and cutting across the fields. The region belonged to them; they lived there as in a conquered territory, enjoying all that the earth and the sky could give them. Miette, with a woman's lack of scruple, did not hesitate to pluck a bunch of grapes, or a cluster of green almonds, from the vines and almond-trees whose boughs brushed her as she passed; and at this Silvere, with his absolute ideas of honesty, felt vexed, although he did not venture to find fault with the girl, whose occasional sulking distressed him. "Oh! the bad girl!" thought he, childishly exaggerating the matter, "she would make a thief of me." But Miette would thereupon force his share of the stolen fruit into his mouth. The artifices he employed, such as holding her round the waist, avoiding the fruit trees, and making her run after him when they were near the vines, so as to keep her out of the way of temptation, quickly exhausted his imagination. At last there was nothing to do but to make her sit down. And then they again began to experience their former stifling sensations. The gloomy valley of the Viorne particularly disturbed them. When weariness brought them to the banks of the torrent, all their childish gaiety seemed to disappear. A grey shadow floated under the willows, like the scented crape of a woman's dress. The children felt this crape descend warm and balmy from the voluptuous shoulders of the night, kiss their temples and envelop them with irresistible languor. In the distance the crickets chirped in the meadows of Sainte-Claire, and at their feet the ripples of the Viorne sounded like lovers' whispers—like the soft cooing of humid lips. The stars cast a rain of sparkles from the slumbering heavens. And, amidst the throbbing of the sky, the waters and the darkness, the children reposing on the grass sought each other's hands and pressed them.

Silvere, who vaguely understood the danger of these ecstasies, would sometimes jump up and propose to cross over to one of the islets left by the low water in the middle of the stream. Both ventured forth, with bare feet. Miette made light of the pebbles, refusing Silvere's help, and it once happened that she sat down in the very middle of the stream; however, there were only a few inches of water, and she escaped with nothing worse than a wet petticoat. Then, having reached the island, they threw themselves on the long neck of sand, their eyes on a level with the surface of the river whose silvery scales they saw quivering far away in the clear night. Then Miette would declare that they were in a boat, that the island was certainly floating; she could feel it carrying her along. The dizziness caused by the rippling of the water amused them for a moment, and they lingered there, singing in an undertone, like boatmen as they strike the water with their oars. At other times, when the island had a low bank, they sat there as on a bed of verdure, and let their bare feet dangle in the stream. And then for hours they chatted together, swinging their legs, and splashing the water, delighted to set a tempest raging in the peaceful pool whose freshness cooled their fever.

These footbaths suggested a dangerous idea to Miette. Nothing would satisfy her but a complete bath. A little above the bridge over the Viorne there was a very convenient spot, she said, barely three or four feet deep and quite safe; the weather was so warm, it would be so nice to have the water up to their necks; besides which, she had been dying to learn to swim for such a long time, and Silvere would be able to teach her.

Silvere raised objections; it was not prudent at night time; they might be seen; perhaps, too they might catch cold. However, nothing could turn Miette from her purpose. One evening she came with a bathing costume which she had made out of an old dress; and Silvere was then obliged to go back to aunt Dide's for his bathing drawers. Their proceedings were characterised by great simplicity. Miette disrobed herself beneath the shade of a stout willow; and when both were ready, enveloped in the blackness which fell from the foliage around them, they gaily entered the cool water, oblivious of all previous scruples, and knowing in their innocence no sense of shame. They remained in the river quite an hour, splashing and throwing water into each other's faces; Miette now getting cross, now breaking out into laughter, while Silvere gave her her first lesson, dipping her head under every now and again so as to accustom her to the water. As long as he held her up she threw her arms and legs about violently, thinking she was swimming; but directly he let her go, she cried and struggled, striking the water with her outstretched hands, clutching at anything she could get hold of, the young man's waist or one of his wrists. She leant against him for an instant, resting, out of breath and dripping with water; and then she cried: "Once more; but you do it on purpose, you don't hold me."

At the end of a fortnight, the girl was able to swim. With her limbs moving freely, rocked by the stream, playing with it, she yielded form and spirit alike to its soft motion, to the silence of the heavens, and the dreaminess of the melancholy banks. As she and Silvere swam noiselessly along, she seemed to see the foliage of both banks thicken and hang over them, draping them round as with a huge curtain. When the moon shone, its rays glided between the trunks of the trees, and phantoms seemed to flit along the river-side in white robes. Miette felt no nervousness, however, only an indefinable emotion as she followed the play of the shadows. As she went onward with slower motion, the calm water, which the moon converted into a bright mirror, rippled at her approach like a silver-broidered cloth; eddies widened and lost themselves amid the shadows of the banks, under the hanging willow branches, whence issued weird, plashing sounds. At every stroke she perceived recesses full of sound; dark cavities which she hastened to pass by;

clusters and rows of trees, whose sombre masses were continually changing form, stretching forward and apparently following her from the summit of the bank. And when she threw herself on her back, the depths of the heavens affected her still more. From the fields, from the distant horizon, which she could no longer see, a solemn lingering strain, composed of all the sighs of the night, was wafted to her.

She was not of a dreamy nature; it was physically, through the medium of each of her senses, that she derived enjoyment from the sky, the river, and the play of light and shadow. The river, in particular, bore her along with endless caresses. When she swam against the current she was delighted to feel the stream flow rapidly against her bosom and limbs. She dipped herself in it yet more deeply, with the water reaching to her lips, so that it might pass over her shoulders, and envelop her, from chin to feet, with flying kisses. Then she would float, languid and quiescent, on the surface, whilst the ripples glided softly between her costume and her skin. And she would also roll over in the still pools like a cat on a carpet; and swim from the luminous patches where the moonbeams were bathing, to the dark water shaded by the foliage, shivering the while, as though she had quitted a sunny plain and then felt the cold from the boughs falling on her neck.

She now remained quite silent in the water, and would not allow Silvere to touch her. Gliding softly by his side, she swam on with the light rustling of a bird flying across the copse, or else she would circle round him, a prey to vague disquietude which she did not comprehend. He himself darted quickly away if he happened to brush against her. The river was now but a source of enervating intoxication, voluptuous languor, which disturbed them strangely. When they emerged from their bath they felt dizzy, weary, and drowsy. Fortunately, the girl declared one evening that she would bathe no more, as the cold water made the blood run to her head. And it was in all truth and innocence that she said this.

Then their long conversations began anew. The dangers to which the innocence of their love had lately been exposed had left no other trace in Silvere's mind than great admiration for Miette's physical strength. She had learned to swim in a fortnight, and often, when they raced together, he had seen her stem the current with a stroke as rapid as his own. He, who delighted in strength and bodily exercises, felt a thrill of pleasure at seeing her so strong, so active and adroit. He entertained at heart a singular admiration for her stout arms. One evening, after one of the first baths that had left them so playful, they caught each other round the waist on a strip of sand, and wrestled for several minutes without Silvere being able to throw Miette. At last, indeed, it was the young man who lost his balance, while the girl remained standing. Her sweetheart treated her like a boy, and it was those long rambles of theirs, those wild races across the meadows, those birds' nests filched from the tree crests, those struggles and violent games of one and another kind that so long shielded them and their love from all impurity.

Then, too, apart from his youthful admiration for his sweetheart's dashing pluck, Silvere felt for her all the compassionate tenderness of a heart that ever softened towards the unfortunate. He, who could never see any forsaken creature, a poor man, or a child, walking barefooted along the dusty roads, without a throb of pity, loved Miette because nobody else loved her, because she virtually led an outcast's hard life. When he saw her smile he was deeply moved by the joy he brought her. Moreover, the child was a wildling, like himself, and they were of the same mind in hating all the gossips of the Faubourg. The dreams in which Silvere indulged in the daytime, while he plied his heavy hammer round the cartwheels in his master's shop, were full of generous enthusiasm. He fancied himself Miette's redeemer. All his reading rushed to his head; he meant to marry his sweetheart some day, in order to raise her in the eyes of the world. It was like a holy mission that he imposed upon himself, that of redeeming and saving the convict's daughter. And his head was so full of certain theories and arguments, that he did not tell himself these things in simple fashion, but became lost in perfect social mysticism; imagining rehabilitation in the form of an apotheosis in which he pictured Miette seated on a throne, at the end of the Cours Sauvaire, while the whole town prostrated itself before her, entreating her pardon and singing her praises. Happily he forgot all these fine things as soon as Miette jumped over the wall, and said to him on the high road: "Let us have a race! I'm sure you won't catch me."

However, if the young man dreamt like this of the glorification of his sweetheart, he also showed such passion for justice that he often made her weep on speaking to her about her father. In spite of the softening effect which Silvere's friendship had had upon her, she still at times gave way to angry outbreaks of temper, when all the stubbornness and rebellion latent in her nature stiffened her with scowling eyes and tightly-drawn lips. She would then contend that her father had done quite right to kill the gendarme, that the earth belongs to everybody, and that one has the right to fire a gun when and where one likes. Thereupon Silvere, in a grave voice, explained the law to her as he understood it, with strange commentaries which would have startled the whole magistracy of Plassans. These discussions took place most often in some remote corner of the Sainte-Claire meadows. The grassy carpet of a dusky green hue stretched further than they could see, undotted even by a single tree, and the sky seemed colossal, spangling the bare horizon with the stars. It seemed to the young couple as if they were being rocked on a sea of verdure. Miette argued the point obstinately; she asked Silvere if her father should have let the gendarme kill him, and Silvere, after a momentary silence, replied that, in such a case, it was better to be the victim than the murderer, and that it was a great misfortune for anyone to kill a fellow man, even in legitimate defence. The law was something holy to him, and the judges had done right in sending Chantegreil to the galleys. At this the girl grew angry, and almost struck her sweetheart, crying out that he was as heartless as the rest. And as he still firmly defended his ideas of justice, she finished by bursting into sobs, and stammering that he was doubtless ashamed of her, since he was always reminding her of her father's crime. These discussions ended in tears, in mutual emotion. But although the child cried, and acknowledged that she was perhaps wrong, she still retained deep within her a wild resentful temper. She once related, with hearty laughter, that she had seen a gendarme fall off his horse and break his leg. Apart from this, Miette only lived for Silvere. When he asked her about her uncle and cousin, she replied that "She did not know;" and if he pressed her, fearing that they were making her too unhappy at the Jas-Meiffren, she simply answered that she worked hard, and that nothing had changed. She believed, however, that Justin had at last found out what made her sing in the morning, and filled her eyes with delight. But she added: "What does it matter? If ever he comes to disturb us we'll receive him in such a way that he won't be in a hurry to meddle with our affairs any more."

Now and again the open country, their long rambles in the fresh air, wearied them somewhat. They then invariably returned to the Aire Saint-Mittre, to the narrow lane, whence they had been driven by the noisy summer evenings, the pungent scent of the trodden grass, all the warm oppressive emanations. On certain nights, however, the path proved cooler, and the winds freshened it so that they could remain there without feeling faint. They then enjoyed a feeling of delightful repose. Seated on the tombstone, deaf to the noise of the children and gipsies, they felt at home again. Silvere had on various occasions picked up fragments of bones, even pieces of skulls, and they were fond of speaking of the ancient burial-ground. It seemed to them, in their lively fancies, that their love had shot up like some vigorous plant in this nook of soil which dead men's bones had fertilised. It had grown, indeed, like those wild weeds, it had blossomed as blossom the poppies which sway like bare bleeding hearts at the slightest breeze. And they ended by fancying that the warm breaths passing over them, the whisperings heard in the gloom, the long quivering which thrilled the path, came from the dead folk sighing their departed passions in their faces, telling them the stories of their bridals, as they turned restlessly in their graves, full of a fierce longing to live and love again. Those fragments of bone, they felt convinced of it, were full of affection for them; the shattered skulls grew warm again by contact with their own youthful fire, the smallest particles surrounded them with passionate whispering, anxious solicitude, throbbing jealousy. And when they departed, the old burial-ground seemed to groan. Those weeds, in which their entangled feet often stumbled on sultry nights, were fingers, tapered by tomb life, that sprang up from the earth to detain them and cast them into each other's arms. That pungent and penetrating odour exhaled by the broken stems was the fertilising perfume, the mighty quintessence of life which is slowly elaborated in the grave, and intoxicates the lovers who wander in the solitude of the paths. The dead, the old departed dead, longed for the bridal of Miette and Silvere.

They were never afraid. The sympathy which seemed to hover around them thrilled them and made them love the invisible beings whose soft touch they often imagined they could feel, like a gentle flapping of wings. Sometimes they were saddened by sweet melancholy, and could not understand what the dead desired of them. They went on basking in their innocent love, amidst this flood of sap, this abandoned cemetery, whose rich soil teemed with life, and imperiously demanded their union. They still remained ignorant of the meaning of the buzzing voices which they heard ringing in their ears, the sudden glow which sent the blood flying to their faces.

They often questioned each other about the remains which they discovered. Miette, after a woman's fashion, was partial to lugubrious subjects. At each new discovery she launched into endless suppositions. If the bone were small, she spoke of some beautiful girl a prey to consumption, or carried off by fever on the eve of her marriage; if the bone were large, she pictured some big old man, a soldier or a judge, some one who had inspired others with terror. For a long time the tombstone particularly engaged their attention. One fine moonlight night Miette distinguished some half-obliterated letters on one side of it, and thereupon she made Silvere scrape the moss away with his knife. Then they read the mutilated inscription: "Here lieth ... Marie ... died ... " And Miette, finding her own name on the stone, was quite terror-stricken. Silvere called her a "big baby," but she could not restrain her tears. She had received a stab in the heart, she said; she would soon die, and that stone was meant for her. The young man himself felt alarmed. However, he succeeded in shaming the child out of these thoughts. What! she so courageous, to dream about such trifles! They ended by laughing. Then they avoided speaking of it again. But in melancholy moments, when the cloudy sky saddened the pathway, Miette could not help thinking of that dead one, that unknown Marie, whose tomb had so long facilitated their meetings. The poor girl's bones were perhaps still lying there. And at this thought Miette one evening had a strange whim, and asked Silvere to turn the stone over to see what might be under it. He refused, as though it were sacrilege, and his refusal strengthened Miette's fancies with regard to the dear phantom which bore her name. She positively insisted that the girl had died young, as she was, and in the very midst of her love. She even began to pity the stone, that stone which she climbed so nimbly, and on which they had sat so often, a stone which death had chilled, and which their love had warmed again.

"You'll see, this tombstone will bring us misfortune," she added. "If you were to die, I should come and lie here, and then I should like to have this stone set over my body."

At this, Silvere, choking with emotion, scolded her for thinking of such mournful things.

And so, for nearly two years, their love grew alike in the narrow pathway and the open country. Their idyll passed through the chilling rains of December and the burning solicitations of July, free from all touch of impurity, ever retaining the sweet charm of some old Greek love-tale, all the naive hesitancy of youth which desires but knows not. In vain did the long-departed dead whisper in their ears. They carried nothing away from the old cemetery but emotional melancholy and a vague presentiment of a short life. A voice seemed to whisper to them that they would depart amidst their virginal love, long ere the bridal day would give them wholly to each other. It was there, on the tombstone and among the bones that lay hidden beneath the rank grass, that they had first come to indulge in that longing for death, that eager desire to sleep together in the earth, that now set them stammering and sighing beside the Orcheres road, on that December night, while the two bells repeated their mournful warnings to one another.

Miette was sleeping calmly, with her head resting on Silvere's chest while he mused upon their past meeting, their lovely years of unbroken happiness. At daybreak the girl awoke. The valley now spread out clearly under the bright sky. The sun was still behind the hills, but a stream of crystal light, limpid and cold as spring-water, flowed from the pale horizon. In the distance, the Viorne, like a white satin ribbon, disappeared among an expanse of red and yellow land. It was a boundless vista, with grey seas of olive-trees, and vineyards that looked like huge pieces of striped cloth. The whole country was magnified by the clearness of the atmosphere and the peaceful cold. However, sharp gusts of wind chilled the young people's faces. And thereupon they sprang to their feet, cheered by the sight of the clear morning. Their melancholy forebodings had vanished with the darkness, and they gazed with delight at the immense expanse of the plain, and listened to the tolling of the two bells that now seemed to be joyfully ringing in a holiday.

"Ah! I've had a good sleep!" Miette cried. "I dreamt you were kissing me. Tell me now, did you kiss me?"

"It's very possible," Silvere replied laughing. "I was not very warm. It is bitterly cold."

"I only feel cold in the feet," Miette rejoined.

"Well! let us have a run," said Silvere. "We have still two good leagues to go. You will get warm."

Thereupon they descended the hill and ran until they reached the high road. When they were below they raised their heads as if to say farewell to that rock on which they had wept while their kisses burned their lips. But they did not again speak of that ardent embrace which had thrilled them so strongly with vague, unknown desire. Under the pretext of walking more quickly they did not even take each other's arm. They experienced some slight confusion when they looked at one another, though why they could not tell. Meantime the dawn was rising around them. The young man, who had sometimes been sent to Orcheres by his master, knew all the shortest cuts. Thus they walked on for more than two leagues, along dingle paths by the side of interminable ledges and walls. Now and again Miette accused Silvere of having taken her the wrong way; for, at times—for a quarter of an hour at a stretch—they lost all sight of the surrounding country, seeing above the walls and hedges nothing but long rows of almond-trees whose slender branches showed sharply against the pale sky.

All at once, however, they came out just in front of Orcheres. Loud cries of joy, the shouting of a crowd, sounded clearly in the limpid air. The insurrectionary forces were only now entering the town. Miette and Silvere went in with the stragglers. Never had they seen such enthusiasm. To judge from the streets, one would have thought it was a procession day, when the windows are decked with the finest drapery to honour the passage of the Canopy. The townsfolk welcomed the insurgents as though they were deliverers. The men embraced them, while the women brought them food. Old men were to be seen weeping at the doors. And the joyousness was of an essentially Southern character, pouring forth in clamorous fashion, in singing, dancing, and gesticulation. As Miette passed along she was carried away by a *farandole*[7] which spread whirling all round the Grand' Place. Silvere followed her. His thoughts of death and his discouragement were now far away. He wanted to fight, to sell his life dearly at least. The idea of a struggle intoxicated him afresh. He dreamed of victory to be followed by a happy life with Miette, amidst the peacefulness of the universal Republic.

The fraternal reception accorded them by the inhabitants of Orcheres proved to be the insurgents' last delight. They spent the day amidst radiant confidence and boundless hope. The prisoners, Commander Sicardot, Messieurs Garconnet, Peirotte and the others, who had been shut up in one of the rooms at the mayor's, the windows of which overlooked the Grand' Place, watched the *farandoles* and wild outbursts of enthusiasm with surprise and dismay.

"The villains!" muttered the Commander, leaning upon a window-bar, as though bending over the velvet-covered hand-rest of a box at a theatre: "To think that there isn't a battery or two to make a clean sweep of all that rabble!"

Then he perceived Miette, and addressing himself to Monsieur Garconnet, he added: "Do you see, sir, that big girl in red over yonder? How disgraceful! They've even brought their mistresses with them. If this continues much longer we shall see some fine goings-on."

Monsieur Garconnet shook his head, saying something about "unbridled passions," and "the most evil days of history." Monsieur Peirotte, as white as a sheet, remained silent; he only opened his lips once, to say to Sicardot, who was still bitterly railing: "Not so loud, sir; not so loud! You will get us all massacred."

7.The farandole is the popular dance of Provence.

As a matter of fact, the insurgents treated the gentlemen with the greatest kindness. They even provided them with an excellent dinner in the evening. Such attentions, however, were terrifying to such a quaker as the receiver of taxes; the insurgents he thought would not treat them so well unless they wished to make them fat and tender for the day when they might wish to devour them.

At dusk that day Silvere came face to face with his cousin, Doctor Pascal. The latter had followed the band on foot, chatting with the workmen who held him in the greatest respect. At first he had striven to dissuade them from the struggle; and then, as if convinced by their arguments, he had said to them with his kindly smile: "Well, perhaps you are right, my friends; fight if you like, I shall be here to patch up your arms and legs."

Then, in the morning he began to gather pebbles and plants along the high road. He regretted that he had not brought his geologist's hammer and botanical wallet with him. His pockets were now so full of stones that they were almost bursting, while bundles of long herbs peered forth from the surgeon's case which he carried under his arm.

"Hallo! You here, my lad?" he cried, as he perceived Silvere. "I thought I was the only member of the family here."

He spoke these last words with a touch of irony, as if deriding the intrigues of his father and his uncle Antoine. Silvere was very glad to meet his cousin; the doctor was the only one of the Rougons who ever shook hands with him in the street, and showed him any sincere friendship. Seeing him, therefore, still covered with dust from the march, the young man thought him gained over to the Republican cause, and was much delighted thereat. He talked to the doctor, with youthful magniloquence, of the people's rights, their holy cause, and their certain triumph. Pascal smiled as he listened, and watched the youth's gestures and the ardent play of his features with curiosity, as though he were studying a patient, or analysing an enthusiasm, to ascertain what might be at the bottom of it.

"How you run on! How you run on!" he finally exclaimed. "Ah! you are your grandmother's true grandson." And, in a whisper, he added, like some chemist taking notes: "Hysteria or enthusiasm, shameful madness or sublime madness. It's always those terrible nerves!" Then, again speaking aloud, as if summing up the matter, he said: "The family is complete now. It will count a hero among its members."

Silvere did not hear him. He was still talking of his dear Republic. Miette had dropped a few paces off; she was still wrapped in her large red pelisse. She and Silvere had traversed the town arm-in-arm. The sight of this tall red girl at last puzzled Pascal, and again interrupting his cousin, he asked him: "Who is this child with you?"

"She is my wife," Silvere gravely answered.

The doctor opened his eyes wide, for he did not understand. He was very shy with women; however, he raised his hat to Miette as he went away.

The night proved an anxious one. Forebodings of misfortune swept over the insurgents. The enthusiasm and confidence of the previous evening seemed to die away in the darkness. In the morning there were gloomy faces; sad looks were exchanged, followed by discouraging silence. Terrifying rumours were now circulating. Bad news, which the leaders had managed to conceal the previous evening, had spread abroad, though nobody in particular was known to have spoken. It was the work of that invisible voice, which, with a word, throws a mob into a panic. According to some reports Paris was subdued, and the provinces had offered their hands and feet, eager to be bound. And it was added that a large party of troops, which had left Marseilles under the command of Colonel Masson and Monsieur de Bleriot, the prefect of the department, was advancing by forced marches to disperse the insurrectionary bands. This news came like a thunderbolt, at once awakening rage and despair. These men, who on the previous evening had been all aglow with patriotic fever, now shivered with cold, chilled to their hearts by the shameful submissiveness of prostrate France. They alone, then, had had the courage to do their duty! And now they were to be left to perish amidst the general panic, the death-like silence of the country; they had become mere rebels, who would be hunted down like wild beasts; they, who had dreamed of a great war, of a whole nation in revolt, and of the glorious conquest of the people's rights! Miserably baffled and betrayed, this handful of men could but weep for their dead faith and their vanished dreams of justice. There were some who, while taunting France with her cowardice, flung away their arms, and sat down by the roadside, declaring that they would there await the bullets of the troops, and show how Republicans could die.

Although these men had nothing now but death or exile before them, there were very few desertions from their ranks. A splendid feeling of solidarity kept them together. Their indignation turned chiefly against their leaders, who had really proved incapable. Irreparable mistakes had been committed; and now the insurgents, without order or discipline, barely protected by a few sentries, and under the command of irresolute men, found themselves at the mercy of the first soldiers that might arrive.

They spent two more days at Orcheres, Tuesday and Wednesday, thus losing time and aggravating the situation. The general, the man with the sabre, whom Silvere had pointed out to Miette on the Plassans road, vacillated and hesitated under the terrible responsibility that weighed upon him. On Thursday he came to the conclusion that the position of Orcheres was a decidedly dangerous one; so towards one o'clock he gave orders to march, and led his little army to the heights of Sainte-Roure. That was, indeed, an impregnable position for any one who knew how to defend it. The houses of Sainte-Roure rise in tiers along a hill-side; behind the town all approach is shut off by enormous rocks, so that this kind of citadel can only be reached by the Nores plain, which spreads out at the foot of the plateau. An esplanade, converted into a public walk planted with magnificent elms, overlooks the plain. It was on this esplanade that the insurgents encamped. The hostages were imprisoned in the Hotel de la Mule-Blanche, standing half-way along the promenade. The night passed away heavy and black. The insurgents spoke of treachery. As soon as it was morning, however, the man with the sabre, who had neglected to take the simplest precautions, reviewed the troops. The contingents were drawn up in line with their backs turned to the plain. They presented a wonderful medley of costume, some wearing brown jackets, others dark greatcoats, and others again blue blouses girded with red sashes. Moreover, their arms were an equally odd collection: there were newly sharpened scythes, large navvies' spades, and fowling-pieces with burnished barrels glittering in the sunshine. And at the very moment when the improvised general was riding past the little army, a sentry, who had been forgotten in an olive-plantation, ran up gesticulating and shouting:

"The soldiers! The soldiers!"

There was indescribable emotion. At first, they thought it a false alarm. Forgetting all discipline, they rushed forward to the end of the esplanade in order to see the soldiers. The ranks were broken, and as the dark line of troops appeared, marching in perfect order with a long glitter of bayonets, on the other side of the greyish curtain of olive trees, there came a hasty and disorderly retreat, which sent a quiver of panic to the other end of the plateau. Nevertheless, the contingents of La Palud and Saint-Martin-de-Vaulx had again formed in line in the middle of the promenade, and stood there erect and fierce. A wood-cutter, who was a head taller than any of his companions, shouted, as he waved his red neckerchief: "To arms, Chavanoz, Graille, Poujols, Saint-Eutrope! To arms, Les Tulettes! To arms, Plassans!"

Crowds streamed across the esplanade. The man with the sabre, surrounded by the folks from Faverolles, marched off with several of the country contingents—Vernoux, Corbiere, Marsanne, and Pruinas—to outflank the enemy and then attack him. Other contingents, from Valqueyras, Nazere, Castel-le-Vieux, Les Roches-Noires, and Murdaran, dashed to the left, scattering themselves in skirmishing parties over the Nores plain.

And meantime the men of the towns and villages that the wood-cutter had called to his aid mustered together under the elms, there forming a dark irregular mass, grouped without regard to any of the rules of strategy, simply placed there like a rock, as it were, to bar the way or die. The men of Plassans stood in the middle of this heroic battalion. Amid the grey hues of the blouses and jackets, and the bluish glitter of the weapons, the pelisse worn by Miette, who was holding the banner with both hands, looked like a large red splotch—a fresh and bleeding wound.

All at once perfect silence fell. Monsieur Peirotte's pale face appeared at a window of the Hotel de la Mule-Blanche. And he began to speak, gesticulating with his hands.

"Go in, close the shutters," the insurgents furiously shouted; "you'll get yourself killed."

Thereupon the shutters were quickly closed, and nothing was heard save the regular, rhythmical tramp of the soldiers who were drawing near.

A minute, that seemed an age, went by. The troops had disappeared, hidden by an undulation of the ground; but over yonder, on the side of the Nores plain, the insurgents soon perceived the bayonets shooting up, one after another, like a field of steel-eared corn under the rising sun. At that moment Silvere, who was glowing with feverish agitation, fancied he could see the gendarme whose blood had stained his hands. He knew, from the accounts of his companions, that Rengade was not dead, that he had only lost an eye; and he clearly distinguished the unlucky man with his empty socket bleeding horribly. The keen recollection of this gendarme, to whom he had not given a thought since his departure from Plassans, proved unbearable. He was afraid that fear might get the better of him, and he tightened his hold on his carbine, while a mist gathered before his eyes. He felt a longing to discharge his gun and fire at the phantom of that one-eyed man so as to drive it away. Meantime the bayonets were still and ever slowly ascending.

When the heads of the soldiers appeared on a level with the esplanade, Silvere instinctively turned to Miette. She stood there with flushed face, looking taller than ever amidst the folds of the red banner; she was indeed standing on tiptoes in order to see the troops, and nervous expectation made her nostrils quiver and her red lips part so as to show her white, eager, gleaming teeth. Silvere smiled at her. But he had scarcely turned his head when a fusillade burst out. The soldiers, who could only be seen from their shoulders upwards, had just fired their first volley. It seemed to Silvere as though a great gust of wind was passing over his head, while a shower of leaves, lopped off by the bullets, fell from the elms. A sharp sound, like the snapping of a dead branch, made him look to his right. Then, prone on the ground, he saw the big wood-cutter, he who was a head taller than the others. There was a little black hole in the middle of his forehead. And thereupon Silvere fired straight before him, without taking aim, reloaded and fired again like a madman or an unthinking wild beast, in haste only to kill. He could not even distinguish the soldiers now; smoke, resembling strips of grey muslin, was floating under the elms. The leaves still rained upon the insurgents, for the troops were firing too high. Every now and then, athwart the fierce crackling of the fusillade, the young man heard a sigh or a low rattle, and a rush was made among the band as if to make room for some poor wretch clutching hold of his neighbours as he fell. The firing lasted ten minutes.

Then, between two volleys some one exclaimed in a voice of terror: "Every man for himself! *Sauve qui peut!*" This roused shouts and murmurs of rage, as if to say, "The cowards! Oh! the cowards!" sinister rumours were spreading—the general had fled; cavalry were sabring the skirmishers in the Nores plain. However, the irregular firing did not cease, every now and again sudden bursts of flame sped through the clouds of smoke. A gruff voice, the voice of terror, shouted yet louder: "Every man for himself! *Sauve qui peut!*" Some men took to flight, throwing down their weapons and leaping over the dead. The others closed their ranks. At last there were only some ten insurgents left. Two more took to flight, and of the remaining eight three were killed at one discharge.

The two children had remained there mechanically without understanding anything. As the battalion diminished in numbers, Miette raised the banner still higher in the air; she held it in front of her with clenched fists as if it were a huge taper. It was completely riddled by bullets. When Silvere had no more cartridges left in his pocket, he ceased firing, and gazed at the carbine with an air of stupor. It was then that a shadow passed over his face, as though the flapping wings of some colossal bird had brushed against his forehead. And raising his eyes he saw the banner fall from Miette's grasp. The child, her hands clasped to her breast, her head thrown back with an expression of excruciating suffering, was staggering to the ground. She did not utter a single cry, but sank at last upon the red banner.

"Get up; come quickly," Silvere said, in despair, as he held out his hand to her.

But she lay upon the ground without uttering a word, her eyes wide open. Then he understood, and fell on his knees beside her.

"You are wounded, eh? tell me? Where are you wounded?"

She still spoke no word; she was stifling, and gazing at him out of her large eyes, while short quivers shook her frame. Then he pulled away her hands.

"It's there, isn't it? it's there."

And he tore open her bodice, and laid her bosom bare. He searched, but saw nothing. His eyes were brimming with tears. At last under the left breast he perceived a small pink hole; a single drop of blood stained the wound.

"It's nothing," he whispered; "I'll go and find Pascal, he'll put you all right again. If you could only get up. Can't you move?"

The soldiers were not firing now; they had dashed to the left in pursuit of the contingents led away by the man with the sabre. And in the centre of the esplanade there only remained Silvere kneeling beside Miette's body. With the stubbornness of despair, he had taken her in his arms. He wanted to set her on her feet, but such a quiver of pain came upon the girl that he laid her down again, and said to her entreatingly: "Speak to me, pray. Why don't you say something to me?"

She could not; she slowly, gently shook her hand, as if to say that it was not her fault. Her close-pressed lips were already contracting beneath the touch of death. With her unbound hair streaming around her, and her head resting amid the folds of the blood-red banner, all her life now centred in her eyes, those black eyes glittering in her white face. Silvere sobbed. The glance of those big sorrowful eyes filled him with distress. He read in them bitter, immense regret for life. Miette was telling him that she was going away all alone, and before their bridal day; that she was leaving him ere she had become his wife. She was telling him, too, that it was he who had willed that it should be so, that he should have loved her as other lovers love their sweethearts. In the hour of her agony, amidst that stern conflict between death and her vigorous nature, she bewailed her fate in going like that to the grave. Silvere, as he bent over her, understood how bitter was the pang. He recalled their caresses, how she had hung round his neck, and had yearned for his love, but he had not understood, and now she was departing from him for evermore. Bitterly grieved at the thought that throughout her eternal rest she would remember him solely as a companion and playfellow, he kissed her on the bosom while his hot tears fell upon her lips. Those passionate kisses brought a last gleam of joy to Miette's eyes. They loved one another, and their idyll ended in death.

But Silvere could not believe she was dying. "No, you will see, it will prove only a trifle," he declared. "Don't speak if it hurts you. Wait, I will raise your head and then warm you; your hands are quite frozen."

But the fusillade had begun afresh, this time on the left, in the olive plantations. A dull sound of galloping cavalry rose from the plain. At times there were loud cries, as of men being slaughtered. And thick clouds of smoke were wafted along and hung about the elms on the esplanade. Silvere for his part no longer heard or saw anything. Pascal, who came running down in the direction of the plain, saw him stretched upon the ground, and hastened towards him, thinking he was wounded. As soon as the young man saw him, he clutched hold of him and pointed to Miette.

"Look," he said, "she's wounded, there, under the breast. Ah! how good of you to come! You will save her."

At that moment, however, a slight convulsion shook the dying girl. A pain-fraught shadow passed over her face, and as her contracted lips suddenly parted, a faint sigh escaped from them. Her eyes, still wide open, gazed fixedly at the young man.

Then Pascal, who had stooped down, rose again, saying in a low voice: "She is dead."

Dead! Silvere reeled at the sound of the word. He had been kneeling forward, but now he sank back, as though thrown down by Miette's last faint sigh.

"Dead! Dead!" he repeated; "it is not true, she is looking at me. See how she is looking at me!"

Then he caught the doctor by the coat, entreating him to remain there, assuring him that he was mistaken, that she was not dead, and that he could save her if he only would. Pascal resisted gently, saying, in his kindly voice: "I can do nothing for her, others are waiting for me. Let go, my poor child; she is quite dead."

At last Silvere released his hold and again fell back. Dead! Dead! Still that word, which rang like a knell in his dazed brain! When he was alone he crept up close to the corpse. Miette still seemed to be looking at him. He threw himself upon her, laid his head upon her bosom, and watered it with his tears. He was beside himself with grief. He pressed his lips wildly to her, and breathed out all his passion, all his soul, in one long kiss, as though in the hope that it might bring her to life again. But the girl was turning cold in spite of his caresses. He felt her lifeless and nerveless beneath his touch. Then he was seized with terror, and with haggard face and listless hanging arms he remained crouching in a state of stupor, and repeating: "She is dead, yet she is looking at me; she does not close her eyes, she sees me still."

This fancy was very sweet to him. He remained there perfectly still, exchanging a long look with Miette, in whose glance, deepened by death, he still seemed to read the girl's lament for her sad fate.

In the meantime, the cavalry were still sabring the fugitives over the Nores plain; the cries of the wounded and the galloping of the horses became more distant, softening like music wafted from afar through the clear air. Silvere was no longer conscious of the fighting. He did not even see his cousin, who mounted the slope again and crossed the promenade. Pascal, as he passed along, picked up Macquart's carbine which Silvere had thrown down; he knew it, as he had seen it hanging over aunt Dide's chimney-piece, and he thought he might as well save it from the hands of the victors. He had scarcely entered the Hotel de la Mule-Blanche, whither a large number of the wounded had been taken, when a band of insurgents, chased by the soldiers like a herd of cattle, once more rushed into the esplanade. The man with the sabre had fled; it was the last contingents from the country who were being exterminated. There was a terrible massacre. In vain did Colonel Masson and the prefect, Monsieur de Bleriot, overcome by pity, order a retreat. The infuriated soldiers continued firing upon the mass, and pinning isolated fugitives to the walls with their bayonets. When they had no more enemies before them, they riddled the facade of the Mule-Blanche with bullets. The shutters flew into splinters; one window which had been left half-open was torn out, and there was a loud rattle of broken glass. Pitiful voices were crying out from within; "The prisoners! The prisoners!" But the troops did not hear; they continued firing. All at once Commander Sicardot, growing exasperated, appeared at the door, waved his arms, and endeavoured to speak. Monsieur Peirotte, the receiver of taxes, with his slim figure and scared face, stood by his side. However, another volley was fired, and Monsieur Peirotte fell face foremost, with a heavy thud, to the ground.

Silvere and Miette were still looking at each other. Silvere had remained by the corpse, through all the fusillade and the howls of agony, without even turning his head. He was only conscious of the presence of some men around him, and, from a feeling of modesty, he drew the red banner over Miette's breast. Then their eyes still continued to gaze at one another.

The conflict, however, was at an end. The death of the receiver of taxes had satiated the soldiers. Some of these ran about, scouring every corner of the esplanade, to prevent the escape of a single insurgent. A gendarme who perceived Silvere under the trees, ran up to him, and seeing that it was a lad he had to deal with, called: "What are you doing there, youngster?"

Silvere, whose eyes were still fixed on those of Miette, made no reply.

"Ah! the bandit, his hands are black with powder," the gendarme exclaimed, as he stooped down. "Come, get up, you scoundrel! You know what you've got to expect."

Then, as Silvere only smiled vaguely and did not move, the other looked more attentively, and saw that the corpse swathed in the banner was that of a girl.

"A fine girl; what a pity!" he muttered. "Your mistress, eh? you rascal!"

Then he made a violent grab at Silvere, and setting him on his feet led him away like a dog that is dragged by one leg. Silvere submitted in silence, as quietly as a child. He just turned round to give another glance at Miette. He felt distressed at thus leaving her alone under the trees. For the last time he looked at her from afar. She was still lying there in all her purity, wrapped in the red banner, her head slightly raised, and her big eyes turned upward towards heaven.

Chapter 6

It was about five o'clock in the morning when Rougon at last ventured to leave his mother's house. The old woman had gone to sleep on a chair. He crept stealthily to the end of the Impasse Saint-Mittre. There was not a sound, not a shadow. He pushed on as far as the Porte de Rome. The gates stood wide open in the darkness that enveloped the slumbering town. Plassans was sleeping as sound as a top, quite unconscious, apparently, of the risk it was running in allowing the gates to remain unsecured. It seemed like a city of the dead. Rougon, taking courage, made his way into the Rue de Nice. He scanned from a distance the corners of each successive lane; and trembled at every door, fearing lest he should see a band of insurgents rush out upon him. However, he reached the Cours Sauvaire without any mishap. The insurgents seemed to have vanished in the darkness like a nightmare.

Pierre then paused for a moment on the deserted pavement, heaving a deep sigh of relief and triumph. So those rascals had really abandoned Plassans to him. The town belonged to him now; it slept like the foolish thing it was; there it lay, dark and tranquil, silent and confident, and he had only to stretch out his hand to take possession of it. That brief halt, the supercilious glance which he cast over the drowsy place, thrilled him with unspeakable delight. He remained there, alone in the darkness, and crossed his arms, in the attitude of a great general on the eve of a victory. He could hear nothing in the distance but the murmur of the fountains of the Cours Sauvaire, whose jets of water fell into the basins with a musical plashing.

Then he began to feel a little uneasy. What if the Empire should unhappily have been established without his aid? What if Sicardot, Garconnet, and Peirotte, instead of being arrested and led away by the insurrectionary band, had shut the rebels up in prison? A cold perspiration broke out over him, and he went on his way again, hoping that Felicite would give him some accurate information. He now pushed on more rapidly, and was skirting the houses of the Rue de la Banne, when a strange spectacle, which caught his eyes as he raised his head, riveted him to the ground. One of the windows of the yellow drawing-room was brilliantly illuminated, and, in the glare, he saw a dark form, which he recognized as that of his wife, bending forward, and shaking its arms in a violent manner. He asked himself what this could mean, but, unable to think of any explanation, was beginning to feel seriously alarmed, when some hard object bounded over the pavement at his feet. Felicite had thrown him the key of the cart-house, where he had concealed a supply of muskets. This key clearly signified that he must take up arms. So he turned away again, unable to comprehend why his wife had prevented him from going upstairs, and imagining the most horrible things.

He now went straight to Roudier, whom he found dressed and ready to march, but completely ignorant of the events of the night. Roudier lived at the far end of the new town, as in a desert, whither no tidings of the insurgents' movements had penetrated. Pierre, however, proposed to him that they should go to Granoux, whose house stood on one of the corners of the Place des Recollets, and under whose windows the insurgent contingents must have passed. The municipal councillor's servant remained for a long time parleying before consenting to admit them, and they heard poor Granoux calling from the first floor in a trembling voice:

"Don't open the door, Catherine! The streets are full of bandits."

He was in his bedroom, in the dark. When he recognised his two faithful friends he felt relieved; but he would not let the maid bring a lamp, fearing lest the light might attract a bullet. He seemed to think that the town was still full of insurgents. Lying back on an arm-chair near the window, in his pants, and with a silk handkerchief round his head, he moaned: "Ah! my friends, if you only knew!—I tried to go to bed, but they were making such a disturbance! At last I lay down in my arm-chair here. I've seen it all, everything. Such awful-looking men; a band of escaped convicts! Then they passed by again, dragging brave Commander Sicardot, worthy Monsieur Garconnet, the postmaster, and others away with them, and howling the while like cannibals!"

Rougon felt a thrill of joy. He made Granoux repeat to him how he had seen the mayor and the others surrounded by the "brigands."

"I saw it all!" the poor man wailed. "I was standing behind the blind. They had just seized Monsieur Peirotte, and I heard him saying as he passed under my window: 'Gentlemen, don't hurt me!' They were certainly maltreating him. It's abominable, abominable."

However, Roudier calmed Granoux by assuring him that the town was free. And the worthy gentleman began to feel quite a glow of martial ardour when Pierre informed him that he had come to recruit his services for the purpose of saving Plassans. These three saviours then took council together. They each re-solved to go and rouse their friends, and appoint a meeting at the cart-shed, the secret arsenal of the reactionary party. Meantime Rougon constantly bethought himself of Felicite's wild gestures, which seemed to betoken danger somewhere. Granoux, assuredly the most foolish of the three, was the first to suggest that there must be some Republicans left in the town. This proved a flash of light, and Rougon, with a feeling of conviction, reflected: "There must be something of Macquart's doing under all this."

An hour or so later the friends met again in the cart-shed, which was situated in a very lonely spot. They had glided stealthily from door to door, knocking and ringing as quietly as possible, and picking up all the men they could. However, they had only succeeded in collecting some forty, who arrived one after the other, creeping along in the dark, with the pale and drowsy countenances of men who had been violently startled from their sleep. The cart-shed, let to a cooper, was littered with old hoops and broken casks, of which there were piles in every corner. The guns were stored in the middle, in three long boxes. A taper, stuck on a piece of wood, illumined the strange scene with a flickering glimmer. When Rougon had removed the covers of the three boxes, the spectacle became weirdly grotesque. Above the fire-arms, whose barrels shown with a bluish, phosphorescent glitter, were outstretched necks and heads that bent with a sort of secret fear, while the yellow light of the taper cast shadows of huge noses and locks of stiffened hair upon the walls.

However, the reactionary forces counted their numbers, and the smallness of the total filled them with hesitation. They were only thirty-nine all told, and this adventure would mean certain death for them. A father of a family spoke of his children; others, without troubling themselves about excuses, turned towards the door. Then, however, two fresh conspirators arrived, who lived in the neighbourhood of the Town Hall, and knew for certain that there were not more than about twenty Republicans still at the mayor's. The band thereupon deliberated afresh. Forty-one against twenty—these seemed practicable conditions. So the arms were distributed amid a little trembling. It was Rougon who took them from the boxes, and each man present, as he received his gun, the barrel of which on that December night was icy cold, felt a sudden chill freeze him to his bones. The shadows on the walls assumed the clumsy postures of bewildered conscripts stretching out their fingers. Pierre closed the boxes regretfully; he left there a hundred and nine guns which he would willingly have distributed; however, he now had to divide the cartridges. Of these, there were two large barrels full in the furthest corner of the cart-shed, sufficient to defend Plassans against an army. And as this corner was dark, one of the gentlemen brought the taper near, whereupon another conspirator—a burly pork-butcher, with immense fists—grew angry, declaring that it was most imprudent to bring a light so close. They strongly approved his words, so the cartridges were distributed in the dark. They completely filled their pockets with them. Then, after they had loaded their guns, with endless precautions, they lingered there for another moment, looking at each other with suspicious eyes, or exchanging glances in which cowardly ferocity was mingled with an expression of stupidity.

In the streets they kept close to the houses, marching silently and in single file, like savages on the war-path. Rougon had insisted upon having the honour of marching at their head; the time had come when he must needs run some risk, if he wanted to see his schemes successful. Drops of perspiration poured down his forehead in spite of the cold. Nevertheless he preserved a very martial bearing. Roudier and Granoux were immediately behind him. Upon two occasions the column came to an abrupt halt. They fancied they had heard some distant sound of fighting; but it was only the jingle of the little brass shaving-dishes hanging from chains, which are used as signs by the barbers of Southern France. These dishes were gently shaking to and fro in the breeze. After each halt, the saviours of Plassans continued their stealthy march in the dark, retaining the while the mien of terrified heroes. In this manner they reached the square in front of the Town Hall. There they formed a group round Rougon, and took counsel together once more. In the facade of the building in front of them only one window was lighted. It was now nearly seven o'clock and the dawn was approaching.

After a good ten minutes' discussion, it was decided to advance as far as the door, so as to ascertain what might be the meaning of this disquieting darkness and silence. The door proved to be half open. One of the conspirators thereupon popped his head in, but quickly withdrew it, announcing that there was a man under the porch, sitting against the wall fast asleep, with a gun between his legs. Rougon, seeing a chance of commencing with a deed of valour, thereupon entered first, and, seizing the man, held him down while Roudier gagged him. This first triumph, gained in silence, singularly emboldened the little troop, who had dreamed of a murderous fusillade. And Rougon had to make imperious signs to restrain his soldiers from indulging in over-boisterous delight.

They continued their advance on tip-toes. Then, on the left, in the police guard-room, which was situated there, they perceived some fifteen men lying on camp-beds and snoring, amid the dim glimmer of a lantern hanging from the wall. Rougon, who was decidedly becoming a great general, left half of his men in front of the guard-room with orders not to rouse the sleepers, but to watch them and make them prisoners if they stirred. He was personally uneasy about the lighted window which they had seen from the square. He still scented Macquart's hand in the business, and, as he felt that he would first have to make prisoners of those who were watching upstairs, he was not sorry to be able to adopt surprise tactics before the noise of a conflict should impel them to barricade themselves in the first-floor rooms. So he went up quietly, followed by the twenty heroes whom he still had at his disposal. Roudier commanded the detachment remaining in the courtyard.

As Rougon had surmised, it was Macquart who was comfortably installed upstairs in the mayor's office. He sat in the mayor's arm-chair, with his elbows on the mayor's writing-table. With the characteristic confidence of a man of coarse intellect, who is absorbed by a fixed idea and bent upon his own triumph, he had imagined after the departure of the insurgents that Plassans was now at his complete disposal, and that he would be able to act there like a conqueror. In his opinion that body of three thousand men who had just passed through the town was an invincible army, whose mere proximity would suffice to keep the bourgeois humble and docile in his hands. The insurgents had imprisoned the gendarmes in their barracks, the National Guard was already dismembered, the nobility must be quaking with terror, and the retired citizens of the new town had certainly never handled a gun in their lives. Moreover, there were no arms any more than there were soldiers. Thus Macquart did not even take the precaution to have the gates shut. His men carried their confidence still further by falling asleep, while he calmly awaited the dawn which he fancied would attract and rally all the Republicans of the district round him.

He was already meditating important revolutionary measures; the nomination of a Commune of which he would be the chief, the imprisonment of all bad patriots, and particularly of all such persons as had incurred his displeasure. The thought of the baffled Rougons and their yellow drawing-room, of all that clique entreating him for mercy, thrilled him with exquisite pleasure. In order to while away the time he resolved to issue a proclamation to the inhabitants of Plassans. Four of his party set to work to draw up this proclamation, and when it was finished Macquart, assuming a dignified manner in the mayor's arm-chair, had it read to him before sending it to the printing office of the "Independant," on whose patriotism he reckoned. One of the writers was commencing, in an emphatic voice, "Inhabitants of Plassans, the hour of independence has struck, the reign of justice has begun——" when a noise was heard at the door of the office, which was slowly pushed open.

"Is it you, Cassoute?" Macquart asked, interrupting the perusal.

Nobody answered; but the door opened wider.

"Come in, do!" he continued, impatiently. "Is my brigand of a brother at home?"

Then, all at once both leaves of the door were violently thrown back and slammed against the walls, and a crowd of armed men, in the midst of whom marched Rougon, with his face very red and his eyes starting out of their sockets, swarmed into the office, brandishing their guns like cudgels.

"Ah! the blackguards, they're armed!" shouted Macquart.

He was about to seize a pair of pistols which were lying on the writing-table, when five men caught hold of him by the throat and held him in check. The four authors of the proclamation struggled for an instant. There was a good deal of scuffling and stamping, and a noise of persons falling. The combatants were greatly hampered by their guns, which they would not lay aside, although they could not use them. In the struggle, Rougon's weapon, which an insurgent had tried to wrest from him, went off of itself with a frightful report, and filled the room with smoke. The bullet shattered a magnificent mirror that reached from the mantelpiece to the ceiling, and was reputed to be one of the finest mirrors in the town. This shot, fired no one knew why, deafened everybody, and put an end to the battle.

Then, while the gentlemen were panting and puffing, three other reports were heard in the courtyard. Granoux immediately rushed to one of the windows. And as he and the others anxiously leaned out, their faces lengthened perceptibly, for they were in nowise eager for a struggle with the men in the guard-room, whom they had forgotten amidst their triumph. However, Roudier cried out from below that all was right. And Granoux then shut the window again, beaming with joy. The fact of the matter was, that Rougon's shot had aroused the sleepers, who had promptly surrendered, seeing that resistance was impossible. Then, however, three of Roudier's men, in their blind haste to get the business over, had discharged their firearms in the air, as a sort of answer to the report from above, without knowing quite why they did so. It frequently happens that guns go off of their own accord when they are in the hands of cowards.

And now, in the room upstairs, Rougon ordered Macquart's hands to be bound with the bands of the large green curtains which hung at the windows. At this, Macquart, wild with rage, broke into scornful jeers. "All right; go on," he muttered. "This evening or to-morrow, when the others return, we'll settle accounts!"

This allusion to the insurrectionary forces sent a shudder to the victors' very marrow; Rougon for his part almost choked. His brother, who was exasperated at having been surprised like a child by these terrified bourgeois, who, old soldier that he was, he disdainfully looked upon as good-for-nothing civilians, defied him with a glance of the bitterest hatred.

"Ah! I can tell some pretty stories about you, very pretty ones!" the rascal exclaimed, without removing his eyes from the retired oil merchant. "Just send me before the Assize Court, so that I may tell the judge a few tales that will make them laugh."

At this Rougon turned pale. He was terribly afraid lest Macquart should blab then and there, and ruin him in the esteem of the gentlemen who had just been assisting him to save Plassans. These gentlemen, astounded by the dramatic encounter between the two brothers, and, foreseeing some stormy passages, had retired to a corner of the room. Rougon, however, formed a heroic resolution. He advanced towards the group, and in a very proud tone exclaimed: "We will keep this man here. When he has reflected on his position he will be able to give us some useful information." Then, in a still more dignified voice, he went on: "I will discharge my duty, gentlemen. I have sworn to save the town from anarchy, and I will save it, even should I have to be the executioner of my nearest relative."

One might have thought him some old Roman sacrificing his family on the altar of his country. Granoux, who felt deeply moved, came to press his hand with a tearful countenance, which seemed to say: "I understand you; you are sublime!" And then he did him the kindness to take everybody away, under the pretext of conducting the four other prisoners into the courtyard.

When Pierre was alone with his brother, he felt all his self-possession return to him. "You hardly expected me, did you?" he resumed. "I understand things now; you have been laying plots against me. You wretched fellow; see what your vices and disorderly life have brought you to!"

Macquart shrugged his shoulders. "Shut up," he replied; "go to the devil. You're an old rogue. He laughs best who laughs last."

Thereupon Rougon, who had formed no definite plan with regard to him, thrust him into a dressing-room whither Monsieur Garconnet retired to rest sometimes. This room lighted from above, had no other means of exit than the doorway by which one entered. It was furnished with a few arm-chairs, a sofa, and a marble wash-stand. Pierre double-locked the door, after partially unbinding his brother's hands. Macquart was then heard to throw himself on the sofa, and start singing the "Ca Ira" in a loud voice, as though he were trying to sing himself to sleep.

Rougon, who at last found himself alone, now in his turn sat down in the mayor's arm-chair. He heaved a sigh as he wiped his brow. How hard, indeed, it was to win fortune and honours! However, he was nearing the end at last. He felt the soft seat of the arm-chair yield beneath him, while with a mechanical movement he caressed the mahogany writing-table with his hands, finding it apparently quite silky and delicate, like the skin of a beautiful woman. Then he spread himself out, and assumed the dignified attitude which Macquart had previously affected while listening to the proclamation. The silence of the room seemed fraught with religious solemnity, which inspired Rougon with exquisite delight. Everything, even the dust and the old documents lying in the corners, seemed to exhale an odour of incense, which rose to his dilated nostrils. This room, with its faded hangings redolent of petty transactions, all the trivial concerns of a third-rate municipality, became a temple of which he was the god.

Nevertheless, amidst his rapture, he started nervously at every shout from Macquart. The words aristocrat and lamp-post, the threats of hanging that form the refrain of the famous revolutionary song, the "Ca Ira," reached him in angry bursts, interrupting his triumphant dream in the most disagreeable manner. Always that man! And his dream, in which he saw Plassans at his feet, ended with a sudden vision of the Assize Court, of the judges, the jury, and the public listening to Macquart's disgraceful revelations; the story of the fifty thousand francs, and many other unpleasant matters; or else, while enjoying the softness of Monsieur Garconnet's arm-chair, he suddenly pictured himself suspended from a lamp-post in the Rue de la Banne. Who would rid him of that wretched fellow? At last Antoine fell asleep, and then Pierre enjoyed ten good minutes' pure ecstasy.

Roudier and Granoux came to rouse him from this state of beatitude. They had just returned from the prison, whither they had taken the insurgents. Daylight was coming on apace, the town would soon be awake, and it was necessary to take some decisive step. Roudier declared that, before anything else, it would be advisable to issue a proclamation to the inhabitants. Pierre was, at that moment, reading the one which the insurgents had left upon the table.

"Why," cried he, "this will suit us admirably! There are only a few words to be altered."

And, in fact, a quarter of an hour sufficed for the necessary changes, after which Granoux read out, in an earnest voice: "Inhabitants of Plassans—The hour of resistance has struck, the reign of order has returned——"

It was decided that the proclamation should be printed at the office of the "Gazette," and posted at all the street corners.

"Now listen," said Rougon; "we'll go to my house; and in the meantime Monsieur Granoux will assemble here the members of the municipal council who had not been arrested and acquaint them with the terrible events of the night." Then he added, majestically: "I am quite prepared to accept the responsibility of my actions. If what I have already done appears a satisfactory pledge of my desire for order, I am willing to place myself at the head of a municipal commission, until such time as the regular authorities can be reinstated. But, in order, that nobody may accuse me of ambitious designs, I shall not reenter the Town Hall unless called upon to do so by my fellow-citizens."

At this Granoux and Roudier protested that Plassans would not be ungrateful. Their friend had indeed saved the town. And they recalled all that he had done for the cause of order: the yellow drawing-room always open to the friends of authority, his services as spokesman in the three quarters of the town, the store of arms which had been his idea, and especially that memorable night—that night of prudence and heroism—in which he had rendered himself forever illustrious. Granoux added that he felt sure of the admiration and gratitude of the municipal councillors.

"Don't stir from your house," he concluded; "I will come and fetch you to lead you back in triumph."

Then Roudier said that he quite understood the tact and modesty of their friend, and approved it. Nobody would think of accusing him of ambition, but all would appreciate the delicacy which prompted him to take no office save with the consent of his fellow-citizens. That was very dignified, very noble, altogether grand.

Under this shower of eulogies, Rougon humbly bowed his head. "No, no; you go too far," he murmured, with voluptuous thrillings of exquisite pleasure. Each sentence that fell from the retired hosier and the old almond-merchant, who stood on his right and left respectively, fell sweetly on his ears; and, leaning back in the mayor's arm-chair, steeped in the odour of officiality which pervaded the room, he bowed to the right and to the left, like a royal pretender whom a *coup d'etat* is about to convert into an emperor.

When they were tired of belauding each other, they all three went downstairs. Granoux started off to call the municipal council together, while Roudier told Rougon to go on in front, saying that he would join him at his house, after giving the necessary orders for guarding the Town Hall. The dawn was now fast rising, and Pierre proceeded to the Rue de la Banne, tapping his heels in a martial manner on the still deserted pavement. He carried his hat in his hand in spite of the bitter cold; for puffs of pride sent all his blood to his head.

On reaching his house he found Cassoute at the bottom of the stairs. The navvy had not stirred, for he had seen nobody enter. He sat there, on the first step, resting his big head in his hands, and gazing fixedly in front of him, with the vacant stare and mute stubbornness of a faithful dog.

"You were waiting for me, weren't you?" Pierre said to him, taking in the situation at a glance. "Well, go and tell Monsieur Macquart that I've come home. Go and ask for him at the Town Hall."

Cassoute rose and took himself off, with an awkward bow. He was going to get himself arrested like a lamb, to the great delight of Pierre, who laughed as he went upstairs, asking himself, with a feeling of vague surprise: "I have certainly plenty of courage; shall I turn out as good a diplomatist?"

Felicite had not gone to bed last night. He found her dressed in her Sunday clothes, wearing a cap with lemon-coloured ribbons, like a lady expecting visitors. She had sat at the window in vain; she had heard nothing, and was dying with curiosity.

"Well?" she asked, rushing to meet her husband.

The latter, quite out of breath, entered the yellow drawing-room, whither she followed him, carefully closing the door behind her. He sank into an arm-chair, and, in a gasping voice, faltered: "It's done; we shall get the receivership."

At this she fell on his neck and kissed him.

"Really? Really?" she cried. "But I haven't heard anything. Oh, my darling husband, do tell me; tell me all!"

She felt fifteen years old again, and began to coax him and whirl round him like a grasshopper fascinated by the light and heat. And Pierre, in the effusion of his triumph, poured out his heart to her. He did not omit a single detail. He even explained his future projects, forgetting that, according to his theories, wives were good for nothing, and that his must be kept in complete ignorance of what went on if he wished to remain master. Felicite leant over him and drank in his words. She made him repeat certain parts of his story, declaring she had not heard; in fact, her delight bewildered her so much that at times she seemed quite deaf. When Pierre related the events at the Town Hall, she burst into a fit of laughter, changed her chair three times, and moved the furniture about, quite unable to sit still. After forty years of continuous struggle, fortune had at last yielded to them. Eventually she became so mad over it that she forgot all prudence.

"It's to me you owe all this!" she exclaimed, in an outburst of triumph. "If I hadn't looked after you, you would have been nicely taken in by the insurgents. You booby, it was Garconnet,

Sicardot, and the others, that had got to be thrown to those wild beasts."

Then, showing her teeth, loosened by age, she added, with a girlish smile: "Well, the Republic for ever! It has made our path clear."

But Pierre had turned cross. "That's just like you!" he muttered; "you always fancy that you've foreseen everything. It was I who had the idea of hiding myself. As though women understood anything about politics! Bah, my poor girl, if you were to steer the bark we should very soon be shipwrecked."

Felicite bit her lip. She had gone too far and forgotten her self-assigned part of good, silent fairy. Then she was seized with one of those fits of covert exasperation, which she generally experienced when her husband tried to crush her with his superiority. And she again promised herself, when the right time should arrive, some exquisite revenge, which would deliver this man into her power, bound hand and foot.

"Ah! I was forgetting!" resumed Rougon, "Monsieur Peirotte is amongst them. Granoux saw him struggling in the hands of the insurgents."

Felicite gave a start. She was just at that moment standing at the window, gazing with longing eyes at the house where the receiver of taxes lived. She had felt a desire to do so, for in her mind the idea of triumph was always associated with envy of that fine house.

"So Monsieur Peirotte is arrested!" she exclaimed in a strange tone as she turned round.

For an instant she smiled complacently; then a crimson blush rushed to her face. A murderous wish had just ascended from the depths of her being. "Ah! if the insurgents would only kill him!"

Pierre no doubt read her thoughts in her eyes.

"Well, if some ball were to hit him," he muttered, "our business would be settled. There would be no necessity to supercede him, eh? and it would be no fault of ours."

But Felicite shuddered. She felt that she had just condemned a man to death. If Monsieur Peirotte should now be killed, she would always see his ghost at night time. He would come and haunt her. So she only ventured to cast furtive glances, full of fearful delight, at the unhappy man's windows. Henceforward all her enjoyment would be fraught with a touch of guilty terror.

Moreover, Pierre, having now poured out his soul, began to perceive the other side of the situation. He mentioned Macquart. How could they get rid of that blackguard? But Felicite, again fired with enthusiasm, exclaimed: "Oh! one can't do everything at once. We'll gag him, somehow. We'll soon find some means or other."

She was now walking to and fro, putting the arm-chairs in order, and dusting their backs. Suddenly, she stopped in the middle of the room, and gave the faded furniture a long glance.

"Good Heavens!" she said, "how ugly it is here! And we shall have everybody coming to call upon us!"

"Bah!" replied Pierre, with supreme indifference, "we'll alter all that."

He who, the night before, had entertained almost religious veneration for the arm-chairs and the sofa, would now have willingly stamped on them. Felicite, who felt the same contempt, even went so far as to upset an arm-chair which was short of a castor and did not yield to her quickly enough.

It was at this moment that Roudier entered. It at once occurred to the old woman that he had become much more polite. His "Monsieur" and "Madame" rolled forth in delightfully musical fashion. But the other habitues were now arriving one after the other; and the drawing-room was fast getting full. Nobody yet knew the full particulars of the events of the night, and all had come in haste, with wondering eyes and smiling lips, urged on by the rumours which were beginning to circulate through the town. These gentlemen who, on the previous evening, had left the drawing-room with such precipitation at the news of the insurgents' approach, came back, inquisitive and importunate, like a swarm of buzzing flies which a puff of wind would have dispersed. Some of them had not even taken time to put on their braces. They were very impatient, but it was evident that Rougon was waiting for some one else before speaking out. He constantly turned an anxious look towards the door. For an hour there was only significant hand-shaking, vague congratulation, admiring whispering, suppressed joy of uncertain origin, which only awaited a word of enlightenment to turn to enthusiasm.

At last Granoux appeared. He paused for a moment on the threshold, with his right hand pressed to his breast between the buttons of his frock-coat; his broad pale face was beaming; in vain he strove to conceal his emotion beneath an expression of dignity. All the others became silent on perceiving him; they felt that something extraordinary was about to take place. Granoux walked straight up to Rougon, through two lines of visitors, and held out his hand to him.

"My friend," he said, "I bring you the homage of the Municipal Council. They call you to their head, until our mayor shall be restored to us. You have saved Plassans. In the terrible crisis through which we are passing we want men who, like yourself, unite intelligence with courage. Come—"

At this point Granoux, who was reciting a little speech which he had taken great trouble to prepare on his way from the Town Hall to the Rue de la Banne felt his memory fail him. But Rougon, overwhelmed with emotion, broke in, shaking his hand and repeating: "Thank you, my dear Granoux; I thank you very much."

He could find nothing else to say. However, a loud burst of voices followed. Every one rushed upon him, tried to shake hands, poured forth praises and compliments, and eagerly questioned him. But he, already putting on official dignity, begged for a few minutes' delay in order that he might confer with Messieurs Granoux and Roudier. Business before everything. The town was in such a critical situation! Then the three accomplices retired to a corner of the drawing-room, where, in an undertone, they divided power amongst themselves; the rest of the visitors, who remained a few paces away, trying meanwhile to look extremely wise and furtively glancing at them with mingled admiration and curiosity. It was decided that Rougon should take the title of president of the Municipal Commission; Granoux was to be secretary; whilst, as for Roudier, he became commander-in-chief of the reorganised National Guard. They also swore to support each other against all opposition.

However, Felicite, who had drawn near, abruptly inquired: "And Vuillet?"

At this they looked at each other. Nobody had seen Vuillet. Rougon seemed somewhat uneasy.

"Perhaps they've taken him away with the others," he said, to ease his mind.

But Felicite shook her head. Vuillet was not the man to let himself be arrested. Since nobody had seen or heard him, it was certain he had been doing something wrong.

Suddenly the door opened and Vuillet entered, bowing humbly, with blinking glance and stiff sacristan's smile. Then he held out his moist hand to Rougon and the two others.

Vuillet had settled his little affairs alone. He had cut his own slice out of the cake, as Felicite would have said. While peeping through the ventilator of his cellar he had seen the insurgents arrest the postmaster, whose offices were near his bookshop. At daybreak, therefore, at the moment when Rougon was comfortably seated in the mayor's arm-chair, he had quietly installed himself in the postmaster's office. He knew the clerks; so he received them on their arrival, told them that he would replace their chief until his return, and that meantime they need be in nowise uneasy. Then he ransacked the morning mail with ill-concealed curiosity. He examined the letters, and seemed to be seeking a particular one. His new berth doubtless suited his secret plans, for his satisfaction became so great that he actually gave one of the clerks a copy of the "Oeuvres Badines de Piron." Vuillet, it should be mentioned, did business in objectionable literature, which he kept concealed in a large drawer, under the stock of heads and religious images. It is probable that he felt some slight qualms at the free-and-easy manner in which he had taken possession of the post office, and recognised the desirability of getting his usurpation confirmed as far as possible. At all events, he had thought it well to call upon Rougon, who was fast becoming an important personage.

"Why! where have you been?" Felicite asked him in a distrustful manner.

Thereupon he related his story with sundry embellishments. According to his own account he had saved the post-office from pillage.

"All right then! That's settled! Stay on there!" said Pierre, after a moment's reflection. "Make yourself useful."

This last sentence revealed the one great fear that possessed the Rougons. They were afraid that some one might prove too useful, and do more than themselves to save the town. Still, Pierre saw no serious danger in leaving Vuillet as provisional postmaster; it was even a convenient means of getting rid of him. Felicite, however, made a sharp gesture of annoyance.

The consultation having ended, the three accomplices mingled with the various groups that filled the drawing-room. They were at last obliged to satisfy the general curiosity by giving detailed accounts of recent events. Rougon proved magnificent. He exaggerated, embellished, and dramatised the story which he had related to his wife. The distribution of the guns and cartridges made everybody hold their breath. But it was the march through the deserted streets and the seizure of the town-hall that most amazed these worthy bourgeois. At each fresh detail there was an interruption.

"And you were only forty-one; it's marvellous!"

"Ah, indeed! it must have been frightfully dark!"

"No; I confess I never should have dared it!"

"Then you seized him, like that, by the throat?

"And the insurgents, what did they say?"

These remarks and questions only incited Rougon's imagination the more. He replied to everybody. He mimicked the action. This stout man, in his admiration of his own achievements, became as nimble as a schoolboy; he began afresh, repeated himself, amidst the exclamations of surprise and individual discussions which suddenly arose about some trifling detail. And thus he continued blowing his trumpet, making himself more and more important as if some irresistible force impelled him to turn his narrative into a genuine epic. Moreover Granoux and Roudier stood by his side prompting him, reminding him of such trifling matters as he omitted. They also were burning to put in a word, and occasionally they could not restrain themselves, so that all three went on talking together. When, in order to keep the episode of the broken mirror for the denouement, like some crowning glory, Rougon began to describe what had taken place downstairs in the courtyard, after the arrest of the guard, Roudier accused him of spoiling the narrative by changing the sequence of events. For a moment they wrangled about it somewhat sharply. Then Roudier, seeing a good opportunity for himself, suddenly exclaimed: "Very well, let it be so. But you weren't there. So let me tell it."

He thereupon explained at great length how the insurgents had awoke, and how the muskets of the town's deliverers had been levelled at them to reduce them to impotence. He added, however, that no blood, fortunately, had been shed. This last sentence disappointed his audience, who had counted upon one corpse at least.

"But I thought you fired," interrupted Felicite, recognising that the story was wretchedly deficient in dramatic interest.

"Yes, yes, three shots," resumed the old hosier. "The pork-butcher Dubruel, Monsieur Lievin, and Monsieur Massicot discharged their guns with really culpable alacrity." And as there were some murmurs at this remark; "Culpable, I repeat the word," he continued. "There are quite enough cruel necessities in warfare without any useless shedding of blood. Besides, these gentlemen swore to me that it was not their fault; they can't understand how it was their guns went off. Nevertheless, a spent ball after ricocheting grazed the cheek of one of the insurgents and left a mark on it."

This graze, this unexpected wound, satisfied the audience. Which cheek, right or left, had been grazed, and how was it that a bullet, a spent one, even, could strike a cheek without piercing it? These points supplied material for some long discussions.

"Meantime," continued Rougon at the top of his voice, without giving time for the excitement to abate; "meantime we had plenty to do upstairs. The struggle was quite desperate."

Then he described, at length, the arrival of his brother and the four other insurgents, without naming Macquart, whom he simply called "the leader." The words, "the mayor's office," "the mayor's arm-chair," "the mayor's writing table," recurred to him every instant, and in the opinion of his audience imparted marvellous grandeur to the terrible scene. It was not at the porter's lodge that the fight was now being waged, but in the private sanctum of the chief magistrate of the town. Roudier was quite cast in to the background. Then Rougon at last came to the episode which he had been keeping in reserve from the commencement, and which would certainly exalt him to the dignity of a hero.

"Thereupon," said he, "an insurgent rushes upon me. I push the mayor's arm-chair away, and seize the man by the throat. I hold him tightly, you may be sure of it! But my gun was in my way. I didn't want to let it drop; a man always sticks to his gun. I held it, like this, under the left arm. All of a sudden, it went off—"

The whole audience hung on Rougon's lips. But Granoux, who was opening his mouth wide with a violent itching to say something, shouted: "No, no, that isn't right. You were not in a position to see things, my friend; you were fighting like a lion. But I saw everything, while I was helping to bind one of the prisoners. The man tried to murder you; it was he who fired the gun; I saw him distinctly slip his black fingers under your arm."

"Really?" said Rougon, turning quite pale.

He did not know he had been in such danger, and the old almond merchant's account of the incident chilled him with fright. Granoux, as a rule, did not lie; but, on a day of battle, it is surely allowable to view things dramatically.

"I tell you the man tried to murder you," he repeated, with conviction.

"Ah," said Rougon in a faint voice, "that's how it is I heard the bullet whiz past my ear!"

At this, violent emotion came upon the audience. Everybody gazed at the hero with respectful awe. He had heard a bullet whiz past his ear! Certainly, none of the other bourgeois who were there could say as much. Felicite felt bound to rush into her husband's arms so as to work up the emotion to boiling point. But Rougon immediately freed himself, and concluded his narrative with this heroic sentence, which has become famous at Plassans: "The shot goes off; I hear the bullet whiz past my ear; and whish! it smashes the mayor's mirror."

This caused complete consternation. Such a magnificent mirror, too! It was scarcely credible! the damage done to that looking-glass almost out-balanced Rougon's heroism, in the estimation of the company. The glass became an object of absorbing interest, and they talked about it for a quarter of an hour, with many exclamations and expressions of regret, as though it had been some dear friend that had been stricken to the heart. This was the culminating point that Rougon had aimed at, the denouement of his wonderful Odyssey. A loud hubbub of voices filled the yellow drawing-room. The visitors were repeating what they had just heard, and every now and then one of them would leave a group to ask the three heroes the exact truth with regard to some contested incident. The heroes set the matter right with scrupulous minuteness, for they felt that they were speaking for history!

At last Rougon and his two lieutenants announced that they were expected at the town-hall. Respectful silence was then restored, and the company smiled at each other discreetly. Granoux was swelling with importance. He was the only one who had seen the insurgent pull the trigger and smash the mirror; this sufficed to exalt him, and almost made him burst his skin. On leaving the drawing-room, he took Roudier's arm with the air of a great general who is broken down with fatigue. "I've been up for thirty-six hours," he murmured, "and heaven alone knows when I shall get to bed!"

Rougon, as he withdrew, took Vuillet aside and told him that the party of order relied more than ever on him and the "Gazette." He would have to publish an effective article to reassure the inhabitants and treat the band of villains who had passed through Plassans as it deserved.

"Be easy!" replied Vuillet. "In the ordinary course the 'Gazette' ought not to appear till to-morrow morning, but I'll issue it this very evening."

When the leaders had left, the rest of the visitors remained in the yellow drawing-room for another moment, chattering like so many old women, whom the escape of a canary has gathered together on the pavement. These retired tradesmen, oil dealers, and wholesale hatters, felt as if they were in a sort of fairyland. Never had they experienced such thrilling excitement before. They could not get over their surprise at discovering such heroes as Rougon, Granoux, and Roudier in their midst. At last, half stifled by the stuffy atmosphere, and tired of ever telling each other the same things, they decided to go off and spread the momentous news abroad. They glided away one by one, each anxious to have the glory of being the first to know and relate everything, and Felicite, as she leaned out of the window, on being left alone, saw them dispersing in the Rue de la Banne, waving their arms in an excited manner, eager as they were to diffuse emotion to the four corners of the town.

It was ten o'clock, and Plassans, now wide awake, was running about the streets, wildly excited by the reports which were circulating. Those who had seen or heard the insurrectionary forces, related the most foolish stories, contradicting each other, and indulging in the wildest suppositions. The majority, however, knew nothing at all about the matter; they lived at the further end of the town, and listened with gaping mouths, like children to a nursery tale, to the stories of how several thousand bandits had invaded the streets during the night and vanished before daybreak like an army of phantoms. A few of the most sceptical said: "Nonsense!" Yet some of the details were very precise; and Plassans at last felt convinced that some frightful danger had passed over it while it slept. The darkness which had shrouded this danger, the various contradictory reports that spread, all invested the matter with mystery and vague horror, which made the bravest shudder. Whose hand had diverted the thunderbolt from them? There seemed to be something quite miraculous about it. There were rumours of unknown deliverers, of a handful of brave men who had cut off the hydra's head; but no one seemed acquainted with the exact particulars, and the whole story appeared scarcely credible, until the company from the yellow drawing-room spread through the streets, scattering tidings, ever repeating the same narrative at each door they came to.

It was like a train of powder. In a few minutes the story had spread from one end of the town to the other. Rougon's name flew from mouth to mouth, with exclamations of surprise in the new town, and of praise in the old quarter. The idea of being without a sub-prefect, a mayor, a postmaster, a receiver of taxes, or authorities of any kind, at first threw the inhabitants into consternation. They were stupefied at having been able to sleep through the night and get up as usual, in the absence of any settled government. Their first stupor over, they threw themselves recklessly into the arms of their liberators. The few Republicans shrugged their shoulders, but the petty shopkeepers, the small householders, the Conservatives of all shades, invoked blessings on those modest heroes whose achievements had been shrouded by the night. When it was known that Rougon had arrested his own brother, the popular admiration knew no bounds. People talked of Brutus, and thus the indiscretion which had made Pierre rather anxious, really redounded to his glory. At this moment when terror still hovered over them, the townsfolk were virtually unanimous in their gratitude. Rougon was accepted as their saviour without the slightest show of opposition.

"Just think of it!" the poltroons exclaimed, "there were only forty-one of them!"

That number of forty-one amazed the whole town, and this was the origin of the Plassans legend of how forty-one bourgeois had made three thousand insurgents bite the dust. There were only a few envious spirits of the new town, lawyers without work and retired military men ashamed of having slept ingloriously through that memorable night, who raised any doubts. The insurgents, these sceptics hinted, had no doubt left the town of their own accord. There were no indications of a combat, no corpses, no blood-stains. So the deliverers had certainly had a very easy task.

"But the mirror, the mirror!" repeated the enthusiasts. "You can't deny that the mayor's mirror has been smashed; go and see it for yourselves."

And, in fact, until night-time, quite a stream of town's-people flowed, under one pretext or another, into the mayor's private office, the door of which Rougon left wide open. The visitors planted themselves in front of the mirror, which the bullet had pierced and starred, and they all gave vent to the same exclamation: "By Jove; that ball must have had terrible force!"

Then they departed quite convinced.

Felicite, at her window, listened with delight to all the rumours and laudatory and grateful remarks which arose from the town. At that moment all Plassans was talking of her husband. She felt that the two districts below her were quivering, wafting her the hope of approaching triumph. Ah! how she would crush that town which she had been so long in getting beneath her feet! All her grievances crowded back to her memory, and her past disappointments redoubled her appetite for immediate enjoyment.

At last she left the window, and walked slowly round the drawing-room. It was there that, a little while previously, everybody had held out their hands to her husband and herself. He and she had conquered; the citizens were at their feet. The yellow drawing-room seemed to her a holy place. The dilapidated furniture, the frayed velvet, the chandelier soiled with fly-marks, all those poor wrecks now seemed to her like the glorious bullet-riddled debris of a battle-field. The plain of Austerlitz would not have stirred her to deeper emotion.

When she returned to the window, she perceived Aristide wandering about the place of the Sub-Prefecture, with his nose in the air. She beckoned to him to come up, which he immediately did. It seemed as if he had only been waiting for this invitation.

"Come in," his mother said to him on the landing, seeing that he hesitated. "Your father is not here."

Aristide evinced all the shyness of a prodigal son returning home. He had not been inside the yellow drawing-room for nearly four years. He still carried his arm in a sling.

"Does your hand still pain you?" his mother asked him, ironically.

He blushed as he answered with some embarrassment: "Oh! it's getting better; it's nearly well again now."

Then he lingered there, loitering about and not knowing what to say. Felicite came to the rescue. "I suppose you've heard them talking about your father's noble conduct?" she resumed.

He replied that the whole town was talking of it. And then, as he regained his self-possession, he paid his mother back for her raillery in her own coin. Looking her full in the face he added: "I came to see if father was wounded."

"Come, don't play the fool!" cried Felicite, petulantly. "If I were you I would act boldly and decisively. Confess now that you made a false move in joining those good-for-nothing Republicans. You would be very glad, I'm sure, to be well rid of them, and to return to us, who are the stronger party. Well, the house is open to you!"

But Aristide protested. The Republic was a grand idea. Moreover, the insurgents might still carry the day.

"Don't talk nonsense to me!" retorted the old woman, with some irritation. "You're afraid that your father won't have a very warm welcome for you. But I'll see to that. Listen to me: go back to your newspaper, and, between now and to-morrow, prepare a number strongly favouring the Coup d'Etat. To-morrow evening, when this number has appeared, come back here and you will be received with open arms."

Then seeing that the young man remained silent: "Do you hear?" she added, in a lower and more eager tone; "it is necessary for our sake, and for your own, too, that it should be done. Don't let us have any more nonsense and folly. You've already compromised yourself enough in that way."

The young man made a gesture—the gesture of a Caesar crossing the Rubicon—and by doing so escaped entering into any verbal engagement. As he was about to withdraw, his mother, looking for the knot in his sling, remarked: "First of all, you must let me take off this rag. It's getting a little ridiculous, you know!"

Aristide let her remove it. When the silk handkerchief was untied, he folded it neatly and placed it in his pocket. And as he kissed his mother he exclaimed: "Till to-morrow then!"

In the meanwhile, Rougon was taking official possession of the mayor's offices. There were only eight municipal councillors left; the others were in the hands of the insurgents, as well as the mayor and his two assessors. The eight remaining gentlemen, who were all on a par with Granoux, perspired with fright when the latter explained to them the critical situation of the town. It requires an intimate knowledge of the kind of men who compose the municipal councils of some of the smaller towns, in order to form an idea of the terror with which these timid folk threw themselves into Rougon's arms. At Plassans, the mayor had the most incredible blockheads under him, men without any ideas of their own, and accustomed to passive obedience. Consequently, as Monsieur Garconnet was no longer there, the municipal machine was bound to get out of order, and fall completely under the control of the man who might know how to set it working. Moreover, as the sub-prefect had left the district, Rougon naturally became sole and absolute master of the town; and thus, strange to relate, the chief administrative authority fell into the hands of a man of indifferent repute, to whom, on the previous evening, not one of his fellow-citizens would have lent a hundred francs.

Pierre's first act was to declare the Provisional Commission "en permanence." Then he gave his attention to the organisation of the national guard, and succeeded in raising three hundred men. The hundred and nine muskets left in the cart-shed were also distributed to volunteers, thereby bringing up the number of men armed by the reactionary party to one hundred and fifty; the remaining one hundred and fifty guards consisted of well-affected citizens and some of Sicardot's soldiers. When Commander Roudier reviewed the little army in front of the town-hall, he was annoyed to see the market-people smiling in their sleeves. The fact is that several of his men had no uniforms, and some of them looked very droll with their black hats, frock-coats, and muskets. But, at any rate, they meant well. A guard was left at the town-hall and the rest of the forces were sent in detachments to the various town gates. Roudier reserved to himself the command of the guard stationed at the Grand'-Porte, which seemed to be more liable to attack than the others.

Rougon, who now felt very conscious of his power, repaired to the Rue Canquoin to beg the gendarmes to remain in their barracks and interfere with nothing. He certainly had the doors of the gendarmerie opened—the keys having been carried off by the insurgents—but he wanted to triumph alone, and had no intention of letting the gendarmes rob him of any part of his glory. If he should really have need of them he could always send for them. So he explained to them that their presence might tend to irritate the working-men and thus aggravate the situation. The sergeant in command thereupon complimented him on his prudence. When Rougon was informed that there was a wounded man in the barracks, he asked to see him, by way of rendering himself popular. He found Rengade in bed, with his eye bandaged, and his big moustaches just peeping out from under the linen. With some high-sounding words about duty, Rougon endeavoured to comfort the unfortunate fellow who, having lost an eye, was swearing with exasperation at the thought that his injury would compel him to quit the service. At last Rougon promised to send the doctor to him.

"I'm much obliged to you, sir," Rengade replied; "but, you know, what would do me more good than any quantity of doctor's stuff would be to wring the neck of the villain who put my eye out. Oh! I shall know him again; he's a little thin, palish fellow, quite young."

Thereupon Pierre bethought himself of the blood he had seen on Silvere's hand. He stepped back a little, as though he was afraid that Rengade would fly at his throat, and cry: "It was your nephew who blinded me; and you will have to pay for it." And whilst he was mentally cursing his disreputable family, he solemnly declared that if the guilty person were found he should be punished with all the rigour of the law.

"No, no, it isn't worth all that trouble," the one-eyed man replied; "I'll just wring his neck for him when I catch him."

Rougon hastened back to the town-hall. The afternoon was employed in taking various measures. The proclamation posted up about one o'clock produced an excellent impression. It ended by an appeal to the good sense of the citizens, and gave a firm assurance that order would not again be disturbed. Until dusk, in fact, the streets presented a picture of general relief and perfect confidence. On the pavements, the groups who were reading the proclamation exclaimed:

"It's all finished now; we shall soon see the troops who have been sent in pursuit of the insurgents."

This belief that some soldiers were approaching was so general that the idles of the Cours Sauvaire repaired to the Nice road, in order to meet and hear the regimental band. But they returned at nightfall disappointed, having seen nothing; and then a feeling of vague alarm began to disturb the townspeople.

At the town-hall, the Provisional Commission had talked so much, without coming to any decision, that the members, whose stomachs were quite empty, began to feel alarmed again. Rougon dismissed them to dine, saying that they would meet afresh at nine o'clock in the evening. He was just about to leave the room himself, when Macquart awoke and began to pommel the door of his prison. He declared he was hungry, then asked what time it was, and when his brother had told him it was five o'clock, he feigned great astonishment, and muttered, with diabolical malice, that the insurgents had promised to return much earlier, and that they were very slow in coming to deliver him. Rougon, having ordered some food to be taken to him, went downstairs, quite worried by the earnestness with which the rascal spoke of the return of the insurgents.

When he reached the street, his disquietude increased. The town seemed to him quite altered. It was assuming a strange aspect; shadows were gliding along the footpaths, which were growing deserted and silent, while gloomy fear seemed, like fine rain, to be slowly, persistently falling with the dusk over the mournful-looking houses. The babbling confidence of the daytime was fatally terminating in groundless panic, in growing alarm as the night drew nearer; the inhabitants were so weary and so satiated with their triumph that they had no strength left but to dream of some terrible retaliation on the part of the insurgents. Rougon shuddered as he passed through this current of terror. He hastened his steps, feeling as if he would choke. As he passed a cafe on the Place des Recollets, where the lamps had just been lit, and where the petty cits of the new town were assembled, he heard a few words of terrifying conversation.

"Well! Monsieur Picou," said one man in a thick voice, "you've heard the news? The regiment that was expected has not arrived."

"But nobody expected any regiment, Monsieur Touche," a shrill voice replied.

"I beg your pardon. You haven't read the proclamation, then?"

"Oh yes, it's true the placards declare that order will be maintained by force, if necessary."

"You see, then, there's force mentioned; that means armed forces, of course."

"What do people say then?"

"Well, you know, folks are beginning to feel rather frightened; they say that this delay on the part of the soldiers isn't natural, and that the insurgents may well have slaughtered them."

A cry of horror resounded through the cafe. Rougon was inclined to go in and tell those bourgeois that the proclamation had never announced the arrival of a regiment, that they had no right to strain its meaning to such a degree, nor to spread such foolish theories abroad. But he himself, amidst the disquietude which was coming over him, was not quite sure he had not counted upon a despatch of troops; and he did, in fact, consider it strange that not a single soldier had made his appearance. So he reached home in a very uneasy state of mind. Felicite, still petulant and full of courage, became quite angry at seeing him upset by such silly trifles. Over the dessert she comforted him.

"Well, you great simpleton," she said, "so much the better, if the prefect does forget us! We shall save the town by ourselves. For my part, I should like to see the insurgents return, so that we might receive them with bullets and cover ourselves with glory. Listen to me, go and have the gates closed, and don't go to bed; bustle about all night; it will all be taken into account later on."

Pierre returned to the town-hall in rather more cheerful spirits. He required some courage to remain firm amidst the woeful maunderings of his colleagues. The members of the Provisional Commission seemed to reek with panic, just as they might with damp in the rainy season. They all professed to have counted upon the despatch of a regiment, and began to exclaim that brave citizens ought not to be abandoned in such a manner to the fury of the rabble. Pierre, to preserve peace, almost promised they should have a regiment on the morrow. Then he announced, in a solemn manner, that he was going to have the gates closed. This came as a relief. Detachments of the national guards had to repair immediately to each gate and double-lock it. When they had returned, several members confessed that they really felt more comfortable; and when Pierre remarked that the critical situation of the town imposed upon them the duty of remaining at their posts, some of them made arrangements with the view of spending the night in an arm-chair. Granoux put on a black silk skull cap which he had brought with him by way of precaution. Towards eleven o'clock, half of the gentlemen were sleeping round Monsieur Garconnet's writing table. Those who still managed to keep their eyes open fancied, as they listened to the measured tramp of the national guards in the courtyard, that they were heroes and were receiving decorations. A large lamp, placed on the writing-table, illumined this strange vigil. All at once, however, Rougon, who had seemed to be slumbering, jumped up, and sent for Vuillet. He had just remembered that he had not received the "Gazette."

The bookseller made his appearance in a very bad humour.

"Well!" Rougon asked him as he took him aside, "what about the article you promised me? I haven't seen the paper."

"Is that what you disturbed me for?" Vuillet angrily retorted. "The 'Gazette' has not been issued; I've no desire to get myself murdered to-morrow, should the insurgents come back."

Rougon tried to smile as he declared that, thank heaven, nobody would be murdered at all. It was precisely because false and disquieting rumours were running about that the article in question would have rendered great service to the good cause.

"Possibly," Vuillet resumed; "but the best of causes at the present time is to keep one's head on one's shoulders." And he added, with maliciousness, "And I was under the impression you had killed all the insurgents! You've left too many of them for me to run any risk."

Rougon, when he was alone again, felt amazed at this mutiny on the part of a man who was usually so meek and mild. Vuillet's conduct seemed to him suspicious. But he had no time to seek an explanation; he had scarcely stretched himself out afresh in his arm-chair, when Roudier entered, with a big sabre, which he had attached to his belt, clattering noisily against his legs. The sleepers awoke in a fright. Granoux thought it was a call to arms.

"Eh? what! What's the matter?" he asked, as he hastily put his black silk cap into his pocket.

"Gentlemen," said Roudier, breathlessly, without thinking of taking any oratorical precautions, "I believe that a band of insurgents is approaching the town."

These words were received with the silence of terror. Rougon alone had the strength to ask, "Have you seen them?"

"No," the retired hosier replied; "but we hear strange noises out in the country; one of my men assured me that he had seen fires along the slope of the Garrigues."

Then, as all the gentlemen stared at each other white and speechless, "I'll return to my post," he continued. "I fear an attack. You had better take precautions."

Rougon would have followed him, to obtain further particulars, but he was already too far away. After this the Commission was by no means inclined to go to sleep again. Strange noises! Fires! An attack! And in the middle of the night too! It was very easy to talk of taking precautions, but what were they to do? Granoux was very near advising the course which had proved so successful the previous evening: that is of hiding themselves, waiting till the insurgents has passed through Plassans, and then triumphing in the deserted streets. Pierre, however, fortunately remembering his wife's advice, said that Roudier might have made a mistake, and that the best thing would be to go and see for themselves. Some of the members made a wry face at this suggestion; but when it had been agreed that an armed escort should accompany the Commission, they all descended very courageously. They only left a few men downstairs; they surrounded themselves with about thirty of the national guards, and then they ventured into the slumbering town, where the moon, creeping over the house roofs, slowly cast lengthened shadows. They went along the ramparts, from one gate to the other, seeing nothing and hearing nothing. The national guards at the various posts certainly told them that peculiar sounds occasionally reached them from the country through the closed gates. When they strained their ears, however, they detected nothing but a distant murmur, which Granoux said was merely the noise of the Viorne.

Nevertheless they remained doubtful. And they were about to return to the town-hall in a state of alarm, though they made a show of shrugging their shoulders and of treating Roudier as a poltroon and a dreamer, when Rougon, anxious to reassure them, thought of enabling them to view the plain over a distance of several leagues. Thereupon he led the little company to the Saint-Marc quarter and knocked at the door of the Valqueyras mansion.

At the very outset of the disturbances Count de Valqueyras had left for his chateau at Corbiere. There was no one but the Marquis de Carnavant at the Plassans house. He, since the previous evening, had prudently kept aloof; not that he was afraid, but because he did not care to be seen plotting with the Rougons at the critical moment. As a matter of fact, he was burning with curiosity. He had been compelled to shut himself up in order to resist the temptation of hastening to the yellow drawing-room. When the footman came to tell him, in the middle of the night, that there were some gentlemen below asking for him, he could not hold back any longer. He got up and went downstairs in all haste.

"My dear Marquis," said Rougon, as he introduced to him the members of the Municipal Commission, "we want to ask a favour of you. Will you allow us to go into the garden of the mansion?"

"By all means," replied the astonished marquis, "I will conduct you there myself."

On the way thither he ascertained what their object was. At the end of the garden rose a terrace which overlooked the plain. A large portion of the ramparts had there tumbled in, leaving a boundless prospect to the view. It had occurred to Rougon that this would serve as an excellent post of observation. While conversing together the members of the Commission leaned over the parapet. The strange spectacle that spread out before them soon made them silent. In the distance, in the valley of the Viorne, across the vast hollow which stretched westward between the chain of the Garrigues and the mountains of the Seille, the rays of the moon were streaming like a river of pale light. The clumps of trees, the gloomy rocks, looked, here and there, like islets and tongues of land, emerging from a luminous sea; and, according to the bends of the Viorne one could now and again distinguish detached portions of the river, glittering like armour amidst the fine silvery dust falling from the firmament. It all looked like an ocean, a world, magnified by the darkness, the cold, and their own secret fears. At first the gentlemen could neither hear nor see anything. The quiver of light and of distant sound blinded their eyes and confused their ears. Granoux, though he was not naturally poetic, was struck by the calm serenity of that winter night, and murmured: "What a beautiful night, gentlemen!"

"Roudier was certainly dreaming," exclaimed Rougon, rather disdainfully.

But the marquis, whose ears were quick, had begun to listen. "Ah!" he observed in his clear voice, "I hear the tocsin."

At this they all leant over the parapet, holding their breath. And light and pure as crystal the distant tolling of a bell rose from the plain. The gentlemen could not deny it. It was indeed the tocsin. Rougon pretended that he recognised the bell of

Beage, a village fully a league from Plassans. This he said in order to reassure his colleagues.

But the marquis interrupted him. "Listen, listen: this time it is the bell of Saint-Maur." And he indicated another point of the horizon to them. There was, in fact, a second bell wailing through the clear night. And very soon there were ten bells, twenty bells, whose despairing tollings were detected by their ears, which had by this time grown accustomed to the quivering of the darkness. Ominous calls rose from all sides, like the faint rattles of dying men. Soon the whole plain seemed to be wailing. The gentlemen no longer jeered at Roudier; particularly as the marquis, who took a malicious delight in terrifying them, was kind enough to explain the cause of all this bell-ringing.

"It is the neighbouring villages," he said to Rougon, "banding together to attack Plassans at daybreak."

At this Granoux opened his eyes wide. "Didn't you see something just this moment over there?" he asked all of a sudden.

Nobody had looked; the gentlemen had been keeping their eyes closed in order to hear the better.

"Ah! look!" he resumed after a short pause. "There, beyond the Viorne, near that black mass."

"Yes, I see," replied Rougon, in despair; "it's a fire they're kindling."

A moment later another fire appeared almost immediately in front of the first one, then a third, and a fourth. In this wise red splotches appeared at nearly equal distances throughout the whole length of the valley, resembling the lamps of some gigantic avenue. The moonlight, which dimmed their radiance, made them look like pools of blood. This melancholy illumination gave a finishing touch to the consternation of the Municipal Commission.

"Of course!" the marquis muttered, with his bitterest sneer, "those brigands are signalling to each other." And he counted the fires complacently, to get some idea, he said, as to how many men "the brave national guard of Plassans" would have to deal with. Rougon endeavoured to raise doubts by saying the villages were taking up arms in order to join the army of the insurgents, and not for the purpose of attacking the town.

But the gentlemen, by their silent consternation, made it clear that they had formed their own opinion, and were not to be consoled.

"I can hear the 'Marseillaise' now," remarked Granoux in a hushed voice.

It was indeed true. A detachment must have been following the course of the Viorne, passing, at that moment, just under the town. The cry, "To arms, citizens! Form your battalions!" reached the on-lookers in sudden bursts with vibrating distinctness. Ah! what an awful night it was! The gentlemen spent it leaning over the parapet of the terrace, numbed by the terrible cold, and yet quite unable to tear themselves away from the sight of that plain which resounded with the tocsin and the "Marseillaise," and was all ablaze with signal-fires. They feasted their eyes upon that sea of light, flecked with blood-red flames; and they strained their ears in order to listen to the confused clamour, till at last their senses began to deceive them, and they saw and heard the most frightful things. Nothing in the world would have induced them to leave the spot. If they had turned their backs, they would have fancied that a whole army was at their heels. After the manner of a certain class of cowards, they wished to witness the approach of the danger, in order that they might take flight at the right moment. Towards morning, when the moon had set and they could see nothing in front of them but a dark void, they fell into a terrible fright. They fancied they were surrounded by invisible enemies, who were crawling along in the darkness, ready to fly at their throats. At the slightest noise they imagined there were enemies deliberating beneath the terrace, prior to scaling it. Yet there was nothing, nothing but darkness upon which they fixed their eyes distractedly. The marquis, as if to console them, said in his ironical way: "Don't be uneasy! They will certainly wait till daybreak."

Meanwhile Rougon cursed and swore. He felt himself again giving way to fear. As for Granoux, his hair turned completely white. At last the dawn appeared with weary slowness. This again was a terribly anxious moment. The gentlemen, at the first ray of light, expected to see an army drawn up in line before the town. It so happened that day that the dawn was lazy and lingered awhile on the edge of the horizon. With outstretched necks and fixed gaze, the party on the terrace peered anxiously into the misty expanse. In the uncertain light they fancied they caught glimpses of colossal profiles, the plain seemed to be transformed into a lake of blood, the rocks looked like corpses floating on its surface, and the clusters of trees took the forms of battalions drawn up and threatening attack. When the growing light had at last dispersed these phantoms, the morning broke so pale, so mournful, so melancholy, that even the marquis's spirits sank. Not a single insurgent was to be seen, and the high roads were free; but the grey valley wore a gruesomely sad and deserted aspect. The fires had now gone out, but the bells still rang on. Towards eight o'clock, Rougon observed a small party of men who were moving off along the Viorne.

By this time the gentlemen were half dead with cold and fatigue. Seeing no immediate danger, they determined to take a few hours' rest. A national guard was left on the terrace as a sentinel, with orders to run and inform Roudier if he should perceive any band approaching in the distance. Then Granoux and Rougon, quite worn out by the emotions of the night, repaired to their homes, which were close together, and supported each other on the way.

Felicite put her husband to bed with every care. She called him "poor dear," and repeatedly told him that he ought not to give way to evil fancies, and that all would end well. But he shook his head; he felt grave apprehensions. She let him sleep till eleven o'clock. Then, after he had had something to eat, she gently turned him out of doors, making him understand that he must go through with the matter to the end. At the town-hall, Rougon found only four members of the Commission in attendance; the others had sent excuses, they were really ill. Panic had been sweeping through the town with growing violence all through the morning. The gentlemen had not been able to keep quiet respecting the memorable night they had spent on the terrace of the Valqueyras mansion. Their servants had hastened to spread the news, embellishing it with various dramatic details. By this time it had already become a matter of history that from the heights of Plassans troops of cannibals had been seen dancing and devouring their prisoners. Yes, bands of witches had circled hand in hand round their caldrons in which they were boiling children, while on and on marched endless files of bandits, whose weapons glittered in the moonlight. People spoke too of bells that of their own accord, sent the tocsin ringing through the desolate air, and it was even asserted that the insurgents had fired the neighbouring forests, so that the whole country side was in flames.

It was Tuesday, the market-day at Plassans, and Roudier had thought it necessary to have the gates opened in order to admit the few peasants who had brought vegetables, butter, and eggs. As soon as it had assembled, the Municipal Commission, now composed of five members only, including its president, declared that this was unpardonable imprudence. Although the sentinel stationed at the Valqueyras mansion had seen nothing, the town ought to have been kept closed. Then Rougon decided that the public crier, accompanied by a drummer, should go through the streets, proclaim a state of siege, and announce to the inhabitants that whoever might go out would not be allowed to return. The gates were officially closed in broad daylight. This measure, adopted in order to reassure the inhabitants, raised the scare to its highest pitch. And there could scarcely have been a more curious sight than that of this little city, thus padlocking and bolting itself up beneath the bright sunshine, in the middle of the nineteenth century.

When Plassans had buckled and tightened its belt of dilapidated ramparts, when it had bolted itself in like a besieged fortress at the approach of an assault, the most terrible anguish passed over the mournful houses. At every moment, in the centre of the town, people fancied they could hear a discharge of musketry in the Faubourgs. They no longer received any news; they were, so to say, at the bottom of a cellar, in a walled hole, where they were anxiously awaiting either deliverance or the finishing stroke. For the last two days the insurgents, who were scouring the country, had cut off all communication. Plassans found itself isolated from the rest of France. It felt that it was surrounded by a region in open rebellion, where the tocsin was ever ringing and the "Marseillaise" was ever roaring like a river that has overflowed its banks. Abandoned to its fate and shuddering with alarm the town lay there like some prey which would prove the reward of the victorious party. The strollers on the Cours Sauvaire were ever swaying between fear and hope according as they fancied that they could see the blouses of insurgents or the uniforms of soldiers at the Grand'-Porte. Never had sub-prefecture, pent within tumble-down walls, endured more agonising torture.

Towards two o'clock it was rumoured that the Coup d'Etat had failed, that the prince-president was imprisoned at Vincennes, and that Paris was in the hands of the most advanced demagogues. It was reported also that Marseilles, Toulon, Draguignan, the entire South, belonged to the victorious insurrectionary army. The insurgents would arrive in the evening and put Plassans to the sword.

Thereupon a deputation repaired to the town-hall to expostulate with the Municipal Commission for closing the gates, whereby they would only irritate the insurgents. Rougon, who was losing his head, defended his order with all his remaining strength. This locking of the gates seemed to him one of the most ingenious acts of his administration; he advanced the most convincing arguments in its justification. But the others embarrassed him by their questions, asking him where were the soldiers, the regiment that he had promised. Then he began to lie, and told them flatly that he had promised nothing at all. The non-appearance of this legendary regiment, which the inhabitants longed for with such eagerness that they had actually dreamt of its arrival, was the chief cause of the panic. Well-informed people even named the exact spot on the high road where the soldiers had been butchered.

At four o'clock Rougon, followed by Granoux, again repaired to the Valqueyras mansion. Small bands, on their way to join the insurgents at Orcheres, still passed along in the distance, through the valley of the Viorne. Throughout the day urchins climbed the ramparts, and bourgeois came to peep through the loopholes. These volunteer sentinels kept up the terror by counting the various bands, which were taken for so many strong battalions. The timorous population fancied it could see from the battlements the preparations for some universal massacre. At dusk, as on the previous evening, the panic became yet more chilling.

On returning to the municipal offices Rougon and his inseparable companion, Granoux, recognised that the situation was growing intolerable. During their absence another member of the Commission had disappeared. They were only four now, and they felt they were making themselves ridiculous by staying there for hours, looking at each other's pale countenances, and never saying a word. Moreover, they were terribly afraid of having to spend a second night on the terrace of the Valqueyras mansion.

Rougon gravely declared that as the situation of affairs was unchanged, there was no need for them to continue to remain there *en permanence*. If anything serious should occur information would be sent to them. And, by a decision duly taken in council, he deputed to Roudier the carrying on of the administration. Poor Roudier, who remembered that he had served as a national guard in Paris under Louis-Philippe, was meantime conscientiously keeping watch at the Grand'-Porte.

Rougon went home looking very downcast, and creeping along under the shadows of the houses. He felt that Plassans was becoming hostile to him. He heard his name bandied about amongst the groups, with expressions of anger and contempt. He walked upstairs, reeling and perspiring. Felicite received him with speechless consternation. She, also, was beginning to despair. Their dreams were being completely shattered. They stood silent, face to face, in the yellow drawing-room. The day was drawing to a close, a murky winter day which imparted a muddy tint to the orange-coloured wall-paper with its large flower pattern; never had the room looked more faded, more mean, more shabby. And at this hour they were alone; they no longer had a crowd of courtiers congratulating them, as on the previous evening. A single day had sufficed to topple them over, at the very moment when they were singing victory. If the situation did not change on the morrow their game would be lost.

Felicite who, when gazing on the previous evening at the ruins of the yellow drawing-room, had thought of the plains of Austerlitz, now recalled the accursed field of Waterloo as she observed how mournful and deserted the place was. Then, as her husband said nothing, she mechanically went to the window—that window where she had inhaled with delight the incense of the entire town. She perceived numerous groups below on the square, but she closed the blinds upon seeing some heads turn towards their house, for she feared that she might be hooted. She felt quite sure that those people were speaking about them.

Indeed, voices rose through the twilight. A lawyer was clamouring in the tone of a triumphant pleader. "That's just what I said; the insurgents left of their own accord, and they won't ask the permission of the forty-one to come back. The forty-one indeed! a fine farce! Why, I believe there were at least two hundred."

"No, indeed," said a burly trader, an oil-dealer and a great politician, "there were probably not even ten. There was no fighting or else we should have seen some blood in the morning. I went to the town-hall myself to look; the courtyard was as clean as my hand."

Then a workman, who stepped timidly up to the group, added: "There was no need of any violence to seize the building; the door wasn't even shut."

This remark was received with laughter, and the workman, thus encouraged, continued: "As for those Rougons, everybody knows that they are a bad lot."

This insult pierced Felicite to the heart. The ingratitude of the people was heartrending to her, for she herself was at last beginning to believe in the mission of the Rougons. She called for her husband. She wanted him to learn how fickle was the multitude.

"It's all a piece with their mirror," continued the lawyer. "What a fuss they made about that broken glass! You know that Rougon is quite capable of having fired his gun at it just to make believe there had been a battle."

Pierre restrained a cry of pain. What! they did not even believe in his mirror now! They would soon assert that he had not heard a bullet whiz past his ear. The legend of the Rougons would be blotted out; nothing would remain of their glory. But his torture was not at an end yet. The groups manifested their hostility as heartily as they had displayed their approval on the previous evening. A retired hatter, an old man seventy years of age, whose factory had formerly been in the Faubourg, ferreted out the Rougons' past history. He spoke vaguely, with the hesitation of a wandering memory, about the Fouques' property, and Adelaide, and her amours with a smuggler. He said just enough to give a fresh start to the gossip. The tattlers drew closer together and such words as "rogues," "thieves," and "shameless intriguers," ascended to the shutter behind which Pierre and Felicite were perspiring with fear and indignation. The people on the square even went so far as to pity Macquart. This was the final blow. On the previous day Rougon had been a Brutus, a stoic soul sacrificing his own affections to his country; now he was nothing but an ambitious villain, who felled his brother to the ground and made use of him as a stepping-stone to fortune.

"You hear, you hear them?" Pierre murmured in a stifled voice. "Ah! the scoundrels, they are killing us; we shall never retrieve ourselves."

Felicite, enraged, was beating a tattoo on the shutter with her impatient fingers.

"Let them talk," she answered. "If we get the upper hand again they shall see what stuff I'm made of. I know where the blow comes from. The new town hates us."

She guessed rightly. The sudden unpopularity of the Rougons was the work of a group of lawyers who were very much annoyed at the importance acquired by an old illiterate oil-dealer, whose house had been on the verge of bankruptcy. The Saint-Marc quarter had shown no sign of life for the last two days. The inhabitants of the old quarter and the new town alone remained in presence, and the latter had taken advantage of the panic to injure the yellow drawing-room in the minds of the tradespeople and working-classes. Roudier and Granoux were said to be excellent men, honourable citizens, who had been led away by the Rougons' intrigues. Their eyes ought to be opened to it. Ought not Monsieur Isidore Granoux to be seated in the mayor's arm-chair, in the place of that big portly beggar who had not a copper to bless himself with? Thus launched, the envious folks began to reproach Rougon for all the acts of his administration, which only dated from the previous evening. He had no right to retain the services of the former Municipal Council; he had been guilty of grave folly in ordering the gates to be closed; it was through his stupidity that five members of the Commission had contracted inflammation of the lungs on the terrace of the Valqueyras mansion. There was no end to his faults. The Republicans likewise raised their heads. They talked of the possibility of a sudden attack upon the town-hall by the workmen of the Faubourg. The reaction was at its last gasp.

Pierre, at this overthrow of all his hopes, began to wonder what support he might still rely on if occasion should require any.

"Wasn't Aristide to come here this evening," he asked, "to make it up with us?"

"Yes," answered Felicite. "He promised me a good article. The 'Independant' has not appeared yet—"

But her husband interrupted her, crying: "See! isn't that he who is just coming out of the Sub-Prefecture?"

The old woman glanced in that direction. "He's got his arm in a sling again!" she cried.

Aristide's hand was indeed wrapped in the silk handkerchief once more. The Empire was breaking up, but the Republic was not yet triumphant, and he had judged it prudent to resume the part of a disabled man. He crossed the square stealthily, without raising his head. Then doubtless hearing some dangerous and compromising remarks among the groups of bystanders, he made all haste to turn the corner of the Rue de la Banne.

"Bah! he won't come here," said Felicite bitterly. "It's all up with us. Even our children forsake us!"

She shut the window violently, in order that she might not see or hear anything more. When she had lit the lamp, she and her husband sat down to dinner, disheartened and without appetite, leaving most of their food on their plates. They only had a few hours left them to take a decisive step. It was absolutely indispensable that before daybreak Plassans should be at their feet beseeching forgiveness, or else they must entirely renounce the fortune which they had dreamed of. The total absence of any reliable news was the sole cause of their anxious indecision. Felicite, with her clear intellect, had quickly perceived this. If they had been able to learn the result of the Coup d'Etat, they would either have faced it out and have still pursued their role of deliverers, or else have done what they could to efface all recollection of their unlucky campaign. But they had no precise information; they were losing their heads; the thought that they were thus risking their fortune on a throw, in complete ignorance of what was happening, brought a cold perspiration to their brows.

"And why the devil doesn't Eugene write to me?" Rougon suddenly cried, in an outburst of despair, forgetting that he was betraying the secret of his correspondence to his wife.

But Felicite pretended not to have heard. Her husband's exclamation had profoundly affected her. Why, indeed, did not Eugene write to his father? After keeping him so accurately informed of the progress of the Bonapartist cause, he ought at least to have announced the triumph or defeat of Prince Louis. Mere prudence would have counselled the despatch of such information. If he remained silent, it must be that the victorious Republic had sent him to join the pretender in the dungeons of Vincennes. At this thought Felicite felt chilled to the marrow; her son's silence destroyed her last hopes.

At that moment somebody brought up the "Gazette," which had only just appeared.

"Ah!" said Pierre, with surprise. "Vuillet has issued his paper!"

Thereupon he tore off the wrapper, read the leading article, and finished it looking as white as a sheet, and swaying on his chair.

"Here, read," he resumed, handing the paper to Felicite.

It was a magnificent article, attacking the insurgents with unheard of violence. Never had so much stinging bitterness, so many falsehoods, such bigoted abuse flowed from pen before. Vuillet commenced by narrating the entry of the insurgents into Plassans. The description was a perfect masterpiece. He spoke of "those bandits, those villainous-looking countenances, that scum of the galleys," invading the town, "intoxicated with brandy, lust, and pillage." Then he exhibited them "parading their cynicism in the streets, terrifying the inhabitants with their savage cries and seeking only violence and murder." Further on, the scene at the town-hall and the arrest of the authorities became a most horrible drama. "Then they seized the most respectable people by the throat; and the mayor, the brave commander of the national guard, the postmaster, that kindly functionary, were—even like the Divinity—crowned with thorns by those wretches, who spat in their faces." The passage devoted to Miette and her red pelisse was quite a flight of imagination. Vuillet had seen ten, twenty girls steeped in blood: "and who," he wrote, "did not behold among those monsters some infamous creatures clothed in red, who must have bathed themselves in the blood of the martyrs murdered by the brigands along the high roads? They were brandishing banners, and openly receiving the vile caresses of the entire horde." And Vuillet added, with Biblical magniloquence, "The Republic ever marches on amidst debauchery and murder."

That, however, was only the first part of the article; the narrative being ended, the editor asked if the country would any longer tolerate "the shamelessness of those wild beasts, who respected neither property nor persons." He made an appeal to all valorous citizens, declaring that to tolerate such things any longer would be to encourage them, and that the insurgents would then come and snatch "the daughter from her mother's arms, the wife from her husband's embraces." And at last, after a pious sentence in which he declared that Heaven willed the extermination of the wicked, he concluded with this trumpet blast: "It is asserted that these wretches are once more at our gates; well then let each one of us take a gun and shoot them down like dogs. I for my part shall be seen in the front rank, happy to rid the earth of such vermin."

This article, in which periphrastic abuse was strung together with all the heaviness of touch which characterises French provincial journalism, quite terrified Rougon, who muttered, as Felicite replaced the "Gazette" on the table: "Ah! the wretch! he is giving us the last blow; people will believe that I inspired this diatribe."

"But," his wife remarked, pensively, "did you not this morning tell me that he absolutely refused to write against the Republicans? The news that circulated had terrified him, and he was as pale as death, you said."

"Yes! yes! I can't understand it at all. When I insisted, he went so far as to reproach me for not having killed all the insurgents. It was yesterday that he ought to have written that article; to-day he'll get us all butchered!"

Felicite was lost in amazement. What could have prompted Vuillet's change of front? The idea of that wretched semi-sacristan carrying a musket and firing on the ramparts of Plassans seemed to her one of the most ridiculous things imaginable.

There was certainly some determining cause underlying all this which escaped her. Only one thing seemed certain. Vuillet was too impudent in his abuse and too ready with his valour, for the insurrectionary band to be really so near the town as some people asserted.

"He's a spiteful fellow, I always said so," Rougon resumed, after reading the article again. "He has only been waiting for an opportunity to do us this injury. What a fool I was to leave him in charge of the post-office!"

This last sentence proved a flash of light. Felicite started up quickly, as though at some sudden thought. Then she put on a cap and threw a shawl over her shoulders.

"Where are you going, pray?" her husband asked her with surprise. "It's past nine o'clock."

"You go to bed," she replied rather brusquely, "you're not well; go and rest yourself. Sleep on till I come back; I'll wake you if necessary, and then we can talk the matter over."

She went out with her usual nimble gait, ran to the post-office, and abruptly entered the room where Vuillet was still at work. On seeing her he made a hasty gesture of vexation.

Never in his life had Vuillet felt so happy. Since he had been able to slip his little fingers into the mail-bag he had enjoyed the most exquisite pleasure, the pleasure of an inquisitive priest about to relish the confessions of his penitents. All the sly blabbing, all the vague chatter of sacristies resounded in his ears. He poked his long, pale nose into the letters, gazed amorously at the superscriptions with his suspicious eyes, sounded the envelopes just like little abbes sound the souls of maidens. He experienced endless enjoyment, was titillated by the most enticing temptation. The thousand secrets of Plassans lay there. He held in his hand the honour of women, the fortunes of men, and had only to break a seal to know as much as the grand vicar at the cathedral who was the confidant of all the better people of the town. Vuillet was one of those terribly bitter, frigid gossips, who worm out everything, but never repeat what they hear, except by way of dealing somebody a mortal blow. He had, consequently, often longed to dip his arms into the public letter-box. Since the previous evening the private room at the post-office had become a big confessional full of darkness and mystery, in which he tasted exquisite rapture while sniffing at the letters which exhaled veiled long-ings and quivering avowals. Moreover, he carried on his work with consummate impudence. The crisis through which the country was passing secured him perfect impunity. If some let-ters should be delayed, or others should miscarry altogether, it would be the fault of those villainous Republicans who were scouring the country and interrupting all communication. The closing of the town gates had for a moment vexed him, but he had come to an understanding with Roudier, whereby the cour-iers were allowed to enter and bring the mails direct to him without passing by the town-hall.

As a matter of fact he had only opened a few letters, the im-portant ones, those in which his keen scent divined some in-formation which it would be useful for him to know before any-body else. Then he contented himself by locking up in a draw-er, for delivery subsequently, such letters as might give inform-ation and rob him of the merit of his valour at a time when the whole town was trembling with fear. This pious personage, in selecting the management of the post-office as his own share of the spoils, had given proof of singular insight into the situation.

When Madame Rougon entered, he was taking his choice of a heap of letters and papers, under the pretext, no doubt, of clas-sifying them. He rose, with his humble smile, and offered her a seat; his reddened eyelids blinking rather uneasily. But Felicite did not sit down; she roughly exclaimed: "I want the letter."

At this Vuillet's eyes opened widely, with an expression of perfect innocence.

"What letter, madame?" he asked.

"The letter you received this morning for my husband. Come, Monsieur Vuillet, I'm in a hurry."

And as he stammered that he did not know, that he had not seen anything, that it was very strange, Felicite continued in a covertly threatening voice: "A letter from Paris, from my son, Eugene; you know what I mean, don't you? I'll look for it myself."

Thereupon she stepped forward as if intending to examine the various packets which littered the writing table. But he at once bestirred himself, and said he would go and see. The ser-vice was necessarily in great confusion! Perhaps, indeed, there might be a letter. In that case they would find it. But, as far as he was concerned, he swore he had not seen any. While he was speaking he moved about the office turning over all the papers. Then he opened the drawers and the portfolios. Felicite waited, quite calm and collected.

"Yes, indeed, you're right, here's a letter for you," he cried at last, as he took a few papers from a portfolio. "Ah! those confounded clerks, they take advantage of the situation to do nothing in the proper way."

Felicite took the letter and examined the seal attentively, apparently quite regardless of the fact that such scrutiny might wound Vuillet's susceptibilities. She clearly perceived that the envelope must have been opened; the bookseller, in his unskilful way, had used some sealing wax of a darker colour to secure it again. She took care to open the envelope in such a manner as to preserve the seal intact, so that it might serve as proof of this. Then she read the note. Eugene briefly announced the complete success of the Coup d'Etat. Paris was subdued, the provinces generally speaking remained quiet, and he counselled his parents to maintain a very firm attitude in face of the partial insurrection which was disturbing the South. In conclusion he told them that the foundation of their fortune was laid, if they did not weaken.

Madame Rougon put the letter in her pocket, and sat down slowly, looking into Vuillet's face. The latter had resumed his sorting in a feverish manner, as though he were very busy.

"Listen to me, Monsieur Vuillet," she said to him. And when he raised his head: "let us play our cards openly; you do wrong to betray us; some misfortune may befall you. If, instead of unsealing our letters—"

At this he protested, and feigned great indignation. But she calmly continued: "I know, I know your school, you never confess. Come, don't let us waste any more words, what interest have you in favouring the Coup d'Etat?"

And, as he continued to assert his perfect honesty, she at last lost patience. "You take me for a fool!" she cried. "I've read your article. You would do much better to act in concert with us."

Thereupon, without avowing anything, he flatly submitted that he wished to have the custom of the college. Formerly it was he who had supplied that establishment with school books. But it had become known that he sold objectionable literature clandestinely to the pupils; for which reason, indeed, he had almost been prosecuted at the Correctional Police Court. Since then he had jealously longed to be received back into the good graces of the directors.

Felicite was surprised at the modesty of his ambition, and told him so. To open letters and risk the galleys just for the sake of selling a few dictionaries and grammars!

"Eh!" he exclaimed in a shrill voice, "it's an assured sale of four or five thousand francs a year. I don't aspire to impossibilities like some people."

She did not take any notice of his last taunting words. No more was said about his opening the letters. A treaty of alliance was concluded, by which Vuillet engaged that he would not circulate any news or take any step in advance, on condition that the Rougons should secure him the custom of the college. As she was leaving, Felicite advised him not to compromise himself any further. It would be sufficient for him to detain the letters and distribute them only on the second day.

"What a knave," she muttered, when she reached the street, forgetting that she herself had just laid an interdict upon the mail.

She went home slowly, wrapped in thought. She even went out of her way, passing along the Cours Sauvaire, as if to gain time and ease for reflection before going in. Under the trees of the promenade she met Monsieur de Carnavant, who was taking advantage of the darkness to ferret about the town without compromising himself. The clergy of Plassans, to whom all energetic action was distasteful, had, since the announcement of the Coup d'Etat, preserved absolute neutrality. In the priests' opinion the Empire was virtually established, and they awaited an opportunity to resume in some new direction their secular intrigues. The marquis, who had now become a useless agent, remained only inquisitive on one point—he wished to know how the turmoil would finish, and in what manner the Rougons would play their role to the end.

"Oh! it's you, little one!" he exclaimed, as soon as he recognized Felicite. "I wanted to see you; your affairs are getting muddled!"

"Oh, no; everything is going on all right," she replied, in an absent-minded way.

"So much the better. You'll tell me all about it, won't you? Ah! I must confess that I gave your husband and his colleagues a terrible fright the other night. You should have seen how comical they looked on the terrace, while I was pointing out a band of insurgents in every cluster of trees in the valley! You forgive me?"

"I'm much obliged to you," said Felicite quickly. "You should have made them die of fright. My husband is a big sly-boots. Come and see me some morning, when I am alone."

Then she turned away, as though this meeting with the marquis had determined her. From head to foot the whole of her little person betokened implacable resolution. At last she was going to revenge herself on Pierre for his petty mysteries, have him under her heel, and secure, once for all, her omnipotence at home. There would be a fine scene, quite a comedy, indeed, the points of which she was already enjoying in anticipation, while she worked out her plan with all the spitefulness of an injured woman.

She found Pierre in bed, sleeping heavily; she brought the candle near him for an instant, and gazed with an air of compassion, at his big face, across which slight twitches occasionally passed; then she sat down at the head of the bed, took off her cap, let her hair fall loose, assumed the appearance of one in despair, and began to sob quite loudly.

"Hallo! What's the matter? What are you crying for?" asked Pierre, suddenly awaking.

She did not reply, but cried more bitterly.

"Come, come, do answer," continued her husband, frightened by this mute despair. "Where have you been? Have you seen the insurgents?"

She shook her head; then, in a faint voice, she said: "I've just come from the Valqueyras mansion. I wanted to ask Monsieur de Carnavant's advice. Ah! my dear, all is lost."

Pierre sat up in bed, very pale. His bull neck, which his unbuttoned night-shirt exposed to view, all his soft, flabby flesh seemed to swell with terror. At last he sank back, pale and tearful, looking like some grotesque Chinese figure in the middle of the untidy bed.

"The marquis," continued Felicite, "thinks that Prince Louis has succumbed. We are ruined; we shall never get a sou."

Thereupon, as often happens with cowards, Pierre flew into a passion. It was the marquis's fault, it was his wife's fault, the fault of all his family. Had he ever thought of politics at all, until Monsieur de Carnavant and Felicite had driven him to that tomfoolery?

"I wash my hands of it altogether," he cried. "It's you two who are responsible for the blunder. Wasn't it better to go on living on our little savings in peace and quietness? But then, you were always determined to have your own way! You see what it has brought us to."

He was losing his head completely, and forgot that he had shown himself as eager as his wife. However, his only desire now was to vent his anger, by laying the blame of his ruin upon others.

"And, moreover," he continued, "could we ever have succeeded with children like ours? Eugene abandons us just at the critical moment; Aristide has dragged us through the mire, and even that big simpleton Pascal is compromising us by his philanthropic practising among the insurgents. And to think that we brought ourselves to poverty simply to give them a university education!"

Then, as he drew breath, Felicite said to him softly: "You are forgetting Macquart."

"Ah! yes; I was forgetting him," he resumed more violently than ever; "there's another whom I can't think of without losing all patience! But that's not all; you know little Silvere. Well, I saw him at my mother's the other evening with his hands covered with blood. He has put some gendarme's eye out. I did not tell you of it, as I didn't want to frighten you. But you'll see one of my nephews in the Assize Court. Ah! what a family! As for Macquart, he has annoyed us to such an extent that I felt inclined to break his head for him the other day when I had a gun in my hand. Yes, I had a mind to do it."

Felicite let the storm pass over. She had received her husband's reproaches with angelic sweetness, bowing her head like a culprit, whereby she was able to smile in her sleeve. Her demeanour provoked and maddened Pierre. When speech failed the poor man, she heaved deep sighs, feigning repentance; and then she repeated, in a disconsolate voice: "Whatever shall we do! Whatever shall we do! We are over head and ears in debt."

"It's your fault!" Pierre cried, with all his remaining strength.

The Rougons, in fact, owed money on every side. The hope of approaching success had made them forget all prudence. Since the beginning of 1851 they had gone so far as to entertain the frequenters of the yellow drawing-room every evening with syrup and punch, and cakes—providing, in fact, complete collations, at which they one and all drank to the death of the Republic. Besides this, Pierre had placed a quarter of his capital at the disposal of the reactionary party, as a contribution towards the purchase of guns and cartridges.

"The pastry-cook's bill amounts to at least a thousand francs," Felicite resumed, in her sweetest tone, "and we probably owe twice as much to the liqueur-dealer. Then there's the butcher, the baker, the greengrocer——"

Pierre was in agony. And Felicite struck him a final blow by adding: "I say nothing of the ten thousand francs you gave for the guns."

"I, I!" he faltered, "but I was deceived, I was robbed! It was that idiot Sicardot who let me in for that by swearing that the Napoleonists would be triumphant. I thought I was only making an advance. But the old dolt will have to repay me my money."

"Ah! you won't get anything back," said his wife, shrugging her shoulders. "We shall suffer the fate of war. When we have paid off everything, we sha'n't even have enough to buy dry bread with. Ah! it's been a fine campaign. We can now go and live in some hovel in the old quarter."

This last phrase had a most lugubrious sound. It seemed like the knell of their existence. Pierre pictured the hovel in the old quarter, which had just been mentioned by Felicite. 'Twas there, then, that he would die on a pallet, after striving all his life for the enjoyment of ease and luxury. In vain had he robbed his mother, steeped his hands in the foulest intrigues, and lied and lied for many a long year. The Empire would not pay his debts—that Empire which alone could save him. He jumped out of bed in his night-shirt, crying: "No; I'll take my gun; I would rather let the insurgents kill me."

"Well!" Felicite rejoined, with great composure, "you can have that done to-morrow or the day after; the Republicans are not far off. And that way will do as well as another to make an end of matters."

Pierre shuddered. It seemed as if some one had suddenly poured a large pail of cold water over his shoulders. He slowly got into bed again, and when he was warmly wrapped up in the sheets, he began to cry. This fat fellow easily burst into tears—gently flowing, inexhaustible tears—which streamed from his eyes without an effort. A terrible reaction was now going on within him. After his wrath he became as weak as a child. Felicite, who had been waiting for this crisis, was delighted to see him so spiritless, so resourceless, and so humbled before her. She still preserved silence, and an appearance of distressed humility. After a long pause, her seeming resignation, her mute dejection, irritated Pierre's nerves.

"But do say something!" he implored; "let us think matters over together. Is there really no hope left us?"

"None, you know very well," she replied; "you explained the situation yourself just now; we have no help to expect from anyone; even our children have betrayed us."

"Let us flee, then. Shall we leave Plassans to- night—immediately?"

"Flee! Why, my dear, to-morrow we should be the talk of the whole town. Don't you remember, too, that you have had the gates closed?"

A violent struggle was going on in Pierre's mind, which he exerted to the utmost in seeking for some solution; at last, as though he felt vanquished, he murmured, in supplicating tones: "I beseech you, do try to think of something; you haven't said anything yet."

Felicite raised her head, feigning surprise; and with a gesture of complete powerlessness she said: "I am a fool in these matters. I don't understand anything about politics, you've told me so a hundred times."

And then, as her embarrassed husband held his tongue and lowered his eyes, she continued slowly, but not reproachfully: "You have not kept me informed of your affairs, have you? I know nothing at all about them, I can't even give you any advice. It was quite right of you, though; women chatter sometimes, and it is a thousand times better for the men to steer the ship alone."

She said this with such refined irony that her husband did not detect that she was deriding him. He simply felt profound remorse. And, all of a sudden, he burst out into a confession. He spoke of Eugene's letters, explained his plans, his conduct, with all the loquacity of a man who is relieving his conscience and imploring a saviour. At every moment he broke off to ask: "What would you have done in my place?" or else he cried, "Isn't that so? I was right, I could not act otherwise." But Felicite did not even deign to make a sign. She listened with all the frigid reserve of a judge. In reality she was tasting the most exquisite pleasure; she had got that sly-boots fast at last; she played with him like a cat playing with a ball of paper; and he virtually held out his hands to be manacled by her.

"But wait," he said hastily, jumping out of bed. "I'll give you Eugene's correspondence to read. You can judge the situation better then."

She vainly tried to hold him back by his night-shirt. He spread out the letters on the table by the bed-side, and then got into bed again, and read whole pages of them, and compelled her to go through them herself. She suppressed a smile, and began to feel some pity for the poor man.

"Well," he said anxiously, when he had finished, "now you know everything. Do you see any means of saving us from ruin!"

She still gave no answer. She appeared to be pondering deeply.

"You are an intelligent woman," he continued, in order to flatter her, "I did wrong in keeping any secret from you; I see it now."

"Let us say nothing more about that," she replied. "In my opinion, if you had enough courage——" And as he looked at her eagerly, she broke off and said, with a smile: "But you promise not to distrust me any more? You will tell me everything, eh? You will do nothing without consulting me?"

He swore, and accepted the most rigid conditions. Felicite then got into bed; and in a whisper, as if she feared somebody might hear them, she explained at length her plan of campaign. In her opinion the town must be allowed to fall into still greater panic, while Pierre was to maintain an heroic demeanour in the midst of the terrified inhabitants. A secret presentiment, she said, warned her that the insurgents were still at a distance. Moreover, the party of order would sooner or later carry the day, and the Rougons would be rewarded. After the role of deliverer, that of martyr was not to be despised. And she argued so well, and spoke with so much conviction, that her husband, surprised at first by the simplicity of her plan, which consisted in facing it out, at last detected in it a marvellous tactical scheme, and promised to conform to it with the greatest possible courage.

"And don't forget that it is I who am saving you," the old woman murmured in a coaxing tone. "Will you be nice to me?"

They kissed each other and said good-night. But neither of them slept; after a quarter of an hour had gone by, Pierre, who had been gazing at the round reflection of the night-lamp on the ceiling, turned, and in a faint whisper told his wife of an idea that had just occurred to him.

"Oh! no, no," Felicite murmured, with a shudder. "That would be too cruel."

"Well," he resumed, "but you want to spread consternation among the inhabitants! They would take me seriously, if what I told you should occur." Then perfecting his scheme, he cried: "We might employ Macquart. That would be a means of getting rid of him."

Felicite seemed to be struck with the idea. She reflected, seemed to hesitate, and then, in a distressful tone faltered: "Perhaps you are right. We must see. After all we should be very stupid if we were over-scrupulous, for it's a matter of life and death to us. Let me do it. I'll see Macquart to-morrow, and ascertain if we can come to an understanding with him. You would only wrangle and spoil all. Good-night; sleep well, my poor dear. Our troubles will soon be ended, you'll see."

They again kissed each other and fell asleep. The patch of light on the ceiling now seemed to be assuming the shape of a terrified eye, that stared wildly and fixedly upon the pale, slumbering couple who reeked with crime beneath their very sheets, and dreamt they could see a rain of blood falling in big drops which turned into golden coins as they plashed upon the floor.

On the morrow, before daylight, Felicite repaired to the town-hall, armed with instructions from Pierre to seek an interview with Macquart. She took her husband's national guard uniform with her, wrapped in a cloth. There were only a few men fast asleep in the guard-house. The doorkeeper, who was entrusted with the duty of supplying Macquart with food, went upstairs with her to open the door of the dressing-room, which had been turned into a cell. Then quietly he came down again.

Macquart had now been kept in the room for two days and two nights. He had had time to indulge in lengthy reflections. After his sleep, his first hours had been given up to outbursts of impotent rage. Goaded by the idea that his brother was lording it in the adjoining room, he had felt a great longing to break the door open. At all events he would strangle Rougon with his own hands, as soon as the insurgents should return and release him. But, in the evening, at twilight, he calmed down, and gave over striding furiously round the little room. He inhaled a sweet odour there; a feeling of comfort relaxed his nerves. Monsieur Garconnet, who was very rich, refined, and vain, had caused this little room to be arranged in a very elegant fashion; the sofa was soft and warm; scents, pomades, and soaps adorned the marble washstand, and the pale light fell from the ceiling with a soft glow, like the gleams of a lamp suspended in an alcove. Macquart, amidst this perfumed soporific atmosphere fell asleep, thinking that those scoundrels, the rich, "were very fortunate, all the same." He had covered himself with a blanket which had been given to him, and with his head and back and arms reposing on the cushions, he stretched himself out on the couch until morning. When he opened his eyes, a ray of sunshine was gliding through the opening above. Still he did not leave the sofa. He felt warm, and lay thinking as he gazed around him. He bethought himself that he would never again have such a place to wash in. The washstand particularly interested him. It was by no means hard, he thought, to keep oneself spruce when one had so many little pots and phials at one's disposal. This made him think bitterly of his own life of privation. The idea occurred to him that perhaps he had been on the wrong track. There is nothing to be gained by associating with beggars. He ought to have played the scamp; he should have acted in concert with the Rougons.

Then, however, he rejected this idea. The Rougons were villains who had robbed him. But the warmth and softness of the sofa, continued to work upon his feelings, and fill him with vague regrets. After all, the insurgents were abandoning him, and allowing themselves to be beaten like idiots. Eventually he came to the conclusion that the Republic was mere dupery. Those Rougons were lucky! And he recalled his own bootless wickedness and underhand intrigues. Not one member of the family had ever been on his side; neither Aristide, nor Silvere's brother, nor Silvere himself, who was a fool to grow so enthusiastic about the Republic and would never do any good for himself. Then Macquart reflected that his wife was dead, that his children had left him, and that he would die alone, like a dog in some wretched corner, without a copper to bless himself with. Decidedly, he ought to have sold himself to the reactionary party. Pondering in this fashion, he eyed the washstand, feeling a strong inclination to go and wash his hands with a certain powder soap which he saw in a glass jar. Like all lazy fellows who live upon their wives or children, he had foppish tastes. Although he wore patched trousers, he liked to inundate himself with aromatic oil. He spent hours with his barber, who talked politics, and brushed his hair for him between their discussions. So, at last, the temptation became too strong, and Macquart installed himself before the washstand. He washed his hands and face, dressed his hair, perfumed himself, in fact went through a complete toilet. He made use in turn of all the bottles, all the various soaps and powders; but his greatest pleasure was to dry his hands with the mayor's towels, which were so soft and thick. He buried his wet face in them, and inhaled, with delight, all the odour of wealth. Then, having pomaded himself, and smelling sweetly from head to foot, he once more stretched himself on the sofa, feeling quite youthful again, and disposed to the most conciliatory thoughts. He felt yet greater contempt for the Republic since he had dipped his nose into Monsieur Garconnet's phials. The idea occurred to him that there was, perhaps, still time for him to make peace with his brother. He wondered what he might well ask in return for playing the traitor. His rancour against the Rougons still gnawed at his heart; but he was in one of those moods when, lying on one's back in silence, one is apt to admit stern facts, and scold oneself for neglecting to feather a comfortable nest in which one may wallow in slothful ease, even at the cost of relinquishing one's most cherished animosities. Towards evening Antoine determined to send for his brother on the following day. But when, in the morning, he saw Felicite enter the room he understood that his aid was wanted, so he remained on his guard.

The negotiations were long and full of pitfalls, being conducted on either side with infinite skill. At first they both indulged in vague complaints, then Felicite, who was surprised to find Macquart almost polite, after the violent manner in which he had behaved at her house on the Sunday evening, assumed a tone of gentle reproach. She deplored the hatred which severed their families. But, in truth, he had so calumniated his brother, and manifested such bitter animosity towards him, that he had made poor Rougon quite lose his head.

"But, dash it, my brother has never behaved like a brother to me," Macquart replied, with restrained violence. "Has he ever given me any assistance? He would have let me die in my hovel! When he behaved differently towards me—you remember, at the time he gave me two hundred francs—I am sure no one can reproach me with having said a single unpleasant word about him. I said everywhere that he was a very good-hearted fellow."

This clearly signified: "If you had continued to supply me with money, I should have been very pleasant towards you, and would have helped you, instead of fighting against you. It's your own fault. You ought to have bought me."

Felicite understood this so well that she replied: "I know you have accused us of being hard upon you, because you imagine we are in comfortable circumstances; but you are mistaken, my dear brother; we are poor people; we have never been able to act towards you as our hearts would have desired." She hesitated a moment, and then continued: "If it were absolutely necessary in some serious contingency, we might perhaps be able to make a sacrifice; but, truly, we are very poor, very poor!"

Macquart pricked up his ears. "I have them!" he thought. Then, without appearing to understand his sister-in-law's indirect offer, he detailed the wretchedness of his life in a doleful manner, and spoke of his wife's death and his children's flight. Felicite, on her side, referred to the crisis through which the country was passing, and declared that the Republic had completely ruined them. Then from word to word she began to bemoan the exigencies of a situation which compelled one brother to imprison another. How their hearts would bleed if justice refused to release its prey! And finally she let slip the word "galleys!"

"Bah! I defy you," said Macquart calmly.

But she hastily exclaimed: "Oh! I would rather redeem the honour of the family with my own blood. I tell you all this to show you that we shall not abandon you. I have come to give you the means of effecting your escape, my dear Antoine."

They gazed at each other for a moment, sounding each other with a look, before engaging in the contest.

"Unconditionally?" he asked, at length.

"Without any condition," she replied.

Then she sat down beside him on the sofa, and continued, in a determined voice: "And even, before crossing the frontier, if you want to earn a thousand-franc note, I can put you in the way of doing so."

There was another pause.

"If it's all above board I shall have no objection," Antoine muttered, apparently reflecting. "You know I don't want to mix myself up with your underhand dealings."

"But there are no underhand dealings about it," Felicite resumed, smiling at the old rascal's scruples. "Nothing can be more simple: you will presently leave this room, and go and conceal yourself in your mother's house, and this evening you can assemble your friends and come and seize the town-hall again."

Macquart did not conceal his extreme surprise. He did not understand it at all.

"I thought," he said, "that you were victorious."

"Oh! I haven't got time now to tell you all about it," the old woman replied, somewhat impatiently. "Do you accept or not?"

"Well, no; I don't accept—I want to think it over. It would be very stupid of me to risk a possible fortune for a thousand francs."

Felicite rose. "Just as you like my dear fellow," she said, coldly. "You don't seem to realise the position you are in. You came to my house and treated me as though I were a mere outcast; and then, when I am kind enough to hold out a hand to you in the hole into which you have stupidly let yourself fall, you stand on ceremony, and refuse to be rescued. Well, then, stay here, wait till the authorities come back. As for me, I wash my hands of the whole business."

With these words she reached the door.

"But give me some explanations," he implored. "I can't strike a bargain with you in perfect ignorance of everything. For two days past I have been quite in the dark as to what's going on. How do I know that you are not cheating me?"

"Bah! you're a simpleton," replied Felicite, who had retraced her steps at Antoine's doleful appeal. "You are very foolish not to trust yourself implicitly to us. A thousand francs! That's a fine sum, a sum that one would only risk in a winning cause. I advise you to accept."

He still hesitated.

"But when we want to seize the place, shall we be allowed to enter quietly?"

"Ah! I don't know," she said, with a smile. "There will perhaps be a shot or two fired."

He looked at her fixedly.

"Well, but I say, little woman," he resumed in a hoarse voice, "you don't intend, do you, to have a bullet lodged in my head?"

Felicite blushed. She was, in fact, just thinking that they would be rendered a great service, if, during the attack on the town-hall, a bullet should rid them of Antoine. It would be a gain of a thousand francs, besides all the rest. So she muttered with irritation: "What an idea! Really, it's abominable to think such things!"

Then, suddenly calming down, she added:

"Do you accept? You understand now, don't you?"

Macquart had understood perfectly. It was an ambush that they were proposing to him. He did not perceive the reasons or the consequences of it, and this was what induced him to haggle. After speaking of the Republic as though it were a mistress whom, to his great grief, he could no longer love, he recapitulated the risks which he would have to run, and finished by asking for two thousand francs. But Felicite abided by her original offer. They debated the matter until she promised to procure him, on his return to France, some post in which he would have nothing to do, and which would pay him well. The bargain was then concluded. She made him don the uniform she had brought with her. He was to betake himself quietly to aunt Dide's, and afterwards, towards midnight, assemble all the Republicans he could in the neighbourhood of the town-hall, telling them that the municipal offices were unguarded, and that they had only to push open the door to take possession of them. Antoine then asked for earnest money, and received two hundred francs. Felicite undertook to pay the remaining eight hundred on the following day. The Rougons were risking the last sum they had at their disposal.

When Felicite had gone downstairs, she remained on the square for a moment to watch Macquart go out. He passed the guard-house, quietly blowing his nose. He had previously broken the skylight in the dressing-room, to make it appear that he had escaped that way.

"It's all arranged," Felicite said to her husband, when she returned home. "It will be at midnight. It doesn't matter to me at all now. I should like to see them all shot. How they slandered us yesterday in the street!"

"It was rather silly of you to hesitate," replied Pierre, who was shaving. "Every one would do the same in our place."

That morning—it was a Wednesday—he was particularly careful about his toilet. His wife combed his hair and tied his cravat, turning him about like a child going to a distribution of prizes. And when he was ready, she examined him, declared that he looked very nice, and that he would make a very good figure in the midst of the serious events that were preparing. His big pale face wore an expression of grave dignity and heroic determination. She accompanied him to the first landing, giving him her last advice: he was not to depart in any way from his courageous demeanour, however great the panic might be; he was to have the gates closed more hermetically than ever, and leave the town in agonies of terror within its ramparts; it would be all the better if he were to appear the only one willing to die for the cause of order.

What a day it was! The Rougons still speak of it as of a glorious and decisive battle. Pierre went straight to the town-hall, heedless of the looks or words that greeted him on his way. He installed himself there in magisterial fashion, like a man who did not intend to quit the place, whatever might happen. And he simply sent a note to Roudier, to advise him that he was resuming authority.

"Keep watch at the gates," he added, knowing that these lines might become public: "I myself will watch over the town and ensure the security of life and property. It is at the moment when evil passions reappear and threaten to prevail that good citizens should endeavour to stifle them, even at the peril of their lives." The style, and the very errors in spelling, made this note—the brevity of which suggested the laconic style of the ancients—appear all the more heroic. Not one of the gentlemen of the Provisional Commission put in an appearance. The last two who had hitherto remained faithful, and Granoux himself, even, prudently stopped at home. Thus Rougon was the only member of the Commission who remained at his post, in his presidential arm-chair, all the others having vanished as the panic increased. He did not even deign to issue an order summoning them to attend. He was there, and that sufficed, a sublime spectacle, which a local journal depicted later on in a sentence: "Courage giving the hand to duty."

During the whole morning Pierre was seen animating the town-hall with his goings and comings. He was absolutely alone in the large, empty building, whose lofty halls reechoed with the noise of his heels. All the doors were left open. He made an ostentatious show of his presidency over a non-existent council in the midst of this desert, and appeared so deeply impressed with the responsibility of his mission that the door-keeper, meeting him two or three times in the passages, bowed to him with an air of mingled surprise and respect. He was seen, too, at every window, and, in spite of the bitter cold, he appeared several times on the balcony with bundles of papers in his hand, like a busy man attending to important despatches.

Then, towards noon, he passed through the town and visited the guard-houses, speaking of a possible attack, and letting it be understood, that the insurgents were not far off; but he relied, he said, on the courage of the brave national guards. If necessary they must be ready to die to the last man for the defence of the good cause. When he returned from this round, slowly and solemnly, after the manner of a hero who has set the affairs of his country in order, and now only awaits death, he observed signs of perfect stupor along his path; the people promenading in the Cours, the incorrigible little householders, whom no catastrophe would have prevented from coming at certain hours to bask in the sun, looked at him in amazement, as if they did not recognize him, and could not believe that one of their own set, a former oil-dealer, should have the boldness to face a whole army.

In the town the anxiety was at its height. The insurrectionists were expected every moment. The rumour of Macquart's escape was commented upon in a most alarming manner. It was asserted that he had been rescued by his friends, the Reds, and that he was only waiting for nighttime in order to fall upon the inhabitants and set fire to the four corners of the town. Plassans, closed in and terror-stricken, gnawing at its own vitals within its prison-like walls, no longer knew what to imagine in order to frighten itself. The Republicans, in the face of Rougon's bold demeanour, felt for a moment distrustful. As for the new town—the lawyers and retired tradespeople who had denounced the yellow drawing-room on the previous evening—they were so surprised that they dared not again openly attack such a valiant man. They contented themselves with saying "It was madness to brave victorious insurgents like that, and such useless heroism would bring the greatest misfortunes upon Plassans." Then, at about three o'clock, they organised a deputation. Pierre, though he was burning with desire to make a display of his devotion before his fellow-citizens, had not ventured to reckon upon such a fine opportunity.

He spoke sublimely. It was in the mayor's private room that the president of the Provisional Commission received the deputation from the new town. The gentlemen of the deputation, after paying homage to his patriotism, besought him to forego all resistance. But he, in a loud voice, talked of duty, of his country, of order, of liberty, and various other things. Moreover, he did not wish to compel any one to imitate him; he was simply discharging a duty which his conscience and his heart dictated to him.

"You see, gentlemen, I am alone," he said in conclusion. "I will take all the responsibility, so that nobody but myself may be compromised. And if a victim is required I willingly offer myself; I wish to sacrifice my own life for the safety of the inhabitants."

A notary, the wiseacre of the party, remarked that he was running to certain death.

"I know it," he resumed solemnly. "I am prepared!"

The gentlemen looked at each other. Those words "I am prepared!" filled them with admiration. Decidedly this man was a brave fellow. The notary implored him to call in the aid of the gendarmes; but he replied that the blood of those brave soldiers was precious, and he would not have it shed, except in the last extremity. The deputation slowly withdrew, feeling deeply moved. An hour afterwards, Plassans was speaking of Rougon as of a hero; the most cowardly called him "an old fool."

Towards evening, Rougon was much surprised to see Granoux hasten to him. The old almond-dealer threw himself in his arms, calling him "great man," and declaring that he would die with him. The words "I am prepared!" which had just been reported to him by his maid-servant, who had heard it at the greengrocer's, had made him quite enthusiastic. There was charming naivete in the nature of this grotesque, timorous old man. Pierre kept him with him, thinking that he would not be of much consequence. He was even touched by the poor fellow's devotion, and resolved to have him publicly complimented by the prefect, in order to rouse the envy of the other citizens who had so cowardly abandoned him. And so both of them awaited the night in the deserted building.

At the same time Aristide was striding about at home in an uneasy manner. Vuillet's article had astonished him. His father's demeanour stupefied him. He had just caught sight of him at the window, in a white cravat and black frock-coat, so calm at the approach of danger that all his ideas were upset. Yet the insurgents were coming back triumphant, that was the belief of the whole town. But Aristide felt some doubts on the point; he had suspicions of some lugubrious farce. As he did not dare to present himself at his parents' house, he sent his wife thither. And when Angele returned, she said to him, in her drawling voice: "Your mother expects you; she is not angry at all, she seems rather to be making fun of you. She told me several times that you could just put your sling back in your pocket."

Aristide felt terribly vexed. However, he ran to the Rue de la Banne, prepared to make the most humble submission. His mother was content to receive him with scornful laughter. "Ah! my poor fellow," said she, "you're certainly not very shrewd."

"But what can one do in a hole like Plassans!" he angrily retorted. "On my word of honour, I am becoming a fool here. No news, and everybody shivering! That's what it is to be shut up in these villainous ramparts. Ah! If I had only been able to follow Eugene to Paris!"

Then, seeing that his mother was still smiling, he added bitterly: "You haven't been very kind to me, mother. I know many things, I do. My brother kept you informed of what was going on, and you have never given me the faintest hint that might have been useful to me."

"You know that, do you?" exclaimed Felicite, becoming serious and distrustful. "Well, you're not so foolish as I thought, then. Do you open letters like some one of my acquaintance?"

"No; but I listen at doors," Aristide replied, with great assurance.

This frankness did not displease the old woman. She began to smile again, and asked more softly: "Well, then, you blockhead, how is it you didn't rally to us sooner?"

"Ah! that's where it is," the young man said, with some embarrassment. "I didn't have much confidence in you. You received such idiots: my father-in-law, Granoux, and the others!—And then, I didn't want to go too far... ." He hesitated, and then resumed, with some uneasiness: "To-day you are at least quite sure of the success of the Coup d'Etat, aren't you?"

"I!" cried Felicite, wounded by her son's doubts; "no, I'm not sure of anything."

"And yet you sent word to say that I was to take off my sling!"

"Yes; because all the gentlemen are laughing at you."

Aristide remained stock still, apparently contemplating one of the flowers of the orange-coloured wall-paper. And his mother felt sudden impatience as she saw him hesitating thus.

"Ah! well," she said, "I've come back again to my former opinion; you're not very shrewd. And you think you ought to have had Eugene's letters to read? Why, my poor fellow you would have spoilt everything, with your perpetual vacillation. You never can make up your mind. You are hesitating now."

"I hesitate?" he interrupted, giving his mother a cold, keen glance. "Ah! well, you don't know me. I would set the whole town on fire if it were necessary, and I wanted to warm my feet. But, understand me, I've no desire to take the wrong road! I'm tired of eating hard bread, and I hope to play fortune a trick. But I only play for certainties."

He spoke these words so sharply, with such a keen longing for success, that his mother recognised the cry of her own blood.

"Your father is very brave," she whispered.

"Yes, I've seen him," he resumed with a sneer. "He's got a fine look on him! He reminded me of Leonidas at Thermopylae. Is it you, mother, who have made him cut this figure?"

And he added cheerfully, with a gesture of determination: "Well, so much the worse! I'm a Bonapartist! Father is not the man to risk the chance of being killed unless it pays him well."

"You're quite right," his mother replied; "I mustn't say anything; but to-morrow you'll see."

He did not press her, but swore that she would soon have reason to be proud of him; and then he took his departure, while Felicite, feeling her old preference reviving, said to herself at the window, as she watched him going off, that he had the devil's own wit, that she would never have had sufficient courage to let him leave without setting him in the right path.

And now for the third time a night full of anguish fell upon Plassans. The unhappy town was almost at its death-rattle. The citizens hastened home and barricaded their doors with a great clattering of iron bolts and bars. The general feeling seemed to be that, by the morrow, Plassans would no longer exist, that it would either be swallowed up by the earth or would evaporate in the atmosphere. When Rougon went home to dine, he found the streets completely deserted. This desolation made him sad and melancholy. As a result of this, when he had finished his meal, he felt some slight misgivings, and asked his wife if it were necessary to follow up the insurrection that Macquart was preparing.

"Nobody will run us down now," said he. "You should have seen those gentlemen of the new town, how they bowed to me! It seems to me quite unnecessary now to kill anybody—eh? What do you think? We shall feather our nest without that."

"Ah! what a nerveless fellow you are!" Felicite cried angrily. "It was your own idea to do it, and now you back out! I tell you that you'll never do anything without me! Go then, go your own way. Do you think the Republicans would spare you if they got hold of you?"

Rougon went back to the town-hall, and prepared for the ambush. Granoux was very useful to him. He despatched him with orders to the different posts guarding the ramparts. The national guards were to repair to the town-hall in small detachments, as secretly as possible. Roudier, that bourgeois who was quite out of his element in the provinces, and who would have spoilt the whole affair with his humanitarian preaching, was not even informed of it. Towards eleven o'clock, the courtyard of the town-hall was full of national guards. Then Rougon frightened them; he told them that the Republicans still remaining in Plassans were about to attempt a desperate *coup de main*, and plumed himself on having been warned in time by his secret police. When he had pictured the bloody massacre which would overtake the town, should these wretches get the upper hand, he ordered his men to cease speaking, and extinguish all lights. He took a gun himself. Ever since the morning he had been living as in a dream; he no longer knew himself; he felt Felicite behind him. The crisis of the previous night had thrown him into her hands, and he would have allowed himself to be hanged, thinking: "It does not matter, my wife will come and cut me down." To augment the tumult, and prolong the terror of the slumbering town, he begged Granoux to repair to the cathedral and have the tocsin rung at the first shots he might hear. The marquis's name would open the beadle's door. And then, in darkness and dismal silence, the national guards waited in the yard, in a terrible state of anxiety, their eyes fixed on the porch, eager to fire, as though they were lying in wait for a pack of wolves.

In the meantime, Macquart had spent the day at aunt Dide's house. Stretching himself on the old coffer, and lamenting the loss of Monsieur Garconnet's sofa, he had several times felt a mad inclination to break into his two hundred francs at some neighbouring cafe. This money was burning a hole in his waistcoat pocket; however, he whiled away his time by spending it in imagination. His mother moved about, in her stiff, automatic way, as if she were not even aware of his presence. During the last few days her children had been coming to her rather frequently, in a state of pallor and desperation, but she departed neither from her taciturnity, nor her stiff, lifeless expression. She knew nothing of the fears which were throwing the pent-up town topsy-turvy, she was a thousand leagues away from Plassans, soaring into the one constant fixed idea which imparted such a blank stare to her eyes. Now and again, however, at this particular moment, some feeling of uneasiness, some human anxiety, occasionally made her blink. Antoine, unable to resist the temptation of having something nice to eat, sent her to get a roast chicken from an eating-house in the Faubourg. When it was set on the table: "Hey!" he said to her, "you don't often eat fowl, do you? It's only for those who work, and know how to manage their affairs. As for you, you always squandered everything. I bet you're giving all your savings to that little hypocrite, Silvere. He's got a mistress, the sly fellow. If you've a hoard of money hidden in some corner, he'll ease you of it nicely some day."

Macquart was in a jesting mood, glowing with wild exultation. The money he had in his pocket, the treachery he was preparing, the conviction that he had sold himself at a good price—all filled him with the self-satisfaction characteristic of vicious people who naturally became merry and scornful amidst their evil practices. Of all his talk, however, aunt Dide only heard Silvere's name.

"Have you seen him?" she asked, opening her lips at last.

"Who? Silvere?" Antoine replied. "He was walking about among the insurgents with a tall red girl on his arm. It will serve him right if he gets into trouble."

The grandmother looked at him fixedly, then, in a solemn voice, inquired: "Why?"

"Eh! Why, he shouldn't be so stupid," resumed Macquart, feeling somewhat embarrassed. "People don't risk their necks for the sake of ideas. I've settled my own little business. I'm no fool."

But aunt Dide was no longer listening to him. She was murmuring: "He had his hands covered with blood. They'll kill him like the other one. His uncles will send the gendarmes after him."

"What are you muttering there?" asked her son, as he finished picking the bones of the chicken. "You know I like people to accuse me to my face. If I have sometimes talked to the little fellow about the Republic, it was only to bring him round to a more reasonable way of thinking. He was dotty. I love liberty myself, but it mustn't degenerate into license. And as for Rougon, I esteem him. He's a man of courage and common-sense."

"He had the gun, hadn't he?" interrupted aunt Dide, whose wandering mind seemed to be following Silvere far away along the high road.

"The gun? Ah! yes; Macquart's carbine," continued Antoine, after casting a glance at the mantel-shelf, where the fire-arm was usually hung. "I fancy I saw it in his hands. A fine instrument to scour the country with, when one has a girl on one's arm. What a fool!"

Then he thought he might as well indulge in a few coarse jokes. Aunt Dide had begun to bustle about the room again. She did not say a word. Towards the evening Antoine went out, after putting on a blouse, and pulling over his eyes a big cap which his mother had bought for him. He returned into the town in the same manner as he had quitted it, by relating some nonsensical story to the national guards who were on duty at the Rome Gate. Then he made his way to the old quarter, where he crept from house to house in a mysterious manner. All the Republicans of advanced views, all the members of the brotherhood who had not followed the insurrectionary army, met in an obscure inn, where Macquart had made an appointment with them. When about fifty men were assembled, he made a speech, in which he spoke of personal vengeance that must be wreaked, of a victory that must be gained, and of a disgraceful yoke that must be thrown off. And he ended by undertaking to deliver the town-hall over to them in ten minutes. He had just left it, it was quite unguarded, he said, and the red flag would wave over it that very night if they so desired. The workmen deliberated. At that moment the reaction seemed to be in its death throes. The insurgents were virtually at the gates of the town. It would therefore be more honourable to make an effort to regain power without awaiting their return, so as to be able to receive them as brothers, with the gates wide open, and the streets and squares adorned with flags. Moreover, none of those present distrusted Macquart. His hatred of the Rougons, the personal vengeance of which he spoke, could be taken as guaranteeing his loyalty. It was arranged that each of them who was a sportsman and had a gun at home should fetch it, and that the band should assemble at midnight in the neighbourhood of the town-hall. A question of detail very nearly put an end to their plans—they had no bullets; however, they decided to load their weapons with small shot: and even that seemed unnecessary, as they were told that they would meet with no resistance.

Once more Plassans beheld a band of armed men filing along close to the houses, in the quiet moonlight. When the band was assembled in front of the town-hall, Macquart, while keeping a sharp look-out, boldly advanced to the building. He knocked, and when the door-keeper, who had learnt his lesson, asked what was wanted, he uttered such terrible threats, that the man, feigning fright, made haste to open the door. Both leaves of it swung back slowly, and the porch then lay open and empty before them, while Macquart shouted in a loud voice: "Come on, my friends!"

That was the signal. He himself quickly jumped aside, and as the Republicans rushed in, there came, from the darkness of the yard, a stream of fire and a hail of bullets, which swept through the gaping porch with a roar as of thunder. The doorway vomited death. The national guards, exasperated by their long wait, eager to shake off the discomfort weighing upon them in that dismal court-yard, had fired a volley with feverish haste. The flash of the firing was so bright, that, through the yellow gleams Macquart distinctly saw Rougon taking aim. He fancied that his brother's gun was deliberately levelled at himself, and he recalled Felicite's blush, and made his escape, muttering: "No tricks! The rascal would kill me. He owes me eight hundred francs."

In the meantime a loud howl had arisen amid the darkness. The surprised Republicans shouted treachery, and fired in their turn. A national guard fell under the porch. But the Republicans, on their side, had three dead. They took to flight, stumbling over the corpses, stricken with panic, and shouting through the quiet lanes: "Our brothers are being murdered!" in despairing voices which found no echo. Thereupon the defenders of order, having had time to reload their weapons, rushed into the empty square, firing at every street corner, wherever the darkness of a door, the shadow of a lamp-post, or the jutting of a stone made them fancy they saw an insurgent. In this wise they remained there ten minutes, firing into space.

The affray had burst over the slumbering town like a thunderclap. The inhabitants in the neighbouring streets, roused from sleep by this terrible fusillade, sat up in bed, their teeth chattering with fright. Nothing in the world would have induced them to poke their noses out of the window. And slowly, athwart the air, in which the shots had suddenly resounded, one of the cathedral bells began to ring the tocsin with so irregular, so strange a rhythm, that one might have thought the noise to be the hammering of an anvil or the echoes of a colossal kettle struck by a child in a fit of passion. This howling bell, whose sound the citizens did not recognise, terrified them yet more than the reports of the fire-arms had done; and there were some who thought they heard an endless train of artillery rumbling over the paving-stones. They lay down again and buried themselves beneath their blankets, as if they would have incurred some danger by still sitting up in bed in their closely-fastened rooms. With their sheets drawn up to their chins, they held their breath, and made themselves as small as possible, while their wives, by their side, almost fainted with terror as they buried their heads among the pillows.

The national guards who had remained at the ramparts had also heard the shots, and thinking that the insurgents had entered by means of some subterranean passage, they ran up helter-skelter, in groups of five or six, disturbing the silence of the streets with the tumult of their excited rush. Roudier was one of the first to arrive. However, Rougon sent them all back to their posts, after reprimanding them severely for abandoning the gates of the town. Thrown into consternation by this reproach—for in their panic, they had, in fact, left the gates absolutely defenceless—they again set off at a gallop, hurrying through the streets with still more frightful uproar. Plassans might well have thought that an infuriated army was crossing it in all directions. The fusillade, the tocsin, the marches and countermarches of the national guards, the weapons which were being dragged along like clubs, the terrified cries in the darkness, all produced a deafening tumult, such as might break forth in a town taken by assault and given over to plunder. It was the final blow of the unfortunate inhabitants, who really believed that the insurgents had arrived. They had, indeed, said that it would be their last night—that Plassans would be swallowed up in the earth, or would evaporate into smoke before daybreak; and now, lying in their beds, they awaited the catastrophe in the most abject terror, fancying at times that their houses were already tottering.

Meantime Granoux still rang the tocsin. When, in other respects, silence had again fallen upon the town, the mournfulness of that ringing became intolerable. Rougon, who was in a high fever, felt exasperated by its distant wailing. He hastened to the cathedral, and found the door open. The beadle was on the threshold.

"Ah! that's quite enough!" he shouted to the man; "anybody would think there was some one crying; it's quite unbearable."

"But it isn't me, sir," replied the beadle in a distressed manner. "It's Monsieur Granoux, he's gone up into the steeple. I must tell you that I removed the clapper of the bell, by his Reverence's order, precisely to prevent the tocsin from being sounded. But Monsieur Granoux wouldn't listen to reason. He climbed up, and I've no idea what he can be making that noise with."

Thereupon Rougon hastily ascended the staircase which led to the bells, shouting: "That will do! That will do! For goodness' sake leave off!"

When he had reached the top he caught sight of Granoux, by the light of the moon which glided through an embrasure; the ex almond dealer was standing there hatless, and dealing furious blows with a heavy hammer. He did so with a right good will. He first threw himself back, then took a spring, and finally fell upon the sonorous bronze as if he wanted to crack it. One might have thought he was a blacksmith striking hot iron—but a frock-coated blacksmith, short and bald, working in a wild and awkward way.

Surprise kept Rougon motionless for a moment at the sight of this frantic bourgeois thus belabouring the bell in the moon-light. Then he understood the kettle-like clang which this strange ringer had disseminated over the town. He shouted to him to stop, but Granoux did not hear. Rougon was obliged to take hold of his frock-coat, and then the other recognising him, exclaimed in a triumphant voice: "Ah! you've heard it. At first I tried to knock the bell with my fists, but that hurt me. For-tunately I found this hammer. Just a few more blows, eh?"

However, Rougon dragged him away. Granoux was radiant. He wiped his forehead, and made his companion promise to let everybody know in the morning that he had produced all that noise with a mere hammer. What an achievement, and what a position of importance that furious ringing would confer upon him!

Towards morning, Rougon bethought himself of reassuring Felicite. In accordance with his orders, the national guards had shut themselves up in the town-hall. He had forbidden them to remove the corpses, under the pretext that it was necessary to give the populace of the old quarter a lesson. And as, while hastening to the Rue de la Banne, he passed over the square, on which the moon was no longer shining, he inadvertently stepped on the clenched hand of a corpse that lay beside the footpath. At this he almost fell. That soft hand, which yielded beneath his heel, brought him an indefinable sensation of dis-gust and horror. And thereupon he hastened at full speed along the deserted streets, fancying that a bloody fist was pursuing him.

"There are four of them on the ground," he said, as he entered his house.

He and his wife looked at one another as though they were astonished at their crime.

The lamplight imparted the hue of yellow wax to their pale faces.

"Have you left them there?" asked Felicite; "they must be found there."

"Of course! I didn't pick them up. They are lying on their backs. I stepped on something soft——"

Then he looked at his boot; its heel was covered with blood. While he was putting on a pair of shoes, Felicite resumed:

"Well! so much the better! It's over now. People won't be inclined to repeat that you only fire at mirrors."

The fusillade which the Rougons had planned in order that they might be finally recognised as the saviours of Plassans, brought the whole terrified and grateful town to their feet. The day broke mournfully with the grey melancholy of a winter-morning. The inhabitants, hearing nothing further, ventured forth, weary of trembling beneath their sheets. At first some ten or fifteen appeared. Later on, when a rumour spread that the insurgents had taken flight, leaving their dead in every gutter, Plassans rose in a body and descended upon the town-hall. Throughout the morning people strolled inquisitively round the four corpses. They were horribly mutilated, particularly one, which had three bullets in the head. But the most horrible to look upon was the body of a national guard, who had fallen under the porch; he had received a charge of the small shot, used by the Republicans in lieu of bullets, full in the face; and blood oozed from his torn and riddled countenance. The crowd feasted their eyes upon this horror, with the avidity for revolting spectacles which is so characteristic of cowards. The national guard was freely recognised; he was the pork-butcher Dubruel, the man whom Roudier had accused on the Monday morning of having fired with culpable eagerness. Of the three other corpses, two were journeymen hatters; the third was not identified. For a long while gaping groups remained shuddering in front of the red pools which stained the pavement, often looking behind them with an air of mistrust, as though that summary justice which had restored order during the night by force of arms, were, even now, watching and listening to them, ready to shoot them down in their turn, unless they kissed with enthusiasm the hand that had just rescued them from the demagogy.

The panic of the night further augmented the terrible effect produced in the morning by the sight of the four corpses. The true history of the fusillade was never known. The firing of the combatants, Granoux's hammering, the helter-skelter rush of the national guards through the streets, had filled people's ears with such terrifying sounds that most of them dreamed of a gigantic battle waged against countless enemies. When the victors, magnifying the number of their adversaries with instinctive braggardism, spoke of about five hundred men, everybody protested against such a low estimate. Some citizens asserted that they had looked out of their windows and seen an immense stream of fugitives passing by for more than an hour. Moreover everybody had heard the bandits running about. Five hundred men would never have been able to rouse a whole town. It must have been an army, and a fine big army too, which the brave militia of Plassans had "driven back into the ground." This phrase of their having been "driven back into the ground," first used by Rougon, struck people as being singularly appropriate, for the guards who were charged with the defence of the ramparts swore by all that was holy that not a single man had entered or quitted the town, a circumstance which tinged what had happened with mystery, even suggesting the idea of horned demons who had vanished amidst flames, and thus fairly upsetting the minds of the multitude. It is true the guards avoided all mention of their mad gallops; and so the more rational citizens were inclined to believe that a band of insurgents had really entered the town either by a breach in the wall or some other channel. Later on, rumours of treachery were spread abroad, and people talked of an ambush. The cruel truth could no longer be concealed by the men whom Macquart had led to slaughter, but so much terror still prevailed, and the sight of blood had thrown so many cowards into the arms of the reactionary party, that these rumours were attributed to the rage of the vanquished Republicans. It was asserted, on the other hand, that Macquart had been made prisoner by Rougon, who kept him in a damp cell, where he was letting him slowly die of starvation. This horrible tale made people bow to the very ground whenever they encountered Rougon.

Thus it was that this grotesque personage, this pale, flabby, tun-bellied citizen became, in one night, a terrible captain, whom nobody dared to ridicule any more. He had steeped his foot in blood. The inhabitants of the old quarter stood dumb with fright before the corpses. But towards ten o'clock, when the respectable people of the new town arrived, the whole square hummed with subdued chatter. People spoke of the other attack, of the seizure of the mayor's office, in which a mirror only had been wounded; but this time they no longer pooh-poohed Rougon, they spoke of him with respectful dismay; he was indeed a hero, a deliverer. The corpses, with open eyes, stared at those gentlemen, the lawyers and householders, who shuddered as they murmured that civil war had many cruel necessities. The notary, the chief of the deputation sent to the town-hall on the previous evening, went from group to group, recalling the proud words "I am prepared!" then used by the energetic man to whom the town owed its safety. There was a general feeling of humiliation. Those who had railed most cruelly against the forty-one, those, especially, who had referred to the Rougons as intriguers and cowards who merely fired shots in the air, were the first to speak of granting a crown of laurels "to the noble citizen of whom Plassans would be for ever proud." For the pools of blood were drying on the pavement, and the corpses proclaimed to what a degree of audacity the party of disorder, pillage, and murder had gone, and what an iron hand had been required to put down the insurrection.

Moreover, the whole crowd was eager to congratulate Granoux, and shake hands with him. The story of the hammer had become known. By an innocent falsehood, however, of which he himself soon became unconscious, he asserted that, having been the first to see the insurgents, he had set about striking the bell, in order to sound the alarm, so that, but for him, the national guards would have been massacred. This doubled his importance. His achievement was declared prodigious. People spoke of him now as "Monsieur Isidore, don't you know? the gentleman who sounded the tocsin with a hammer!" Although the sentence was somewhat lengthy, Granoux would willingly have accepted it as a title of nobility; and from that day forward he never heard the word "hammer" pronounced without imagining it to be some delicate flattery.

While the corpses were being removed, Aristide came to look at them. He examined them on all sides, sniffing and looking inquisitively at their faces. His eyes were bright, and he had a sharp expression of countenance. In order to see some wound the better he even lifted up the blouse of one corpse with the very hand which on the previous day had been suspended in a sling. This examination seemed to convince him and remove all doubt from his mind. He bit his lips, remained there for a moment in silence, and then went off for the purpose of hastening the issue of the "Independant," for which he had written a most important article. And as he hurried along beside the houses he recalled his mother's words: "You will see to-morrow!" Well, he had seen now; it was very clever; it even frightened him somewhat.

In the meantime, Rougon's triumph was beginning to embarrass him. Alone in Monsieur Garconnet's office, hearing the buzzing of the crowd, he became conscious of a strange feeling, which prevented him from showing himself on the balcony. That blood, in which he had stepped, seemed to have numbed his legs. He wondered what he should do until the evening. His poor empty brain, upset by the events of the night, sought desperately for some occupation, some order to give, or some measure to be taken, which might afford him some distraction. But he could think about nothing clearly. Whither was Felicite leading him? Was it really all finished now, or would he still have to kill somebody else? Then fear again assailed him, terrible doubts arose in his mind, and he already saw the ramparts broken down on all sides by an avenging army of the Republicans, when a loud shout: "The insurgents! The insurgents!" burst forth under the very windows of his room. At this he jumped up, and raising a curtain, saw the crowd rushing about the square in a state of terror. What a thunderbolt! In less than a second he pictured himself ruined, plundered, and murdered; he cursed his wife, he cursed the whole town. Then, as he looked behind him in a suspicious manner, seeking some means of escape, he heard the mob break out into applause, uttering shouts of joy, making the very glass rattle with their wild delight. Then he returned to the window; the women were waving their handkerchiefs, and the men were embracing each other. There were some among them who joined hands and began to dance. Rougon stood there stupefied, unable to comprehend it all, and feeling his head swimming. The big, deserted, silent building, in which he was alone, quite frightened him.

When he afterwards confessed his feelings to Felicite, he was unable to say how long his torture had lasted. He only remembered that a noise of footsteps, re-echoing through the vast halls, had roused him from his stupor. He expected to be attacked by men in blouses, armed with scythes and clubs, whereas it was the Municipal Commission which entered, quite orderly and in evening dress, each member with a beaming countenance. Not one of them was absent. A piece of good news had simultaneously cured all these gentlemen. Granoux rushed into the arms of his dear president.

"The soldiers!" he stammered, "the soldiers!"

A regiment had, in fact, just arrived, under the command of Colonel Masson and Monsieur de Bleriot, prefect of the department. The gunbarrels which had been observed from the ramparts, far away in the plain, had at first suggested the approach of the insurgents. Rougon was so deeply moved on learning the truth, that two big tears rolled down his cheeks. He was weeping, the great citizen! The Municipal Commission watched those big tears with most respectful admiration. But Granoux again threw himself on his friend's neck, crying:

"Ah! how glad I am! You know I'm a straightforward man. Well, we were all of us afraid; it is not so, gentlemen? You, alone, were great, brave, sublime! What energy you must have had! I was just now saying to my wife: 'Rougon is a great man; he deserves to be decorated.'"

Then the gentlemen proposed to go and meet the prefect. For a moment Rougon felt both stunned and suffocated; he was unable to believe in this sudden triumph, and stammered like a child. However, he drew breath, and went downstairs with the quiet dignity suited to the solemnity of the occasion. But the enthusiasm which greeted the commission and its president outside the town-hall almost upset his magisterial gravity afresh. His name sped through the crowd, accompanied this time by the warmest eulogies. He heard everyone repeat Granoux's avowal, and treat him as a hero who had stood firm and resolute amidst universal panic. And, as far as the Sub-Prefecture, where the commission met the prefect, he drank his fill of popularity and glory.

Monsieur de Bleriot and Colonel Masson had entered the town alone, leaving their troops encamped on the Lyons road. They had lost considerable time through a misunderstanding as to the direction taken by the insurgents. Now, however, they knew the latter were at Orcheres; and it would only be necessary to stop an hour at Plassans, just sufficient time to reassure the population and publish the cruel ordinances which decreed the sequestration of the insurgents' property, and death to every individual who might be taken with arms in his hands. Colonel Masson smiled when, in accordance with the orders of the commander of the national guards, the bolts of the Rome Gate were drawn back with a great rattling of rusty old iron. The detachment on duty there accompanied the prefect and the colonel as a guard of honour. As they traversed the Cours Sauvaire, Roudier related Rougon's epic achievements to the gentlemen—the three days of panic that had terminated with the brilliant victory of the previous night. When the two processions came face to face therefore, Monsieur de Bleriot quickly advanced towards the president of the Commission, shook hands with him, congratulated him, and begged him to continue to watch over the town until the return of the authorities. Rougon bowed, while the prefect, having reached the door of the Sub-Prefecture, where he wished to take a brief rest, proclaimed in a loud voice that he would not forget to mention his brave and noble conduct in his report.

In the meantime, in spite of the bitter cold, everybody had come to their windows. Felicite, leaning forward at the risk of falling out, was quite pale with joy. Aristide had just arrived with a number of the "Independant," in which he had openly declared himself in favour of the Coup d'Etat, which he welcomed "as the aurora of liberty in order and of order in liberty." He had also made a delicate allusion to the yellow drawing-room, acknowledging his errors, declaring that "youth is presumptuous," and that "great citizens say nothing, reflect in silence, and let insults pass by, in order to rise heroically when the day of struggle comes." He was particularly pleased with this sentence. His mother thought his article extremely well written. She kissed her dear child, and placed him on her right hand. The Marquis de Carnavant, weary of incarcerating himself, and full of eager curiosity, had likewise come to see her, and stood on her left, leaning on the window rail.

When Monsieur de Bleriot offered his hand to Rougon on the square below Felicite began to weep. "Oh! see, see," she said to Aristide. "He has shaken hands with him. Look! he is doing it again!" And casting a glance at the windows, where groups of people were congregated, she added: "How wild they must be! Look at Monsieur Peirotte's wife, she's biting her handkerchief. And over there, the notary's daughter, and Madame Massicot, and the Brunet family, what faces, eh? how angry they look! Ah, indeed, it's our turn now."

She followed the scene which was being acted outside the Sub-Prefecture with thrills of delight, which shook her ardent, grasshopper-like figure from head to foot. She interpreted the slightest gesture, invented words which she was unable to catch, and declared that Pierre bowed very well indeed. She was a little vexed when the prefect deigned to speak to poor Granoux, who was hovering about him fishing for a word of praise. No doubt Monsieur de Bleriot already knew the story of the hammer, for the retired almond-dealer turned as red as a young girl, and seemed to be saying that he had only done his duty. However, that which angered Felicite still more was her husband's excessive amiability in presenting Vuillet to the authorities. Vuillet, it is true, pushed himself forward amongst them, and Rougon was compelled to mention him.

"What a schemer!" muttered Felicite. "He creeps in everywhere. How confused my poor dear husband must be! See, there's the colonel speaking to him. What can he be saying to him?"

"Ah! little one," the marquis replied with a touch of irony, "he is complimenting him for having closed the gates so carefully."

"My father has saved the town," Aristide retorted curtly. "Have you seen the corpses, sir?"

Monsieur de Carnavant did not answer. He withdrew from the window, and sat down in an arm-chair, shaking his head with an air of some disgust. At that moment, the prefect having taken his departure, Rougon came upstairs and threw himself upon his wife's neck.

"Ah! my dear!" he stammered.

He was unable to say more. Felicite made him kiss Aristide after telling him of the superb article which the young man had inserted in the "Independant." Pierre would have kissed the marquis as well, he was deeply affected. However, his wife took him aside, and gave him Eugene's letter which she had sealed up in an envelope again. She pretended that it had just been delivered. Pierre read it and then triumphantly held it out to her.

"You are a sorceress," he said to her laughing. "You guessed everything. What folly I should have committed without you! We'll manage our little affairs together now. Kiss me: you're a good woman."

He clasped her in his arms, while she discreetly exchanged a knowing smile with the marquis.

Chapter 7

It was not until Sunday, the day after the massacre at Sainte-Roure, that the troops passed through Plassans again. The prefect and the colonel, whom Monsieur Garconnet had invited to dinner, once more entered the town alone. The soldiers went round the ramparts and encamped in the Faubourg, on the Nice road. Night was falling; the sky, overcast since the morning, had a strange yellow tint, and illumined the town with a murky light, similar to the copper-coloured glimmer of stormy weather. The reception of the troops by the inhabitants was timid; the bloodstained soldiers, who passed by weary and silent, in the yellow twilight, horrified the cleanly citizens promenading on the Cours. They stepped out of the way whispering terrible stories of fusillades and revengeful reprisals which still live in the recollection of the region. The Coup d'Etat terror was beginning to make itself felt, an overwhelming terror which kept the South in a state of tremor for many a long month. Plassans, in its fear and hatred of the insurgents, had welcomed the troops on their first arrival with enthusiasm; but now, at the appearance of that gloomy taciturn regiment, whose men were ready to fire at a word from their officers, the retired merchants and even the notaries of the new town anxiously examined their consciences, asking if they had not committed some political peccadilloes which might be thought deserving of a bullet.

The municipal authorities had returned on the previous evening in a couple of carts hired at Sainte-Roure. Their unexpected entry was devoid of all triumphal display. Rougon surrendered the mayor's arm-chair without much regret. The game was over; and with feverish longing he now awaited the recompense for his devotion. On the Sunday—he had not hoped for it until the following day—he received a letter from Eugene. Since the previous Thursday Felicite had taken care to send her son the numbers of the "Gazette" and "Independant" which, in special second editions had narrated the battle of the night and the arrival of the prefect at Plassans. Eugene now replied by return of post that the nomination of a receivership would soon be signed; but added that he wished to give them some good news immediately. He had obtained the ribbon of the Legion of Honour for his father. Felicite wept with joy. Her husband decorated! Her proud dream had never gone as far as that. Rougon, pale with delight, declared they must give a grand dinner that very evening. He no longer thought of expense; he would have thrown his last fifty francs out of the drawing-room windows in order to celebrate that glorious day.

"Listen," he said to his wife; "you must invite Sicardot: he has annoyed me with that rosette of his for a long time! Then Granoux and Roudier; I shouldn't be at all sorry to make them feel that it isn't their purses that will ever win them the cross. Vuillet is a skinflint, but the triumph ought to be complete: invite him as well as the small fry. I was forgetting; you must go and call on the marquis in person; we will seat him on your right; he'll look very well at our table. You know that Monsieur Garconnet is entertaining the colonel and the prefect. That is to make me understand that I am nobody now. But I can afford to laugh at his mayoralty; it doesn't bring him in a sou! He has invited me, but I shall tell him that I also have some people coming. The others will laugh on the wrong side of their mouths tomorrow. And let everything be of the best. Have everything sent from the Hotel de Provence. We must outdo the mayor's dinner."

Felicite set to work. Pierre still felt some vague uneasiness amidst his rapture. The Coup d'Etat was going to pay his debts, his son Aristide had repented of his faults, and he was at last freeing himself from Macquart; but he feared some folly on Pascal's part, and was especially anxious about the lot reserved for Silvere. Not that he felt the least pity for the lad; he was simply afraid the matter of the gendarme might come before the Assize Court. Ah! if only some discriminating bullet had managed to rid him of that young scoundrel! As his wife had pointed out to him in the morning, all obstacles had fallen away before him; the family which had dishonoured him had, at the last moment, worked for his elevation; his sons Eugene and Aristide, those spend-thrifts, the cost of whose college life he had so bitterly regretted, were at last paying interest on the capital expended for their education. And yet the thought of that wretched Silvere must come to mar his hour of triumph!

While Felicite was running about to prepare the dinner for the evening, Pierre heard of the arrival of the troops and determined to go and make inquiries. Sicardot, whom he had questioned on his return, knew nothing; Pascal must have remained to look after the wounded; as for Silvere, he had not even been seen by the commander, who scarcely knew him. Rougon therefore repaired to the Faubourg, intending to make inquiries there and at the same time pay Macquart the eight hundred francs which he had just succeeded in raising with great difficulty. However, when he found himself in the crowded encampment, and from a distance saw the prisoners sitting in long files on the beams in the Aire Saint-Mittre, guarded by soldiers gun in hand, he felt afraid of being compromised, and so slunk off to his mother's house, with the intention of sending the old woman out to pick up some information.

When he entered the hovel it was almost night. At first the only person he saw there was Macquart smoking and drinking brandy.

"Is that you? I'm glad of it," muttered Antoine. "I'm growing deuced cold here. Have you got the money?"

But Pierre did not reply. He had just perceived his son Pascal leaning over the bed. And thereupon he questioned him eagerly. The doctor, surprised by his uneasiness, which he attributed to paternal affection, told him that the soldiers had taken him and would have shot him, had it not been for the intervention of some honest fellow whom he did not know. Saved by his profession of surgeon, he had returned to Plassans with the troops. This greatly relieved Rougon. So there was yet another who would not compromise him. He was evincing his delight by repeated hand-shakings, when Pascal concluded in a sorrowful voice: "Oh! don't make merry. I have just found my poor grandmother in a very dangerous state. I brought her back this carbine, which she values very much; I found her lying here, and she has not moved since."

Pierre's eyes were becoming accustomed to the dimness. In the fast fading light he saw aunt Dide stretched, rigid and seemingly lifeless, upon her bed. Her wretched frame, attacked by neurosis from the hour of birth, was at length laid prostrate by a supreme shock. Her nerves had so to say consumed her blood. Moreover some cruel grief seemed to have suddenly accelerated her slow wasting-away. Her pale nun-like face, drawn and pinched by a life of gloom and cloister-like self-denial, was now stained with red blotches. With convulsed features, eyes that glared terribly, and hands twisted and clenched, she lay at full length in her skirts, which failed to hide the sharp outlines of her scrawny limbs. Extended there with lips closely pressed she imparted to the dim room all the horror of a mute death-agony.

Rougon made a gesture of vexation. This heart-rending spectacle was very distasteful to him. He had company coming to dinner in the evening, and it would be extremely inconvenient for him to have to appear mournful. His mother was always doing something to bother him. She might just as well have chosen another day. However, he put on an appearance of perfect ease, as he said: "Bah! it's nothing. I've seen her like that a hundred times. You must let her lie still; it's the only thing that does her any good."

Pascal shook his head. "No, this fit isn't like the others," he whispered. "I have often studied her, and have never observed such symptoms before. Just look at her eyes: there is a peculiar fluidity, a pale brightness about them which causes me considerable uneasiness. And her face, how frightfully every muscle of it is distorted!"

Then bending over to observe her features more closely, he continued in a whisper, as though speaking to himself: "I have never seen such a face, excepting among people who have been murdered or have died from fright. She must have experienced some terrible shock."

"But how did the attack begin?" Rougon impatiently inquired, at a loss for an excuse to leave the room.

Pascal did not know. Macquart, as he poured himself out another glass of brandy, explained that he had felt an inclination to drink a little Cognac, and had sent her to fetch a bottle. She had not been long absent, and at the very moment when she returned she had fallen rigid on the floor without uttering a word. Macquart himself had carried her to the bed.

"What surprises me," he said, by way of conclusion, "is, that she did not break the bottle."

The young doctor reflected. After a short pause he resumed: "I heard two shots fired as I came here. Perhaps those ruffians have been shooting some more prisoners. If she passed through the ranks of the soldiers at that moment, the sight of blood may have thrown her into this fit. She must have had some dreadful shock."

Fortunately he had with him the little medicine-case which he had been carrying about ever since the departure of the insurgents. He tried to pour a few drops of reddish liquid between aunt Dide's closely-set teeth, while Macquart again asked his brother: "Have you got the money?"

"Yes, I've brought it; we'll settle now," Rougon replied, glad of this diversion.

Thereupon Macquart, seeing that he was about to be paid, began to moan. He had only learnt the consequence of his treachery when it was too late; otherwise he would have demanded twice or thrice as much. And he complained bitterly. Really now a thousand francs was not enough. His children had forsaken him, he was all alone in the world, and obliged to quit France. He almost wept as he spoke of his coming exile.

"Come now, will you take the eight hundred francs?" said Rougon, who was in haste to be off.

"No, certainly not; double the sum. Your wife cheated me. If she had told me distinctly what it was she expected of me, I would never have compromised myself for such a trifle."

Rougon laid the eight hundred francs upon the table.

"I swear I haven't got any more," he resumed. "I will think of you later. But do, for mercy's sake, get away this evening."

Macquart, cursing and muttering protests, thereupon carried the table to the window, and began to count the gold in the fading twilight. The coins tickled the tips of his fingers very pleasantly as he let them fall, and jingled musically in the darkness. At last he paused for a moment to say: "You promised to get me a berth, remember. I want to return to France. The post of rural guard in some pleasant neighbourhood which I could mention, would just suit me."

"Very well, I'll see about it," Rougon replied. "Have you got the eight hundred francs?"

Macquart resumed his counting. The last coins were just clinking when a burst of laughter made them turn their heads. Aunt Dide was standing up in front of the bed, with her bodice unfastened, her white hair hanging loose, and her face stained with red blotches. Pascal had in vain endeavoured to hold her down. Trembling all over, and with her arms outstretched, she shook her head deliriously.

"The blood-money! the blood-money!" she again and again repeated. "I heard the gold. And it is they, they who sold him. Ah! the murderers! They are a pack of wolves."

Then she pushed her hair aback, and passed her hand over her brow, as though seeking to collect her thoughts. And she continued: "Ah! I have long seen him with a bullet-hole in his forehead. There were always people lying in wait for him with guns. They used to sign to me that they were going to fire... . It's terrible! I feel some one breaking my bones and battering out my brains. Oh! Mercy! Mercy! I beseech you; he shall not see her any more—never, never! I will shut him up. I will prevent him from walking out with her. Mercy! Mercy! Don't fire. It is not my fault. If you knew——"

She had almost fallen on her knees, and was weeping and entreating while she stretched her poor trembling hands towards some horrible vision which she saw in the darkness. Then she suddenly rose upright, and her eyes opened still more widely as a terrible cry came from her convulsed throat, as though some awful sight, visible to her alone, had filled her with mad terror.

"Oh, the gendarme!" she said, choking and falling backwards on the bed, where she rolled about, breaking into long bursts of furious, insane laughter.

Pascal was studying the attack attentively. The two brothers, who felt very frightened, and only detected snatches of what their mother said, had taken refuge in a corner of the room. When Rougon heard the word gendarme, he thought he understood her. Ever since the murder of her lover, the elder Macquart, on the frontier, aunt Dide had cherished a bitter hatred against all gendarmes and custom-house officers, whom she mingled together in one common longing for vengeance.

"Why, it's the story of the poacher that she's telling us," he whispered.

But Pascal made a sign to him to keep quiet. The stricken woman had raised herself with difficulty, and was looking round her, with a stupefied air. She remained silent for a moment, endeavouring to recognise the various objects in the room, as though she were in some strange place. Then, with a sudden expression of anxiety, she asked: "Where is the gun?"

The doctor put the carbine into her hands. At this she raised a light cry of joy, and gazed at the weapon, saying in a soft, sing-song, girlish whisper: "That is it. Oh! I recognise it! It is all stained with blood. The stains are quite fresh to-day. His red hands have left marks of blood on the butt. Ah! poor, poor aunt Dide!"

Then she became dizzy once more, and lapsed into silent thought.

"The gendarme was dead," she murmured at last, "but I have seen him again; he has come back. They never die, those blackguards!"

Again did gloomy passion come over her, and, shaking the carbine, she advanced towards her two sons who, speechless with fright, retreated to the very wall. Her loosened skirts trailed along the ground, as she drew up her twisted frame, which age had reduced to mere bones.

"It's you who fired!" she cried. "I heard the gold... . Wretched woman that I am! ... I brought nothing but wolves into the world—a whole family—a whole litter of wolves! ... There was only one poor lad, and him they have devoured; each had a bite at him, and their lips are covered with blood... . Ah! the accursed villains! They have robbed, they have murdered... . And they live like gentlemen. Villains! Accursed villains!"

She sang, laughed, cried, and repeated "accursed villains!" in strangely sonorous tones, which suggested a crackling of a fusillade. Pascal, with tears in his eyes, took her in his arms and laid her on the bed again. She submitted like a child, but persisted in her wailing cries, accelerating their rhythm, and beating time on the sheet with her withered hands.

"That's just what I was afraid of," the doctor said; "she is mad. The blow has been too heavy for a poor creature already subject, as she is, to acute neurosis. She will die in a lunatic asylum like her father."

"But what could she have seen?" asked Rougon, at last venturing to quit the corner where he had hidden himself.

"I have a terrible suspicion," Pascal replied. "I was going to speak to you about Silvere when you came in. He is a prisoner. You must endeavour to obtain his release from the prefect, if there is still time."

The old oil-dealer turned pale as he looked at his son. Then, rapidly, he responded: "Listen to me; you stay here and watch her. I'm too busy this evening. We will see to-morrow about conveying her to the lunatic asylum at Les Tulettes. As for you, Macquart, you must leave this very night. Swear to me that you will! I'm going to find Monsieur de Bleriot."

He stammered as he spoke, and felt more eager than ever to get out into the fresh air of the streets. Pascal fixed a penetrating look on the madwoman, and then on his father and uncle. His professional instinct was getting the better of him, and he studied the mother and the sons, with all the keenness of a naturalist observing the metamorphosis of some insect. He pondered over the growth of that family to which he belonged, over the different branches growing from one parent stock, whose sap carried identical germs to the farthest twigs, which bent in divers ways according to the sunshine or shade in which they lived. And for a moment, as by the glow of a lightning flash, he thought he could espy the future of the Rougon-Macquart family, a pack of unbridled, insatiate appetites amidst a blaze of gold and blood.

Aunt Dide, however, had ceased her wailing chant at the mention of Silvere's name. For a moment she listened anxiously. Then she broke out into terrible shrieks. Night had now completely fallen, and the black room seemed void and horrible. The shrieks of the madwoman, who was no longer visible, rang out from the darkness as from a grave. Rougon, losing his head, took to flight, pursued by those taunting cries, whose bitterness seemed to increase amidst the gloom.

As he was emerging from the Impasse Saint-Mittre with hesitating steps, wondering whether it would not be dangerous to solicit Silvere's pardon from the prefect, he saw Aristide prowling about the timber-yard. The latter, recognising his father, ran up to him with an expression of anxiety and whispered a few words in his ear. Pierre turned pale, and cast a look of alarm towards the end of the yard, where the darkness was only relieved by the ruddy glow of a little gipsy fire. Then they both disappeared down the Rue de Rome, quickening their steps as though they had committed a murder, and turning up their coat-collars in order that they might not be recognised.

"That saves me an errand," Rougon whispered. "Let us go to dinner. They are waiting for us."

When they arrived, the yellow drawing-room was resplendent. Felicite was all over the place. Everybody was there; Sicardot, Granoux, Roudier, Vuillet, the oil-dealers, the almond-dealers, the whole set. The marquis, however, had excused himself on the plea of rheumatism; and, besides, he was about to leave Plassans on a short trip. Those bloodstained bourgeois offended his feelings of delicacy, and moreover his relative, the Count de Valqueyras, had begged him to withdraw from public notice for a little time. Monsieur de Carnavant's refusal vexed the Rougons; but Felicite consoled herself by resolving to make a more profuse display. She hired a pair of candelabra and ordered several additional dishes as a kind of substitute for the marquis. The table was laid in the yellow drawing-room, in order to impart more solemnity to the occasion. The Hotel de Provence had supplied the silver, the china, and the glass. The cloth had been laid ever since five o'clock in order that the guests on arriving might feast their eyes upon it. At either end of the table, on the white cloth, were bouquets of artificial roses, in porcelain vases gilded and painted with flowers.

When the habitual guests of the yellow drawing-room were assembled there they could not conceal their admiration of the spectacle. Several gentlemen smiled with an air of embarrassment while they exchanged furtive glances, which clearly signified, "These Rougons are mad, they are throwing their money out of the window." The truth was that Felicite, on going round to invite her guests, had been unable to hold her tongue. So everybody knew that Pierre had been decorated, and that he was about to be nominated to some post; at which, of course, they pulled wry faces. Roudier indeed observed that "the little black woman was puffing herself out too much." Now that "prize-day" had come this band of bourgeois, who had rushed upon the expiring Republic—each one keeping an eye on the other, and glorying in giving a deeper bite than his neighbour—did not think it fair that their hosts should have all the laurels of the battle. Even those who had merely howled by instinct, asking no recompense of the rising Empire, were greatly annoyed to see that, thanks to them, the poorest and least reputable of them all should be decorated with the red ribbon. The whole yellow drawing-room ought to have been decorated!

"Not that I value the decoration," Roudier said to Granoux, whom he had dragged into the embrasure of a window. "I refused it in the time of Louis-Philippe, when I was purveyor to the court. Ah! Louis-Philippe was a good king. France will never find his equal!"

Roudier was becoming an Orleanist once more. And he added, with the crafty hypocrisy of an old hosier from the Rue Saint-Honore: "But you, my dear Granoux; don't you think the ribbon would look well in your button-hole? After all, you did as much to save the town as Rougon did. Yesterday, when I was calling upon some very distinguished persons, they could scarcely believe it possible that you had made so much noise with a mere hammer."

Granoux stammered his thanks, and, blushing like a maiden at her first confession of love, whispered in Roudier's ear: "Don't say anything about it, but I have reason to believe that Rougon will ask the ribbon for me. He's a good fellow at heart, you know."

The old hosier thereupon became grave, and assumed a very affable manner. When Vuillet came and spoke to him of the well-deserved reward that their friend had just received, he replied in a loud voice, so as to be heard by Felicite, who was sitting a little way off, that "men like Rougon were an ornament to the Legion of Honour." The bookseller joined in the chorus; he had that morning received a formal assurance that the custom of the college would be restored to him. As for Sicardot, he at first felt somewhat annoyed to find himself no longer the only one of the set who was decorated. According to him, none but soldiers had a right to the ribbon. Pierre's valour surprised him. However, being in reality a good-natured fellow, he at last grew warmer, and ended by saying that the

Napoleons always knew how to distinguish men of spirit and energy.

Rougon and Aristide consequently had an enthusiastic reception; on their arrival all hands were held out to them. Some of the guests went so far as to embrace them. Angele sat on the sofa, by the side of her mother-in-law, feeling very happy, and gazing at the table with the astonishment of a gourmand who has never seen so many dishes at once. When Aristide approached, Sicardot complimented his son-in-law upon his superb article in the "Independant." He restored his friendship to him. The young man, in answer to the fatherly questions which Sicardot addressed to him, replied that he was anxious to take his little family with him to Paris, where his brother Eugene would push him forward; but he was in want of five hundred francs. Sicardot thereupon promised him the money, already foreseeing the day when his daughter would be received at the Tuileries by Napoleon III.

In the meantime, Felicite had made a sign to her husband. Pierre, surrounded by everybody and anxiously questioned about his pallor, could only escape for a minute. He was just able to whisper in his wife's ear that he had found Pascal and that Macquart would leave that night. Then lowering his voice still more he told her of his mother's insanity, and placed his finger on his lips, as if to say: "Not a word; that would spoil the whole evening." Felicite bit her lips. They exchanged a look in which they read their common thoughts: so now the old woman would not trouble them any more: the poacher's hovel would be razed to the ground, as the walls of the Fouques' enclosure had been demolished; and they would for ever enjoy the respect and esteem of Plassans.

But the guests were looking at the table. Felicite showed the gentlemen their seats. It was perfect bliss. As each one took his spoon, Sicardot made a gesture to solicit a moment's delay. Then he rose and gravely said: "Gentlemen, on behalf of the company present, I wish to express to our host how pleased we are at the rewards which his courage and patriotism have procured for him. I now see that he must have acted upon a heaven-sent inspiration in remaining here, while those beggars were dragging myself and others along the high roads. Therefore, I heartily applaud the decision of the government.... Let me finish, you can then congratulate our friend... . Know, then, that our friend, besides being made a chevalier of the Legion of Honour, is also to be appointed to a receiver of taxes."

There was a cry of surprise. They had expected a small post. Some of them tried to force a smile; but, aided by the sight of the table, the compliments again poured forth profusely.

Sicardot once more begged for silence. "Wait one moment," he resumed; "I have not finished. Just one word. It is probable that our friend will remain among us, owing to the death of Monsieur Peirotte."

Whilst the guests burst out into exclamations, Felicite felt a keen pain in her heart. Sicardot had already told her that the receiver had been shot; but at the mention of that sudden and shocking death, just as they were starting on that triumphal dinner, it seemed as if a chilling gust swept past her face. She remembered her wish; it was she who had killed that man. However, amidst the tinkling music of the silver, the company began to do honour to the banquet. In the provinces, people eat very much and very noisily. By the time the *releve* was served, the gentlemen were all talking together; they showered kicks upon the vanquished, flattered one another, and made disparaging remarks about the absence of the marquis. It was impossible, they said, to maintain intercourse with the nobility. Roudier even gave out that the marquis had begged to be excused because his fear of the insurgents had given him jaundice. At the second course they all scrambled like hounds at the quarry. The oil-dealers and almond-dealers were the men who saved France. They clinked glasses to the glory of the Rougons. Granoux, who was very red, began to stammer, while Vuillet, very pale, was quite drunk. Nevertheless Sicardot continued filling his glass. For her part Angele, who had already eaten too much, prepared herself some sugar and water. The gentlemen were so delighted at being freed from panic, and finding themselves together again in that yellow drawing-room, round a good table, in the bright light radiating from the candelabra and the chandelier—which they now saw for the first time without its fly-specked cover—that they gave way to most exuberant folly and indulged in the coarsest enjoyment. Their voices rose in the warm atmosphere more huskily and eulogistically at each successive dish till they could scarcely invent fresh compliments. However, one of them, an old retired master-tanner, hit upon this fine phrase—that the dinner was a "perfect feast worthy of Lucullus."

Pierre was radiant, and his big pale face perspired with triumph. Felicite, already accustoming herself to her new station in life, said that they would probably rent poor Monsieur Peirotte's flat until they could purchase a house of their own in the new town. She was already planning how she would place her future furniture in the receiver's rooms. She was entering into possession of her Tuileries. At one moment, however, as the uproar of voices became deafening, she seemed to recollect something, and quitting her seat she whispered in Aristide's ear: "And Silvere?"

The young man started with surprise at the question.

"He is dead," he replied, likewise in a whisper. "I was there when the gendarme blew his brains out with a pistol."

Felicite in her turn shuddered. She opened her mouth to ask her son why he had not prevented this murder by claiming the lad; but abruptly hesitating she remained there speechless. Then Aristide, who had read her question on her quivering lips, whispered: "You understand, I said nothing—so much the worse for him! I did quite right. It's a good riddance."

This brutal frankness displeased Felicite. So Aristide had his skeleton, like his father and mother. He would certainly not have confessed so openly that he had been strolling about the Faubourg and had allowed his cousin to be shot, had not the wine from the Hotel de Provence and the dreams he was building upon his approaching arrival in Paris, made him depart from his habitual cunning. The words once spoken, he swung himself to and fro on his chair. Pierre, who had watched the conversation between his wife and son from a distance, understood what had passed and glanced at them like an accomplice imploring silence. It was the last blast of terror, as it were, which blew over the Rougons, amidst the splendour and enthusiastic merriment of the dinner. True, Felicite, on returning to her seat, espied a taper burning behind a window on the other side of the road. Some one sat watching Monsieur Peirotte's corpse, which had been brought back from Sainte-Roure that morning. She sat down, feeling as if that taper were heating her back. But the gaiety was now increasing, and exclamations of rapture rang through the yellow drawing-room when the dessert appeared.

At that same hour, the Faubourg was still shuddering at the tragedy which had just stained the Aire Saint-Mittre with blood. The return of the troops, after the carnage on the Nores plain, had been marked by the most cruel reprisals. Men were beaten to death behind bits of wall, with the butt-ends of muskets, others had their brains blown out in ravines by the pistols of gendarmes. In order that terror might impose silence, the soldiers strewed their road with corpses. One might have followed them by the red trail which they left behind.[8] It was a long butchery. At every halting-place, a few insurgents were massacred. Two were killed at Sainte-Roure, three at Ocheres, one at Beage. When the troops were encamped at Plassans, on the Nice road, it was decided that one more prisoner, the most guilty, should be shot. The victors judged it wise to leave this fresh corpse behind them in order to inspire the town with respect for the new-born Empire. But the soldiers were now weary of killing; none offered himself for the fatal task. The prisoners, thrown on the beams in the timber-yard as though on a camp bed, and bound together in pairs by the hands, listened and waited in a state of weary, resigned stupor.

At that moment the gendarme Rengade roughly opened a way for himself through the crowd of inquisitive idlers. As soon as he heard that the troops had returned with several hundred insurgents, he had risen from bed, shivering with fever, and risking his life in the cold, dark December air. Scarcely was he out of doors when his wound reopened, the bandage which covered his eyeless socket became stained with blood, and a red streamlet trickled over his cheek and moustache. He looked frightful in his dumb fury with his pale face and blood-stained bandage, as he ran along closely scrutinising each of the prisoners. He followed the beams, bending down and going to and fro, making the bravest shudder by his abrupt appearance. And, all of a sudden: "Ah! the bandit, I've got him!" he cried.

---

8. Though M. Zola has changed his place in his account of the insurrection, that account is strictly accurate in all its chief particulars. What he says of the savagery both of the soldiers and of their officers is confirmed by all impartial historical writers.—EDITOR.

He had just laid his hand on Silvere's shoulder. Silvere, crouching down on a beam, with lifeless and expressionless face, was looking straight before him into the pale twilight, with a calm, stupefied air. Ever since his departure from Sainte-Roure, he had retained that vacant stare. Along the high road, for many a league, whenever the soldiers urged on the march of their captives with the butt-ends of their rifles, he had shown himself as gentle as a child. Covered with dust, thirsty and weary, he trudged onward without saying a word, like one of those docile animals that herdsmen drive along. He was thinking of Miette. He ever saw her lying on the banner, under the trees with her eyes turned upwards. For three days he had seen none but her; and at this very moment, amidst the growing darkness, he still saw her.

Rengade turned towards the officer, who had failed to find among the soldiers the requisite men for an execution.

"This villain put my eye out," he said, pointing to Silvere. "Hand him over to me. It's as good as done for you."

The officer did not reply in words, but withdrew with an air of indifference, making a vague gesture. The gendarme understood that the man was surrendered to him.

"Come, get up!" he resumed, as he shook him.

Silvere, like all the other prisoners, had a companion attached to him. He was fastened by the arm to a peasant of Poujols named Mourgue, a man about fifty, who had been brutified by the scorching sun and the hard labour of tilling the ground. Crooked-backed already, his hands hardened, his face coarse and heavy, he blinked his eyes in a stupid manner, with the stubborn, distrustful expression of an animal subject to the lash. He had set out armed with a pitchfork, because his fellow villagers had done so; but he could not have explained what had thus set him adrift on the high roads. Since he had been made a prisoner he understood it still less. He had some vague idea that he was being conveyed home. His amazement at finding himself bound, the sight of all the people staring at him, stupefied him still more. As he only spoke and understood the dialect of the region, he could not imagine what the gendarme wanted. He raised his coarse, heavy face towards him with an effort; then, fancying he was being asked the name of his village, he said in his hoarse voice:

"I come from Poujols."

A burst of laughter ran through the crowd, and some voices cried: "Release the peasant."

"Bah!" Rengade replied; "the more of this vermin that's crushed the better. As they're together, they can both go."

There was a murmur.

But the gendarme turned his terrible blood-stained face upon the onlookers, and they slunk off. One cleanly little citizen went away declaring that if he remained any longer it would spoil his appetite for dinner. However some boys who recognised Silvere, began to speak of "the red girl." Thereupon the little citizen retraced his steps, in order to see the lover of the female standard-bearer, that depraved creature who had been mentioned in the "Gazette."

Silvere, for his part, neither saw nor heard anything; Rengade had to seize him by the collar. Thereupon he got up, forcing Mourgue to rise also.

"Come," said the gendarme. "It won't take long."

Silvere then recognised the one-eyed man. He smiled. He must have understood. But he turned his head away. The sight of the one-eyed man, of his moustaches which congealed blood stiffened as with sinister rime, caused him profound grief. He would have liked to die in perfect peace. So he avoided the gaze of Rengade's one eye, which glared from beneath the white bandage. And of his own accord he proceeded to the end of the Aire Saint-Mittre, to the narrow lane hidden by the timber stacks. Mourgue followed him thither.

The Aire stretched out, with an aspect of desolation under the sallow sky. A murky light fell here and there from the copper-coloured clouds. Never had a sadder and more lingering twilight cast its melancholy over this bare expanse—this wood-yard with its slumbering timber, so stiff and rigid in the cold. The prisoners, the soldiers, and the mob along the high road disappeared amid the darkness of the trees. The expanse, the beams, the piles of planks alone grew pale under the fading light, assuming a muddy tint that vaguely suggested the bed of a dried-up torrent. The sawyers' trestles, rearing their meagre framework in a corner, seemed to form gallows, or the uprights of a guillotine. And there was no living soul there excepting three gipsies who showed their frightened faces at the door of their van—an old man and woman, and a big girl with woolly hair, whose eyes gleamed like those of a wolf.

Before reaching the secluded path, Silvere looked round him. He bethought himself of a far away Sunday when he had crossed the wood-yard in the bright moonlight. How calm and soft it had been!—how slowly had the pale rays passed over the beams! Supreme silence had fallen from the frozen sky. And amidst this silence, the woolly-haired gipsy girl had sung in a low key and an unknown tongue. Then Silvere remembered that the seemingly far-off Sunday was only a week old. But a week ago he had come to bid Miette farewell! How long past it seemed! He felt as though he had not set foot in the wood-yard for years. But when he reached the narrow path his heart failed him. He recognised the odour of the grass, the shadows of the planks, the holes in the wall. A woeful voice rose from all those things. The path stretched out sad and lonely; it seemed longer to him than usual, and he felt a cold wind blowing down it. The spot had aged cruelly. He saw that the wall was moss-eaten, that the verdant carpet was dried up by frost, that the piles of timber had been rotted by rain. It was perfect devastation. The yellow twilight fell like fine dust upon the ruins of all that had been most dear to him. He was obliged to close his eyes that he might again behold the lane green, and live his happy hours afresh. It was warm weather; and he was racing with Miette in the balmy air. Then the cruel December rains fell unceasingly, yet they still came there, sheltering themselves beneath the planks and listening with rapture to the heavy plashing of the shower. His whole life—all his happiness—passed before him like a flash of lightning. Miette was climbing over the wall, running to him, shaking with sonorous laughter. She was there; he could see her, gleaming white through the darkness, with her living helm of ink-black hair. She was talking about the magpies' nests, which are so difficult to steal, and she dragged him along with her. Then he heard the gentle murmur of the Viorne in the distance, the chirping of the belated grasshoppers, and the blowing of the breeze among the poplars in the meadows of Sainte-Claire. Ah, how they used to run! How well he remembered it! She had learnt to swim in a fortnight. She was a plucky girl. She had only had one great fault: she was inclined to pilfering. But he would

have cured her of that. Then the thought of their first embraces brought him back to the narrow path. They had always
ended by returning to that nook. He fancied he could hear the
gipsy girl's song dying away, the creaking of the last shutters,
the solemn striking of the clocks. Then the hour of separation
came, and Miette climbed the wall again and threw him a kiss.
And he saw her no more. Emotion choked him at the thought:
he would never see her again—never!

"When you're ready," jeered the one-eyed man; "come,
choose your place."

Silvere took a few more steps. He was approaching the end
of the path, and could see nothing but a strip of sky in which
the rust-coloured light was fading away. Here had he spent his
life for two years past. The slow approach of death added an in-
effable charm to this pathway which had so long served as a
lovers' walk. He loitered, bidding a long and lingering farewell
to all he loved; the grass, the timber, the stone of the old wall,
all those things into which Miette had breathed life. And again
his thoughts wandered. They were waiting till they should be
old enough to marry: Aunt Dide would remain with them. Ah! if
they had fled far away, very far away, to some unknown village, where the scamps of the Faubourg would no longer have
been able to come and cast Chantegreil's crime in his
daughter's face. What peaceful bliss! They would have opened
a wheelwright's workshop beside some high road. No doubt, he
cared little for his ambitions now; he no longer thought of
coachmaking, of carriages with broad varnished panels as
shiny as mirrors. In the stupor of his despair he could not remember why his dream of bliss would never come to pass. Why
did he not go away with Miette and aunt Dide? Then as he
racked his memory, he heard the sharp crackling of a fusillade;
he saw a standard fall before him, its staff broken and its folds
drooping like the wings of a bird brought down by a shot. It
was the Republic falling asleep with Miette under the red flag.
Ah, what wretchedness! They were both dead, both had bleeding wounds in their breasts. And it was they—the corpses of his
two loves—that now barred his path of life. He had nothing left
him and might well die himself. These were the thoughts that
had made him so gentle, so listless, so childlike all the way
from Sainte-Roure. The soldiers might have struck him, he

would not have felt it. His spirit no longer inhabited his body. It was far away, prostrate beside the loved ones who were dead under the trees amidst the pungent smoke of the gunpowder.

But the one-eyed man was growing impatient; giving a push to Mourgue, who was lagging behind, he growled: "Get along, do; I don't want to be here all night."

Silvere stumbled. He looked at his feet. A fragment of a skull lay whitening in the grass. He thought he heard a murmur of voices filling the pathway. The dead were calling him, those long departed ones, whose warm breath had so strangely perturbed him and his sweetheart during the sultry July evenings. He recognised their low whispers. They were rejoicing, they were telling him to come, and promising to restore Miette to him beneath the earth, in some retreat which would prove still more sequestered than this old trysting-place. The cemetery, whose oppressive odours and dark vegetation had breathed eager desire into the children's hearts, while alluringly spreading out its couches of rank grass, without succeeding however in throwing them into one another's arms, now longed to imbibe Silvere's warm blood. For two summers past it had been expecting the young lovers.

"Is it here?" asked the one-eyed man.

Silvere looked in front of him. He had reached the end of the path. His eyes fell on the tombstone, and he started. Miette was right, that stone was for her. *"Here lieth ... Marie ... died ... "* She was dead, that slab had fallen over her. His strength failing him, he leant against the frozen stone. How warm it had been when they sat in that nook, chatting for many a long evening! She had always come that way, and the pressure of her foot, as she alighted from the wall, had worn away the stone's surface in one corner. The mark seemed instinct with something of her lissom figure. And to Silvere it appeared as if some fatalism attached to all these objects—as if the stone were there precisely in order that he might come to die beside it, there where he had loved.

The one-eyed man cocked his pistols.

Death! death! the thought fascinated Silvere. It was to this spot, then, that they had led him, by the long white road which descends from Sainte-Roure to Plassans. If he had known it, he would have hastened on yet more quickly in order to die on that stone, at the end of the narrow path, in the atmosphere where he could still detect the scent of Miette's breath! Never had he hoped for such consolation in his grief. Heaven was merciful. He waited, a vague smile playing on is face.

Mourgue, meantime, had caught sight of the pistols. Hitherto he had allowed himself to be dragged along stupidly. But fear now overcame him, and he repeated, in a tone of despair: "I come from Poujols—I come from Poujols!"

Then he threw himself on the ground, rolling at the gendarme's feet, breaking out into prayers for mercy, and imagining that he was being mistaken for some one else.

"What does it matter to me that you come from Poujols?" Rengade muttered.

And as the wretched man, shivering and crying with terror, and quite unable to understand why he was going to die, held out his trembling hands—his deformed, hard, labourer's hands—exclaiming in his patois that he had done nothing and ought to be pardoned, the one-eyed man grew quite exasperated at being unable to put the pistol to his temple, owing to his constant movements.

"Will you hold your tongue?" he shouted.

Thereupon Mourgue, mad with fright and unwilling to die, began to howl like a beast—like a pig that is being slaughtered.

"Hold your tongue, you scoundrel!" the gendarme repeated.

And he blew his brains out. The peasant fell with a thud. His body rolled to the foot of a timber-stack, where it remained doubled up. The violence of the shock had severed the rope which fastened him to his companion. Silvere fell on his knees before the tombstone.

It was to make his vengeance the more terrible that Rengade had killed Mourgue first. He played with his second pistol, raising it slowly in order to relish Silvere's agony. But the latter looked at him quietly. Then again the sight of this man, with the one fierce, scorching eye, made him feel uneasy. He averted his glance, fearing that he might die cowardly if he continued to look at that feverishly quivering gendarme, with blood-stained bandage and bleeding moustache. However, as he raised his eyes to avoid him, he perceived Justin's head just above the wall, at the very spot where Miette had been wont to leap over.

Justin had been at the Porte de Rome, among the crowd, when the gendarme had led the prisoners away. He had set off as fast as he could by way of the Jas-Meiffren, in his eagerness to witness the execution. The thought that he alone, of all the Faubourg scamps, would view the tragedy at his ease, as from a balcony, made him run so quickly that he twice fell down. And in spite of his wild chase, he arrived too late to witness the first shot. He climbed the mulberry tree in despair; but he smiled when he saw that Silvere still remained. The soldiers had informed him of his cousin's death, and now the murder of the wheelwright brought his happiness to a climax. He awaited the shot with that delight which the sufferings of others always afforded him—a delight increased tenfold by the horror of the scene, and a feeling of exquisite fear.

Silvere, on recognising that vile scamp's head all by itself above the wall—that pale grinning face, with hair standing on end—experienced a feeling of fierce rage, a sudden desire to live. It was the last revolt of his blood—a momentary mutiny. He again sank down on his knees, gazing straight before him. A last vision passed before his eyes in the melancholy twilight. At the end of the path, at the entrance of the Impasse Saint-Mittre, he fancied he could see aunt Dide standing erect, white and rigid like the statue of a saint, while she witnessed his agony from a distance.

At that moment he felt the cold pistol on his temple. There was a smile on Justin's pale face. Closing his eyes, Silvere heard the long-departed dead wildly summoning him. In the darkness, he now saw nothing save Miette, wrapped in the banner, under the trees, with her eyes turned towards heaven. Then the one-eyed man fired, and all was over; the lad's skull burst open like a ripe pomegranate; his face fell upon the stone, with his lips pressed to the spot which Miette's feet had worn—that warm spot which still retained a trace of his dead love.

And in the evening at dessert, at the Rougons' abode, bursts of laughter arose with the fumes from the table, which was still warm with the remains of the dinner. At last the Rougons were nibbling at the pleasures of the wealthy! Their appetites, sharpened by thirty years of restrained desire, now fell to with wolfish teeth. These fierce, insatiate wild beasts, scarcely entering upon indulgence, exulted at the birth of the Empire—the dawn of the Rush for the Spoils. The Coup d'Etat, which retrieved the fortune of the Bonapartes, also laid the foundation for that of the Rougons.

Pierre stood up, held out his glass, and exclaimed: "I drink to Prince Louis—to the Emperor!"

The gentlemen, who had drowned their jealousies in champagne, rose in a body and clinked glasses with deafening shouts. It was a fine spectacle. The bourgeois of Plassans, Roudier, Granoux, Vuillet, and all the others, wept and embraced each other over the corpse of the Republic, which as yet was scarcely cold. But a splendid idea occurred to Sicardot. He took from Felicite's hair a pink satin bow, which she had placed over her right ear in honour of the occasion, cut off a strip of the satin with his dessert knife, and then solemnly fastened it to Rougon's button-hole. The latter feigned modesty, and pretended to resist. But his face beamed with joy, as he murmured: "No, I beg you, it is too soon. We must wait until the decree is published."

"Zounds!" Sicardot exclaimed, "will you please keep that! It's an old soldier of Napoleon who decorates you!"

The whole company burst into applause. Felicite almost swooned with delight. Silent Granoux jumped up on a chair in his enthusiasm, waving his napkin and making a speech which was lost amid the uproar. The yellow drawing-room was wild with triumph.

But the strip of pink satin fastened to Pierre's button-hole was not the only red spot in that triumph of the Rougons. A shoe, with a blood-stained heel, still lay forgotten under the bedstead in the adjoining room. The taper burning at Monsieur Peirotte's bedside, over the way, gleamed too with the lurid redness of a gaping wound amidst the dark night. And yonder, far away, in the depths of the Aire Saint-Mittre, a pool of blood was congealing upon a tombstone.

22845793R00183

Printed in Great Britain
by Amazon